Charles K. Adams, Herbert B. Adams, William F. Allen

Methods of Teaching History

Volume 1

Charles K. Adams, Herbert B. Adams, William F. Allen

Methods of Teaching History
Volume 1

ISBN/EAN: 9783337168094

Printed in Europe, USA, Canada, Australia, Japan

Cover: Foto ©Paul-Georg Meister /pixelio.de

More available books at **www.hansebooks.com**

Pedagogical Library.

EDITED BY G. STANLEY HALL.

VOL. I.

METHODS OF TEACHING HISTORY.

BY

A. D. WHITE, W. F. ALLEN, C. K. ADAMS, JOHN W. BURGESS, J. R. SEELEY, H. B. ADAMS, E. EMERTON, G. S. MORRIS, R. T. ELY, A. B. HART, W. C. COLLAR, J. T. CLARKE, W. E. FOSTER, AND OTHERS.

SECOND EDITION, ENTIRELY RECAST AND REWRITTEN.

BOSTON:
GINN, HEATH, AND COMPANY.
1885.

COPYRIGHT, 1883,
BY GINN, HEATH, & CO.

J. S. CUSHING & CO., PRINTERS, 115 HIGH STREET, BOSTON.

CONTENTS.

	PAGE.
INTRODUCTION	V

By the EDITOR.

METHODS OF TEACHING AMERICAN HISTORY 1
By Dr. A. B. HART, Harvard University.

THE PRACTICAL METHOD IN HIGHER HISTORICAL INSTRUCTION 31
By Professor EPHRAIM EMERTON, of Harvard University.

ON METHODS OF TEACHING POLITICAL ECONOMY 61
By Dr. RICHARD T. ELY, Johns Hopkins University.

HISTORICAL INSTRUCTION IN THE COURSE OF HISTORY AND POLITICAL SCIENCE AT CORNELL UNIVERSITY 73
By President ANDREW D. WHITE, Cornell University.

ADVICE TO AN INEXPERIENCED TEACHER OF HISTORY . . . 77
By W. C. COLLAR, A.M., Head Master of Roxbury Latin School.

A PLEA FOR ARCHÆOLOGICAL INSTRUCTION 89
By JOSEPH THACHER CLARKE, Director of the Assos Expedition.

THE USE OF A PUBLIC LIBRARY IN THE STUDY OF HISTORY . 105
By WILLIAM E. FOSTER, Librarian of the Providence Public Library.

SPECIAL METHODS OF HISTORICAL STUDY 113
By Professor HERBERT B. ADAMS, Johns Hopkins University.

THE PHILOSOPHY OF THE STATE AND OF HISTORY 149
By Prof. GEORGE S. MORRIS, Michigan and Johns Hopkins Universities.

THE COURSES OF STUDY IN HISTORY, ROMAN LAW, AND POLITICAL ECONOMY AT HARVARD UNIVERSITY . . . 167
By Dr. HENRY E. SCOTT, Harvard University.

CONTENTS.

	PAGE.
THE TEACHING OF HISTORY	193
By Professor J. R. SEELEY, Cambridge University, Eng.	
ON METHODS OF TEACHING HISTORY	203
By Professor C. K. ADAMS, Michigan University.	
ON METHODS OF HISTORICAL STUDY AND RESEARCH IN COLUMBIA UNIVERSITY	215
By Professor JOHN W. BURGESS, Columbia University.	
PHYSICAL GEOGRAPHY AND HISTORY	223
WHY DO CHILDREN DISLIKE HISTORY?	227
By THOMAS WENTWORTH HIGGINSON.	
GRADATION AND THE TOPICAL METHOD OF HISTORICAL STUDY	231
PART I.—HISTORICAL LITERATURE AND AUTHORITIES	239
II.—BOOKS FOR COLLATERAL READING	296
III.—SCHOOL TEXT-BOOKS	303
SUPPLEMENT	309
HISTORY TOPICS	323
By Professor W. F. ALLEN, Wisconsin University.	
BIBLIOGRAPHY OF CHURCH HISTORY (see special index to this article)	337
By Rev. JOHN ALONZO FISHER, Johns Hopkins University.	

INTRODUCTION.

THIS book was intended to be the first of a series entitled a *Pedagogical Library*, devoted to methods of teaching, one volume of which was to be occupied with each of the more important branches of instruction in grammar and high schools. The design and plan of the work was not to produce systematic treatises, and still less to develop anything ultimate or absolute in method; but to gather together, in the form most likely to be of direct practical utility to teachers, and especially students and readers of history, generally, the opinions and modes of instruction, actual or ideal, of eminent and representative specialists in each department. The present volume has been an unremunerated work of love on the part of each writer, and the appearance of subsequent volumes in the series is not yet assured. It should be added that the articles are printed in the order in which they were received by the editor.

Teachers in whom a methodic interest has been awakened will find many useful hints in the following books, pamphlets, and articles:—

Georg Gottfried Gervinus. Grundzüge der Historik. Leipzic, 1837. pp. 95.

F. Jacobi. Grundzüge einer neuen Methode für den vaterländischen Geschichtsunterricht in deutschen Schulen. Nürnberg, 1839.

F. Seckel. Der vaterländische Geschichtsunterricht in unseren Elementarschulen. Koblenz, 1842.

F. W. Miquel. Beiträge eines mit der Herbart'schen Pädagogik befreundeten Schulmannes zur Lehre vom biographischen Geschichtsunterricht auf Gymnasien. Anrich, 1847.

L. ... Grundzüge einer Methodik des geschichtlichen Unterrichts auf Gymnasien. Leipzig, 1847.

C. Peter. Der Geschichtsunterricht auf Gymnasien. Ein methodischer Versuch. Halle, 1849.

W. Assman. Das Studium der Geschichte. Braunschweig, 1849.

H. v. Sybel. Ueber den Stand der neueren deutschen Geschichtschreibung. Marburg, 1856.

J. F. C. Campe. Geschichte und Unterricht in der Geschichte. Leipzig, 1859.

Friedrich Karl Biedermann. Der Geschichts-Unterricht in der Schule, seine Mängel und ein Vorschlag zu seiner Reform. Braunschweig, 1860. pp. 45.

G. Weber. Der Geschichtsunterricht in Mittelschulen. Heidelberg, 1861.

Anon. Ueber die Nothwendigkeit einer gründlichen Reform des Lehrplans für den Geschichtsunterricht auf Real- und höheren Burgerschulen. Neuwied, 1870.

M. Lazarus. Ueber die Ideen in der Geschichte. Berlin, 1872.

J. G. Droysen. Grundriss der Historik. Leipzig, 1868. pp. 38.

Rudolph Foss, Realschule Director. Wie ist der Unterricht in der Geschichte mit dem Geographischen Unterricht zu verbinden. Dargelegt an der Darstellung der Mark Brandenburg. Eine Anleitung für Lehrer und reiferen Schülern. Mit Karten. Berlin, 1874. pp. 48.

K. F. Eberhardt. Zur Methode und Technik des Geschichtsunterrichts auf den Seminarien. Eisenach, 1874.

O. A. Gräfllich. Beitrag zur Methodik des Geschichtsunterrichtes an höheren Lehranstalten. Löbau, 1874.

C. Radenhausen. Osiris. Weltgesetze in der Weltgeschichte. Hamburg, 1875.

F. Muster, Hauptlehrer in Köln. Die Geschichte in der Volkschule; eine von der Diesterweg-Stiftung in Berlin prämiirte Concurrenzschrift. Köln, 1876. pp. 78.

F. Krieger. Der Geschichtsunterricht in Volks-, Bürger- und Fortbildungsschulen. Eine Anleitung zur richtigen Ertheilung der Geschichte. Nürnberg, 1876.

R. Mayr. Die philosophische Geschichtsauffassung der Neuzeit. Wien, 1877.

F. L. W. Herbst, Recter der Kön. Landesschule Pforta. Die Neure und Neueste Geschichte auf Gymnasien. Mainz, 1877. pp. 40.

Ottokar Lorenz, Wirkl. Mitgleid der K. Akademie der Wissenschaften. Friedrich Christoph Schlosser und ueber einige Aufgaben und Principien der Geschichtschreibung. Wien, 1878. pp. 91.

Clemens Nohl. Ueber die Nothwendigkeit einer gründlichen Reform des Lehrplans für den Geschichtsunterricht auf Real- und höheren Bürgerschulen. Neuweid.

H. Nohascheck. Ueber der Geschichts-Unterricht in einer Volkschule von acht Klassen. Ein methodischer Versuch. Mainz, 1878. pp. 38.

F. Jodl. Die Culturgeschichtsschreibung, ihre Entwickelung und ihr Problem. Halle, 1878.

H. Doergens. Grundlinien einer Wissenschaft der Geschichte. Leipzig, 1878.

M. Lazarus. Erziehung und Geschichte. Breslau & Leipzig, 1881. pp. 51.

E. F. Oscar-Jäger. Bemerkungen ueber den Geschichtlichen Unterricht. Beigabe zu dem "Hilfsbuch für den ersten Unterricht in alten Geschichte." Für Lehrer der Geschichte an Höheren Schulen. Wiesbaden, 1882. pp. 47.

Anon. Wie Studirt Man classische Philologie und Geschichte. Leipzic, 1884.

Maurenbrecher. Geschichte und Politik. 1884.

Keferstein. Historiches Wissen und historiche Bildung. Ziller's päd. Jahrbuch XIII., p. 130, *et seq.*

Zillig. Der Geschichtliche Unterricht in den elementaren Erziehung Schulen. Ziller's päd. Jahrbuch, XIV., p. 89, et seq.

K. J. Eberhardt. Ueber Geschichts-Unterricht in Rein's päd. Studien. Heft 4.

E. Blume. Geschichts-Unterricht auf den Seminarien Rein's päd. Studien.

P. Frédéricq. De L'enseignement Supérieur de l'histoire en Allemagne. Revue de L'instruction publique en Belgique, 1882. pp. 18-79

P. Frédéricq. L'enseignement Supérieur de l'histoire à Paris. Revue Internationale de L'enseignement, 1883. p. 742.

See also, Alte und neue Ansichten ueber die Ziele des Geschichts-Unterrichts. *Von F. Noack.* "Pädagogische Archiv," 1883, Apr. 6. Der Lernstoff in Geschichtlichen Unterricht. *Von E. Stutzer. Ibid.* 2 Aug. *Seignobos*, Revue Internationale, 1881, X., and also in *Revue*, Internationale de L'enseignement, Tome I., p. 565, and Aug., 1884. *Krauth's.* Revue d'instruction publique en Belgique, XIX. The Study of History, its Lets and Hindrances, by *E. A. Freeman.* 1879. See also his recent inaugural address at Oxford, both of which are, however, little but reiterations of his theory of the unity, through Roman institutions, of Ancient and Modern history.

In America nothing has heretofore been published of such value as "Methods of Historical Study," by Dr. H. B. Adams, in the Johns Hopkins University Studies, in "Historical and Political Science," which he edits. Baltimore, 1884. pp. 136. Also C. K. Adams's "Manual of Historical Study." The former work is in part Dr. Adams's contribution to the present volume. See, too, Mr. Atkinson's lectures on "History and the Study of History." For teachers of the young Adams's Historical Chart, and for all Tillinghast's translation of Ploetz's "Epitome of Ancient, Mediæval, and Modern History," Boston, 1844, will be useful. Also, "Instruction in History," by Dr. G. Diesterweg, printed in the first edition of this book, but omitted and now published separately. Boston, 1884.

Many of the systematic German treatises on pedagogy also contain suggestive chapters or sections devoted to the didactics of history; of these, Kehr and Schrader may be mentioned as representatives.

History was chosen for the subject of the first volume of this educational library because, after much observation in the schoolrooms of many of the larger cities in the eastern part of our country, the editor, without having a hobby about its relative importance or being in any sense an expert in history, is convinced that no subject so widely taught is, on the whole, taught so poorly.

Most text-books now in use are dry compilations, and yet are far more closely adhered to than even the best should be in this department. Teachers of history generally give instruction also in several other often unrelated branches; and, worst of all perhaps, history is crowded into a single term or year. Two radical changes, which have long since been found practicable in schools of corresponding grades in Germany, are greatly needed here. First, there should be in all the larger towns special teachers, who should go from room to room, or from one schoolhouse to another, and give instruction in history alone. They might qualify and be examined in higher and higher grades of work, and this would tend to give to their vocation a professional spirit and character. It is not impossible that, eventually thus, the way into the professors' chairs in our colleges and universities might be as open to teachers here, who have worked their way up through such an apprenticeship, as it is in Germany. The teacher's mind must be kept saturated with its spirit, stored with copious illustrations of its varied lessons, by wide and diligent reading, or history cannot be taught effectively to the young. The high educational value of history is too great to be left to teachers who merely hear recitations, keeping the finger on the place in the text-book, and only asking the questions conveniently printed for them in the margin or back of the book, — teachers, too, who know that their present method is a good illustration of how history ought not to be taught, and who would do better if opportunity were afforded them. Nowhere is so much of the time spent on text-books by pupils lost on school artifacts, mistaken for perplexities inherent in the subject itself. When we reflect that what men think of the world depends on what they know of it, it is not surprising that the wider altruistic and ethical interests, which it is a special function of history to develop, rarely become strong enough to control narrower and more isolated and selfish aims in life.

Secondly, the time devoted to historical study in the public schools should be increased. So slow is historical comprehension, and so independent of all cram-work, that even the time now given to history would probably be more advantageously used if distributed over more months or years, by devoting to it a correspondingly less number of hours per week; though this could not be said of most studies, and is not true of the examinable elements in this. We have not yet in this country considered the problem of adapting historical material to the earlier phases of the development of the childish mind from the first years of school life, as Ziller and his pupils, especially Rein, Pickel, and Scheller, have done in their recent *Pädagogische Studien*. The child's love of stories, they hold, is the earliest manifestation of historic interest, and should be developed by systematic story-telling, which, since the much-lauded invention of Herr Güttenburg, has become a lost art. So important is this art, that normal schools should give special training in it, and it should be made, with respect to young classes, the culmination of pedagogic skill. These writers have selected and arranged twelve of Grimm's tales, and would bring nearly the whole work of school the first year about these, upon the principle of the well-known concentration method of the late Professor Ziller. They are to be told and retold, and then reproduced by the children item by item, and moral and religious sentiments, as well as all manner of material information and illustrative object-lessons, made to centre about them. The next year connected stories from Robinson Crusoe are treated in the same way, till the child comes to almost identify itself with the hero, and repeat with him the slow progress, not unlike that of the race, from destitution to comfort and comparative civilization by the use of powers which every child feels itself possessed of and as competent as Robinson to put forth under like circumstances for his own amelioration. Later select tales from the Old Testament are made the focal points of the school work. Thus the unity of the child's mind is secured from distracting special studies, which with advancing school years become more and more independent and isolated. Selections from the Odyssey, the Norse sagas, tales from Shakespeare, Herodotus, Livy, Xenophon, etc., follow,—all stimulating the historical sense, and creating centres of interest before technical instruction in history begins.

A teacher who has a prescribed period of history in which to qualify pupils in a given time should elect a method with the greatest care. For certain periods and for certain ages it may be best to group all the material about the biographies of eminent men; for others, about important battles; while a purely pragmatic narrative may again be most effective. With somewhat older children, the investigating method, which follows the order and describes the process of search and discovery of historic facts; or the discussive method, which applies a body of historic material to the determination or elucidation of a problem of the present; or the other presentative methods which Droysen has enumerated, may have peculiar pedagogic merit. No rules can be laid down here or anywhere in pedagogy to be followed blindly. What is essential is that the teacher shall know and ponder many good methods, so that he may have a wide repertory of means from which to choose the best for the attainment of his ends.

A purely colorless presentation of facts, such as used to be postulated, is clearly impossible for the average teacher, and, could it be secured, would rob his instruction of most of its value and interest, — and yet it is the safest of all ideals. Teachers of the grades here contemplated seem just now peculiarly liable to hobbies which sometimes actually deform the pupil's historic sense, and illustrate the danger of great ideas to minds not well disciplined for them. Some who have very lately caught the national idea of Freeman, Stubbs, etc., do scanty justice to Norman influence in English history. Others, who have realized the pregnant sense in which "history is past politics," forget the other sense in which the history of the world has been at nearly every point very different from the history of the conscious purposes of the leaders in its movements, and that "while men thought they were doing this thing by these means, it was later seen that they were really doing quite other things by very different means." Physical geography, as important perhaps for a correct understanding of historic events as some knowledge of the senses and the brain is for mental science, is very apt to be too much neglected or, though far more rarely, to be made too prominent. History, a wise teacher has said in substance, is neither a theophany, or a series of special providences, nor a play of absolute ideas on the one hand, nor the product of material necessity on the other. This dualism is not normal, and a true pedagogy, like a true philosophy of history, will tend to reconcile and not to emphasize it. If a teacher feels the need of a philosophy of history as a background for his methods and as a safeguard against one-sidedness, he will hardly find a saner one than in the chapters of the third volume of Lotze's *Microcosm*, which opens up a broad and safe middle way between extremes, like those of Hegel and Helwald; but let him remember that philosophic ideas, while they may often enliven historic work, are dangerous if premature, and should be made centres of historic interest only quite late in the pupil's mental development.

The liberality of the publishers has made it possible to eliminate from the second about half the material of the first edition and to substitute new matter to an extent which somewhat enlarges the volume, and of a kind which it is believed so increases its value and utility that readers of the old edition will find this essentially a new work. If the methods detailed in the first edition were mainly for advanced historical training, or for teaching "not so much history, as how to study history," the present collection of essays will, it is hoped, prove of service to teachers of all grades.

G. STANLEY HALL.

JOHNS HOPKINS UNIVERSITY, *Dec.* 16, 1884.

METHODS OF TEACHING AMERICAN HISTORY.

By Dr. A. B. Hart, Harvard University.

CONSIDERING the thought which has been devoted to the deduction of general principles, applicable to history as a science, wherever taught, it seems almost presuming to assume that there are any peculiar methods of teaching American history. It is always well, however, to test principles by finding out whether they may be adapted to a particular case; and if any history meets with special difficulties, and needs a special treatment, it is that of our own country.

In the first place, it is almost always the first, and often the last, branch of the subject to be pursued at all. In the second place, there exists not only a negative ignorance as to the facts on which it is based, but too often a positive misinformation, — a structure to be pulled down before one can begin to build. It is only necessary to turn to the *Congressional Globe*, or to the columns of a newspaper, to find out that public men know a great many things about the history of the United States which never happened. Where there is good will to learn the truth, there is usually an untrained helplessness about using books. Where there is discrimination, and a readiness to choose the best, there is a lack of trustworthy authorities in compact form. The luminous brief histories with which the Germans abound simply do not exist in America. After 1820, there is no narrative history which can be used as a college text-book; and, till Von Holst wrote, there was no critical history whatever.

Yet no country can boast of a richer or more instructive past: it is full of interesting detail; it has, in the slavery contest, the most dramatic episode of the century; it abounds in questions which have nowhere else been worked out; no other government ever had more revenue than it could spend; no other country ever disposed of the soil of half a continent; no other people ever successfully developed a strong federation. To Americans the great questions of national policy are of peculiar interest, because capable of personal association. To give an example: one of the students at Harvard, who is writing a thesis on the fugitive slave law, has gone for information to a man who had been tried under that law before the student's father. Thus American history has, at home, a presumption in its favor. It is important not only to the American, but for any student of political science. It appeals to that practical side of the American character, which is likely to prefer a subject which has an evident use beyond collegiate life. Finally, the authorities are easy to find, wherever there is a library; and there is no lack of interesting questions waiting for investigators.

American history will, therefore, be studied more than other history; it is not learned without study; it is worth studying for itself; it appeals to Americans; and the materials are at hand. The next question is, How shall it be studied? The question naturally divides itself into a discussion of general principles, arrangement and division, purpose, point of view, manner of instruction, helps to the student, and tests.

First of all, it is necessary to lay down certain fundamental principles in such form as to leave them sharply defined in the minds of the students. They may be so framed as to correct a few of the more dangerous popular errors about the real relations of the United States to other countries.

It might be well to draw up and print some such list as the following: —

FUNDAMENTAL PRINCIPLES OF AMERICAN HISTORY.

1. **No** nation has a **history disconnected** from that of the rest of the world: the United States is closely related, in point of time, with previous ages; in point of space, with other civilized countries.

2. **Institutions are a growth**, and not a creation: the Constitution of the United States itself is constantly changing with the changes in public opinion.

3. Our institutions are **Teutonic in origin**: they have come to us through English institutions.

4. The growth of our institutions has been **from local to central**: the general government can, therefore, be understood only in the light of the early history of the country.

5. The **principle of union** is of slow growth in America: the Constitution was formed from necessity, and not from preference.

6. Under a **federal form of government** there must inevitably be a perpetual contest of authority between the States and the general government: hence the two opposing doctrines of States-rights and of nationality.

7. **National political parties** naturally appeal to the federal principle when in power, and to the local principle when out of power.

8. When parties become distinctly sectional, a **trial of strength** between a part of the States and the general government must come sooner or later.

To descend from the abstract to the concrete, perhaps no better way can be found for suggesting a method for the study of American history than to describe the methods actually in use in Harvard College. It is to be borne in mind that the system is still incomplete and imperfect, and that a part only of the devices to be enumerated have been put into operation.

Beginning with 1884, two full courses, each consisting of three lectures a week, will be given. Together they are to cover the whole period from the earliest settlements to the Civil War; although intended to form a systematic whole, each is to be complete in itself. The first course (1600–1789) is intended for a small number of students, and will be suggestive rather than didactic. The point of view will be: first, the origin of our local institutions; and, later on, the nature of the Constitution, as illustrated by the preceding history of the United Colonies and United States. The second course (1789–1861) is one of the larger electives in college; what follows may be considered as applying more particularly to this course, — the history of the United States under the Constitution.

From 1775 down, a course on American history ought to be primarily for instruction. If human nature were otherwise, if the fitting schools gave a different preparation, another method might be followed. As it is, few students know anything positive about institutions; how should they, without any good elementary text-books? Our political treatises and speeches show the lack of knowledge, and the danger of generalizing without it. Van Buren's "Political Parties" is an example of a book which thus assumes history instead of teaching it. On the other hand, it is quite as undesirable for the student to accept the instructor's generalizations ready-made. With bright students it is perfectly possible, after putting clearly before them the facts and the deductions of both sides, to extract from them an independent judgment. They may be required to read specific references, and then to submit, in brief form, a written opinion embodying their own conclusions. It is, of course, essential not to turn the lecture-room into a primary meeting by discussing political parties as they now exist. Part of the duty of the instructor is to point out the evils in our political system; but having once based his deduction on ascertained facts, he may safely leave the application to the student. The suggestive method is not to be left out of sight; but suggestions must follow and not precede knowledge. In the present state of the preparatory schools, the present want of textbooks, the present superficiality of more general works, the present mass of ill-digested material, if the instructor does not himself supply accurate and detailed information, his students will not have it.

With all the restrictions thus laid upon him, it is still possible for the instructor to select a point of view which will oblige his students to think, and to see the relation of one part of history to another; it is, the comparison of the past with the present. No history is better adapted to the method than our own; no treatment lends more life to a course, or appeals more strongly to young minds. The connection between a subject under discussion, and the same subject in our present system, is always useful in itself and fructifying to the mind. To give a specific instance: After a lecture on Jackson's removals, and the effect of the system thus introduced, the students were last year required to submit a written suggestion for a remedy. The results were crude, but thoughtful, and in some cases shrewd and far-seeing. Care should be taken, however, to preserve the consistency of the course; it is a mistake to work from the present backward. If each topic, as it comes up in its logical order, is sketched out clear to its present status, the connection of events with each other need not be broken.

The only practicable form of instruction at Harvard seems to be that of lectures. The classes are too large for recitations, even did proper text-books exist. In lectures alone can the instructor arrange the proportions of the course himself. In connection with lectures the student may be led to use many books, instead of two or three, or half a dozen. The lectures are all, or nearly all, delivered by the instructor; it is only in rare cases that a student may have looked up a subject in such detail that he can profitably lecture (not read a thesis) before the class. The method, in a word, is the topical. The precise scope of the course for the year 1883–84 may be seen by the following: —

TOPICS FOR A COURSE OF EIGHTY-SIX LECTURES ON THE POLITICAL AND CONSTITUTIONAL HISTORY OF THE UNITED STATES.[1]

1. **Introductory.** — Methods of the course. Suggestions on note-taking and on habits of study.
2. **Preliminary Conceptions.** — What is history? What is a Constitution? What is the United States?
3. **Authorities.** — Official publications. Legal. Newspapers. Biographies. Works of statesmen. Constitutional treaties. General histories.
4. **Constitution of England** at the outbreak of the Revolution. Theoretical. Actual. Conventional: *Esprit des Lois*, XI., chaps. i.-vi. Institutions of the United States derived from England.
5. **The Colonies.** — Government by England. Local government. Application of English law. The issue in the Revolution.
6. **Union of the Colonies.** — Early schemes.
7. **Colonial Union accomplished.** — Difficulties in 1775. Reasons in 1775. Origin of the revolutionary government. Sovereign powers exercised. Limitations.
8. **Independence.** — Early suggestions. Preparatory steps. Nature and bearing. New State governments. Union older than the States.

---

[1] The list is condensed from the "Outline" printed by the class in 1883–84; only those required references appear which are appended to the main heads of the lectures; there are many others in the original. The course for 1884–85 begins later, and comes ten years further down.

9. **The Confederation.** — Formation. Powers. Defects: *Story*, § 265.

10. **Conflicts of the Confederation.** — Theories of power over States. Attempts to assert authority. Violations by States. Violations by Congress.

11. **Weakness of the States.** — In their relations to the people. In the relations of people to the States.

12. **Proposed Amendment of the Articles of Confederation.** — By grants of particular powers. By grants of coercive power. By change in the form of the government.

13. **The Constitutional Convention.** — Call. Preliminaries. Task. Parties. Sources. Propositions. Development of action on individuals.

14. **Scope of the Constitution.** — Questions settled. Questions unsettled. Questions imperfectly settled.

15. **Origin and Nature of the Constitution.** — Ratification. " Who made the Constitution?" " What is the Constitution?"

16. **The United States in 1789.** — Geography, — social, economic, political. Origin of parties.

17. **Organization of the Government.** — Expiration of the Confederation: *J. C.*, XIII. 170. Elections: *McMaster*, I. 525–32; *Schouler*, I. 70–73, 82–85. Congress: *Snow*, 13–14. The executive: *Snow*, 15–17. The judiciary: *Snow*, 17–18.

18. **Early Constitutional Questions.** — Oath. Citizenship. Amendments. Indians. Territories.

19. **Acts for putting into Effect Clauses of the Constitution.** — Revenue: *McMaster*, I. 544, 55; *Schouler*, I. 86–93, 187. Navigation and commerce.

20. **Same, continued.** — Defence and preservation of order. General welfare of the United States.

21. **Questions relating to the States.** — Assumption and capital: *McMaster*, I. 574–85; *Von Holst*, I. 80–89. Apportionment: *Hildreth*, IV. 303; *Schouler*, I. 188–89.

22. **Same, continued.** — Slavery: *Von Holst*, I. 272–309. Fugitive slaves: *Von Holst*, I. 309–15. New States: *Hildreth*, IV. 117, 209, 268, 326. Suits against States: *Schouler*, I. 273–74.

23. **Constitutional Questions of National Policy.** — Protec-

tion: *Hildreth*, IV. 65-76; *Schouler*, I. 87-90. National bank: *Schouler*, I. 159-62; *Snow*, 24-27; *Story*, §§ 1231-66.

24. Washington's First Administration. — Appointments: *Schouler*, I. 93, 107-9. Washington's character and policy: *Von Holst*, II. 80-83. Quarrels in the cabinet: *Morse's Jeff.*, 96-145; *Lodge's Ham.*, 140-48. Investigation of Hamilton: *Lodge*, 148-52; *Schouler*, I. 175, 216-20.

25. Foreign Relations: France and England. — Neutrality question: *Von Holst*, I. 106-12; *Lodge's Ham.*, 153-66. Complications with France: *Schouler*, I. 246-55, and *Lodge*, 166-75; *Morse's Jeff.*, 146-65, and *Von Holst*, I. 113-18. Complication with England: *Hildreth*, IV. 410-43. Preparations for war: *Schouler*, I. 266-73; *Lodge*, 175-80.

26. Whiskey Rebellion. — Causes: *Adams's Gallatin*, 86-93. Constitutional question of coercion. Suppression. Effects.

27. Jay Treaty. Legislation. Election. — Conclusion of a treaty with England: *Von Holst*, I. 122-28; *Schouler*, I. 308-18. General legislation. Retirement of Washington: *Schouler*, I. 327-31; *Von Holst*, I. 32-37.

28. Foreign Affairs: Spain and France. — Relations with Spain: *Hildreth*, IV. 131-36, 569; V. 238-39. X. Y. Z. affair: *Gilman's Monroe*, 44-68; *Schouler*, I. 317-26, 345-51, 374-91.

29. Alien and Sedition Acts. — Third naturalization act: *Schouler*, I. 393; *Hildreth*, V. 213-14, 216. Alien Act: *Story*, §§ 1293-94; *Schouler*, I. 394-99. Alien Enemies Act. Sedition Act: *Schouler*, I. 396-404; *Von Holst*, I. 141-43; *Hildreth*, V. 225-32. Application of the acts: *Schouler*, I. 420-21, 448-50; *Hildreth*, V. 247-50, 352, 365, 368.

30. Virginia and Kentucky Resolutions. History. — Origin. Kentucky Resolutions: *Von Holst*, I. 143-45; *Hildreth*, V. 272-76; *Jeff.*, XI. 464-69. Virginia Resolutions: *Schouler*, I. 422-24; *Hildreth*, V. 276-77. Action of other States: *Hildreth*, V. 296-97. Second Kentucky Resolutions: *Hildreth*, V. 319-20. Madison's Report: *Hildreth*, V. 319-21; *Von Holst*, I. 147. Was forcible resistance intended? *Von Holst*, I. 156-58.

31. The Supreme Arbiter. — Necessity of some final tribunal. Distinction between judicial and political cases. Controversies between departments of the general government. Controversies between citizens. Controversies to which States are parties.

32. **Interposition as a Remedy for Usurpation.** — Other remedies. Interposition as a remedy: *Von Holst*, I. 150–69; *Madison*, IV. 95–106.

33. **Fall of the Federal Party.** — Unpopularity of the administration. Unpopularity of Congress: *Hildreth*, V. 414. Dissensions within the party: *Lodge's Ham.*, 188–236; *Schouler*, I. 166–75. Election of 1801: *Lodge*, 194–201; *Von Holst*, I. 168–78. Triumph over federal principles: *Von Holst*, I. 178–83; *Hildreth*, V. 415–18.

34. **Policy of the Republican Party.** — Administrative: *Snow*, 69–76; *Cook's Notes*, 148–62; *Schouler*, II. 2–15. Legislative: *Snow*, 76–79; *Cook's Notes*, 163–68; *Schouler*, II. 15–26. Tripolitan war: *Cook's Notes*, 167–68; *Schouler*, II. 16–18.

35. **The Public Lands.** — Jurisdiction before the Revolution: *H. B. Adams*, in *Maryland Historical Society Fund Publication*, No. 11; *Blunt's Historical Sketch*. Question of national jurisdiction. Administration before 1789. Alienation before 1789. Land system of the United States.

36. **The Louisiana Annexation.** — Previous changes of ownership: *Morse's Jeff.*, 231–39. Negotiations: *Morse's Jeff.*, 239–46; *Gilman's Monroe*, 74–85; *Schouler*, II. 37–51; *Adams's Randolph*, 75–81. Treaty of cession completed: *Gilman's Monroe*, 85–93; *Stevens's Gallatin*, 201–2. Constitutionality of the treaty: *Story*, §§ 1277–83.

37. **"New England Plot of 1803-4."** — Early suggestions of separation. Causes of dissatisfaction. Evidences of a "plot": *Adams's New England Federalism*; *Von Holst*, I. 193–95. Effect of the "plot": *Von Holst*, I. 197–99.

38. **Republican Legislation and Administration.** — Impeachment of the judges: *Hildreth*, V. 511–12, 540–44; *Adams's Randolph*, 131–53. Election of 1804: *Schouler*, II. 59, 66; *Morse's Jeff.*, 268–71. The Territories. Finance and defence: *Adams's Gallatin*, 348–49, 352–55. Internal improvements: *Stevens's Gallatin*, 300; *Adams's Gallatin*, 352–54.

39. **Burr's Conspiracy.** — Burr's plans: *Hildreth*, v. 594–603; *Randall's Jeff.*, III. 173–78. The expedition: *Hildreth*, v. 603–24; *Randall's Jeff.*, III. 179–86. Habeas corpus cases: *Hildreth*, v. 612–13; *Randall's Jeff.*, III. 194–98. Prosecution for treason: *Hildreth*, v. 668–73; *Story*, §§ 1790–97. Enforcement Act.

40. **Neutral Trade and the Embargo.** — Foreign aggression: *Hildreth*, v. 646–49; *Schouler*, II. 151–56. Jefferson's policy: *Hildreth*, v. 653–65, 674–86; *Schouler*, II. 133–51. The embargo: *Schouler*, II. 156–65; *Hildreth*, VI. 35–44.

41. **Failure of Jefferson's Policy.** — Enforcement: *Schouler*, II. 185–94; *Hildreth*, VI. 108–24; *Von Holst*, I. 209–13. Repeal: *Morse's Jeff.*, 310–20; *Schouler*, II. 194–98; *Hildreth*, VI. 124–36; *Von Holst*, I. 214–25. Result of Jefferson's administration: *Schouler*, II. 198–201; *Hildreth*, VI. 138–43.

42. **Madison's First Term.** — General policy: *Schouler*, II. 279–81; *Stevens's Gallatin*, 305–11. Foreign relations. Impending war: *Von Holst*, I. 225–30.

43. **Review of the First Half Year.**

44. **War of 1812.** — Preliminaries: *Von Holst*, I. 226–30; *Snow*, 100–103; *Von Holst's Calhoun*, 12–26; *Schouler*, II. 315–17. Declaration of war: *Von Holst*, I. 230–42; *Schouler*, II. 348–56. Progress: *Snow*, 103–108; *Schouler*, II. 356–75; *Roosevelt*. The militia question: *Dwight*, 233–57; *Story*, §§ 1204–10.

45. **War of 1812.** — Unpopularity in New England: *Von Holst*, I. 243–54. Hartford convention: *Von Holst*, I. 254–72; *Adams's New England Federalism*, 245. Close of the war: *Schouler*, II. 402–19, 438–44; *Hildreth*, VI. 545–66. Martial law: *North American Review*, XCIII. 486, 501–504.

46. **End of the War of 1812.** — Peace of Ghent: *Schouler*, II. 434–38. Results of the war: *Von Holst*, I. 273–77. The bank: *Snow*, 109–10, 124–25; *Bolles's Financial History*, II. 278–82, 317–29; *Sumner's American Currency*, 68–79; *Von Holst*, I. 382–88.

47. **Monroe's Administration. Internal Policy.** — " Era of good feeling:" *Schouler*, II. 458–63; *Gilman's Monroe*, 125–40. Tariff of 1816: *Snow*, 118–24; *Von Holst*, I. 396–400; *Bolles*, II. 359–74 (*Protectionist view*). Internal improvements. Constitutional question: *Von Holst*, I. 388–96.

48. **Relations with Spain.**—West Florida question: *Hildreth*, VI. 223-28, 310. East Florida question: *Sumner's Jackson*, 49-72. Texas question: *Von Holst*, II. 548-58.

49. **Slavery (1789-1820). Remedies.** — Emancipation: *Goodell's Slavery and Anti-Slavery; Von Holst*, I. 273-300. Colonization: *Von Holst*, I. 329-33. Abolition.

50. **Regulation of Slavery.** — *Von Holst*, I. 302-39. Slave-trade: *Von Holst*, I. 315-28. Growth of slavery. Fugitive slaves: *Von Holst*, I. 310-15. Petitions. Territories.

51. **The Missouri Question.** — Rivalry of North and South: *Von Holst*, I. 340-56. Status of Missouri. Arkansas Territorial Act: *Von Holst*, I. 372-74. First Missouri debate.

52. **Missouri Compromise.** — Second debate, *Hildreth*, VI. 682-98. The compromise: *Von Holst*, I. 370-81; *Benton's View*, I. 5. Nature and effect of the compromise: *Adams's Memoirs*, V. 3-13; *Benton*, I. 8-10. The Missouri Constitution: *Hildreth*, VI. 703, 706-12.

53. **Constitutional Decisions.** — McCullough v. Maryland: *Marshall*, 160-87; *Van Santvoord's Chief Justices*, 459-65. Dartmouth College case: *Marshall*, 188-220; *Van Santvoord's Chief Justices*, 450-55. Cohens v. Virginia: *Marshall*, 221-61; *Van Santvoord's Chief Justices*, 466-69. Effect of the decisions.

54. **American Policy of European States.** — Colonies. Revolt of the Spanish Colonies. Schemes of foreign intervention.

55. **Monroe Doctrine. Occasion.** — European intervention in Spain. English proposition for joint declaration. Plan of a European Congress. Cuban question. Republican spirit. Russian complications. Traditional foreign policy of the United States: *Gilman's Monroe*, 162-66.

56. **Monroe Doctrine. Enunciation.** — Preliminary discussion: *Gilman's Monroe*, 167-74. The declaration: *Gilman's Monroe*, 150-62; *Von Holst*, I. 419-21. Effect of the declaration. Exposition of the declaration. Historical development.

57. **Tariff, and Election of 1824.** — Tariff: *Von Holst*, I. 396-404. The election: *Von Holst*, II. 1-9.

58. **Adams's Administration. Opposition.** — Opposition formed: *Sargent, Public Men and Events*, 106-14. Panama mission: *Von*

Holst, I. 409-33. Amendment for Presidential elections: *Benton*, I. 37, 78-80. Attempt to control patronage: *Benton*, I. 80-87. Anti-Masonic party. Attack on the expenditures. General internal policy of Adams: *Morse's Adams*, 199-213.

59. **Creek Controversy.**— Early difficulties. Negotiations with the Creeks: *Von Holst*, I. 433-35. Controversy about the survey: *Von Holst*, I. 435-43; *Benton*, I. 58-60. Second controversy: *Von Holst*, I. 441-48.

60. **Accession of Jackson.**— Tariff of 1828: *Von Holst*, I. 459-63. Election of Jackson: *Sumner*, 114-18. Jackson's policy: *Von Holst*, II. 9-12. Internal events of Jackson's first administration: *Sumner*, 139-63; *Von Holst*, II. 27-31.

61. **Removals. Internal Improvements. Public Lands.**— Removals: *Von Holst*, II. 13-27. Internal improvements: *Sumner's Jackson*, 191-94; *Von Holst*, I. 389-96. Public lands: *Sumner's Jackson*, 109, 184-91.

62. **Cherokee Controversy.**— Origin of the difficulty: *Sumner*, 49, 179. Conflict with Georgia: *Von Holst*, I. 448-49. Georgian encroachments permitted: *Sumner*, 180-81; *Von Holst*, I. 449-51. Conflict with the supreme court: *Von Holst*, I. 452-58.

63. **The Bank Controversy.** — History of the bank: *Sumner's Jackson*, 224-36. Hostility of Jackson: *Von Holst*, II. 31-36; *Sumner's Jackson*, 236-44; *Benton*, I. 229-29. Struggle for a charter: *Von Holst*, II. 36-43; *Sumner's Jackson*, 244-49, 258-74. Jackson's veto: *Von Holst*, II. 43-55; *Sumner's Jackson*, 274-75.

64. **Distribution.** — Dickerson's distribution bills. Proceeds of public lands scheme. Clay's distribution bill: *Benton*, I. 275-78. Clay's bill revived: *Benton*, I. 362. Pocket veto: *Benton*, I. 365-69. Calhoun's scheme: *Von Holst*, II. 187-88. Constitutional question.

65. **The Nullification Movement** — Precedents: *Sumner's Jackson*, 212-16. Agitation by Calhoun: *Von Holst*, I. 459-75; *Sumner's Jackson*, 216-22. Tariff of 1832: *Von Holst*, I. 471; *Sumner's Jackson*, 222. Action of South Carolina: *Von Holst*, I. 475-77. Action of the Executive of the United States.

66. **Nullification Crisis and Discussion (1832-33).** — Issue joined. Is nullification constitutional? *Von Holst*, I. 465-75.

67. **Nullification. Force Bill and Compromise.** — Principle

of Coercion. The Force Bill: *Von Holst*, I. 484–90; *Sumner*, 285–87. The compromise: *Von Holst*, I. 490–92, 497–501. The settlement: *Von Holst*, I. 501–503; *Sumner*, 288–90.

68. **The Deposits.**—Attack on the bank renewed: *Benton*, I. 86–89, 294–96; *Sumner's Jackson*, 291–94. "Removal of the deposits": *Von Holst*, II. 51–55; *Sumner's Jackson*, 294–309. Constitutionality of the removal: *Story, Life and Letters*, II. 155–58; *Von Holst*, II. 55–68.

69. **Censure and Protest.**—Censure of the President: *Sumner's Jackson*, 309–11. Jackson's protest: *Sumner*, 311; *Von Holst*, II. 70–76. Expunging resolutions: *Sumner*, 313–14; *Von Holst*, II. 68–70. Bank controversy continued: *Sumner*, 309, 310, 312, 314–21.

70. **Anti-Slavery Agitation.**—Agitation in the North: *Von Holst*, II. 80–87. Opposition in the North: *Von Holst*, II. 97–110. Opposition in the South: *Von Holst*, II. 110–121. The mails: *Von Holst*, II. 121–36. Petitions.

71. **Finances and Deposit.**—Banks and currency. Deposit act. French indemnity.

72. **Texas.**—Boundaries: *Von Holst*, II. 548–51. Importance to slavery: *Von Holst*, II. 551–58, 569. Independence: *Von Holst*, II. 558–85. Recognition by the United States: *Von Holst*, II. 585–88.

73. **End of the "Reign of Jackson."**—Judiciary in Jackson's administration. Election of 1836. Jackson's influence: *Sumner's Jackson*, 277–80, 385–86.

74. **Van Buren's Administration.**—Character and policy: *Von Holst*, II. 147–72. Panic of 1837. Public Funds. Caroline affair: *Lodge's Webster*, 247–49, 252, 255.

75. **The Whigs and Tyler.**—Election of 1840: *Von Holst*, II. 360–405. Harrison's policy: *Von Holst*, II. 406–12. Tyler and the bank: *Von Holst*, II. 412–26. Breach with Tyler: *Von Holst*, II. 426–39. Finances: *Von Holst*, II. 440–51. Tariff of 1842: *Von Holst*, II. 451–64.

76. **North-Eastern Boundary.**—The dispute. Negotiations. Northern boundary. Treaty of Washington: *Lodge's Webster*, 253–60.

77. **Slavery: International and Interstate Status.**—Legal aspect of slavery. Restriction of the slave-trade. International status of slaves in the United States. International status of slaves on the high seas. Interstate status of slavery.

78. **Polk's Election and Administration.** — Election of 1844. Polk's internal administration. Tariff of 1846: *Von Holst*, III. 276–81.

79. **Northwestern Boundary.**— Conflicting claims: *Von Holst*, III. 29–36, 39–40. Joint occupation with Great Britain: *Von Holst*, III. 36–44; *Barrows*, 67–76. American settlements established: *Von Holst*, III. 44–53. "Fifty-four forty or fight." Treaty of Washington.

80. **Annexation of Texas.** — Jackson's policy. Recognition only: *Lecture* 72. Van Buren's policy: *Von Holst*, II. 599–612. Tyler's policy: *Von Holst*, II. 612–14, 625–43. Annexation in the campaign of 1844: *Von Holst*, II. 677–90, 702–709. Annexation by joint resolution: *Von Holst*, II. 709–14; *Greeley*, I. 171–73.

81. **Causes of the Mexican War.** — Breach of neutrality by the United States: *Von Holst*, II. 571–85. Recognition of Texas: *Lecture* 72. Question of claims: *Von Holst*, II. 592–601, 604–606, 627, 631–36, 681. Jones's attack on Monterey: *Von Holst*, II. 615–20. Annexation of Texas: *Von Holst*, II. 680, III. 80–82. Occupation of Texas: *Von Holst*, III. 93–99. Claim up to the Rio Grande: *Von Holst*, III. 84–93; *Cal.* III. 574–79. Greed for California: *Von Holst*, III. 108–13.

82. **Mexican War.**— Preliminaries. Military operations. Peace of Guadeloupe Hidalgo: *Von Holst*, III.

83. **Territorial Slavery.** — Comparison of North and South. Constitutional question of territorial slavery. Application to new territory.

84. **The Crisis of 1848–49.** — Election of 1848. Status of the slavery question.

85. **Compromise of 1850.** — Compromise proposed. Attitude of public men: *Greeley*, 203–207. Compromise carried: *Von Holst*, III. 515–61. Who won the victory? *Von Holst*, III. 561–62.

86. **Review of the Second Half Year.**

It will be noticed that there are but few distinctively biographical sketches in the course just outlined. The deficiency is supplied in part by constant reference to the character and motives of the actors in the historical drama; it is further supplied by references to *brief* biographies, particularly the excellent American Statesmen Series. Nevertheless, the course might be improved by systematically taking up one man after another, in connection with some event in which he was particularly concerned. Such a plan has been elaborated in the following

Topics for a Course of Twenty Lectures.[1]

1. The United States in 1789.
2. Organization and consolidation of the government.—Hamilton.
3. Foreign relations and neutrality.—Washington.
4. Fall of the Federal party.—John Adams.
5. Public lands and the annexation of Louisiana.—Gallatin.
6. Neutral trade and the embargo.—Jefferson.
7. War of 1812 and its results.—Madison.
8. Slavery and the Missouri Compromise.—Monroe.
9. Florida purchase and the Monroe doctrine.—John Quincy Adams.
10. Jackson's election and the spoils system.—Van Buren.
11. The United States Bank and the Sub-treasury.—Jackson.
12. Conflicts with States, and nullification.—Calhoun.
13. The tariff, surplus revenue, and internal improvements.—Clay.
14. The anti-slavery movement.—Giddings.
15. Annexation of Texas, and the Mexican War.—Polk.
16. Completion of the boundaries of the United States.—Benton.
17. Compromise of 1850.—Webster.
18. Kansas-Nebraska struggle.—Douglas.
19. The slavery issue, and election of 1860.—Seward.
20. Causes of the Civil War.—Jefferson Davis.

In connection with the lectures several aids for the student have been put in operation. The chief ones are: a printed

---

[1] This course has been arranged for the Swain Free School of New Bedford, Mass.

"outline"; helps on note-taking; maps; diagrams; and helps on thesis writing.

The "outline," of which a sample follows, is prepared by the instructor, and printed, at the expense of those of the class who choose to subscribe for it, under the direction of a committee of their own number. The cost has been about a dollar and a half a page. It is printed in paragraphs, so as readily to catch the eye; it is printed on one side, so that the successive lectures may be detached and put among the students' notes, each in its proper place; it is printed in advance, so that the student may have it before him while he listens. The following is the outline for the first four lectures of the course for 1884-85: —

NOTE. — Opposite each heavy-face heading are noted several brief references, any one of which is sufficient for a general outline of the topic taken up in that section; the more detailed references, in the body of the text, are intended for the convenience of those who desire to go deeper into the history of the period.

1. PROVINCIAL GOVERNMENT AND COLONIAL UNION (1612-1765).

Introduction. The Federal building as we find it.
1. The site — territory.
2. The builders — "the people."
3. Materials — institutions.
4. The plan — the Constitution.
5. The agent — a personified head.
6. The purpose — government.

I. The Land: *Frothingham, Rise of the Republic,* 1-5.
1. In 1620: the wilderness and its inhabitants. *Map.*
2. In 1765: the British Colonies. *Map.*
3. Who owned the land? *Story's Commentaries,* §§ 1-38.

II. The People: *Lodge, English Colonies in America,* ch. II., ch. XVIII.; *McMaster, History of the People of the United States.* I., ch. I.

1. The race: sturdiness of the Anglo-Saxons.
2. Immigration: causes and distribution. *Map.*
3. Population: increase and settlement. *Diagram.*

III. Free Institutions: *Frothingham,* 11–32; *Bancroft,* II., ch. XVII.
1. Rights of Englishmen: *Story,* §§ 146–58.
2. English representative institutions.
3. Principle of self-government: *Porter, Outlines of the Constitutional History of the United States,* 1–36.
4. **Special Colonial Institutions:** *Story's Commentaries,* §§ 159–67.
   a. "Provincial governments."
   b. "Proprietary governments."
   c. "Charter governments."
5. Control by the home government: *Lecky, History of the Eighteenth Century,* II. 2, III. 272, 299; *Bancroft,* III. 1–12, 100–108; *Story,* §§ 183–97.

IV. Attempts to form Colonial Unions: *Porter,* 36–37.
1643. "The United Colonies of New England": *Lodge,* 351–58.
1696–1752. Various English and American plans: *Frothingham,* 111–16.
1754. Congress of Albany — Franklin's scheme: *Frothingham,* 132–40.
1765. Informal union in the Stamp-Act Congress: *Frothingham,* 177–89.
Why union was difficult.

II. REVOLUTIONARY UNION AND INDEPENDENCE. (1765–1776.)

I. Union Accomplished: *Von Holst, History of the United States,* I. 1–20.
   A. The Way Prepared: *Frothingham,* 266–86, 320–39; *Lodge,* 476–91.
   1. Why union was possible.
   2. Effect of the Stamp-Act Congress.
   3. 1772–73. Committees of Correspondence.
   4. 1774. First Continental Congress, union still voluntary: *Journals of Congress,* I. 3–67.

B. **1775-81. A General Government in the Second Continental Congress**: *Lodge*, 498–500, 510–21; *Frothingham*, 466–90.

"The form of the structure."
1. What was Congress? *Story*, § 201; *Frothingham*, 420.
2. What was Congress authorized to do? *Journal of Congress*, I. 73–78.
3. What did Congress do? *Story*, §§ 202–205, 214–17; *Diagram*. Conduct of the war — Foreign affairs: *Hildreth's United States*, III. 76–98.
   General governing powers. Direction of the States.
4. What Congress could not do.

II. **Independence Accomplished**: *Von Holst*, I. 20–35; *Hildreth*, III. 124–39.
   A. **The Way Prepared**: *Frothingham*, 496–539; *Bancroft*, VIII. 381–93, 431–62.
      Early predictions and suggestions.
      Loyalty at the beginning of the Revolution.
      1775. May 31. Mecklenburg resolutions.
         Nov. 3. N. H. advised to form a government.
      1776. March–June. Instructions of the States.
         May 15. Congress votes for independence.
   B. **The Declaration of Independence**: *Frothingham*, 539–60; *Morse's Life of Jefferson*, 26–40.
      1. Who made it? *Jefferson*, I. 9–26.
      2. By what authority? *Story*, §§ 205–13.
      3. Its influence.
      4. Its nature and bearing: *Bancroft*, VIII. 462–75.
      5. Who was made "independent": *Story*, § 213.

III. STATE GOVERNMENTS AND IMPERFECT UNION.
(1776–1786.)

I. **The States.**
   A. **What is a State?** *Story*, §§ 207–209.
   B. **Birth of the States**: *Hildreth*, III. 374–95; *Curtis, History of the Constitution of the United States*, I. 37, 116–20.
      Colonies left without government.

1775-76. Advice of Congress: *Frothingham*, 443-44, 447-51.
Adoption of State constitutions: *Frothingham*, 491-96, 506, 563-68.

C. **Is the Union Older than the States?** *Von Holst*, I. 7-11: *Story*, §§ 210-13; *Curtis*, I. 37-40, 122.
State rights view. *Calhoun's Works*, I. 190.
Temporary purpose view: *Jefferson in Von Holst*, I. 7 n.
National view: *Lincoln's Message, July* 4, 1861.

II. **The Confederation**: *Von Holst*, I. 20-46; *Story*, §§ 218-42.

A. **Articles of Confederation.** "The plan of the structure"; *Hildreth*, III. 395-410.
1775-77. Suggestions and drafts: *Curtis*, I. 104, 124-30.
1777. Nov. 15. Congress adopts the Articles: *Frothingham*, 569-79.
The Territorial disputes: *H. B. Adams in Maryland Historical Society Publications; Curtis*, I. 131-40; *Map*.
1781. March 1. The Confederation in effect. *Map*.
Powers granted — Powers withheld: *Curtis*, I. 140-49.

B. **Defects of the Confederation**: *Story*, § 265.
1. In form.
2. In powers granted.
3. In means of carrying out its powers.
4. Weakness and timidity.

C. **Violations of the Articles of Confederation**: *Elliot Debates*, V. 207-208.
1. The States do not perform their duties. *Diagrams*.
2. Congress oversteps its powers: *The Federalist*, No. 39.
3. The States quarrel with each other: *McMaster*, I. 210.

III. **Union of States in a Confederation a Failure**: *McMaster*, I., ch. III.; *Schouler, History of the United States*, I. 19-34; *Story*, §§ 243-71.
Debts unpaid; Newburg Addresses: *Bancroft, History of the Constitution of the United States*, I. 76-101; *Curtis*, I. 155-74.
Commerce unprotected: *Curtis*, I. 276-90.
Treaty unfulfilled: *Curtis*, I. 249-50.
State governments oppressive: *Bancroft, Constitution*, I. 228-41.

The people rebellious: *McMaster*, I. 294-351.
Western territory ungoverned: *Curtis*, I. 291-308.
Threatened withdrawal of the West: *Curtis*, I. 309-27.
The plan must be altered or the building abandoned.

IV. A NATIONAL GOVERNMENT AND THE UNION. (1781-1789.)
I. **Attempt to Improve the Articles of Confederation**: *Curtis*, I. 328-79.
   A. By granting Particular Powers.
      1781. Five per cent scheme: *Bancroft, Constitution*, I. 34-45.
      1783. Revenue scheme: *Curtis*, I. 233-48.
      1784. Commercial scheme: *Curtis*, I. 276-90; *Bancroft, Constitution*, I. 184-209.
      1787. North-west Ordinance.
   B. By granting Powers of Enforcement.
   C. By altering the Form of the Government.
      1. To a monarchy. (Morris.)
      2. To a centralized government.
      3. To a closer federal government: *Bancroft, Constitution*, I. 146-67.
II. **The Philadelphia Convention**: *Von Holst*, I. 47-53; *Frothingham*, 589-97; *Hildreth*, III. 482-526; *Bancroft, Constitution*, II. 3-222; *Curtis, Constitution*, II. 3-187; *McMaster*, I. 438-53.
Early suggestions of a Convention: *Bancroft, Constitution*, I. 11-76.
Annapolis Convention and formal call: *Curtis*, I. 340-79.
   1. Powers of the Convention: *Curtis*, II. 3-17.
   2. Its task.
   3. Its difficulties.
   4. Its compromises.
   5. Its product, — the "**New Roof**": *Von Holst*, I. 64-79; *Frothingham*, 597-610.
      a. A "government" established: in practical form.
      b. A government with power over individuals.
      c. A government with power to protect itself.
      d. A government which could govern; **purpose** of the structure.

IV. **Acceptance of the Constitution**: *Von Holst,* I. 53–63 ; *McMaster,* I. 454–501; *Curtis,* II. 491–604 ; *Bancroft, Constitution,* II. 225–350.
  1. Process. (1787–88.)
  2. Who ratified it? *Elliot,* I. 319–35.
  3. Who were the people of the United States? *Federalist,* No. 39; *Calhoun's Works,* VI. 151–52; *Elliot,* IV. 499–510 ; *Story,* §§ 362, 463.
  4. 1789. April 6. The new government in effect. *Map.*

As will at once be seen, the outline is meant to guide, and not to be memorized. Indeed, it is purposely cast into a negative form, which shall not convey too much direct information. The advantages of the system are many. It is an aid to intelligent note-taking : the references are verified by the committee, and annoying errors in getting down the references given by the lecturer are avoided ; and since most of the citations are thus before him, the student may follow the lecture more closely. A convenient means of reference and cross-reference to the notes themselves is provided. The lecturer is saved the necessity of putting tables and chronologies on the board, and the arrangement and sequence of his thought is made perfectly clear. To the student it is a skeleton ready to be clothed from his own reading, or always at hand hereafter for a more elaborate study of any topic that may become interesting to him. A further advantage is, that it is possible, together with the outline, to have printed other helps or suggestions, such as do not strictly fall within the scope of the lectures. Such are the

PRINCIPLES OF CONSTITUTIONAL DISCUSSION.

I. Distinguish clearly into which of the following **departments of Controversy** the question falls.
  1. **Origin of the Constitution**: including the question of its form.

2. **Scope of the Constitution**: usually, but not always, a discussion of the extent of legislative powers.
3. **Interpreter of the Constitution**: always involving the judiciary powers and the jurisdiction of the United States Courts.
4. **Execution of the Constitution**: particularly relating to the executive powers, but including others.

II. Observe the **two aspects** selected by the two great schools of Constitutional exposition, — the loose constructionists and strict constructionists.
1. Origin. *a.* Did "**the people**" form the Constitution?
        b. Is it a "**Compact**"?
Discussed particularly in 1791 and 1830.
2. Scope. *a.* Are there "**Constructive powers**"?
        b. Are powers limited to "**express grants**"?
Discussed particularly in 1791, 1799, 1803, 1819, 1833, 1842.
3. Interpreter. *a.* Is the Supreme Court the "**Common arbiter**"?
        b. Can States "**interpose**" to make acts void?
Discussed particularly in 1799, 1815.
4. Execution. *a.* Can the United States "**coerce**" the execution of its acts?
        b. Can States by "**secession**" make themselves independent?
Question raised in 1861. It involves the question of allegiance.

III. Draw arguments from four **sources**.
1. **Nature of government** in general.
2. **Words of the Constitution.**
3. **Opinions.**
    a. Testimony of "the fathers."
    b. Views of statesmen and jurists.
    c. Decisions of the Supreme Court.
4. **Usage**, as shown in the history of the United States.

IV. Keep in mind and avoid certain **difficulties**.
1. **Confusion of arguments** among the different departments of controversy.
2. Possibility of bringing strong **proofs of contrary aspects**.
3. Change of **party views** and party arguments.

The main purpose of the "outline" is, however, to direct, or rather to suggest, the reading of the students. The range of references in any of the larger courses in history is restricted by three difficulties: one mechanical, one temporal, and one general. In the first place, no library has a sufficient number of copies of original sources to furnish fifty or a hundred men with working materials; recourse must therefore be had to easily accessible books, which the student may own or borrow. In the second place, allowing a fair proportion of study hours to the subject of American history, there is time for reading, but not for research, collation, and selection of authorities. The difficulty is made greater by the overwhelming mass of undigested details: the instructor owes it to his students to select the really significant events for them, and to send them direct to a passage where these events may be found described. If time is to be found for original investigation, the field must be restricted. Here comes in the third difficulty. To refer a student in a general way to a library or an alcove, or a work, or even a volume, for information, is, in average cases, to make sure that he will get none: the moral repugnance to deciding what to do first and where to begin, is great enough, without adding the discouragement of having to select one's materials. It is, of course, a good thing for a man to read books which are not very useful, and to handle and recognize many that he cannot read. But, as a practical matter of fact, ordinary students cannot be got to investigate in a course covering so much ground; and, indeed, where there is so much trash, it is unfair to turn them into an intellectual cornfield, to help themselves. The references therefore should be specific and limited: there should be no excuse for not taking hold somewhere. The first class of references in the outline is made up of those opposite the sub-heads of the lectures; many are given in the list of topics quoted above. They are to common books; they are precise; they are limited; the student is held responsible for one, at least, on every sub-topic. The second class of references, in the body of the outline, is intended for the more ambitious students, or for special work; the references are chiefly to the sources.

In arranging the references, care is taken to introduce the reader to a variety of authors, and to refer often to books which take a different view from that presented in the lectures. The whole plan rather takes for granted some system of "reserved books," by which the books most often cited are kept altogether for use in the library, or may be drawn out only over night. The one book on which most reliance is placed is Von Holst's. No writer has so thoroughly studied and digested the enormous mass of material; no writer searches more carefully for the hidden springs of action; none is so suggestive. He assumes, however, a general knowledge of the history of the country, which must be supplied by other reading or from the lectures.

Neither the outline nor the study of the references is considered sufficient. Students are expected to take careful notes, and to complete them out of their own reading. As an assistance to the somewhat difficult labor, a system is recommended: it is designed to spare as much time from the manual labor of writing as may be, and thus to leave as much as possible for study.

Suggestions for taking Notes.

1. Have a regular **system**.
2. If you have worked out a system of **your own** which satisfies you, do not change it.
3. **Shorthand** is not a great convenience, unless the notes are afterwards put into a form which may be read by any one.

4. A system of recognizable **abbreviations** is desirable.

5. Take notes **all the time** during the lecture.

6. A word-for-word reproduction of what you hear is much less valuable to you than your own **condensed form**, embodying the lecturer's ideas.

7. Distinguish in your own mind the **heads of the lecture** as it proceeds, and paragraph your notes accordingly.

8. Aim to set down the **substance of general statements**, in your own words, rather than to note a part of each sentence.

9. Practise getting the **exact words** of significant phrases or quotations.

10. If you miss something important, **ask to have it repeated**.

11. If you lose a lecture, **fill up the blank** immediately, from the note-book of a fellow-student.

12. After each lecture, go over your notes, and clearly **indicate the heads**: (*a*) by catch-words in the margin; or (*b*) by underlining words.

13. Once a week **review** the notes taken since the previous review.

14. Make out a brief **table of contents**, as you go along, referring to pages of your note-books.

[*For courses, in any subject, made up chiefly of lectures with parallel readings, the following specific system is recommended.*]

1. Use a **note-book** ruled in three vertical columns : a narrower one next the outer edge; the remaining space on each page equally divided. Let there be a broad horizontal line an inch or more from the top.

2. Enter your **notes** in the middle column; dates and headings (if desired) in the outer column.

3. **Do not rewrite** the notes taken in class.

4. Enter abstracts or quotations from your **later readings** in the inner column, each opposite the passage in the notes which it is meant to illustrate.

5. Across the top of the page write a **running heading** in two, three, or four members, summarizing the matter on the page; *e.g.*, " History, — Methods, — Note-Taking."

6. Begin to write on the right side of the opened book, and **begin each** distinct general **head** on a new leaf.

7. Each leaf being thus **complete in itself** may at any time be detached and used in another connection; or others may be interleaved, without disturbing the logical connection.

8. Copy or reproduce **tables, diagrams, or maps** before the succeeding lecture.

One of the most important aids to the study of American history is the use of maps. A large outline map should be painted on a movable blackboard; it is sufficient to indicate the coasts, and a few great water-courses, and the State boundary lines. By using colored crayons, it is easy, in a few minutes, to present any desired general maps, on a scale large enough to be seen at a distance of forty feet. Where a larger scale is desired, or the field is out of the limits of the United States, sketches may be made on the blackboard, or permanent maps on thick paper. It is much simpler than it seems to draw rough maps on a large scale: even those who are not draughtsmen will find no difficulty. A roll of strong manila paper, a few colored crayons, or, better still, water colors, a yard-stick, and a small map on which rectangles may be lightly ruled, are all the materials necessary. For the student's use, the signal-service weather-map, which costs eighteen cents a dozen, is exactly what is needed: with a few colored pencils he can reproduce the large map; and, at the end of the year, he will have a historical atlas of his own.

The first use of the maps is to illustrate the territorial development of the country, by bringing before the eye the successive cessions and purchases. At the same time, the perplexing boundary controversies may be made clear. The close connection between annexations and the inner political history of the country is often brought out in startling relief, when presented to the eye. Next comes the internal development of the country. Successive maps, dated say ten years apart, may show the extent of settlement, and the formation of Territories and States. Even political affairs may sometimes be strikingly mapped out: thus, a series of maps showing the distribution of the Presidential vote in each succeeding election will forever fix in the mind the slow growth of sectional parties. Special maps may be used for a variety of purposes. The theatre of wars and campaigns, detailed boundary controversies, proposed sites for the national capital, schemes of internal improvements, — these and many like subjects may be made to appeal to the eye.

Another form of illustration, equally useful, and much less generally known, is the use of graphic charts. A set of coördinate lines, ruled on a blackboard, or perhaps on the back of the movable map, and a dozen colored crayons, are all that is necessary. The student can use cross-section paper and a few colored pencils. All the various forms of graphic charts can be put in use: curves, blocks, squares, triangles, circles, or shaded maps. The easiest subject to illustrate is the growth of population: a curve may be drawn in five minutes which will leave on the mind a clearer notion of the progress of the United States than could half a dozen pages of print. Two similar curves will show ineffaceably the comparative growth of the sections; another diagram may show a comparison between the population of this and of other countries: and the student will never forget how the United States has outstripped most European powers if he has once seen its rocket's path plotted out. In like manner, the apportionment of representatives to the States and sections may be represented, or the status of political parties in Congress. A most suggestive diagram may be made of the changes in the rank of States, reckoning by population. Then come revenue, expenditure, and debt: they may be compared with each other, or with similar statistics in other countries. By the same system may be shown the territorial extension of the United States, and the division of the acquisitions between the sections. The depreciation of paper currency, the number of banks, and other economic phenomena may be clearly shown. The sales of the available public lands, appropriations for internal improvements, are examples of similar possibilities. In the census atlas of 1874, and the census reports of 1870 and 1880, may be found a variety of such charts. It is even possible to represent certain great political doctrines by diagram: thus the different theories as to the ratification of the Constitution may be defined from each other by a few simple drawings.

Only one aid for the student remains to be described. To require theses is to expect more than the average student can give, in time and thought. It is well, however, to encourage them; and it will almost always be found that the best writer has also the best general knowledge of the course. The only general instruction given in connection with the course is summed up in the

Hints to Thesis Writers.

1. Be sure you are willing to do the necessary **work**.
2. Select a **subject** which interests you, if possible in a limited field, but over a long period.
3. Begin by noting the chief **authorities**.
   a. Furnished by the instructor.
   b. In Poole's Index and the Q. P. Indexes.
   c. In the Subject Catalogue.

    d. In other classified library catalogues.
    e. In accessible bibliographies.
    Write the title, author (with initials), place, and date.
4. Have a **system of note-taking**.
    a. Note only one subject on each piece of paper.
    b. Note the authority, volume, and page, for each quotation or abstract.
    c. Preferably use loose sheets, arranging as you go.
5. From the general authorities, make out a **synopsis** of the chief points which are to be studied, observing:
    a. New authorities and references for extension of details;
    b. Chronological development;
    c. Salient sub-heads of your subject.
6. Extend the **details** which appear to you to need further examination. If necessary make synopses of the sub-heads. Make *references* for other sub-heads, but abstract them later.
7. **Arrange** your sheets of notes in a logical form, sub-heads under main heads. Choose between chronological or topical arrangement, or a combination.
8. **Compose** the thesis.
    a. First settling the proportions.
    b. Introducing striking quotations.
    c. Giving exact references for all important statements of fact.
9. **Write** only on one side of your paper, and leave space for your foot-notes on the same page as the text which they illustrate.
10. Do your work throughout as though it were to appear in print.
11. Add a **bibliography** of authorities, with brief remarks on the bearing of the most important.

The value of the work to the student needs no argument: and the results at Harvard have been such as to justify the system. Those who engage in it find their interest in the whole field aroused; they are quicker to seize on the great principles of the subject, and, in some cases, they do work of real scientific value.

The means employed to keep students up to their work may be very briefly described. The first is a series of written exercises. Perhaps the most helpful are the brief written suggestions on questions raised in the lectures, to which reference has already been made. They can be arranged so as to call for a little original thinking. The second test is a system of brief examinations, — perhaps ten or fifteen minutes, once a week; they may be contrived to require the application of principles, developed in the lectures, to new specific cases. A third means, the recitation or quiz, takes time from the lectures, and is nearly impossible in a large class. The main dependence is on the regular examinations, twice a year. Questions can always be so framed as to call for thought rather than for a memory of details; and an opportunity may be given to put most of the time on two or three general questions, testing the knowledge of the whole subject.

THE PRACTICAL METHOD IN HIGHER HISTORICAL INSTRUCTION.

BY EPHRAIM EMERTON, OF HARVARD UNIVERSITY.

IN the academic teaching of history three possible methods of instruction suggest themselves at once: the recitation, the lecture, and original work. We may assume for the present that the discussion as to the value of recitation from a book is practically at an end. While admitting that the power of accurate re-statement of a thing learned is valuable to the student, the common sense of most has concluded that the time spent by an educated man in listening to such repetition is an actual loss to science, and that the brighter students of a class can employ themselves very much more profitably than in hearing the mistakes of their duller mates. Adding to this that the learning of what is contained in any one book, especially on a subject admitting wide difference in point of view, can go but little way toward widening or deepening a man's mental capacity, and remembering that such acquisition is usually easiest to shallow minds, we may at once relegate recitations to their proper place, namely, in elementary instruction, where they ought to be insisted upon with unbending severity.

The historical lecture, while liable to great abuses, has certainly its well-defined use, and, therefore, its right to be. It should not be designed to convey definite and detailed information. That is the evil in Germany. Men of mediocre — even men of splendid talents often commit the glaring mistake of spending four or five hours a week in the dreary recitation of facts which their hearers could gather in one-tenth of the time from printed books. Perhaps the book might even be the work of the very lecturer who is now making his capital pay him a double interest. I recall a course of lectures on German History given by a man whose name, standing among the very highest in Germany, served to fill his auditorium with a keenly-expectant audience. In the course of a fortnight a dozen hearers might have been counted, scattered about among the nearly empty benches. The instinct of the students had shown them that he was not offering them anything which they could not gain more easily elsewhere.

The justification of academic lectures on history, is that they shall contain *suggestion*, which shall enable students to do their own reading intelligently, and, therefore, profitably. They should contain the result of varied reading and research, summarizing the outcome of long controversies, showing how events of one period explain and are explained by those of another. It would take the inexperienced student weeks of reading to grasp the meaning of men and events which his instructor may present to him in a paragraph. Not that this presentation can ever be accepted as a substitute for the student's own reading, but that it forms the almost indispensable condition of a wise and profitable use of historical works. Reading alone soon becomes repulsive and wearisome because one sees no way out of it. All books seem alike dreary and stale; but let the living word of a living man once illumine the whole study with its invigorating rays, and the student finds his reading filled with a meaning he never dreamed of.

The danger here I have already hinted at. Goethe saw it clearly enough:

> "Denn was man schwarz auf weiss besitzt
> Kann man getrost nach Hause tragen,"

says the already half-conventionalized scholar to his infernal counsellor. The scholar cannot be wiser than his master. If a mere unthinking note-taking be accepted as sufficient effort on his part, he would be more than human if he made a greater one. Doubtless the result will disappoint him. He will find himself at the end of his studies wretchedly equipped for any scholarly work; he will wonder why this is so, but he cannot be expected to reach the reason. Let him be assured that the reason is a very simple one: his mind has never been called upon for independent, individual effort, and it is only the mind of a rare genius which works without being called upon. It would seem an astonishing proposition at this day that chemistry or physics could be taught without a laboratory, and yet it is not so very long since laboratories were either not used at all, or so very little as to be scarce worth mentioning. Experiment and demonstration by the instructor to his class go very little way. The student must have his chemicals and his apparatus in his own hands before he can have any realizing sense of the meaning of his science. Men have learned this in regard to physical study. In every new school of learning a well-equipped laboratory is as much a necessity as a well-trained teacher. It remains to apply the same method to other branches of education. Here we are concerned with history only, and the conclusion is inevitable, that historical teaching, to be effective, must not confine itself to lectures, but must supplement these by the method of original work.

Attention has recently been called to this subject by two

articles[1] by Professor Paul Frédéricq, lately of Liège, now of Ghent, who, in the years 1881 and 1882, visited the principal universities of Germany, and the various schools of Paris, to observe the methods of higher instruction in history. These articles are, as the author informs us, merely a traveller's notes, without any pretence at completeness or profundity. I have made use of them for certain statistical information not elsewhere easily accessible. Their grace of style and amiability of tone make them altogether quite attractive reading.

The phrase employed by Professor Frédéricq for the peculiar institution he was observing is the "*cours pratique*," as opposed to the usual lecture-course, which he calls the "*cours théorique*." The term "Practice-course" seems to me really an improvement upon the various originals employed in the different German universities, though these original terms have each an historical significance which the men who made them and have handed them down would doubtless be sorry to lose. The "Gesellschaften" (societies), "Seminaria" (training schools), and "Uebungen" (exercises) of Germany appear all together in M. Frédéricq's report as "cours pratiques" (practice-courses). His word expresses the actual fact that these classes now form a regular part of the university work; are numbered among its published courses of instruction, and are counted as such, to the credit of both professors and students. The German terms, on the other hand, express the fact of their development out of originally voluntary and, one may say, extra-academic exercises. The Gesellschaft implies a society of students grouped about a

---

[1] "De l'Enseignement Supérieur de l'Histoire." Gand, 1882, pp. 49. In the "Revue de l'Instruction publique en Belgique."
"L'Enseignement Supérieur de l'Histoire à Paris," Paris, 1883, pp. 61. In the "Revue International de l'Enseignement." July 15, 1883.

professor, and working with him in lines of special research, and under conditions not imposed by academic rules, but growing out of the common enthusiasm for the study in hand. Their relation to their teacher reminds one of the early mediæval relation of the university student to his lecturer. It is personal, feudal almost, for there is a bond of mutual service here which adds its force to distinguish these classes from their contemporaries, grouped in the ordinary lecture-room, and learning from the spoken word. While there a certain tradition, if not fixed statute, has determined the attitude of the student to the imposing being who talks at him *ex cathedra*, here all is voluntary, free, unconventional. This is a society, a club, presided over by a professor, but composed, not of subject students, but of "members," of whom the guiding scholar, chancing to be a professor, is the chief.

The word "Seminarium" brings us to another phase of the institution we are studying. The primitive society became a training-school. The German, with his hard-headed practical sense, having allowed university teaching to crystallize into the form of a lecture-system, saw an escape from its deadening influence upon the mind in this new form of instruction. This enthusiasm of the individual student was now to be made practical. The name "Seminarium" denotes the fertilizing power of the historical "Gesellschaft" on the intellectual life of Germany. Out of these training-schools came the men who gave to historical science in Germany, and through Germany to the world, the impulse under which it is now moving.

But by this time the voluntary association had become a recognized feature of university life. The professor conducted a Seminarium as a matter of course, and the student who meant to distinguish himself in the department entered one or more seminaria equally as a matter of course. And now comes the third of the distinctive names — the oldest in point of time — to express sharply the marked difference in *kind* of work done here from that of the ordinary classroom. "Uebungen" still denotes the practical character of the Seminar work, and is the one term from which M. Frédéricq has derived his "cours pratique." Its meaning is that uppermost in the student's mind. Elsewhere he is a listener, here he is a worker; no longer a mere receiver of another man's thought, he becomes an investigator, a discoverer, a creator.

The founder of practice-courses as an adjunct to higher historical instruction is the veteran professor Leopold Ranke, now, in his eighty-ninth year, laboring with juvenile enthusiasm and power on his crowning work, a History of the World. As early as 1830 Ranke began to gather about him such students as desired to learn the method of historical investigation, inviting them to a weekly meeting at his house. These meetings appear upon the Berlin university programme of that day as "exercitationes historicae." This private class in Ranke's study became in the truest sense of the word the seminarium for all future historical work in Germany. Among its early members were Waitz, Duncker, Giesebrecht, Sybel, Adolf Schmidt, Wattenbach, and many others whose names have become synonyms for powerful and honest work in opening up the record of the past. These men, called to various universities, carried with them the practice-course as their chief instrument in spreading the doctrine of true historical method which the great master Ranke had taught them. They have now become veterans in their turn, and their pupils, an army of still younger men, have carried out still more widely the theory of the practical method.

At first the subject most often treated was the history of Germany's heroic age, the mediæval empire; but soon, under the leadership of the elder Droysen, modern history found its place, and at present no department of historical research is without its practice-course as a supplement to theoretical teaching. At Berlin there are regularly six or eight such courses, led by men like Mommsen, Droysen, Wattenbach, Weizsächer, Bresslau, and Hassel. Other universities follow with a number of courses proportioned to their strength in the department of history.

Any one familiar with the inner working of these classes feels at once that here is the true life of the historical department. Here it is that the professor reveals himself to his select pupils as a fellow-worker with them. He is at work upon inquiries which are to bear fruit in his own publication, and these young men are made to feel that they are contributing personally, by their researches, to the completion of these works. The method of procedure is practically the same in the various universities and under the various teachers. Indeed, it is but one method employed with endless diversity, according to the character of the man in whose hands it may be. The essential principle of the practice-course is to lead the student back from the ordinary presentation of history as a completed whole in standard narratives to the original sources from which these narratives have been composed. To the ordinary student, higher as well as lower, the study of history means the reading of narratives describing men and events in the form of more or less entertaining stories. He fancies that he has passed from elementary to higher study when he reads somewhat biggei books and more of them. Even the German " Gymnast" is liable to this error. He may bring it with him to the university; he may even retain it there so long as he confines himself to the hearing of lectures and collateral reading, — but the moment he passes the door of the seminarium his error falls from him as by magic. The charm which has heretofore surrounded the names of great historians vanishes. He learns to accept nothing on their word. He demands the proof of every assertion, or if, as is often the case, proof be impossible, he demands at least evidence as to degree of probability. And this he does not blindly, not in the spirit of mere carping criticism, but intelligently, under the guidance of men who are themselves makers of books, and who are on the watch at every step to detect a flaw in his argument, an error in his judgment, or a gap in his powers of perception. Thus he becomes *trained*, not merely *learned*, as we use that phrase to describe a man who has taken in an enormous amount of material, without regard to his ability to use it. The German Seminarist is armed at all points to grapple with his material wherever he may find it.

The ordinary course of the Seminar work is somewhat as follows. The professor assigns to each member some topic for investigation, usually some controverted point upon which various opinions may be possible. Often these topics are selected from a limited period, so that the various researches will cross each other at many points. Thus each student becomes familiar with the authorities used by all the others, and is able to form an intelligent judgment of their work. As the term progresses, any student may be called upon to criticise the work of every other. Ordinarily the result of each investigation is presented in the form of a written dissertation, which is read by its author, and publicly criticised, first by a member of the class selected beforehand for the purpose, then by other members at their pleasure, and finally by the professor himself. It is evident that this criticism is by no means the least useful part of the work. It is dealt out with an unsparing hand. Indeed, M. Frédéricq informs us that Professors Droysen and Mommsen refused to admit him to the exercises of their Seminars, excusing this apparent want of courtesy by saying that the presence of a stranger might be a check upon the unlimited criticism which was there the rule.

I had the good fortune to be, during one year, a regular member of the practice-course of the elder Droysen in Berlin, and can thoroughly confirm the impression received by M. Frédéricq. The criticism was free and unrestrained to the verge of savagery. I well remember one unhappy youth, who ought never to have been there, whose productions were received with a mixture of derision and scathing logical analysis which, to a member of a less thick-skinned race, would have been torture. At the same time, I cannot help bearing testimony to the uniform consideration which I, as a stranger and a foreigner, received from students and professor alike. The inspiration of the Saturday evenings spent amidst that vigorous intellectual jousting has entered into every moment of subsequent study, and been a constant support in the effort to carry on the impulse there received.

The papers thus produced, especially by students who have been for several terms members of the Seminar, are often of more than passing value, are actual contributions to historical science. The younger Droysen began some time since to publish the more important papers contributed in his class at Halle, and an association of university professors is now carrying on a similar work, with a larger scope, and a wider promise of usefulness. One can well understand that the prospect of such distinction must be a keen spur to the diligence and activity of mind of many a student, who, under the ordinary conditions of the lecture-room, would never have risen above his fellows.

Within a few years a distinction has arisen between what we may call private and public practice-courses. The former are such as I have been describing, in which the membership is determined by the professor's judgment as to the capacity and promise of the individual student.

The public courses mark an innovation upon the original plan. Certain professors, strongly impressed with the absolute importance of the practice-course as an agent in instruction, and wishing to extend its advantages to as many students as possible, obtained from their governments sufficient appropriations of money to provide working-rooms for their classes, to furnish these rooms with reference libraries, and with all necessary appliances for study, and also to establish scholarships for regularly enrolled members. This system, while offering great attractions to a large body of students, has met with violent opposition from the more conservative professors to whom the traditions of the practice-course, as established by Ranke, had become especially dear. To their minds, the substitution of state control for the personal relation of the instructor to the student must endanger the essential and vital principle of the Gesellschaft. In short, they believed that the very nature of the association implied the membership of picked men only, and more especially of such as proposed to make historical work the business of their lives. However this may be, the two systems are now in operation side by side, and the future must determine which is based upon the truer foundation. Thus far, I incline to believe that the conservatives have the best of the argument.

But it must not be supposed that the practice-course in its essential theory has escaped criticism and opposition. The point is made, and with much show of reason, that German historical writing has within the last two generations steadily lost in breadth of view and in power of effective presentation, while its gain has been steadily in the direction of minute and careful investigation of narrow and narrowing details. Perhaps the most striking illustration of the truth of this criticism is the fact that we are still without a satisfactory treatment of the history of Germany as a whole, while the number of treatises, large and small, upon detached periods or single institutions is simply distracting. There is scarcely a point in the whole range of German history which has not given rise to at least a Gymnasium-program or a Doctor-dissertation. It seems as if the very minuteness of the research into the records of the Fatherland had frightened everyone away from the task of moulding this whole mass into an available and comprehensive form.

Now the charge is made that the cause of this deficiency in graphic power among German historians to-day is the belittling influence of the training in the Seminar. Certain it is that both leaders and followers in the work of disinterring the German record from its long burial, and of preparing it for use in the world, have been the men who organized and developed the practice-course. We may admit further, that if the practice-course had not been, the *Monumenta* of Pertz, and the host of investigations leading up to and based upon that colossal undertaking, could scarcely have been produced. But I incline to think that this character of minute investigation does not imply the entire absence of graphic skill or breadth of historic insight. It is rather the evidence of a deeply-felt reaction from the false methods, — the dramatic form, the partisan purpose, the rhetorical elaboration, which mark the historical writing of the eighteenth century. The falseness of that method was so strongly felt that men avoided consciously any approach toward brilliant presentation. Germans especially did not care to cultivate a kind of ability which seemed to them of questionable value. Before philosophizing about the record, the record must be had; and so the last half century has been a time of accumulation and preparation of material upon which future philosophies of history may, if one pleases, be constructed. The distinctive character of German historical science has been an absolute devotion to the discovery of historical documents; to comparing them, and thus ascertaining their value; and then to publishing them in a form convenient for the use of scholars.

If one must choose between a school of history whose main characteristic is *esprit*, and one which rests upon a faithful and honest effort to base its whole narration upon the greatest attainable number of recorded facts, we cannot long hesitate. This character of diligence and honesty of research into the actual story of the past has been stamped upon Germany by the work of the seminary. Training has taken the place of brilliancy, and the whole civilized world is to-day reaping the benefit. Doubtless, if this mechanical skill were to be the sole object of instruction, the result would be most unsatisfactory. After all, it is the power of arranging and combining his material which makes the great historian. Ranke himself is the triumphant vindication of his system. Let one but read the modest words of his preface to the German History, where he speaks of mastering the contents of something like a hundred folio volumes of proceedings of the Diet in one library, and as many more in another, before putting pen to paper, and then let one turn to his narrative, in which the spoils of this gigantic research are utilized with telling power, and one sees how in the hands of the master these two elements — minute research and gift of presentation — are combined to produce a truly great historical work.

So it must be with instruction, — the training of the hand must not exclude the culture of the mind. Nor does this seem to be, even in Germany, a threatening danger. With Treitschke, lecturing in an improvised auditorium to seven hundred students; with Droysen, holding three hundred to a course of lectures on modern European history; with Georg Voigt delighting a crowded audience in Leipzig with his brilliant picture of the French Revolution, — there can be no fear that the student will be left without inspiration to broad and liberal reflection upon the great movements of history. Admitting a certain tendency to narrowness in the technical training of the seminary, there is the widest opportunity for counteracting it and making it effective by the broader view and the more comprehensive range of the public lecture.

The following table, compiled from the "Deutscher Universitäts-Kalender," shows the amount of historical instruction offered in 1883-4 by the seven German universities which pay most attention to the subject. The proportion of practice-courses to theoretical teaching may easily be perceived.

	Universal.	Oriental.	Greek and Roman.	Mediæval.	Modern.	Contemporary.	German.	Local.	France.	England.	Italy.	Slavs.	Sources & Method.	Diplomatics.	Palæography.	Chronology.	Practice-Courses.	Total.	Geography.
BERLIN	1	1	2	1	4	1	2	1Pr.	1		1	3						8 26	4
LEIPSIC			1	4	1	2		4 1Pr.		1		2		1				8 25	4
HALLE			3	4	1	1	4			1		1	1	1				4 21	2
BRESLAU	1		1	2	1			2Pr.	1	1								5 14	1
GÖTTINGEN			2	2		4								1	1			4 14	2
BONN			3	2	1							2		1				4 13	2
HEIDELBERG				1		3		1					1					2 8	

But perhaps the best proof of the value of the practical method in historical teaching is its progress and its success in countries outside of Germany, notably in France.[1] Until within twenty years, there had scarcely been such a thing as real historical instruction in France. There were, to be sure, at the ancient Collège de France, courses of history, held by men of distinguished excellence as historians and lecturers; but, strange as it sounds to our ears, these lectures were not addressed to students at all. They were held in open halls, where all the world might come, and the audience, varying with each lecture, was composed of women, travellers, and old men, of whom many chose this opportunity for their afternoon nap. If here and there a young man was seen, he was in no relation to the lecturer. He had only to take his notes, and do the best he could with them.

It is evident that this sort of historical treatment of any subject must be wholly wanting in every element of fruitfulness. It could never produce men, who, in their time, should become effective teachers and writers. The glaring absurdity of such a system was visible to all the rising generation of scholars, but the method of reform was doubtful. The process finally adopted was to go around the ancient forms, and to establish new schools upon a different basis. This process has now been going on, with interruptions, from the time of the first Napoleon. The final result is a complex of schools, each with a certain purpose, with a separate government support, its own buildings or rooms, and its own pupils. And yet, so often do the purposes of these schools cross each other, that their separation cannot be kept complete, and simply causes a vast and inexcusable waste of money,

---

[1] The details of the French system are taken mainly from Professor Frédéricq's article.

time, and energy. No less than five different schools in Paris are devoted wholly or in part to the study of history.

1. The Collège de France, dating from the time of Francis I., continues, almost unchanged, the traditions of the past. M. Frédéricq heard some of the most distinguished scholars of France lecturing in enormous halls to a score or so of chance hearers, of whom scarce one could have had any serious scholarly purpose.

2. The Faculté des Lettres, the successor of the ancient Sorbonne, occupies the building which still perpetuates the name of that venerable institution. Here, too, until within a few years, the instruction was mainly intended for *hearers* rather than for *pupils;* but now, mainly through the energy of Victor Duruy, as minister of public instruction under Napoleon III., the substitution of pupils for hearers has become almost complete, and many of the more serious courses are now designated as *cours fermés*, to which admission can be had only on the written order of the Dean. The same general purpose has been followed in the appointment of promising young scholars as *maîtres de conférences*, a position corresponding somewhat to that of the *privatdocent* in the German University. Students under the Faculté des Lettres are in training for a special diploma as teachers of history. This diploma has existed only since 1880, and marks the recognition of history as one among the sciences demanding trained teachers.

3. The École des Chartes was founded in 1821, but lived a precarious existence until 1847, when it was provided with sufficient quarters and a competent staff of instructors. Here we may learn especially the method of historical research. Instruction is given in palæography, romance languages, bibliography and classification of libraries and archives, diplomatics, political, administrative, and judicial institutions

of France, the civil and canon law, and the archæology of the middle ages. Here is to be found at least as great, if not a greater opportunity, for preparation in the art of writing history, than can be obtained at any German university. The excellent "Bibliothèque de l'École des Chartes" contains the work of professors, pupils, and graduates.

4. The École Normale Supérieure dates back beyond the Revolution, but was also first placed upon a sound working basis in 1847. History enters here as part of a general course for all students during two years, and may be made a specialty during the third and final year. During this third year, pupils may attend courses in the other schools. The distinct purpose of the École Normale is the preparation of teachers. Only a limited number of pupils can enter each year, — perhaps one in every six or seven applicants, — a curious instance of protecting industry.

5. The École Pratique des Hautes Études was another creation of Minister Duruy in the year 1868. The condition of French advanced teaching, even as late as that, was such that M. Duruy, in presenting his plan to the Emperor, was forced to say that a student in Paris, however able lecturers he might hear, and however many and excellent books might be accessible to him, was left altogether without the personal guidance necessary to apply his study most effectively. This was true of all subjects. The remedy suggested by the minister was to offer, in addition to all the valuable and interesting instruction then given, a series of practice-courses, which, taken together, should form the École Pratiques des Hautes Études. One of the four branches of this school was that of history and philology. Beginning with but few pupils, the historical and philological branch of the Hautes Études now numbers twenty-five professors, and offers more than fifty practice-courses. Before presenting the plan for

this new departure, a systematic study of methods in use in other countries was made, and, of course, one sees clearly where the real model was found. The *Conférence* of France is the "Seminar" of Germany. The most prominent leaders in the new movement have themselves studied in Germany. M. Alfred Maury is director of this department, aided by M. Gabriel Monod, known to all the world of scholars as the editor, first of the "Revue Critique," and afterwards, of the "Revue Historique," altogether the leading historical periodical of the world. From the beginning, the administration has been largely in the hands of young and comparatively little known men, who were in sympathy with the practical method, and had no ambition to become historical orators in the grand style of the previous generation. Thus, to the brilliant and vivacious Frenchman, as well as to the more stolid and plodding German, it has become clear, that to make a science fruitful, productive of new work and new men, it must be made *practical*. The record of the past, as it lies there in inscriptions, institutions, legal records, names of places, coins, systems of chronology, as well as in consciously written histories, must be put into the hands of students, and they must be trained in the way to use them.

There is something positively pathetic in the words of M. Lavisse, in the year 1880, to the pupils of the Faculté des Lettres.[1]

"I recall the time when I was a candidate for the historical diploma, and, better still, the time, far less remote, when I watched the third-year pupils of the École Normale at their work. At the beginning of the year they set themselves bravely at their task, without a breathing-space from

---

[1] Quoted by M. Frédéricq, from the "Revue Internationale de l'Enseignement" for February 15, 1881.

morning till night. They helped each other, but each did the burden of his work for himself. The study-room was filled with books borrowed from the emptied shelves of the library. The drawers were filled with well-arranged piles of notes. Their comrades, who were preparing for other examinations, especially in philosophy, where the demand was less burdensome, made fun of the unhappy historical students, whom they considered as mere day-laborers. But they held out bravely. History, thank God, has so potent a charm that it helps one to bear fatigue, as the hope of discovering a vast new horizon sustains the weary traveller who climbs painfully the steep mountain side! But some of the travellers give out, and I have scarce known one of our future historians who was not overcome by discouragement on his way. It comes when one has passed over the grand questions which attracted him at first, and finds that he has barely glanced at their surface, while he is already pressed upon by a throng of new ones, less important, but any one of which may, as we say, 'be given.' 'Do you think, sir,' they say to the tutor, 'that we shall have this question? or this?' and the tutor cannot always say 'No.' There comes a moment when the student feels that he is going to drown himself. He loses his head, and begins to draw up lists of the kings of Egypt, the sultans of Turkey, or the Hansa cities, and rushes feverishly from the successors of Alexander to those of Charlemagne, from the Samnite war to the wars of the Roses, from the tributaries of the Danube to those of the Mississippi, from Hanno and Pytheas to Livingstone and Nachtigal, taking Marco Polo on the way. He comes down from books to outlines, and from outlines to manuals. He keeps before him the lyceum program; he divides it into numbers, and marks off twenty or thirty numbers on which he is prepared. There remain a hundred about which he knows not a word. He comes up to his examination jaded out, and, what is worse, trained to wretched habits. which may lead his mind astray forever, and disgust him with all honest work."

Out of this slough of despair and self-deception French students have been rescued through the influence of the German Seminar system, applied with that wider tact which might have been expected from a people more susceptible to general ideas, and less in danger of becoming mechanical in their methods.

We are thus brought to the point toward which all that I have said thus far has been tending,—the possibility of usefulness for the historical practice-course in America. It will be generally admitted that our historical instruction is at least in an undeveloped condition. Whether as a reflection of the ultra-American notion that we here are independent of all tradition, have nothing to learn from the experience of the past, or for whatever reason, the fact is that history forms an extremely unimportant element in our plans of education. The New England colleges require for admission only a nodding acquaintance with Greek and Roman history, an amount of knowledge which may be readily taken in through the pores while " reading " classic authors. Of European and American history the ordinary Freshman has a colossal ignorance. Within these Eastern colleges themselves the situation is not very much better. It would be idle to assert that history has as yet reached anything like an equality with classics, mathematics, or science, either in the amount of time devoted to it or in the character of the men to whom its teaching is entrusted. As to the average

Western college, the attention paid to history is simply infinitely small, and may be neglected. Until within a few years such a thing as a special preparation for teaching history had not been heard of. Any classical instructor could teach the history of Greece or Rome, no matter if he had never in his life looked into his classics with any other purpose than to solve grammatical puzzles. Any "cultivated gentleman" could teach European history; and as for America, one might suppose a knowledge of its history to form a part of those innate ideas some philosophers tell us about, for all the effort visible to compass it by way of education.[1]

Within these few years a very great change has taken place. The leaven of the German method has begun to work among us. Young Americans at German universities, becoming impressed with the value of the system of instruction there, saw the hope of occupation and usefulness in transplanting this method to our shores. They threw themselves with a new energy into the study of history as a science by itself, and their enthusiasm was rewarded by finding on their return that the leading colleges of their own land had kept pace with the demand of the time and were ready to employ them. The number of these younger scholars is not very great. The road is an arduous one; the rewards tardy and never dazzling. But, in spite of obstacles, the number of devoted scholars in this field is increasing. They are reasonably certain of finding employment. The lesser colleges must follow in the footsteps of the greater; where classes of history do not exist, they will be created. The elementary

---

[1] Since the above was written, attention has been called to the defects in American historical teaching by President Eliot of Harvard University, in an address at Johns Hopkins University, printed in the "Century" magazine for June, 1884.

teaching must become better and more widely diffused as the students of our colleges go out from under enthusiastic teachers to become teachers in their turn. So far as quantity goes, we may well believe that the future of historical teaching in our country is secure. It is now with quality that we are concerned. As soon as a branch of science takes a recognized place upon the college programme, the question of method becomes of the first importance.

If my argument as to recitations and lectures shall have been approved, it follows that the method of original work remains as the indispensable supplement to whatever other means of instruction the wise teacher may employ. I am aware that there is an intelligent opposition to this view. There are educators who maintain that the original work of college students is in itself of so little value that it is a mere waste of time. These youngsters cannot be expected to produce anything better than what now exists, and would much better spend their time in learning the best of what has been done. "As well advise students of Shakespeare," said an accomplished professor of English, "to practise themselves in composing plays, in the hope of some day producing something better than their master."

But this line of argument wholly misses the point at issue. It is not for the sake of the immediate results that the practice-course is to be commended. The student in chemistry does not expect to gain from his own early and awkward experiments any new or startling results. He only aims to comprehend, as one can only do by personal experiment, those laws of chemical action already laid down by previous investigation. So the student of history may not expect to arrive at new results during the time of his apprenticeship, but he will certainly learn how other men have arrived at their results, and will thus know how to measure these at their true value. We may even go a step further. Just as here and there a rarely gifted mind, working patiently through hands and eyes in the chemical laboratory, may strike out a truth which has escaped the experience of the past, so the vigorous mind, working out by means of original investigation problems of history, may here and there light upon a conclusion which shall at once elevate his work to the rank of distinguished excellence.

In natural science we have come to recognize the absolute necessity of practical methods, and the expression of this is found in the countless chemical, physical, zoölogical, and geological laboratories now used even in the most elementary scientific instruction.

But, now, are not these illustrations of a great general law of education? Do they not declare that in moral science, as well as in physical, the practical method of instruction is the only effectual method? I believe that underneath all schemes and devices and systems and theories of education there lies one single great principle, — that one learns, in any true sense of the word, only that to which he puts the whole force of his own mind. We might throw away all our machinery, and still the man who should put the force of his mind upon the similarities of structure in flowers could produce a system of botany. Without a laboratory or a book the human mind would be capable of results, great because original, if it should turn itself with single devotion to dissecting animals, breaking and comparing stones, watching the developments of fœtal life, or following out any other of those processes by which our present knowledge of the material world has been gained. And, conversely, given all our magnificent machinery of instruction, and the mind which does not apply *itself* to the problems before it, which is content to simply absorb what is offered to it without vigorous action of its own, may pass through the mill from hopper to bin without any change, excepting that, like the grain, it has grown smaller in the process. I take it that one very strong reason for the popularity of physical science in these latter years is found in its method of study. The senses are reached more easily than the reflecting powers. Minds to which history, philosophy, law, seem mere accumulations of learning in books,— learning which is to be got at only by years of reading and remembering,— are attracted instantly by the manual processes which introduce them into the study of natural law. And until lately they have been justified in supposing that all those branches of study which they somewhat sneeringly, perhaps, designate as culture studies, were nothing but masses of fictitious learning, founded upon nothing, and leading to nothing.

If we think for a moment of the slough into which the study of language had fallen twenty-five years ago, and out of which it has not yet wholly freed itself, we can understand why the phrase "classical study" had come to be almost a reproach. What has redeemed linguistic study from its downfall has been the use of new methods, practical methods in acquiring language, and the application of this acquired knowledge to the discovery of new truth in archæology, ethnology, and in every other branch of human learning. Now, instead of aimlessly cramming a Greek grammar into their pupils, enlightened teachers are teaching them to read and write Greek, then to use Greek, and thus to love and appreciate Greek. Or, if we glance at political science, we find that where twenty-five years ago there was one teacher, now there are a dozen, and we see again that men are learning no longer by studying so many pages a day out of a book, but by putting their own powers of mind upon questions whose solution can be reached by no other process.

Wise teachers of philosophy are forcing their students to grapple with problems of the mind, and so giving them power to follow and appreciate the work of those who have gone before.

Thus everywhere we see the conviction gaining ground that the method of practice is indeed the only effectual method. Laboratories in natural science, the "natural method" of learning language, instruction by topics instead of by text-books, — all these are parts of one movement towards a higher and more effectual standard of instruction. How does it stand now with history? Perhaps more than any other study, history has suffered, and is suffering, from that misconception I have alluded to, that it means only a dreary mass of facts, dates, and events, strung along like so many beads on a chain, and with no more distinction in value or meaning. It is the rarest thing to find a man who has any idea whatever about the materials of historical writing, or of the methods used in dealing with these materials. Even educated men are inclined to regard history as a collection of stories merely, more or less entertaining to read, but not having any really serious bearing upon the present active life of men. That there is a science of history, with its apparatus, its schools, its devotees, and its great results already reached, is an extremely unfamiliar fact.

A professor of chemistry once asked me to explain what original work in history could mean. He had supposed that all history was in the books, and that all one had to do was to read these. One could not, he fancied, make new history as one made new experiments and discovered new relations in his own science. The answer made to him may be in place here. Original work in history consists in an inquiry into the sources of authority for a given period or for a given statement or series of statements. Every conscientious his-

HIGHER HISTORICAL INSTRUCTION. 55

torian of to-day goes through such a process in preparing his narrative, but this process is not final. The mass of material for any period or for any series of events is so great that the powers of one man in one lifetime are not sufficient to grapple with it. There must still be a multitude of special investigations which he cannot pursue, a multitude of points still left obscure. These furnish the subjects for the original work of the future. A history of the world, for example, is to the historical scholar not a final account of what has happened since the world began, but rather a vast encyclopedia of problems awaiting solution. He cannot meet them all; he must content himself with selecting one or two upon which he shall spend the labor of a life.

Now the practical question is, how can this original work be made a fruitful means of instruction in our higher schools? In answering this question, we may be guided by the experience of Germany. It is our problem to secure the advantages and avoid the dangers to which I have already called attention. Emphasis was laid, it will be remembered, upon the voluntary character of the various associations which were classed together under the name of practice-courses. This voluntary character must be retained whenever the practice-course is made at home among us. It is inconceivable that whole classes of students should be called upon to do original work in any subject with any prospect of success. The practice-course is not designed to replace more ordinary methods of instruction but to supplement them. It presupposes an election of studies by which it should be possible to bring only devoted students under its influence. With these conditions, it should be the duty and the pride of every historical instructor to conduct, at the side of his theoretical courses, another for practice in the especial line of work he is engaged upon. Supposing there be at a given college no professor of ancient history, then classical instructors should make it their business to guide their most promising pupils in historical research, using as materials the classic authors, who would thus become living sources of knowledge to them, instead of being, as they too often are, mere collections of grammatical puzzles. History and literature would both be the gainers, each lighting up the other and filling it with unthought-of meanings.

As to mediæval history, both of England and the continent, its materials lie before us almost complete. The industry of the recent awakening has turned with especial interest to this field. It would be possible for any American teacher to put before his students the volumes of original mediæval sources from which all existing histories have been written, and to guide them into independent use of these materials in the criticism of written books and in preparing dissertations of their own. In modern European history, the case is somewhat more difficult, the mass of material increasing enormously, and far surpassing the powers of printing to place it all before the reading public. But here, too, very much has been done. The chief reports of ambassadors, correspondence of princes, pamphlets, literature of the time, can be procured, and its complicated story be unravelled.

But the field which should prove most attractive and remunerative to the American scholar is the growth and development of our own institutions. Here the material, ponderous as it is, lies all within our grasp. The same hunting-grounds invite us as those which led on European scholars of an earlier day. In every corner of America are to be found documents of every description bearing upon the formative period of our national life. Here are problems not beyond the strength of any vigorous student. Besides hearing lectures and reading books, let such students as can be convinced of its usefulness be brought together into a practice-course where they shall be brought face to face with actual records, and be called upon to solve a few of the unsolved problems which confront the future historian of America. What a mass of conflicting evidence will gather about the case of Fitz-John Porter! The historian of the next generation will stand appalled before it; but it will be his duty, and that of the student also, to analyze the conflict of motives which has produced this conflict of evidence. Now the past is full of such cases. The "rights" of scarce any historical question are fully understood. It is not enough to say to students, Bancroft or Hildreth or Von Holst is right or wrong on this point. To impress them with the fact, we must put into their hands the very documents from which these authors drew their argument, and let them draw their own. For the lecture to a large class, the statement might be enough, all that a majority of the hearers might be able to assimilate, but there should be among them some few capable of being inspired to more thorough work. These few should be encouraged. They should become the intimates of their instructor. He should see in them the companions of his own researches and the sure reward of his own industry. They should see in him their leader in a road which is to take them up out of a boyish way into a manly way of study.

And what is more, they will and do come to look upon each other, teacher and scholar, in this manly way. The work of the teacher is relieved of its worst element of drudgery, and the work of the student loses *its* worst element also, — that of mere memorizing and repeating. Both enter together, out of the realm of pedagogy into the world of letters. Nothing impressed M. Frédéricq so much, both in

Germany and France, as the free and familiar footing upon which professor and student met in the practice-courses. There was no mystery about it. Both were, for the time, upon the same level. In America, the same result will be more easily attainable.

I can recall only with gratitude the inspiration which came from the generous enthusiasm of those young men who have sat with me about the green table in the Harvard College library, working over, with a pure scholarly spirit, the dusty record of the middle ages. What a sense of discovery when they found themselves touching the very thought of the men who lived through the events they describe! What a triumph when they proved this book, bearing the imposing name of some famous scholar of our day, to be a tissue of gaps and errors! Nor could a scholar ask for any ampler reward than the repeated assurance of these young men that this power of independent thought was the best fruit of their student lives.

One apparent obstacle to success in America lies in our almost universal system of grading students, by which all efforts, after a true scholarly standard, are hampered, and many of them wholly defeated. It may well be imagined, that, to very many persons controlling our higher education, it would seem like dangerous favoritism for a professor to surround himself with picked students for a definite purpose. How shall these especial students be rewarded in marks? How can we measure their work so that neither they nor their fellows shall suffer by the comparison? It would not be surprising if such petty considerations as these should actually prevent the adoption of the method I am suggesting. The hope is that the distrust of all individual rank in college, which has now become evident in several of our leading institutions, will spread so widely that this primal curse of our whole educational system will soon disappear.

Another obstacle, greater still perhaps, lies in the deep-seated dread of putting pen to paper, which generally marks the American student. Writing appears to him oftenest as a kind of extra work. It suggests compositions with all their train of absurdities. It is to him a thing apart from his ordinary studies, instead of being, as it should be, an instrument, the most useful instrument, in pursuing those studies. Our boys, for instance, may be forced to study Latin for years without writing one Latin sentence. The young German, on the other hand, must write constantly, so that form becomes a thing of nature to him, and writing is only what it ought to be, a means of education. The practice-course, to be successful, must be reinforced by early training in similar kinds of practice, and by the presence of similar exercises in related fields of study. If the time spent in what is called "English" in colleges were spent upon the use of English in the pursuit of other studies, the results could hardly fail to benefit immensely both the studies and the English itself. In a word, the time must be hoped for when in all the moral sciences as well as in the physical, *practice in production* shall supplement the reception of information. The man to whom Harvard College owes an impulse in this direction, which has never been lost, used to say. "If there is any one thing I despise more than another, it is information." Another man, who is now giving his life towards stamping upon a great American university this character of independent, original investigation. said to me, "Our young men make a mistake in not writing. What if their productions are immature? They are at least production, and their very immaturity will be of service in pointing the way to better things."

What the laboratory is to physical science, that the library must be to moral science. The library must become, not a store-house of books, but a place for work. Books must exist not so much to be read as to be studied, compared, digested, made to serve in the development of new truth by the method of practice with them. One unfamiliar with student life would be surprised at the unwillingness to use other books than those presented by their instructors. Numbers of students pass through college without knowing how to consult the library catalogue. Instruction by means of text-books, even with wide suggestion of collateral reading, can bring a student into relation with but few minds, can give him almost no power of getting out of books the material wanted for a given purpose. The practice-course alone, calling upon a student to use dozens of books, though probably never to read one, must go far toward giving him right ideas about their value. He sees how men before him have gone to work, and his inevitable loss of faith in the infallibility of printing may be counted as his greatest gain.

The danger pointed out in Germany, that a wholly practical method must lead to a loss in breadth and vigor of grasp upon the whole broad subject of history, is one we are not likely to fall into. Our danger lies rather in the opposite direction, and it is from this danger that we must look to the practice-course to relieve us. M. Frédéricq laments the entire absence of practice-courses in Belgium. We are somewhat better off than that. Johns Hopkins is not the only American university which has taken a step in the right direction. In all, perhaps a half-dozen have done something already, so that it seems not without reason to hope that before very long every historical professor in America will consider his practice-course as much an essential to successful work as his lecture or recitation.

ON METHODS OF TEACHING POLITICAL ECONOMY.

BY RICHARD T. ELY, JOHNS HOPKINS UNIVERSITY.

IT is easy to compress into the compass of a single sentence all the information needed to qualify any man of fair native ability and liberal education to teach political economy as it was taught eight years ago in one of the proudest institutions in the United States. The information in question is this: Buy Mrs. Fawcett's "Political Economy for Beginners"; see that your pupils do the same; then assign them once a week a chapter to be learned; finally, question them each week on the chapter assigned the week before, using the questions found at the end of the chapter, and not omitting the puzzles which follow the more formal questions; as it is a test of the academical learning and grasp of economic science of a senior to have a puzzling problem like this hurled at him: "Is the air in a diving-bell wealth; and, if so, why?"

Let no one suppose this description satirical or exaggerated. It is the literal truth; and the hour a week for a part of a year of such instruction was absolutely all the teaching of political economy done in any department of the rich and powerful college. It is scarcely necessary to describe the state in which the students' minds were left. They learned by heart a few truisms, as, *e.g.*, that it is a good thing to be honest, diligent, and frugal; that products are divided between capitalists, laborers, and landlords; and that values being defined as certain relations of things to one another, there cannot be a general rise or a general fall in values; and they acquired an imperfect comprehension of certain great fundamental facts, like the Ricardian theory of rent and the Malthusian doctrine of population. This, with not a very high opinion of political economy, was the sum-total of results for the student, and prepared him for the degree of A.B. first, and afterward for that of A.M. In our national banks we have a wonderful and unique economic institution, but they were not once mentioned, nor was a single allusion made to the financial history of this great country. And yet this instruction was to fit the élite of the youth of the land for the duties of citizenship!

This is a true picture of one way to teach political economy, and it is a method of instruction for which a high salary was paid. Is it a state of things entirely exceptional? It is to be feared not. A preface to Amasa Walker's "Science of Wealth," edited 1872, contains these words, which seem to have met with very general approbation: "Although desirable that the instructor should be familiar with the subject himself, it is by no means indispensable. With a well-arranged text-book in the hands of both teacher and pupil, with suitable effort on the part of the former and attention on the part of the latter, the study may be profitably pursued. We have known many instances where this has been done in colleges and other institutions highly to the satisfaction and advantage of all parties concerned."

The writer holds that better things than this are possible, even in a high school; and it is certain that political economy ought to be taught in every school of advanced grade in the land.[1] The difficulties are by no means insuperable. It is, in fact, easy to interest young people in economic discussions which keep close to the concrete, and ascend only gradually from particulars to generals.

The writer has indeed found it possible to entertain a school-room full of boys, varying in age from five to sixteen, with a discourse on two definitions of capital, — one taken from a celebrated writer, and the other from an obscure pamphlet on socialism by a radical reformer. As the school was in the country, illustrations were taken from farm life, such as corn-planting and harvesting, and from the out-door sports of the boys, such as trapping for rabbits. Some common familiar fact was kept constantly in the foreground, and thus the attention of the youngest lad was held.

Perhaps money is as good a subject as any for an opening lecture to bright boys and girls, and the writer would recommend a course of procedure somewhat like this: Take into the class-room the different kinds of money in use in the United States, both paper and coin, and ask questions about them, and talk about them. Show the class a greenback and a national bank-note, and ask them to tell you the difference. After they have all failed, as they probably will, ask some one to read what is engraved on the notes, after which the difference may be further elucidated. Silver and gold certificates may be discussed, and the distinction made clear between the bullion and face value of the five-cent piece, etc. Other talks, interesting and familiar, about alloys, the extent to which pennies and small coins are legal tender, the char-

---

[1] In Belgium it has been proposed to introduce political economy even into the elementary schools; and in view of the immense importance of the economic problems which will one day be pressing for solution in the United States, it is to be hoped that such a proposal at some future time will not be Utopian in our country.

acter of the trade-dollar, etc., etc., will occupy several hours, and delight the class.[1] The origin of money is a topic which will instruct and entertain the scholars for an hour. Various kinds of money should be mentioned; and it is possible you may find examples of curious kinds of money in some hill town not very remote, *e.g.*, eggs, and you are very likely to find several kinds of money in use among the boys and girls, *e.g.*, pins. In one boarding-school, near Baltimore, bits of butter, served the boys at meals in quantities less than they desired, passed as money, and quite an extensive use of bills and orders, "negotiable instruments," was established.[2] After this, a work like Jevons's "Money and the Mechanism of Exchange,"[3] or at least parts of it, will interest the pupils.

Banking very properly comes under the head of political economy, performing as it does most important functions in industrial life; and the most prominent banking institutions in this country are the national banks, which have also played an important rôle in our history. There is likely to be one in every town where there is a high school, and it is well to continue the course of instruction with the village national

---

[1] The teacher will find the necessary information in the Revised Statutes of the United States (Government Printing Office, Washington, D.C.), which should be in the school library. It is contained in more convenient shape in the "Laws of the United States relating to Loans and the Currency" and "Instructions and Regulations in Relation to the Transaction of Business at the Mints and Assay Offices of the United States." These pamphlets, like most other government publications, can be obtained gratis of the congressman of the district in which the school is situated. They are kept on sale by various book-dealers in Washington.

[2] *Cf.* Mr. John Johnston's instructive paper, "Rudimentary Society among Boys," published in the "Johns Hopkins University Studies in Historical and Political Sciences," second series, No. XI., edited by Dr. Herbert B. Adams.

[3] This is published in paper covers in the Humboldt Library for forty cents, as well as in the "International Scientific Series" of D. Appleton & Co.

bank. Procure for this purpose "The National Bank Act,"[1] and study it with your class in connection with reports and advertisements and circulars of the village bank. You will find a certain minimum number of directors prescribed by law: ascertain the number in the bank in question, and their functions. Some members of the class will be acquainted with them, and all the class will know of them, and this will give a personal interest to the study. Then compare the amount of capital required with the actual amount, and have the class ascertain from the law the amount of bank-notes which the bank could receive from the comptroller of the currency, and the actual circulation. After the various features of the bank have been examined, it is desirable that some bright boy should write a history of the bank, to read before the class, and afterwards, perhaps, to publish in the village paper. Files of the paper, to which the editor will doubtless give access, will contain all the published reports of the bank, as well as the proceedings and the village talk about the bank at its foundation. If officers of the bank are properly approached, they will assist with hints and information. In this way the pupils will acquire a new interest in banks; and when they pass by the national bank, it will never again seem quite the same lifeless institution. From the history of one national bank it is easy to pass over to the history of national banks in this country, and to a description of the State banking systems, which preceded the national banking system.[2] Then the student may be glad to read what General Walker says on banks, in his "Politi-

---

[1] A government publication; also published by the Homans Publishing Company, 251 Broadway. Care should be taken to secure the latest edition, as there have been various changes in the banking laws.

[2] For this purpose the teacher should consult the reports of the comptroller of the currency, especially for the years 1875 and 1876.

cal Economy," and in his "Money, Trade, and Industry,"[1] and a work like Bagehot's "Lombard Street" will not be without attractions.[2]

Taxes can be studied in the town or village. The pupils can learn from their fathers what the taxes are, how they are assessed and collected, and what part of the revenues is used for village purposes, what part for schools, what part for the county, and what part for the State. In any village it cannot be difficult to induce one of the assessors to explain before the class in political economy the principles upon which he does his work. All the pupils can then write essays about taxation in the said place, and perhaps one of them will be able to write a financial history of the town. In this way the pupils will be prepared for the perusal of a work like the "Report on Local Taxation," prepared by Messrs. Wells, Dodge, and Cuyler.[3] It may be learned from the reports of the Secretary of the Treasury[4] how the expenses of the federal government are defrayed. In this way a complete view of taxation in the United States is obtained,[5] and in many respects a small town or village offers better facilities for such a course than a large city, where manners are less simple, and where city officials for well-known reasons often show a manifest unwillingness to impart information. This course will teach pupils to observe economic phenomena, will impart to them an interest in financial questions, and will prepare them in later years to deal with large problems. As Carl Ritter prepared himself for his

---

[1] Published by Henry Holt & Co., New York.
[2] Published by the Scribners, New York.
[3] Published by Harper & Brothers, New York.
[4] Government publications.
[5] The United States Census Reports contain valuable information, and every high school should be provided with copies.

great geographical work by the study of the geography of Frankfort,[1] so bright pupils, beginning with the study of local finance, will learn how to deal with even the difficult problems of war finance when they arise.

The two great impelling causes of economic study have ever been financial difficulties of government and social problems, or discontent with the condition of social classes, coupled with a desire to improve this unsatisfactory condition, and it is with these two kinds of topics that political economy chiefly deals. In a manner similar in principle to that described, the administration of public charity and its relation to private charity may be studied in the town and county. If poorhouses, insane asylums, hospitals, etc., are in the vicinity, and can be visited, so much the better. The manner of caring for the criminal classes may be studied locally. Reports of State boards of charities will enable the pupils to connect local with State charities.[2]

Then there is the ordinary laborer. Let the pupils describe his manner of living, his wages, etc. If the school is a mixed one, some young girl of sufficient tact will be found to visit the ordinary laborers in their homes, to talk with them, and obtain their ideas. In some towns a real laboring population can scarcely be said to exist; but factory towns afford favorable opportunities for studies of this character. Many a Massachusetts factory town furnishes an excellent field for such study, and the reports of the Massachusetts Bureau of Labor Statistics will be found helpful.

---

[1] This illustration is taken from Dr. Adams's paper, v. p. 161 of first edition.

[2] Teachers and pupils will find much useful information in the large work of Dr. Wines, entitled "The State of Prisons and of Child-Saving Institutions in the Civilized World," Cambridge (Mass.), 1880.

A book like "Work and Wages," by Thorold Rogers,[1] will then be enjoyed by many of the class.[2]

After part or all of this ground has been gone over, it will then be time to take up the more systematic study of political economy. The work described might be gone over in exercises once a week, extending through one year, and the second year a systematic course might follow; and this is not too much time for so all-important a study in a high school. There are few good text-books of political economy, but for the English-speaking student the writer would recommend Francis A. Walker's " Political Economy," or Laveleye's " Elements of Political Economy," with additions by Taussig.[3] Here is an admirable high-school course sketched out. All the works referred to ought to be accessible to the *teacher, and should be mastered before he begins to teach.*[4] This may seem like requiring a great deal; but preparation is as necessary in a teacher of political economy as in a teacher of mathematics; and it is as absurd to venture to teach political economy, without a knowledge of the subject, as to teach trigonometry without a knowledge of trigonometry. It is because this has been attempted that such contempt has been thrown on the study of political economy, and that the science is in such a sad condition.

---

[1] Published by G. P. Putnam's Sons, New York.

[2] In his "French and German Socialism" (Harper & Brothers), the writer has attempted to give a brief sketch of the more prominent Utopian theories in a manner adapted to school and college use. Albert Shaw has described admirably an American communistic society in his "Icaria: A Chapter in the History of Communism." Published by G. P. Putnam's Sons.

[3] If there is sufficient time, Walker's larger work is preferable; if less time can be devoted to the study, Laveleye's is better. The teacher should have both. Laveleye's "Political Economy" is published by the Putnams, New York.

[4] Let one who proposes to teach political economy master, first of all, F. A. Walker's "Political Economy."

For a more advanced course, a preliminary training in logic is advisable, as the discussion of deductive and inductive methods, of conceptions and definitions, etc., will otherwise hardly be intelligible.[1] Besides this, the training one obtains in the study of logic is excellent preparation for much of the work required in political economy. It teaches students to analyze conceptions, to combine elements, and to reason closely. The writer has often felt that a want of this training in his pupils was an obstacle in his way.

The more profound one's knowledge of history the better for teacher in high school or college. This economic life, this working, buying, selling, this getting a living, is only one part of the historical life of a people; and the more that is known about the whole, the better will each part be understood.

For the advanced investigation, a knowledge of foreign languages, especially of German, is indispensable. Roscher,[2] Wagner,[3] Knies,[4] Schmoller,[5] Schönberg,[6] and Leroy-Beaulieu[7] should be studied.

Colleges and universities ought also to provide periodicals like the "Jahrbücher für Nationalökonomie und Statistik," "Jahrbuch für Gesetzgebung, Verwaltung und Volkswirthschaft," the "Tübinger Zeitschrift für die Gesammte Staatswissenchaft," the "Journal des Économistes," the English "Economist," "Bradstreets," and the "Banker's Magazine."

---

[1] The two little works by Thomas Fowler, "Deductive Logic" and "Inductive Logic," published in the Clarendon Press Series, Oxford, are recommended.
[2] System der Volkswirthschaft.
[3] Lehrbuch der politischen Oekonomie.
[4] Die politische Oekonomie vom geschichtlichen Standpubkte, and his "Geld und Credit."
[5] Ueber einige Grundfragen des Rechts und der Volkswirthschaft.
[6] Handbuch der politischen Oekonomie.
[7] Traité de la science des finances.

The teacher of college students, who ought always himself to be an original worker, *should be perfectly independent.* It is doubtless owing largely to a lack of independence on the part of the teacher that political economy has not made more progress in this country. *Men are too often employed to teach free trade or to teach protection, — and as usually taught, it is difficult to tell which of the two is more unscientific, — or to teach Henry C. Carey's system, or teach monometallism or bimetallism, whereas the teacher should be encouraged in the pursuit of truth, regardless of where it strikes.*

Independence is nowhere more necessary than in the study of economics. A new theory of the iota subscript does not move the mass of men profoundly, but a new theory of taxation is bound to call forth from some one the cry "heresy." In fact, as there are always large and powerful classes interested in the present condition of things, every change proposed, no matter what it is, is certain to meet with a storm of opposition. Ignorance, prejudice, and selfishness have always combined in their attacks on every political economist who has contributed to the advance of his science.

The political economist requires likewise, if he is to do his best work, a salary which shall enable him to mingle with the world, to become, to a certain extent, a man of the world, in order that he may the better understand the world with which he deals. He ought further to be able to travel and conduct investigations in industrial regions at home and abroad. So important is travel, indeed, that one great French school, that of Le Play, has made travel the chief method of investigation.[1]

---

[1] The following note on Le Play may be interesting in this connection: In 1829 Le Play began a series of journeys, which continued for over fifty years, and extended themselves into all parts of Europe, and even into the regions of Asiatic semi-civilization. These travels have borne plenteous

The thoroughly equipped teacher of political economy ought, in addition to his qualifications in history and philosophy, including chiefly logic, to be a careful student of the principles of law. Evidence and practice, and the formal details of law, are not of great importance to him; but real-estate law, the law of contract and of banking, etc., are. The political economist lays the basis for legal study, he tells the reason why such and such legal institutions, e.g., private property in land, exist, and should exist; but he can manifestly lay a much better basis if he knows the superstructure which is to be erected thereon.[1]

A legal friend, at the same time a political economist, recommends the following course in law for advanced students of political economy: "Blackstone's Commentaries."[2]

fruits, of which the most prominent are the following: the publication of numerous works, the establishment of a method of study in social science, and the foundation of a school. Le Play's method, which he calls "La Méthode social," centres in what may be called the doctrine of travel. The quintessence of his theory is, that it is as essential for the economist to observe economic phenomena as for the mineralogist to observe minerals. The economist, however, not being able to gather together and arrange in a laboratory manufactories, laborers' quarters in cities, agricultural villages, extensive mines, and the commercial phenomena of a great port, must travel to them, observe the manifestations of social and individual life which are there to be seen, and classify the results thus obtained in such manner that instructive and useful generalization may be drawn therefrom. The most important among the works of Le Play bears the title "les Ouvriers Européens," in which the author describes from actual observation the minutest details of separate laborers' households in every part of Europe. The third service to science, which these journeys enabled Le Play to render, consists in the foundation of a school, called "L'École de la Paix Sociale," which manifests its activity in various ways, of which the most striking is the publication of their semi-monthly organ, "La Réforme Sociale."

[1] In many German universities every law-student is obliged to take a course in political economy. The study of political economy is likewise obligatory in French law-schools.
[2] Chase's edition is one volume.

which should be thoroughly digested; Parson on "Contracts"; Washburn on "Real Estate," Benjamin on "Sales of Personal Property," and Bispham on "Equity." I would add, at least, Morse on "Banks and Banking," Cooley on "Taxation," and Morawetz on "Corporations."

Only one point more remains to be mentioned. The best original economic work is, for the most part, expensive. Laws, government reports, as blue-books and financial statements, and all sorts of original documents are required. Much economic work can be done only in connection with a learned institution or a government office, or by a very wealthy person. Any university which would have good work on the part of its teachers of political economy must not begrudge the expense of material as necessary to the economist as chemicals to the chemist. Of course, it cannot be expected that an American college will provide the political economist with a special library of seventy thousand volumes, like the Library of the Prussian Statistical Bureau; but it is doubtful whether a fair working university library of political economy can be produced for less than five thousand dollars.[1]

---

[1] It will readily be understood that a university library, designed to aid original research, is something quite different from a high-school library. One hundred dollars would purchase economic books which would answer fairly well the needs of a high school.

HISTORICAL INSTRUCTION IN THE COURSE OF HISTORY AND POLITICAL SCIENCE AT CORNELL UNIVERSITY.

By Andrew D. White, Cornell University.

THE theory and practice of historical instruction in Cornell University may be outlined as follows: —

1. The basis of historical study among university students is to be found in the necessities of their general development as men, and of their special development as citizens preparing to take positions of influence among the civilizing activities of their land and time.

2. As to the general system upon which a course extending through four years is conducted, the first step is to enable the student to secure some adequate general knowledge of the simpler fundamental facts in that evolution of man and of society in the past which best aids in solving the problems regarding the evolution of both in the future. This is done, as regards ancient history, by a rapid survey of the main ancient nations; as regards mediaeval history, by a study of the general transition from the ancient to the mediaeval period, and of the more important and fruitful elements, institutions, and men developed in mediaeval life; as regards modern history, by a study of the transition from the mediæval to the modern period in leading modern nations, and

especially by attention to the movements, phases of thought and action, institutions, epochs, and men in these which throw most light on the evolution of existing society.

3. As to special work, having in view the education of the student as a man and citizen, there naturally comes next the more careful study of such nations, epochs, movements, systems, phases, or tendencies as bear most directly on the world of thought and action in which the student is to live and move and have his being. These subjects for special study are frequently found in ancient, mediaeval, or general modern history, but students are especially encouraged to devote their most careful labor to subjects which have to do most directly with thought and action in their own country.

4. As to the practical plan pursued, the general knowledge of ancient and mediaeval history, and of the history of England, — considered as a typical example of a great modern state, — is given in the lower classes by text-books, with supplementary lectures by the resident professors, and occasional courses of lectures by others. This elementary knowledge is afterward developed in the advanced classes by various courses of lectures upon the more important nations and periods, supplemented by recommendations as to the examination of authorities and general reading, and by "seminary exercises" calculated to increase the familiarity of students with important sources, and to stimulate their investigation of these.

5. As to methods of teaching, it is taken for granted that the student must be directly interested in his work, and that he is not to be considered a passive recipient of facts and ideas flung at him by his instructors. Efforts are constantly made to trace back important events and institutions through the various stages of their development, and to make suggestive comparisons between different phases of progress

in the same nation, and between similar phases in different nations. In general modern history and in American history, while pains is taken to present the framework and connections historically, the filling-in is largely biographical. It is believed that history is thus more surely made living and real, that the development of principles and events is more firmly planted into the thinking of students, and that the ethical content of events may be grasped as it can be in no other way.

6. The importance of leading the student to make individual investigation into original sources is fully recognized; but it is felt that such special investigations are likely to be narrow and poor, in fact, to be simply those of an attorney's clerk preparing a case, unless there has been some large preliminary study of human events, and some good philosophical conception of the values and relations of these; that to promote special investigation among young men not matured by broad historical studies, and by thought upon these, is simply to train up annalists or historical special pleaders. To guard against this danger, it is thought best to advise, first, that such individual investigations be made as a rule in the latter years of the course; and, secondly, that they be made upon points of permanent and direct interest in the history with which American citizens have most directly to do; more especially in the constitutional history of England, and in the general, political, and constitutional history of the United States.

7. During the entire course of four years efforts are made to keep up the interest of the student, and to increase his power of looking upon historical events and developments from various points of view. It is for this reason that such special lecturers as Goldwin Smith, James Anthony Froude, Hermann von Holst, Edward A. Freeman, George W.

Greene, Charles Kendall Adams, and others have at various times been called to supplement the work of the resident professors.

8. Instruction in political science, international law, and the great literatures, ancient and modern, is brought as far as possible into connection with historical study. As to literature, courses of general reading are suggested which shall aid in making history a living study, and not a mere "swallowing of formulas."

9. As to the philosophy of history, efforts are made from the first to stimulate the student to find in the progress of the world's affairs philosophical principles and underlying laws, and toward the end of the course a special series of lectures on the subject is delivered for the benefit of those thus matured in general and special historical work.

10. To sum up as regards the connection of theory with method, the effort is, first, to proceed from the simple to the complex by the survey of single nations in ancient history and single elements in mediaeval history before taking up with more minuteness the complicated history of the modern world; and, in modern history, to study nations and even individuals separately before grouping all together; secondly, to proceed from the concrete to the abstract by a large use of the biographical method before presenting extended chains of historical events; and, thirdly, to proceed from the empirical to the rational by encouraging students to draw philosophical principles out of events before any connected discussion upon the philosophy of history is given as a whole.

ADVICE TO AN INEXPERIENCED TEACHER OF HISTORY.

By W. C. Collar, A.M., Head Master of Roxbury Latin School.

YOU contemplate your task with a kind of despairing shudder, and it is not strange. If we except the instructors in a relatively small number of city high schools, the American teacher who is a college graduate is supposed to be equipped for instructing in most branches of human knowledge, or, to speak guardedly, at least in languages, ancient and modern, physical and natural science, mathematics, history, and English literature.

History has been with you a favorite pastime rather than a subject of severe, absorbing, protracted study. You have read a good number of standard histories of ancient and modern times without attempting to make a careful and minute study of any one nation or period, and this you rightly feel is a very slender preparation for the weighty responsibilities that you are now to assume. For you have not to teach a definite portion of a well-defined subject in accordance with tried and accepted methods, or even under the guidance of certain established principles of historical instruction. The teaching of history has hardly yet reached the scientific stage. Both the What and the How are to be largely of your own invention. The subject itself is vast. It opens in many and far-reaching vistas that lose themselves in a tortuous complexity. Where is a clue to be found? Evidently time, reading, observation, experiment, reflection, judgment will all be needed.

Then what of the class of minds to be taught? For instruction must be adapted to the condition and needs of your pupils, or it will count for little. It is said that "the German pupil at the age of fifteen or sixteen has been able to complete two distinct surveys of universal history." It will not be safe to assume any such amount of knowledge and training in the case of high-school scholars of that age with us. Their acquaintance with history is most likely limited to a meagre outline of facts in English history, and such a knowledge of United States' history as may be got from the study of a manual like Anderson's or Berard's. It is hardly necessary to say that the imagination has not probably been cultivated by their contact with history, still less have they any developed historical sense, any notion of the continuity of history, and most likely no love whatever of historical reading. It is fortunate if they do not think of history as a mere collection of dry facts, without interest or significance,—a dreary, barren study, to be cast aside and done with as soon as possible. How often does one hear from children the exclamation, "Oh! I hate history!" Or from grown persons, "I never could get interested in history."

Finally, account must be taken of the school time allotted to history. This reveals perhaps the most discouraging feature of all. I have found three hours a week for a year too little time for Greek and Roman history alone; but that, I am sure, would seem in most high schools a liberal, if not excessive, allowance of time for a much wider range. The statement made in another essay in this volume, that "In America, history is generally crowded into one or two terms, or at most into a single year," is probably within the mark.

Such, then, are some of the conditions under which you must work. A consciousness of inadequate preparation, insufficient time, and pupils without historical training. The situation is not exhilarating; but neither is it without hope. Certainly it is of the utmost importance first to appreciate clearly under what limitations one must work, and then to conceive definitely the kind and amount of work to be done. To supply your own lack of knowledge and training will be the slow task of years; but nothing is so satisfying and stimulating as the consciousness of progress. This is the one of the conditions enumerated that it lies in your own power to change, and you may be sure that on the increasing depth and fulness and freshness of your own knowledge will depend in large measure the interest and progress of your pupils, that is, the power and success of your instruction, and accordingly your own satisfaction in your work.

Let us suppose the subject of ancient history is assigned to you. The field is immense, and the time is absurdly inadequate. But it is only the Hebrews, the Greeks, and the Romans, whose history and literatures are of great interest and importance to us; and many as are the points of contact of these nations with Egypt, Phœnicia, Assyria, Persia, and a few other oriental peoples, some incidental notice only of these relations will suffice. Thus, the area is at once greatly circumscribed. And even Hebrew history must not be permitted to occupy a relatively large place; partly because a considerable portion of it is not important; partly because what is of the greatest value to us requires, for its comprehension and appreciation, a degree of mental training and maturity. The Hebrews have transmitted to us their conceptions of God, of religion, and of morality. Their thoughts, beliefs, aspirations, emotions, have entered into our inmost being, and constantly affect our outward life and conduct. Their ecstasy of joy, of triumph, of hope; their passion of remorse, of sorrow, of despair, have been embalmed in our sacred music, and hallowed by the most tender and solemn associations of religion. Their language and their imagery have permeated our literature and color our daily speech. But it would be vain to attempt to show a class of beginners the immensity of the influence for good, and likewise for evil, that has been wrought upon us through the ages, by the faith, the ethics, the laws, the literature of that strange people. Of these things, a partial, fragmentary, or even incidental treatment must suffice.

But to be more precise. As a basis for such instruction, as circumstances allow, it is enough to read with a class, first, the life and work of Moses, contained in the first twenty-four chapters of Exodus, and the first three and the thirty-fourth chapters of Deuteronomy; second, the first eleven chapters of Joshua; and, finally, the life of David.

It is necessary to assume some familiarity with Bible stories; though how so many intelligent boys and girls, accustomed to attendance at Sunday-schools, grow up without such familiar knowledge is something of a mystery. The discovery, some years ago, that in a class of thirty bright boys of about fourteen years of age, only three understood an allusion to the story of Ruth and Boaz, led to my laying out a course of Bible reading in my own school for each year of a six years' curriculum.

Thus far, we have considered the nature and scope of your work, and have pointed out some of the limitations imposed by circumstances for which you are not responsible, but which you must not disregard. It is time to speak of the method of teaching. But the method must be determined in the main by the object aimed at. If the object is to deposit in the mind the greatest number possible of historical facts, there is perhaps no better way than to confine the instruction to drill upon the contents of a manual by question and answer, with frequent examinations in writing. Such a method would probably be effective in two ways: it would give learners positive knowledge, or the semblance of it, and it would pretty certainly make them hate history. I do not hesitate to say that the ultimate purpose of school instruction should be to incite an interest in history, and to create a love for historical reading. If this is a correct view, it gives the key to right methods; and, from other essays in this volume, you will gather many useful suggestions. Only consider well what hints you can use. Remember that your task is not that of a college professor. It is very different, and it is much more difficult. Therefore, many excellent methods described by eminent teachers of history in the preceding essays you may be unable to put in practice. You have to deal with minds less mature and less capable of independent study; and you cannot probably send your pupils to a well-furnished library for reading and research. Perhaps what is contained in this volume, in answer to the question "How shall history be taught?" is most directly helpful. Let me try to add some suggestions derived from my own experience.

I will suppose that your pupils have some brief manual of Roman or Greek history, like "Creighton's Primer of Roman History," or "Smith's Smaller History of Greece." First read over the lesson assigned for the next day, or portions of it, with the class; indicate briefly what is of greater and what of less importance; make such explanations as are needful for an intelligent comprehension of the text, and indicate what dates should be committed to memory.

A word may be here most conveniently said on the subject of chronology. A few dates should be well fixed in the memory; they should be carefully selected by the teacher, and some explanation given of their significance. But "a few," you will say, is a little indefinite. Of course, opinions will differ as to the number of indispensable dates in any history, though there might be a general assent to the principle of requiring the pupil to commit as few as possible. Of the two hundred and fifty dates given in "Smith's Smaller History of Greece," I insist on fifteen, and I think the number might be reduced to ten. But if learners are properly taught, they will, of course, be able to determine a great many dates approximately. For example, a boy who has clearly understood the cause, purpose, and results of the Confederacy of Delos could not possibly place it in time far wrong, with reference to great events before and after it; and a single important date in the century well remembered would enable him to fix very nearly its absolute time.

Remembering that you must make history interesting, to that end use all available means to produce vivid impressions. This is a trite remark, but it will bear repeating. Casts, models, coins, photographs, relief maps, may not be at your command; but maps of some sort you must have. Historical instruction, without the constant accompaniment of geography, has no solid foundation,—"is all in the air." The imagination must be stirred; the sympathies must be quickened. How? I answer, first, by drawing with judgment from your own stores of knowledge. An interesting, but perhaps not historically important, incident is merely alluded to, or not mentioned at all in the manual used by the class. Tell the story in all its details. You might read it in a form more perfect from a literary point of view, but you ought to be able to tell it in a way far more impressive, and that is the main thing. For events of a different class, I should, following suggestions more than once made in this volume, read from original, and, if possible, from contemporary records. What a vivid idea, for instance, will be got of the plague at Athens from the reading of a few pages from "Thucydides," with a word or two added from modern medical studies of that scourge. The opportunity and the advantage of studying history from original documents is one strong reason why I have advised the study of a small portion of Hebrew history, though I am not ignorant what modern criticism has established regarding the age and authorship of those writings. It is not necessary, however, to communicate to a class knowledge for which they are not prepared.

But for awakening the sympathies and moving the imagination of children, I attach greater importance to the aid to be derived from imaginative literature, particularly poetry. Poetry gives life and reality to history. History describes, poetry paints; and this is often true of poetry that ranks neither in the first nor in the second order. For years I have found it very useful to have Macaulay's "Lays of Ancient Rome" read in connection with the mythical part of Roman History. There is nothing like the magic charm, whether of sublimity or pathos, that poetry lends to historical events, persons, and places. Who can read Milman's magnificent ode on the Israelites crossing the Red Sea without a consciousness, if he reflects upon it, of a fresh and more vivid realization of a scene familiar to his imagination from childhood? How Scott's beautiful hymn, sung by Rebecca in "Ivanhoe," makes us see, as the Scripture narrative never did, the slow onward toiling of the Israelites through the rocky fastnesses and over the sandy deserts of Arabia, guided by the pillar of cloud by day and the pillar of fire by night!

At the distance of forty years I recall the emotion, the tears, with which I read in our country school reading-book a poem which I have never since seen, entitled "Jugurtha in Prison," beginning,

"Well, is the rack prepared, the pincers heated?"

I knew nothing of Jugurtha, neither when he lived nor in what part of the world, nor what he had done that he was to be starved to death in prison. It is true, in this particular case, that if I had known what a scamp Jugurtha was, my sympathies for him would have been considerably less ardent ; but in that case they would only have been transferred to his brothers, whom he had so foully murdered.

With what a swell of patriotic pride, too, did I use as a boy to recite, —

> "Departed spirits of the mighty dead,
> Ye that at Marathon and Leuctra bled."

"Marathon and Leuctra" signified nothing to me. I had not the remotest idea who the "mighty dead" were who had fallen there, but I felt as if it would have been a joy to have shed my blood with them.

Do not make the mistake, which I am afraid is a common one, of teaching the history of one ancient nation as if it had no relation to that of any other. To point out relations, to contrast and compare times, institutions, events, men, is one of the most delightful and most useful parts of the teacher's work. To encourage pupils to discover likenesses and differences is to promote thinking, to enlarge the mental horizon, to induce a habit of mind of inestimable value. Take, for example, the fundamental laws of the Hebrews, the Greeks, and the Romans; their constitutions, which embodied and expressed their most striking and distinctive national characteristics. It would be easy to show, how on the one hand the Mosaic constitution, the Decalogue, aimed to make men moral and religious; while on the other the Greek and Roman constitutions sought to form men into soldiers, and to make them into members of a body politic. Hence the importance of private conduct under the one, and its relative unimportance under the other, with all the far-reaching consequences that followed. In the study of Greek history a comparison of the two rival states, Athens and Sparta, in spirit and policy, and the tracing of the immediate and remote effects on themselves and all Hellas, will not only impart increased interest, by bringing into clearer relief the essential characteristics, the heroism, the selfishness, the hardihood, the cruelty, the narrowness of the one, and the intelligence, love of knowledge and beauty, but also, alas! the sensuality, levity, and weakness of the other; but it will suggest many an important lesson, and will be an excellent preparation for the reading of modern history with a more intelligent observation and reflection.

Again, how interesting is the comparison in detail of the growth of the Athenian constitution under Solon, Cleisthenes, and Pericles, with that slowly evolved among the Romans after the beginning made by Servius Tullus, by the struggle for two centuries between the patricians and plebeians. There is the same exclusive possession of political rights on the part of the nobles, and accordingly the same control of government by the few for their own benefit and pleasure; the same misery, poverty, and indebtedness of the lower classes; the same struggle to escape from intolerable burdens, and then to share equally with the more fortunate the rights of citizenship, that meant so much in ancient times; the same shifting of the basis and condition of political privileges from birth to wealth, estimated, observe, in both cases, by the amount or income of property in land; and finally the same issue, the turning of the tables, the ultimate predominance of the people, and the transference of the sceptre of power from the noble by birth to the rich. And can there be a more interesting lesson in history than to continue this analogy, and trace the upward struggle of the common people in England? There the same contest has been going on for six hundred years; the same forces are at work, and there are many signs that the same results will follow.

I have anticipated in the last few sentences the only additional suggestion that I can now permit myself to make. I mean the comparison of ancient with modern history. According to Herbert Spencer, there is no thinking without a consciousness of similitude, and no knowing without a perception of relation, difference, and likeness. If, then, comparison, conscious or unconscious, is a necessary condition of knowledge, is one in danger of pressing the comparative method of historical study too far? Explicit comparisons at every step are not necessary, and the strict limitations of time must not be forgotten. I have never failed to awaken interest by such comparisons, whether in the study of ancient or modern history, even when the basis of knowledge on the part of pupils was of the slenderest. But a striking parallelism pointed out here and there will be enough to give direction to the thoughts in reading history, to lead pupils, as has already been observed, to see and follow out analogies themselves, to bring home to the consciousness what is far away, and to recognize in what appears new and strange what is known or even familiar. Let me illustrate.

Suppose the topic for a lesson has been the Sicilian Expedition. There is hardly to be found a more thrilling narrative than that by the great Greek historian, and the reading of some pages from Thucydides may well occupy a half-hour. A class will hardly find in their course in ancient history so conspicuous an example of the utter disastrous failure of an important undertaking through the irresolution and incapacity of a leader. Let the teacher now tell the story of the Peninsula Campaign of McClellan in our late Rebellion, to illustrate how history is repeated in events and in the characters of men. Nicias was a man of upright character and respectable talents, but as a general cautious to timidity, and in a pinch incapable of coming to a decision. He was one of those men who are always thought to be sure to do great things, without its being possible to tell what inspires such confidence. He had the resources of the state at his back, and to support him the unflinching determination of his countrymen to win. He was ably seconded by his subordinates, and he *almost* achieved a great success. But at the last moment victory slipped from his grasp, and the hopeless ruin of all his plans quickly followed. Such, at least in the opinion of many, was McClellan, and so ended disastrously his strategy of the spade. As the elder Nicias barely missed capturing Syracuse, so did the modern Nicias all but take Richmond.

Again, at first, a boy or girl would not see much likeness in the characters of the Romans and the English. But reflection, aided by the hints and questions of the teacher, would bring out a surprising number of points of resemblance, and it would appear that the English might be fairly called the Romans of the modern world. There is at bottom the same solidity, massiveness, and sobriety of nature. The same indomitable will and tenacity of purpose is characteristic of the two peoples. They are alike in their respect for woman, their domesticity, their love of old-fashioned ways and things, their arrogance, their dislike of foreigners. They have above all other nations a genius for law and government.

> Tu regere imperio populos, Romane, memento,
> Hae tibi erunt artes; pacisque imponere morem,
> Parcere subjectis, et debellare superbos.

In many ways their defects and limitations are the same. The brusqueness, harshness, and indifference to the rights and feelings of others which foreigners complain of in the English, seem to have been traits of the Romans. Cato, a typical Roman, was willing that the prayer of the Achæan exiles should be granted that they might return to their own country after having languished seventeen years in prison, but he gave his consent in these gracious words: "Have we nothing better to do than to sit here all day long debating whether a parcel of worn-out Greeks shall be carried to their graves here or in Achaia?" Both are incapable of the highest excellence in certain forms of art. Matthew Arnold is fond of repeating of a large part of his countrymen, that they are characterized by "a defective type of religion, a narrow range of intellect and knowledge, a stunted sense of beauty, a low standard of manners." This seems to be equally true of the Roman Philistine, and, I imagine, true of a far larger part of the whole body of the Romans than of the English.

Our aim has been to show how to give life and reality to history, and we have seen that the methods by which this end may be reached are also those by which the greatest benefits are to be derived from historical study; I mean the culture of the imagination, the quickening of the sympathies, the elevation of the moral nature, the forming of mental habits of observation, comparison, and reflection, and finally an increased interest in history and general literature.

A Plea for Archæological Instruction.

By Joseph Thacher Clarke.

"*Die Werkstätte eines grossen Künstlers entwickelt den keimenden Philosophien, den keimenden Dichter, mehr als der Hörsaal des Weltweisen und des Kritikers.*" — Letter of Goethe to Oeser, 1768.

IT has long been evident that, as matters now stand, a living interest in classical antiquity is difficult to introduce in the studies of youth, and almost impossible to maintain in the busy life of later years. To some men of acknowledged intelligence it appears inadvisable to devote even that attention to classical attainment hitherto customary in our educational systems. Such complaints, that the study of the ancient languages is not productive of adequate results are not new, and unfortunately are not without foundation.

Teachers of long experience in the University of Cambridge tell us "it is quite usual to find among advanced classical students so complete an absence of the feeling of the reality of ancient life that they will sometimes in construing put into the mouth of one of the characters of history or fiction a sentiment in ludicrous disaccord with his position and with what might have been expected, and will do so without the slightest sense of incongruity." If the case elsewhere is otherwise, it certainly is not more favorable than with so great and so typical an institution.

This absence of the feeling of *reality*, this want of acquaintance with the actual circumstances of the life of the Greeks and Romans, touches the secret of the entire matter. We must admit that, in this regard, there is indeed the need of improvement, almost of a revolution, in the presentation of the classics to the student and to the public if these branches are to hold their own against the pressure brought to bear upon them by the absorbing utilitarianism of our age. Such an improvement can only proceed from a rejuvenation of philological studies by that living knowledge of antiquity gained by practical archæology. A means of adapting classical instruction to the needs and tastes of present generations has long been sought, and has gradually become more and more needful. An increase of the direct study of ancient life, which unites the advantages of philological scholarship and the exact research of natural science, is the only satisfactory resort in the present emergency. Archæology is that combination of tangible acquisition with intellectual attainment which is the ideal compromise between the conflicting principles. Not long ago a prominent statesman spoke of archæology as a "great and healthgiving" science. In this application it may truly bear out his curious characterization.

It is not difficult to demonstrate that the real disease of modern classical instruction,—notably in our own country, which is entirely without archæological study,—is this very want of the sense of reality, resulting from the omission of what Boeckh has termed the material discipline of the science of antiquity. The history of classical learning, during the last four centuries, shows clearly that, without frequent and systematic research among the material remains of earlier life, the real intercourse of modern generations with antiquity steadily declines. The want of archæological investigations during the ages succeeding the first great impulse of the

Renaissance, and of that intelligent understanding only to be derived from discoveries thus made, resulted in the stagnation and pedantic lifelessness of all classic learning which is so characteristic of the sixteenth and seventeenth centuries. The promising beginning of antique research made in the Quatrocento, by Italian architects and travellers.— Brunelleschi, Bracciolini, Squarcione, and particularly Cyriacus of Ancona,— did not meet with encouragement sufficient to insure the position of archæological investigations during the following ages. Even as late as the time of Millin, scholars did not generally recognize the fact that the study of ancient monuments of art is the study of one of the chief expressions of human genius and attainment; did not perceive that a knowledge of the monuments alone could lift the veil by which the earlier civilizations were shrouded.

This inability to recognize and enter into the actual life of the ancients led to the appearance of that great and yet deplorable race of scholars who, Cyclop-like, lacked the eye of practical acquaintance with the material remains of those civilizations to whose literary vestiges they devoted an erudition not since surpassed. Philologists and philosophers stretched and contracted the few facts of antique civilization known to them until they fitted as best they might the Procrustean beds of their preconceived theories. In all branches of intellectual attainment there was a lack of practical knowledge which it is difficult to comprehend. Erasmus, besides his mother tongue, could only speak Latin, and did not even understand the languages of France, Italy, or England, although he had lived long in those countries. Duval, at the court of Francis I. of Austria, could repeat the names and alleged dates of all the rulers of Egypt. Greece, and Rome, but could not tell how many Imperial Electors were living, and did not even know the beautiful sisters of the Emperor Joseph, — who himself excused the scholar with the explanation: "But then my sisters are not antiques." Perhaps the greatest corypheus of this school of pedants was, however, one Hermann Conring, who wrote something over two hundred "opera" and "opuscula," and whose epitaph in the little churchyard of Helmstädt, after enumerating his many attainments and more titles, concludes : "multus putes conditos? Unus est, Conringius, Saeculi Miraculum !" But who to-day gives a thought to this Wonder of his Century, with all his learning?

The study of the classics with these men of the schools, even more than with our own, was dominated by a purely philological and literary spirit, to the exclusion of practical, that is to say of archæological and definite historical conceptions. Scholars had come to regard the words of the ancients more than their meaning, even as style rather than matter still generally decides the choice of classical reading. In their limited minds they were always ready to measure the importance of archæological study by the meagre information they had concerning its materials.

One of the first effects of this misjudgment was the neglect and decay of the ill-arranged collections of antiques then existing. The lamentable fate which befell so many of the Arundel marbles is a striking instance of the lack of general interest in archæological studies at the time. Early in the seventeenth century the collection had been brought from the Cyclades to England by a fortunate chance ; but its value could not then be worthily appreciated. The influence of this unrivalled accession of antiques to one of the chief centres of European thought is hardly perceptible in the intellectual life of those times. The statues and reliefs in vain appealed to the learned world : " Be not so blind ; we, too, are that Hellas which ye seek."

The continental museums of this period, while accumulating worthless curiosities and bric-à-brac of all kinds, dwindled in character to the discouraging cabinets of varieties which were the idle delight of every petty potentate. There was no conception of the great value of such collections as indices of former development. A representative work of this misdirected antiquarianism is Martorelli's notorious volume of 800 quarto pages on an antique ink-stand found at Portici, in which bulky work there is nothing of practical importance, nothing definite, even in regard to antique ink-stands.

When a superficial knowledge of Greek antiquities or costume was acquired, it was only to play an ignoble part in the masquerades of Louis Quatorze. Even as late as the time of Gessner, in the first years of the eighteenth century, these branches of learning were generally held in such low esteem, that he, the learned Rector of the Thomas-Schule, Göttingen Professor, and President of the wisest existing Academy of Sciences, seriously recommended a study of the classics to the *homines elegantes* of his day; that they might thereby be enabled rightly to comprehend the elaborate displays of fire-works then in vogue, and dilate with learned emotions before the complicated and tasteless structures of white-of-egg and tinsel placed by the sugar bakers upon the tables of the great!

Such was the debased state of classical instruction, which resulted from a neglect of that material discipline of antiquity, assured by the researches of the archæologist and by the practical investigations of the explorer. The rise of *humaniora* in Germany and France is due to the more just recognition of the unity of classical studies.

Apart from the futility of such comparisons, no archæologist would go so far as to maintain that the group from the eastern gable of the Temple of Zeus, at Olympia, is more majestic than a Pindaric ode; that the Victory from Samothrace is a more spirited creation than the warlike chorus of Œdipous at Kolonos; or that, for instance, the agora and fortifications at Assos convey a higher conception of the civic and military life of Greece than do the works of Xenophon. But it is right to insist upon the fact that the thoughts of the Greek poets and historians are presented in a difficult language, — the full force and delicacy of which are only to be appreciated after years of devoted study, — while the unrivalled monuments of art of that people speak directly to the intellect and heart of the modern observer. It would be wrong indeed to assert that the language of Greek architecture and sculpture, and of all other archæological materials as well, speaks alike to all; for archæology also has its grammar and lexicon. Still, it remains true that its interest is more immediate and more accessible.

Every teacher of the classics knows how much a reference to an antique monument, or a description à *propos* of an otherwise obscure passage, increases the interest and reality, even of the driest author. Such explanations awaken attention, and give that vivacity of conception so dependent upon the imagination. A line of Pindar or Theokritos thus acquires the living and picturesque value of modern verse. Names of things not in use to-day are met with frequently in the usual school authors, and may be, in fact generally are, mechanically translated, without conveying even the most vague idea of their real signification. But let the objects, or even an adequate representation of them, be shown to the class, and, thenceforth, the pupil will see in the word the thing itself, — its shape, color, and, above all, its character.

Now, archæology stands in the same relation to all antique literature as does the object to the word in the case referred to. Such brilliant discoveries upon ancient sites, as the last generation has witnessed, give us that feeling of the inadequacy of our theoretical information, which is the greatest stimulant to advance. They open new and far-stretching regions, and may be pronounced the only specific for that common and most dangerous tendency of the human mind to form a system from a few facts accidentally known, and then lapse into self-satisfied sterility.

Another reason why the position of archæology should become important in our modern plans of study is to be found in the fact that, although political research attained the full perfection of its apparatus in antique fields, historians have long been inclined to relinquish the prosecution of Greek and Roman history to classical, and particularly to archæological specialists, who are better prepared to consider the monumental and epigraphical testimony afforded by the remains now daily brought to light. The present representatives of classical science cannot be too thankful that so many great masters of historical induction have bestowed upon it the comprehensiveness of their methods. In return for this, it now devolves upon epigraphists and archæologists to increase the supply of materials for the determination of the political and social relations of ancient life.

What better illustration of the brilliant advance of the wealthy cities on the Lydian and Mysian sea-board during the latter half of the fourth century B.C. have we than the appearance and peculiar transformation of Attic architecture and sculpture in Asia Minor during this period? And how could the political union of the small autocratic states to one world-wide dominion be exemplified and defined without an understanding of the art and material culture of the Hellenistic and earlier Roman epochs? In view of these tasks it almost appears that, as Littré has said, the true end of all erudition is to furnish materials for the science of history. Our age has no greater honor than the zeal with which all branches of learning work in concert to recover the riches of the past from the shadow of oblivion; recognizing the intellectual physiognomy of extinct races by the traces of its material expression. It is by the acquirement of such knowledge that we are put in full possession of the attainments of previous generations, and become capable of increasing and improving this inheritance.

In this regard, archaeology, though late, is not least in rank among the sister sciences. Not one furnishes to this grand history more varied and more solid materials, or adds to the picture of former greatness firmer outlines and brighter colors. Indeed, as a handmaid of History, Archaeology is more trustworthy than Literature. A monument of assured authenticity is the most indisputable witness to the contemporary fact which it asserts. An author, on the other hand, may have been content to follow a groundless tradition, to speak on hearsay, sometimes even may have knowingly misrepresented the truth. Moreover, the date of a document does not necessarily indicate either the age or the general acceptance of the fact recorded, still less of the idea which inspired it; while a work of art involuntarily and unconsciously furnishes us with this information. The artist of a complex and imitative age may, it is true, attempt to mislead his generation in regard to the spirit of his design. As we see, to-day he may even succeed with many of those before whom he displays his archaistic or foreign work. But he cannot deceive the trained discrimination of the later historian of art.

Every form given to a material by man is the envelope or sign of a thought. Thoughts thus expressed are translated by archaeology, which science may consequently be defined as the study of all visible monuments of early human activity; it excludes from its limits only the spoken and written languages of the past. It is thus the science which alone can teach us the most remote history of the race; for, while man has not always written, he has, from the first days of his existence, fashioned the materials which surrounded him to accommodate them to his needs, unconsciously impressing upon them the evidence of his conceptions and abilities. Hence, no object, however insignificant it may appear to untrained eyes, is deemed by the archæologist unworthy his study. He regards, with a respectful and almost tender curiosity, the smallest vestige of an earlier age, for in it he recognizes some human thought. The minutiæ of archæological methods are often ridiculed by the vulgar; nothing is more easy than to jest at an uncomprehended activity of any kind. The justification lies in the result. Those researches are surely not in vain by which we are enabled to decipher a single line of the nearly obliterated pages of early human history.

It is owing to those self-sacrificing explorers who for the last hundred years have followed in the footsteps of Stuart and Revett, that we have to-day in archæology a new science, which, in perfection of apparatus and results, may be proudly ranked with comparative anatomy: that branch of research which practical archæology most closely resembles in point of method. For, as the naturalist from a handful of bones can present the image and describe the very habits of an animal which for thousands of years has had no representative on earth, so can the classically educated architect reconstruct the buildings of extinct civilizations by study of their overthrown and widely scattered stones. And as the anatomist sees in the varieties of species certain stages of advance dependent on environing conditions, — so does the student of antique sculpture note in the monuments of the

Asiatic sea-board, of Ægina, and of Attica, the development of artistic conceptions and technical execution. These observations gradually grow to a history of a perfectly parallel human advance, a warning and directing guide.

The great advantage of archæological studies in pedagogical respects lies in the fact that, although the ultimate subject of research is the human mind, it deals primarily with the tangible facts and institutions of antiquity. For the purposes of instruction it has all the advantages of the concrete over the abstract. *Non scholae, sed vitae.* Any man who builds a house, or drives a horse, will do it the better for knowing how houses were arranged, or horses trained, in the antique world. This must surely be the manner in which the out-of-door Greeks would themselves have desired to be studied. It has often been remarked that no race has ever lived upon whose life external surroundings worked with deeper effect. More than any other people the Hellenes had a highly developed sense of the beautiful, and they found the delights to be derived from this appreciation as much in their works of art as in their poetry and eloquence. Certainly no people was ever so surrounded by works of its own hands, and these works influenced most decisively the great body of the Greek public, for whom the scrolls which contained the writings of their comparatively few authors were far out of reach. It was not merely a literary education which raised the citizens of Athens to the eminence of the Pheidian age; it was not the wisdom of their writers, but of their artists which occupied the most prominent place in the minds of the Greek people. Archæology and the history of art teach us to comprehend Hellenic genius as expressed in these most characteristic works, which may be of a like beneficent influence upon our receptive and cosmopolitan generation.

To study exclusively the literary aspects of Greek life, to refuse classical archæology its high place in the unity of Hellenic studies, is to refuse to profit by those lessons of antiquity most needed by modern civilization.

In consideration of these many and varied advantages,— I may even say of this imperative necessity,— it is certainly most deplorable that there is to-day absolutely no recognized archæological instruction in the United States. A barrier like the Chinese Wall seems to separate those who study antiquity in its written works from those who seek its genius in material creations. One American university has, in the strength of its youth, lifted itself upon tip-toe to glance over the wall; but from one domain to the other there is no regularly established communication, no widely open gates.

With this state of things the verdict of the most enlightened minds concerning the results of our pedagogical systems ought not to surprise us. What M. Renan has said is only just: "The United States has created considerable popular instruction without any serious higher instruction, and will long have to expiate this fault by its intellectual mediocrity, its vulgarity of manners, its superficial spirit, its lack of general intelligence." Our own Lowell has stated the fact more tersely: "Americans are the most common-schooled and the least cultivated people in the world."

The gradual advance of archæology in the academical instruction of Europe during the last hundred years indicates one of the most important lines of improvement. The sixteen most prominent universities of Germany, for instance, have regular chairs of archæology, and there are doubtless others which have escaped the inquiry of the present writer. Even ten years ago, when Meyer and Stark were complaining so bitterly of the history of art, "that Cinderella among modern sciences," being neglected by native universities, there were independent professorships of this branch, in addition to the regular archæological instruction, at Berlin, Bonn, Königsberg, Leipzig, Munich, Strassburg, Prague, Tübingen, Vienna, and Zurich.

France, England, and Italy follow this example. There exist no better arguments concerning the importance of archæological studies in the higher curriculum than those delivered by M. George Perrot upon accepting the newly created chair of archæology at the Sorbonne, and by Mr. Percy Gardener upon being called to a similar position at Cambridge.

Even so small a university as that of Bucharest has a chair of archæology. The fifteen lectures delivered by Professor Odobescu on the pedagogic importance of this science and its history up to the time of Montfaucon[1] are well worthy the attention of those interested in the subject. The Roumanian language — though it presents no serious difficulties to one acquainted with the other daughters of the Latin — has not hitherto been much needed by scholars for purposes of reference; the appearance in it of such a work indicates the rapid advance of archæological studies beyond the narrow limits to which the last generation saw them confined. In view of this example, given by a state which until so very recently was between the upper and nether millstones of Oriental misrule and disturbance, we must cease to lay that flattering unction to our American souls which has too often been found in the "newness" of our country and its institutions.

The decree which founded the *École d'Athènes* gave a

---

[1] A. L. Odobescu, Istoria Archeologiei, Studiu Intraductiou la Acésta Sciintia. Bucharesci, 1877.

great and enduring impulse to these studies in France; let us hope that our new American School at Athens may become something more than a philological seminary, and develop the broad interests of its well-arranged predecessors. For it is in Greece itself, amongst the vestiges of Hellenic civilization, that the study of its antiquities is pursued to the greatest advantage. Indeed, the chief difficulty of archæological studies lies in the fact that, in order to enjoy and fully to understand the material remains of antiquity, it is necessary to see them often, and to study them closely. By the magic of a few lines of Homer, of Euripides, of Catullus, the master of ancient languages carries his hearers on the wings of imagination to the classical world. But the archæologist and the historian of art are less free from the material. The thoughts which they study are embodied in a tangible form, of which a mere description is necessarily insufficient. It is not difficult to lay out a plan of archæological study, aided by that admirable scheme of academic instruction founded by Hermann[1] upon K. O. Müller's great work, by Gerhard's similar schedule of lectures,[2] and by useful hints to be derived from later pedagogical treatises.[3] The difficulty lies rather in providing adequate illustrations for the historical and descriptive course determined upon. Hence an imperative requirement is the formation of a collection of antiquities, which is to archæ-

---

[1] Schema akademischer Vorträge über Archäologie, oder Geschichte der Kunst des klassischen Alterthums. Von Dr. K. Fr. Hermann. Göttingen, 1844.

[2] Grundriss der Archaeologie, fuer Vorlesungen, nach Mueller's Handbuch. Von Ed. Gerhard. Berlin, 1853.

[3] One of many: Vorschläge zu einer Methode des ästhetischen Unterrichts, nebst Beispielen. Mit besonderer Hervorhebung der Griechen. Von Rudolf Menge. In the Pädagogische Studien, Von Dr. Wilhelm Rein. Heft XII. Eisenach.

ology what a laboratory is to chemistry. In this respect also the example is given by European countries. As late as 1850 Gerhard could scarcely find material in Berlin for the illustration of his lectures; but in 1873 only five of the German universities (the inferior establishments of Erlangen, Giessen, Marburg, Münster, and Rostock) were without archaeological collections intended for the purposes of instruction. Many of these have gradually grown to great importance, Bonn, Breslau, and Würzburg possessing antiques of inestimable value. Even the preparatory schools of Germany often have admirably complete collections of casts, — as, for instance, that in the little town of Schulpforta, the catalogue of which, by Benndorf, is a work of independent scientific interest.

For the illustration of the history of classical sculpture such a collection should consist of types chosen to represent the characteristics of different centuries and of various schools, rather than of those elegant and familiar figures which please at first sight. These examples should be arranged as far as possible in chronological order, so as to exhibit the modifications of technical methods and style, the gradual development of artistic means, the advance from the archaic to the highest perfection, and, finally, the affectation and insincerity of work which led to the decadence. Without such collections, or the far less trustworthy aid of engravings and photographs, the history of antique art and archaeology can only be pursued at the expense of laborious journeys, impossible to most students, which even the professional explorer has continually to recommence.

Much has already been done in Europe to give to classical studies their true importance and to enable them to exercise their peculiarly salutary influence upon our generation; but far more remains. We have improved, it is true, upon the narrow pedantry of Conring and Gessner, to whom the texts were everything. The science of antiquity has become something more than that *suffisance purement livresque* ridiculed by Montaigne. But practical explorations are still not sufficiently encouraged, and archaeological instruction as yet has not attained its worthy place.

The great Winckelmann stood on the portal between the past and the present of classical learning. It was the suggestiveness of his historical methods that first pointed out the way which has led from the tasteless and unprofitable collector's mania of the Roccoco to the eminence of true archaeological science. But even in his exposition much was empirical, disconnected, and hopelessly entangled. The purely literary accounts of artistic development in Egypt, Mesopotamia, Phœnicia, and Greece obscured rather than enlightened the scholars of the last century, and were ever before their eyes like distorting fogs.

As late as the time of Zoega and Visconti the field of archæology was a promised land, — seen by them with much the feelings of Moses upon Mount Pisgah. It has first become possible to the younger generation of to-day to enter into full possession of the milk and honey of Greek perfection. And this possibility is almost wholly due to the investigations of practical workers upon classic soil, and to those archæological scholars who have taught the world the true value of the materials thus obtained.

THE USE OF A PUBLIC LIBRARY IN THE STUDY OF HISTORY.

BY WM. E. FOSTER, LIBRARIAN OF THE PROVIDENCE PUBLIC LIBRARY.

IT would be a mistake to assume that the usefulness of such an institution as a public library is manifested exclusively, or even chiefly, in connection with any one line of investigation. On the contrary, the demands made upon it represent the widest variety of studies and researches. At the same time, some of its methods have been found to adapt themselves with peculiar directness to the requirements of historical study.

For the sake of brevity, the instances cited below are drawn in every case from the experience of a single library;[1] yet many of the phases of the work here indicated may no doubt be met with in other libraries; and there would seem to be no inherent reason why they are not applicable to libraries in general.

From the outset there has been a definite purpose to maintain a concert of action, and a mutual understanding, between this library, on the one hand, and, on the other, such institutions and agencies as a local historical society, courses of study in college and in the public schools, private schools, local debating societies, private historical classes, and bodies

---

[1] The Providence Public Library.

of students pursuing the admirable courses of the Society to
Encourage Studies at Home, and similar plans of study. In
the college just referred to — Brown University — topics are
regularly assigned for theme-writing, not only in the department of history, but in that of English literature and English
composition. In one of these departments from the outset,
and in the other during a great portion of the time, a memorandum of the topics assigned has been invariably sent to the
public library; and carefully prepared lists of references to
authorities have thereupon been made. Naturally a large
share of the topics in both the departments above mentioned
may be described as distinctly historical; in many cases,
however, biographical or literary. The lists of references
thus prepared have not merely been forwarded to the college
class, but have also been placed on file at the library, for the
use of the students. Gradually, moreover, an extension of
this system to the requirements of the other readers and
students named above — those of the public and private
schools, etc. — has grown up, in which the same method
is followed with greater or less elaborateness. The aim has
been, in short, to observe diligently the nature and extent of
the actual demands upon the library for specific assistance of
this kind, and then to meet it in the fullest possible manner.

But this is only one phase of the work; for the aim has
been not merely to meet such a demand, but to create it as
well. For instance, it has been the unbroken practice, from
the very first day on which the library was opened,[1] to post a
series of "daily notes" on current events and topics. A
newspaper slip, cut in nearly every instance from the morning paper of the current date, is posted on the bulletin-board
in the public portion of the library; and under this are

---

[1] In 1873.

grouped references to authorities, — in many instances citing volume and page, — which illustrate, or supplement, or in some way bear upon this topic. Opposite each entry, moreover, the reader finds the book-number, by which to apply for the work in question; and this he is very likely to do. It is, in fact, a slice out of the catalogue which is thus presented to the attention of readers each morning, but the references are on a much more minute plan than would be possible in any ordinary catalogue. What relation, it may be asked, has this to the study of history? In the first place, most of the topics thus presented, distinctly illustrate Mr. Freeman's suggestion, that "History is past politics; and politics present history"; and during the past six years cases in point have been the "Berlin Congress," "Nihilism in Russia," the "Operations in Egypt," etc. In the second place, it has been found that the works in the library, to which the references have thus been made, are, in a very large percentage of instances, works of standard history.

The most significant fact in connection with this system of suggestions and assistance is the completeness with which it has been recognized and used by the readers. These daily notes, hanging always in a well-recognized place, near the entrance, have from the first been regularly scanned; and the extent to which the suggestions have actually been put in practice has been at all times an appreciable feature in the intelligent use made of the library. But this "daily" system, though the earliest of the library's schemes of suggesting lines of reading, has not been the only one. From it, as a basis, have been developed several very interesting outgrowths, in some instances unforeseen. (1) It was found that these daily lists had, in the eyes of the readers, a more than ephemeral value. They were not merely examined on the day when posted, but were consulted weeks after, by those who remembered having seen on a given day a list on a given subject. So many, moreover, were the instances in which a desire was expressed to make copies of the more extended lists, that the copying process known as the hektograph was introduced, and thus a number of copies could be supplied to those who desired them. (2) To the surprise of the librarian, the number of readers who could thus be supplied (70 or 75) was soon found to be too limited, and resort was had to printing them. At first this was only at rare intervals, and in special cases, but in 1880 the practice was begun — and since continued without interruption — of regular weekly printed lists in each of two local daily newspapers. This has proved an eminently practical and successful measure. The library's "constituency," so to speak, consisting of the local public, has, placed under its eyes each week, whether visiting the library in person or not, a memorandum of reading, in certain specified lines. As a matter of fact, it is noticed that in a large number of instances readers come to the library with these weekly lists in their hands, which they have cut from their newspaper, and which they plainly use as a species of order-list. (3) The next step is of curious interest as illustrating the repeatedly demonstrated fact, that the usefulness of such an institution is not limited by the district or municipality in which it is situated. In response to numerous requests, several of the more extended lists were printed in the "Library Journal" (New York), and elsewhere, in 1880. In 1881, however, was begun the regular monthly issue of the periodical entitled the "Monthly Reference Lists."

This periodical, published at a specified subscription-price, began with a subscription-list which was chiefly local, but which has gradually widened to include readers in all parts of this country, and several in Europe. Among the historical lists which have appeared in this, from month to month, have been references on such current topics as "The Stability of the French Republic," "The German Empire," "European Interests in Egypt," "Indian Tribes in the United States," etc. At the same time a very general demand for references in connection with topics which may be called standard, rather than current, has led to the furnishing of lists on such subjects as "The Unification of Italy,' "The Closing Years of the Roman Republic," "The Plantagenets in England," and "Tendencies of Local Self-government in the United States." Other topics again, like "Elements of Unity in South-Eastern Europe," stand for the interest awakened by historical lectures like those of Mr. Freeman; while still others, like "Yorktown," plainly connect themselves with the recurrence of some anniversary.

Certainly not the least noteworthy of the phases of recent historical research has been the newly-awakened interest in the study of American history, and very naturally the reading and study connected with public libraries have reflected this fact. Four years ago the librarian prepared for use in connection with several of the schools, a series of lists on American history, covering (1) the early stages of colonial history, (2) the adoption of the constitution, and (3) United States history since 1789. The first set of these lists (on the colonies) has been printed, in part, in the "Library Journal"; the second (on the constitution), in "Economic tract, No. 2," issued by the Society for Political Education, in 1881; while the third (on the administrations since 1789), has for the past year been published, month by month, in the "Monthly Reference Lists"; a separate list being devoted to the administration of each successive president. In thus re-issuing them, the librarian has wished to render them as distinctly adapted to the use of readers as possible;

and the proofs have accordingly passed, month by month, under the eyes of accomplished historical investigators at Cambridge, New Haven, Ithaca, Princeton, Baltimore, Ann Arbor, and Madison.

Perhaps there is no more significant feature connected with an institution like a public library, than the fact that its service is rendered alike to the intelligent reader and to the untrained mind; to the specialist and to the general reader. What has been the fact in connection with the class last named? Greatly to the librarian's satisfaction, it has been found that one of the results of this systematic plan of assistance and suggestions, is actually to awaken an interest where none existed, and to supply a clue to historical researches, which may be followed out, with greater or less comprehensiveness, by the reader himself. In repeated instances coming under the librarian's own observation, this result has been noted, and it is of course impossible to say in how many other instances it may have been the case. And, in truth, it is not at all strange that it should be so. These daily, weekly, and monthly references, on topics of *current* interest, are precisely in the line of what is at the time uppermost in the thought of the public; and it is for this reason that they appeal to the interested attention of a very wide circle of readers with so much more than ordinary directness.

A study of library methods like these, moreover, reveals the very marked extent to which a public library becomes almost of necessity an agency in the diffusion of knowledge. Given a certain portion of the library's constituency who are known to be desirous of certain aids to advanced research; given also the desired aids. Who is to say that the only ones who will avail themselves of these aids are the skilled students for whom they are primarily supplied? The reverse has, in fact, been found to be the case, by actual observation. The references in connection with college themes, for instance, placed on file at the library, where they may be used by any one, have indeed been constantly used by the students themselves; but they have also been used to a very marked extent by the general public. There should be observed, of course, on the one hand, a caution against " shooting above the heads of the public "; but there is a no less important necessity, on the other, for not undervaluing the intelligence of readers, and for supplying what may even be regarded as a mental stimulus or impulse. In historical studies, as in other fields of investigation, there can be little doubt that a public library may so ally itself (to quote from Mr. Charles Francis Adams, Jr.) with certain " wide, deep currents of popular taste," and with the pervasive spirit of the time, as to become a constant force in the progress towards better results.

SPECIAL METHODS OF HISTORICAL STUDY[1]

AS PURSUED AT THE JOHNS HOPKINS UNIVERSITY AND FORMERLY AT SMITH COLLEGE.

BY PROFESSOR HERBERT B. ADAMS, JOHNS HOPKINS UNIVERSITY.

THE main principle of historical training at the Johns Hopkins University is to encourage independent thought and research. Little heed is given to text-books, or the mere phraseology of history, but all stress is laid upon clear and original statements of fact and opinion, whether the student's own or the opinion of a consulted author. The comparative method of reading and study is followed by means of assigning to individual members of the class separate topics, with references to various standard works. These topics are duly reported upon by the appointees, either *ex tempore*, with the the aid of a few notes, or in formal papers, which are discussed at length by the class. The oral method has been found to afford a better opportunity than essays for question and discussion, and it is in itself a good means of individual training, for the student thereby learns to think more of substance than of form. Where essays are written, more time

[1] This article contains extracts from a paper on "History: Its Place in American Colleges," originally contributed in October, 1879, to *The Alumnus*, a literary and educational quarterly then published in Philadelphia, but now suspended and entirely out of print. A few extracts have also been made from an article on "Co-operation in University Work," in the second number of *The Johns Hopkins University Studies in Historical and Political Science*. But the body of the article is new, and was written by request, for the purpose of suggesting to teachers how the study of History might be made more interesting and vital by beginning upon home ground, with the investigation of local life and its widening relations.

is usually expended on style than on the acquisition of facts. If the student has a well-arranged brief, like a lawyer's, and a head full of ideas, he will express himself at least intelligibly, and clearness and elegance will come with sufficient practice. The *ex tempore* method, with a good brief or abstract (which may be dictated to the class) is one of the best methods for the teacher as well as for the student. The idea should be, in both cases, to personify historical science in the individual who is speaking upon a given topic. A book or an essay, however symmetrical it may be, is often only a fossil, a lifeless thing; but a student or teacher talking from a clear head is a fountain of living science. A class of bright minds quickly discern the difference between a phrase-maker and a man of ideas.

As an illustration of the kind of subjects in mediæval history studied in 1878, independently of any text-book, by a class of undergraduates, from eighteen to twenty-two years of age, the following list of essay-topics is appended:—

1. Influence of Roman law during the middle ages. (Savigny, Sir Henry Maine, Guizot, Hadley.)
2. The kingdom of Theodoric, the East Goth. (Milman, Gibbon, Freeman.)
3. The conversion of Germany. (Merivale, Milman, Trench.)
4. The conversion of England. (Bede, Milman, Freeman, Montalembert, Trench.)
5. The civilizing influence of the Benedictine Monks. (Montalembert, Gibbon, Milman.)
6. Cloister and cathedral schools. (Einhard, Guizot, Mullinger.)
7. The origin and character of mediæval universities. (Green, History of England; Lacroix; various university histories.)
8. Modes of legal procedure among the early Teutons. (Waitz, J. L. Laughlin, Lea.)
9. Report of studies in "Anglo-Saxon Law." (Henry Adams *et al.*)

HISTORICAL STUDY. 115

10. Origin of Feudalism.   Feudal rights, aids, and incidents. (Guizot, Hallam, Stubbs, Digby, Maine, Waitz, Roth.)
11. Evils of Feudalism.   (Authorities as above.)
12. Benefits of Feudalism.   (As above.)
13. The Saxon Witenagemot and its historical relation to the House of Lords.   (Freeman, Stubbs, Hallam, Guizot.)
14. Origin of the House of Commons.   (Pauli, Creighton, and authorities above stated.)
15. Origin of communal liberty.   (Hegel, Städteverfassung von Italien; Testa, Communes of Lombardy; Wauters, Les libertés communales; Stubbs, Freeman, Guizot, et al.)

At Smith College, an institution founded at Northampton, Massachusetts, by a generous woman, in the interest of the higher education of her sex, the study of history is pursued by four classes in regular gradation, somewhat after the college model. The First, corresponding to the "Freshman" class, study oriental or ante-classic history, embracing the Stone Age, Egypt, Palestine, Phœnicia, the empires of Mesopotamia and ancient India. This course was pursued in 1879 by dictations and *ex tempore* lectures on the part of the teacher, and by independent reading on the part of the pupils. The first thing done by the teacher in the introduction to the history of any of the above-mentioned countries, was to explain the sources from which the history of that country was derived, and then to characterize briefly the principal literary works relating to it, not omitting historical novels, like Ebers' "Egyptian Princess," or "Uarda." Afterwards, the salient features, in Egyptian history, for example, were presented by the instructor, under distinct heads, such as geography, religion, art, literature, and chronology. Map-drawing by and before the class was insisted upon; and, in connection with the foregoing subjects, books or portions of books were recommended for private reading. For instance, on the "Geography of Egypt," fifty pages of Herodotus were assigned in Rawlinson's translation. This, and other reading, was done in the so-called "Reference Library," which was provided with all the books that were recommended. An oral account of such reading was sooner or later demanded from each pupil by the instructor, and fresh points of information were thus continually brought out. The amount of positive fact acquired by a class of seventy-five bright young women bringing together into one focus so many individual rays of knowledge, collected from the best authorities, is likely to burn to ashes the dry bones of any text-book, and to keep the instructor at a white heat.

As an illustration of the amount of reading done *in one term* of ten weeks by this class of beginners in history, the following fair specimen of the lists handed in at the end of the academic year of 1879 is appended. The reading was of course by topics: —

EGYPT.

Unity of History (Freeman).
Geography (Herodotus).
Gods of Egypt (J. Freeman Clarke).
Manners and Customs (Wilkinson).
Upper Egypt (Klunzinger).
Art of Egypt (Lübke).
Hypatia (Kingsley).
Egyptian Princess (Ebers).

PALESTINE.

Sinai and Palestine, 40 pages (Stanley).
History of the Jews (extracts from Josephus).
The Beginnings of Christianity, Chap. VII. (Fisher).
Religion of the Hebrews (J. Freeman Clarke).

PHŒNICIA, ASSYRIA, ETC.

Phœnicia, 50 pages (Kenrick).
Assyrian Discoveries (George Smith).
Chaldean Account of Genesis (George Smith).
Assyrian Architecture (Fergusson).
Art of Central Asia (Lübke).

In the Second, or "Sophomore" class, classic history was pursued by means of the History Primers of Greece and Rome, supplemented by lectures and dictations, as the time would allow. The Junior class studied mediaeval history in much the same way, by text-books (the Epoch Series) and by lectures. Both classes did excellent work of its kind, but it was not the best kind; for little or no stimulus was given to original research. And yet, perhaps, to an outsider, fond of old-fashioned methods of recitation, these classes would have appeared better than the First class. They did harder work, but it was less spontaneous and less scientific. The fault was a fault of method.

With the Senior class the method described as in use at the Johns Hopkins University was tried with marked success. With text-books on modern history as a guide for the whole class, the plan was followed out of assigning to individuals subjects with references for private reading and for an oral report of about fifteen minutes' length. The class took notes on these reports or informal student-lectures as faithfully as on the extended remarks and more formal lectures of the instructor. This system of making a class lecture to itself is, of course, very unequal in its immediate results, and sometimes unsatisfactory; but, as a system of individual training for advanced pupils, it is valuable as a means both of culture and of discipline. Contrast the good to the individual student of any amount of mere text-book memorizing or idle note-taking with the positive culture and wide acquaintance with books, derived *in ten weeks* from such a range of reading as is indicated in the following *bona fide* report by one member of the Senior class (1879), who afterwards was a special student of history for two years in the "Annex" at Harvard College, and who in 1881 returned to Smith College for her degree of Ph.D. First are given the subjects assigned to this young woman for research, and the reading done by her in preparation for report to the class; and then is given the list of her general reading in connection with the class work of the term. Other members of the class had other subjects and similar reports: —

I. — SUBJECTS FOR RESEARCH.

1. *Anselm and Roscellinus.*
   Milman's Latin Christianity, Vol. IV., pp. 190–225.
   Ueberweg's History of Philosophy, Vol. I., pp. 271–385.
2. *Platonic Academy at Florence.*
   Roscoe's Life of Lorenzo di Medici, Vol. I., p. 30 *et seq.*
   Burckhardt's Renaissance, Vol. I.
   Villari's Machiavelli, Vol. I., p. 205 *et seq.*
3. *Colet.*
   Seebohm's Oxford Reformers.
4. *Calvin.*
   Fisher's History of the Reformation (Calvin).
   Spalding's History of the Reformation (Calvin).
   D'Aubigné's History of the Reformation, Vol. I., book 2, chap. 7.
5. *Frederick the Great.*
   Macaulay's Essay on Frederick the Great.
   Lowell's Essay on Frederick the Great.
   Ency. Brit. Article on Frederick the Great.
   Menzel's History of Germany (Frederick the Great).
   Carlyle's Frederick the Great (parts of Vols. I., II., III.).
6. *Results of the French Revolution.*
   French Revolution (Epoch Series).

HISTORICAL STUDY. 119

II.—GENERAL READING.

Roscoe's Life of Leo X. (one-half of Vol. I.).
Mrs. Oliphant's Makers of Florence (on cathedral builders, Savonarola, a Private Citizen, Michel Angelo).
Symonds' Renaissance (Savonarola).
Walter Pater's Renaissance (Leonardo da Vinci).
Hallam's Middle Ages (on Italian Republics).
Benvenuto Cellini's Autobiography (about one-half).
Burckhardt's Renaissance (nearly all).
Vasari's Lives of the Painters (da Vinci, Alberti).
Lowell's Essay on Dante.
Carlyle's Essay on Dante.
Trench's Mediæval Church History (Great Councils of the West, Huss and Bohemia, Eve of the Reformation).
Fisher's History of the Reformation (Luther).
White's Eighteen Christian Centuries (16th).
Macaulay's Essay on Ranke's History of the Popes.
Lecky's European Morals (last chapter).
Seebohm's Era of the Protestant Revolution.
Froude's Short Studies on Great Subjects (studies on the times of Erasmus and Luther, the Dissolution of the Monasteries).
Spalding's History of the Reformation (chapter on Luther).
Carlyle's Essay on Luther and Knox.
Hosmer's German Literature (chapters on Luther, Thirty Years' War, Minnesingers and Mastersingers).
Gardiner's Thirty Years' War.
Morris's Age of Anne.
George Eliot's Romola (about one-half).
Hawthorne's Marble Faun (parts).

It is but fair to say in reference to this vast amount of reading, that it represents the chief work done by the above-mentioned young lady during the summer term, for her class exercises were mainly lectures requiring little outside study. The list will serve not merely as an illustration of Senior work in history at Smith College, but also as an excellent guide for a course of private reading on the *Renaissance and Reformation*. No more interesting or profitable course can be followed than a study of the Beginnings of Modern History. With Symonds' works on the "Renaissance in Italy," Burckhardt's "Civilization of the Period of the Renaissance" (English translation), and Seebohm's "Era of the Protestant Revolution" (Epoch series) for guide-books, a college instructor can indicate to his pupils lines of special investigation more grateful than text-book "cramming," more inspiring than lectures or dictations. The latter, though good to a certain extent, become deadening to a class when its members are no longer stimulated to original research, but sink back in passive reliance upon the authority of the lecturer. That method of teaching history which converts bright young pupils into note-taking machines is a bad method. It is the construction of a poor text-book at the expense of much valuable time and youthful energy. Goethe satirized this, the fault of German academic instruction, in Mephistopheles' counsel to the student, who is advised to study well his notes, in order to see that the professor says nothing which he hasn't said already: —

> Damit ihr nachher besser seht,
> Dass er nichts sagt, als was im Buche steht;
> Doch euch des Schreibens ja befleisst,
> Als dictirt' euch der Heilig' Geist!

The simple-minded student assents to this counsel, and says it is a great comfort to have everything in black and white, so that he can carry it all home. But no scrap-book of facts can give wisdom, any more than a tank of water can form a running spring. It is, perhaps, of as much consequence to teach a young person *how* to study history as to teach him history itself.

The above notes were written in the summer of 1879, and

were published in October of that year, after the author's return to Baltimore. Subsequent experience at Smith College, in the spring terms of 1880 and 1881, when the lecturer's four years' partial connection with Smith College terminated, showed the necessity of a reference library for each class, the resources of the main collection in the reading-room having proved inadequate to the growing historical needs of the college. Instead of buying text-books, the members of each class, with the money which text-books would have cost, formed a library fund, from which a book committee purchased such standard works (often with duplicate copies) as the lecturer recommended. The class libraries were kept in places generally accessible; for example, in the front halls of the "cottage" dormitories. Each class had its own system of rules for library administration. Books that were in greatest demand could be kept out only one or two days. The amount of reading by special topics accomplished in this way in a single term was really most remarkable. Note-books with abstracts of daily work were kept, and finally handed in as a part of the term's examination. Oral examinations upon reading, pursued in connection with the lectures, were maintained throughout the term, and, at the close, a written examination upon the lectures and other required topics, together with a certain range of optional subjects, fairly tested the results of this voluntary method of historical study. The amount of knowledge acquired in this way would as much surpass the substance of any system of lectures or any mere text-book acquisitions as a class library of standard historians surpasses an individual teacher or any historical manual. This method of study is practicable in any high-school class of moderate size. If classes are generous, they will leave their libraries to successors, who can thus build up a collection for historical reference within the school itself, which will thus become a seminary of living science.

A development of the above idea of special libraries for class use was the foundation in Baltimore, at the Johns Hopkins University, in 1881-2, of a special library for the study of American Institutional History by college graduates. There was nothing really new about the idea except its application. German universities have their *seminarium* libraries distinct from the main university library, although often in the same building. In Baltimore the special library was established in the lecture-room where the class meets. The design of the collection was to gather within easy reach the chief authorities used in class work and in such original investigations as were then in progress. The special aim, however, was to bring together the statutory law and colonial archives of the older States of the Union, together with the journals of Congress, American State papers, and the writings and lives of American statesmen. The statutes of England and parliamentary reports on subjects of particular interest were next secured. Then followed, in December, 1882, the acquisition of the Bluntschli Library of three thousand volumes, with many rare pamphlets and Bluntschli's manuscripts, including his notes taken under Niebuhr the historian, and under Savigny the jurist. This library of the lamented Dr. Bluntschli, professor of constitutional and international law in Heidelberg, was presented to the Johns Hopkins University by German citizens of Baltimore; and it represents, not only in its transfer to America, but in its very constitution, the internationality of modern science. Here is a library, which, under the care of a great master, developed from the narrow chronicles of a Swiss town and canton into a library of cosmopolitan character, embracing many nations in its scope. Into this inheritance the Seminary Library of American Institutional History has now entered. Although the special work of the Seminary will still be directed toward American themes, yet it will be from the vantage-ground of the Bluntschli Library, and with the knowledge that this great collection was the outgrowth of communal studies similar to those now in progress in Baltimore.

A word may be added in this connection touching the nature of graduate-work in history at the Johns Hopkins University. What was said in the early part of this article applied only to undergraduates, who develop into the very best class of graduate students now present at the University. The idea of a co-operative study of American local institutions, by graduate students representing different sections of country, evolved very naturally from the Baltimore environment. Germinant interest in the subject originated in a study of New England towns, in a spring sojourn for four years at Smith College, Northampton, Mass., and in summer tours along the New England coast; but the development of this interest was made possible by associations in Baltimore with men from the South and the West, who were able and willing to describe the institutions of their own States for purposes of comparison with the institutions of other States. Thus it has come about that the parishes, districts, and counties of Maryland, Virginia, and the Carolinas are placed historically side by side with the townships of the West and the towns and parishes of New England; so that, by and by, all men will see how much these different sections have in common.

There is a great variety of subjects pertaining to American local life in its rural and municipal manifestations. Not only the history of local government, but the history of schools, churches, charities, manufactures, industries, prices, economics, municipal protection, municipal reforms, local taxation, representation, administration, poor laws, liquor laws, labor laws, and a thousand and one chapters of legal and social history are yet to be written in every State. Johns Hopkins students have selected only a few topics like towns, parishes, manors, certain state systems of free schools, a few phases of city government, a few French and Indian villages in the North-west, certain territorial institutions, Canadian feudalism, the town institutions of New England (to a limited extent); but there is left historical territory enough for student immigration throughout the next hundred years. The beauty of science is that there are always new worlds to discover. And at the present moment there await the student pioneer vast tracts of American institutional and economic history almost as untouched as were once the forests of America, her coal measures and prairies, her mines of iron, silver, and gold. Individual and local effort will almost everywhere meet with quick recognition and grateful returns. But scientific and cosmopolitan relations with college and university centres, together with the generous co-operation of all explorers in the same field, will certainly yield the most satisfactory results both to the individual and to the community which he represents.

It is highly important that isolated students who desire to co-operate in this kind of work should avail themselves of the existing machinery of local libraries, the local press, local societies, and local clubs. If such things do not exist, the most needful should be created. No community is too small for a book club and for an association of some sort. Local studies should always be connected in some way with the life of the community, and should always be used to quicken that life to higher consciousness. A student, a teacher, who prepares a paper on local history or some social question, should read it before the village lyceum or some literary club or an association of teachers. If encouraged to believe his work of any general interest or permanent value, he should print it in the local paper or in a local magazine, perhaps an educational journal, without aspiring to the highest popular monthlies, which will certainly reject all purely local contributions by unknown contributors. It is far more practicable to publish by local aid in pamphlet form or in the proceedings of associations and learned societies, before which such papers may sometimes be read.

From a variety of considerations, the writer is persuaded that one of the best introductions to history that can be given in American high schools, and even in those of lower grade, is through a study of the community in which the school is placed. History, like charity, begins at home. The best American citizens are those who mind home affairs and local interests. "That man's the best cosmopolite who loves his native country best." The best students of universal history are those who know some one country or some one subject well. The family, the hamlet, the neighborhood, the community, the parish, the village, town, city, county, and state are historically the ways by which men have approached national and international life. It was a preliminary study of the geography of Frankfort-on-the-Main that led Carl Ritter to study the physical structure of Europe and Asia, and thus to establish the new science of comparative geography. He says: "Whoever has wandered through the valleys and woods, and over the hills and mountains of his own state, will be the one capable of following a Herodotus in his wanderings over the globe." And we may say, as Ritter said of the science of geography, the first step in history is to know thoroughly the district where we live. In America, Guyot has represented for many years this method of teaching geography. Huxley, in his Physiography, has introduced pupils to a study of Nature as a whole, by calling attention to the physical features of the Thames valley and the wide range of natural phenomena that may be observed in any English parish. Humboldt long ago said in his Cosmos: "Every little nook and shaded corner is but a reflection of the whole of Nature." There is something very suggestive and very quickening in such a philosophy of Nature and history as regards every spot of the earth's surface, every pebble, every form of organic life, from the lowest mollusk to the highest phase of human society, as a perfect microcosm, perhaps an undiscovered world of suggestive truth. But it is important to remember that all these things should be studied in their widest relations. Natural history is of no significance if viewed apart from Man. Human history is without foundation if separated from Nature. The deeds of men, the genealogy of families, the annals of quiet neighborhoods, the records of towns, states, and nations are *per se* of little consequence to history unless in some way these isolated things are brought into vital connection with the progress and science of the world. To establish such connections is sometimes like the discovery of unknown lands, the exploration of new countries, and the widening of the world's horizon.

American local history should first be studied as a contribution to national history. This country will yet be viewed and reviewed as an organism of historic growth, developing from minute germs, from the very protoplasm of state life. And some day this country will be studied in its international relations, as an organic part of a larger organism now vaguely called the World State, but as surely developing through the operation of economic, legal, social, and scientific forces as the American Union, the German and British Empires are evolving into higher forms. American history in its widest relations is not to be written by any one man nor by any one generation of men. Our history will grow with the nation and with its developing consciousness of internationality. The present possibilities for the real progress of historic and economic science lie, first and foremost, in the development of a generation of economists and practical historians, who realize that history is past politics and politics present history; secondly, in the expansion of the local consciousness into a fuller sense of its historic worth and dignity, of the cosmopolitan relations of modern local life, and of its own wholesome conservative power in these days of growing centralization. National and international life can best develop upon the constitutional basis of local self-government in church and state.

The work of developing a generation of specialists has already begun in the college and the university. The development of local consciousness can perhaps be best stimulated through the common school. It may be a suggestive fact that the school committee of Great Barrington, Mass., lately voted (*Berkshire Courier*, Sept. 6, 1882) to introduce into their village high school,[1] in the hands of an Amherst graduate, in connection with Nordhoff's "Politics for Young Americans" and Jevons' "Primer of Political Economy," the article upon "The Germanic Origin of New England Towns," which was once read in part before the Village Improvement Society of Stockbridge, Mass., Aug. 24, 1881, and published in the *Pittsfield Evening Journal* of that day. Local demand really occasioned a university supply of the article[2] in question. The possible connection between the

---

[1] The catalogue of the Great Barrington High School (1882) shows that the study of history and politics is there founded, as it should be, upon a geographical basis.

[2] *Johns Hopkins University Studies in Historical and Political Science*, II. "The Germanic Origin of New England Towns." (Now out of print, 1884.)

college and the common school is still better illustrated by the case of Professor Macy, of Iowa College, Grinnell, who is one of the most active pioneers in teaching "the real homely facts of government," and who in 1881 published a little tract on Civil Government in Iowa, which is now used by teachers throughout that entire State in preparing their oral instructions for young pupils, beginning with the township and the county, the institutions that are "nearest and most easily learned." A special pupil of Professor Macy's — Albert Shaw, A.B., Iowa College, 1879 — is now writing a similar treatise on Civil Government in Illinois, for school use in that State. There should be such a manual for every State in the Union.

But the writer would like to see a text-book which not only explains, as does Principal Macy, " the real homely facts of government," but which also suggests how those facts came to be. A study of the practical workings of local government and of the American Constitution is the study of politics which every young American ought to pursue. But a study of the origin and development of American institutions is a study of history in one of its most important branches. It is not necessary that young Americans should grapple with " the Constitution " at the very outset. Their forefathers put their energies into the founding of villages, towns, and plantations before they thought of American independence. Their first country this side of the Atlantic was the colony; in some instances, the county. It is not unworthy of sons to study the historic work of fathers who constructed a nation upon the solid rock of local self-government in church and state.

If young Americans are to appreciate their religious and political inheritance, they must learn its intrinsic worth. They must be taught to appreciate the common and lowly things around them. They should grow up with as profound respect for town and parish meetings as for the State legislature, not to speak of the Houses of Congress. They should recognize the majesty of the law, even in the parish constable as well as in the high sheriff of the county. They should look on selectmen as the head men of the town, the survival of the old English reeve and four best men of the parish. They should be taught to see in the town common or village green a survival of that primitive institution of land-community upon which town and state are based. They should be taught the meaning of town and family names; how the word "town" means, primarily, a place *hedged in* for purposes of defence; how the picket-fences around home and house-lot are but a survival of the primitive *town* idea; how *home, hamlet*, and *town* live on together in a name like *Hampton*, or *Home-town*. They should investigate the most ordinary things, for these are often the most archaic. For example, there is the village pound, which Sir Henry Maine says is one of the most ancient institutions, "older than the king's bench, and probably older than the kingdom." There, too, are the field-drivers (still known in New England), the ancient town herdsmen, village shepherds, and village swineherds (once common in this country), who serve to connect our historic life with the earliest pastoral beginnings of mankind.

It would certainly be an excellent thing for the development of historical science in America if teachers in our public schools would cultivate the historical spirit in their pupils with special reference to the local environment. Something more than local history can be drawn from such sources. Take the Indian relics, the arrow-heads which a boy has found in his father's field or which may have been given him by some antiquary: here are texts for familiar talks by the teacher upon the "Stone Age" and the progress of the world from savage beginnings. Indian names still linger upon our landscapes, upon our mountains, rivers, fields, and meadows, affording a suggestive parallel between the "exterminated" natives of England and New England. What a quickening impulse could be given to a class of bright pupils by a visit to some scene of ancient conflict with the Indians, like that at Bloody Brook in South Deerfield, Mass., or to such an interesting local museum as that in Old Deerfield, where is exhibited, in a good state of preservation, the door of an early settler's house, — a door cut through by Indian tomahawks. A multitude of historical associations gather around every old town and hamlet in the land.

There are local legends and traditions, household tales, stories told by grandfathers and grandmothers, incidents remembered by "the oldest inhabitants." But above all in importance are the old documents and manuscript records of the first settlers, the early pioneers, the founders of our towns. Here are sources of information more authentic than tradition, and yet often entirely neglected. If teachers would simply make a few extracts from these unpublished records, they would soon have sufficient materials in their hands for elucidating local history to their pupils and fellow-townsmen. The publication of such extracts in the local paper is one of the best ways to quicken local interest in matters of history. Biographies of "the first families," of the various ministers, doctors, lawyers, "Squires," "Generals," "Colonels," college graduates, school-teachers, and leading citizens, -- these are all legitimate and pleasant means of kindling historical interest in the community and in the schools. The town fathers, the fathers of families, and all their sons and daughters will quickly catch the bearings of this kind of historical study, for it takes hold upon the life of the community and quickens not only pride in the past but hope for the future.

In order to study history it is not necessary to begin with dead men's bones, with Theban dynasties, the kings of Assyria. the royal families of Europe, or even with the presidents of the United States. These subjects have their importance in certain connections, but for beginners in history there are perhaps other subjects of greater interest and vitality. The most natural entrance to a knowledge of the history of the world is from a local environment through widening circles of interest, until, from the rising ground of the present, the broad horizon of the past comes clearly into view. There is hardly a subject of contemporary interest which, if properly studied, will not carry the mind back to a remote antiquity, to historic relations as wide as the world itself. A study of the community in which the student dwells will serve to connect that community not only with the origin and growth of the State and Nation, but with the mother-country, with the German fatherland, with village communities throughout the Aryan world, — from Germany and Russia to old Greece and Rome; from these classic lands to Persia and India. Such modern connections with the distant Orient are more refreshing than the genealogy of Darius the son of Hystaspes.

I would not be understood as disparaging ancient or old-world history, for, if rightly taught, this is the most interesting of all history; but I would be understood as emphasizing the importance of studying the antiquity which survives in the present and in this country. America is not such a new world as it seems to many foreigners. Geologists tell us that our continent is the oldest of all. Historians like Mr. Freeman declare that if we want to see Old England we must go to New England. Old France survives in French Canada.

In Virginia, peculiarities of the West Saxon dialect are still preserved. Professor James A. Harrison, of Lexington, Virginia, writes me that in Louisiana and Mississippi, where upon old French and Spanish settlements the English finally planted, there are "sometimes three traditions superimposed one on the other." Men like George W. Cable and Charles Gayarré have been mining to good advantage in such historic strata. If American students and teachers are equally wise, they will look about their own homes before visiting the land of Chaldæa.

The main difficulty with existing methods of teaching history seems to be that the subject is treated as a record of dead facts, and not as a living science. Pupils fail to realize the vital connection between the past and the present; they do not understand that ancient history was the dawn of a light which is still shining on; they do not grasp the essential idea of history, which is the growing self-knowledge of a living, progressive age. Etymologically and practically, the study of history is simply a learning by inquiry. According to Professor Droysen, who was one of the most eminent historians in Berlin, the historical method is merely *to understand by means of research*. Now it seems entirely practicable for every teacher and student of history to promote, in a limited way, the "know thyself" of the nineteenth century by original investigation of things not yet fully known, and by communicating to others the results of his individual study. The pursuit of history may thus become an active instead of a passive process, — an increasing joy instead of a depressing burden. Students will thus learn that history is not entirely bound up in text-books; that it does not consist altogether in what this or that learned authority has to say about the world. What the world believes concerning itself, after all that men have written, and what the student thinks of the world, after viewing it with the aid of guide-books and with his own eyes,—these are matters of some moment in the developmental process of that active self-knowledge and philosophic reflection which make history a living science instead of a museum of facts and of books "as dry as dust." Works of history, the so-called standard authorities, are likely to become dead specimens of humanity unless they continue in some way to quicken the living age. But written history seldom fails to accomplish this end, and even antiquated works often continue their influence if viewed as progressive phases of human self-knowledge. Monuments and inscriptions can never grow old so long as the race is young. New meaning is put into ancient records; fresh garlands are hung upon broken statues; new temples are built from classic materials; and the world rejoices at its constant self-renewal.

Since the publication of the foregoing pages, in the first edition of this book, I have elsewhere described, in greater detail, certain special methods of historical study. The following abstract is taken from the "Johns Hopkins University Studies in Historical and Political Science," Second Series, Numbers I. and II. "Methods of Historical Study," page 137:—

1. *The Topical Method.*—If there is any guiding principle in the study of historical as well as of natural science, it is "The way to that which is general is through that which is special." It makes little difference with what class of facts the student begins, provided they are not too complex for easy apprehension. The point is that universal history may be approached in a great variety of special ways, any one of which may be as good as another. They are like the Brahminical philosopher's idea of different religious revelations,—gates leading into the same city. All roads

lead to Rome, and all roads lead to history. But while this general truth remains, it also remains true that there is a certain practical advantage in beginning historical study with that which is nearest and most familiar. A man's own family, community, country, and race, are the most natural objects of historical interest, because man is born into such associations, and because an historical knowledge of them will always be the most valuable form of historical culture, for these subjects most concern our own life, our past, present, and future. In history, as in biology, live specimens are usually better than dead ones. *Life* is of supreme interest to history, as it is to biology; hence those nations and men that have made the present what it is will always be the best topics for historical study.

I should be inclined to recommend, in beginning the study of history by any special method of approach, like the history of America or the history of Egypt, that teacher and class begin work upon the geography of the United States, or of the Nile valley. Then, after a thorough consideration of the lay of the land, comes naturally the topic of the people, the first inhabitants. After the topics of a chosen land and of a chosen people should come the subject of the sources of that people's history. What memorials of themselves have the primitive inhabitants of America or of Egypt left behind them? It is of great importance in the pedagogical process of teaching history that the student should learn the origin of written history, how manuals and standard histories are constructed; otherwise, the student will look upon the book or manual as a final authority. He should, on the contrary, look at all written history as simply a current, more or less colored by human prejudice, a current which has come down, like the Nile or the Mississippi, from some higher and more original source than the passing stream. Such a consciousness leads the student to further inquiry, to a habit of mind like that of explorers who sought the sources of the Nile or of the Congo.

Professor Moses Coit Tyler, of Cornell University, has prepared the following brief account of a special class-course, which admirably illustrates the topical method: " Perhaps it may be a peculiarity in my work as a teacher of History here that I am permitted to give my whole attention to American history. At any rate, this fact enables me to organize the work of American history so as to cover, more perfectly than I could otherwise do, the whole field, from the prehistoric times of this continent down to the present, with a minuteness of attention varying, of course, as the importance of the particular topic varies. I confess that I adopt for American history the principle which Professor Seeley, of Cambridge, is fond of applying to English history, namely, that while history should be thoroughly scientific in its method, its object should be practical. To this extent I believe in history with a tendency. My interest in our own past is chiefly derived from my interest in our own present and future ; and I teach American history, not so much to make historians as to make citizens and good leaders for the State and the Nation. From this point of view, I decide upon the selection of historical topics for special study. At present I should describe them as the following: The native races, especially the Mound-builders and the North-American Indians ; the alleged Pre-Columbian discoveries ; the origin and enforcement of England's claim to North America, as against competing European nations ; the motives and methods of English colony-planting in America in the seventeenth and eighteenth centuries ; the development of ideas and institutions in the American colonies, with particular reference to religion, education, industry, and civil freedom; the grounds of inter-colonial isolation and of inter-colonial fellowship; the causes and progress of the movement for colonial independence; the history of the formation of the national constitution; the origin and growth of political parties under the constitution; the history of slavery as a factor in American politics, culminating in the civil war of 1861–65. On all these subjects, I try to generate and preserve in myself and my pupils such an anxiety for the truth, that we shall prefer it even to national traditions or the idolatries of party.

"As to methods of work, I doubt if I have anything to report that is peculiar to myself, or different from the usage of all teachers who try to keep abreast of the times. I am an eclectic. I have tried to learn all the current ways of doing this work, and have appropriated what I thought best suited to our own circumstances. As I have students of all grades, so my methods of work include the recitation, the lecture, and the seminary. I have found it impossible by the two former to keep my students from settling into a merely passive attitude; it is only by the latter that I can get them into an attitude that is inquisitive, eager, critical, originating. My notion is that the lecturing must be reciprocal. As I lecture to them, so must they lecture to me.

"We are all students and all lecturers. The law of life with us is co-operation in the search after the truth of history."

2. *The Comparative Method.*—A great impulse was given to the historical sciences by the introduction of the comparative method into the study of philology, mythology, religion, law, and institutions. It seemed as though the horizon of all these fields suddenly widened, and as if the world of human thought and research were expanding into new realms. "Before the great discoveries of modern science,"

says Freeman, "before that greatest of all its discoveries which has revealed to us the unity of Aryan speech, of Aryan religion, and Aryan political life, the worn-out superstitions about 'ancient' and 'modern' ought to pass by like the spectres of darkness. . . . The range of our political vision becomes wider when the application of the comparative method sets before us the *ekklesia* of Athens, the *comitia* of Rome, as institutions, not merely analogous, but absolutely the same thing, parts of the same common Aryan heritage, as the ancient assemblies of our own land. We carry on the tale as we see that it is out of those assemblies that our modern parliaments, our modern courts of justice, our modern public gatherings of every kind, have grown." ("On the Study of History," Fortnightly Review, March 1, 1881.)

It would be a fine thing for American students, if, in studying special topics in the history of their own country, they would occasionally compare the phases of historic truth here discovered with similar phases of discovery elsewhere; if, for example, the colonial beginnings of North America should be compared with Aryan migrations westward into Greece and Italy, or again with the colonial systems of Greece and of the Roman Empire, or of the English Empire to-day, which is continuing in South Africa and Australia and in Manitoba, the same old spirit of enterprise which colonized the Atlantic seaboard of North America. It would interest young minds to have parallels drawn between English colonies, Grecian commonwealths, Roman provinces, the United Cantons of Switzerland, and the United States of Holland. To be sure, these various topics would require considerable study on the part of teacher and pupil, but the fathers of the American constitution, Madison, Hamilton, and others, went over such ground in preparing the platform of our present federal government.

But my special plea is for the application of the comparative method to the use of historical literature. Students should learn to view history in different lights and from various standpoints. Instead of relying passively upon the *ipse dixit* of the school-master, or of the school-book, or of some one historian, pupils should learn to judge for themselves by comparing evidence. Of course some discretion should be exercised by the teacher in the case of young pupils; but even children are attracted by different versions of the same tale or legend, and catch at new points of interest with all the eagerness of original investigators. The scattered elements of fact or tradition should be brought together as children piece together the scattered blocks of a map. The criterion of all truth, as well as of all art, is *fitness*. Comparison of different accounts of the same historic event would no more injure boys and girls than would a comparative study of the four gospels. On the contrary, such comparisons strengthen the judgment, and give it greater independence and stability. In teaching history, altogether too much stress has been laid, in many of our schools, upon mere forms of verbal expression in the text-book, as though historic truth consisted in the repetition of what some author had said. It would be far better for the student to read the same story in several different forms, and then to give his own version. The latter process would be an independent historical view based upon a variety of evidence. The memorizing of "words, words," prevents the assimilation of facts, and clogs the mental processes of reflection and private judgment.

The prosecution of the comparative method in the study of history requires an increase of facilities beyond the meagre text-books now in use. While by no means advocating the abolition of all manuals, chronologies, and general sketches of history, I would strongly urge the establishment of class-libraries for historical reference. This special practice would be quite in harmony with the growing custom of equipping public schools with special libraries. It is a practice which the interest of publishers and the good sense of all friends of education would tend to foster. At Smith College, Harvard College, and at the Johns Hopkins University, the comparative method of study in history and other subjects has long been in operation. In Cambridge and in Baltimore, certain books are reserved from the main library of the university for class-use. In Baltimore, such reservations are occasionally supplemented by drafts on other libraries in the city, and by private contributions. The books are read in the university reading-room, but are taken out by special arrrangement, for a limited time, when there is no other demand.

3. *The Co-operative Method.* — It is not possible, within the limits of this paper, to describe the development of that new system of writing history, which is based upon the economic principles of division of labor and final co-operation. The time was when individual historians, monks and chroniclers, grappled boldly with the history of the whole world. There are still compilers of text-books for schools and colleges who attempt to epitomize the deeds of men from creation down to the present day. Indeed, the greatest of living historians, Leopold von Ranke, is now rapidly reviewing universal history in a work which already embraces several volumes, and which he hopes to finish soon, being now at the age of eighty-nine, so that he may resume more special work. But, in spite of this extraordinary example, which seems to defy the weakness of age and the will of fate, it may be said with confidence that the day of universal histories by individual men is past. The day for

the special and co-operative treatment of history by countries, epochs, and monographic themes is already here. We see a co-operative tendency in the best school-books. The history even of a single nation is now recognized as too vast a thing for one man to handle in a truly scientific manner, although special results of individual research are still co-ordinated in popular ways. The most notable example of the co-operative method in universal history is the new monographic history of the world, edited by Professor Wilhelm Oncken, but composed by the most eminent specialists in Germany. One man writes the history of Egypt in the light of modern research; another that of Persia; a third reviews the history of Greece, giving the latest results of Grecian archaeological investigations; others revise Roman history and the early history of Germanic peoples.

This co-operative method has lately been applied in Schönberg's great work on political economy, and was applied many years ago to a dictionary of political science by the late Dr. J. C. Bluntschli, of Heidelburg. Under his editorial guidance, contributions were made by French and German specialists to a great variety of subjects relating to European history and politics. Bluntschli's example has been followed in this country by the publication of Lalor's "Cyclopaedia of Political Science, Political Economy, and of the Political History of the United States." In America, the co-operative method of writing history has long been in quiet operation. Perhaps one of the earliest and most fruitful examples was that of the Massachusetts Historical Society, which, in the latter part of the last century, began to encourage the writing of New England town history upon principles of local co-operation. The contributions of parish ministers and local antiquaries were published in the proceedings of the society, and proved the humble beginnings of that remarkable series of town histories, which have now specialized the constitution of New England into a vast number of village republics, each one thought worthy of independent treatment. Co-operation has entered even the local domain, e.g., the history of Boston, after passing through various individual hands, has lately been rewritten by a group of specialists, working under the editorial direction of Professor Justin Winsor, of Harvard College. This method is now proposed in Providence and other cities. It has been extended by Justin Winsor to the whole country, for the "Narrative and Critical History of the United States," which he is now editing, is made up of monographs by the best specialists that the country affords.

The urgent plea, then, for the co-operative method which I would make is this: apply it to the study of general history in classes. Experience at the Johns Hopkins University and at Smith College has shown the advantage of this method for classes with a short period of time at their command, who nevertheless desire to cover a goodly stretch of historical territory. The method, in its practical operation, consists of a division of labor in a class guided by an instructor, who undertakes to direct special work into co-operative channels. The student, while to some extent upon the common ground of text-books, or prescribed authors, and while taking notes upon class-lectures, of a special character, carries on investigations in close connection with the general course. Written reports are submitted to a critic for correction, are read before an elocutionist for the sake of training in the art of presentation, and are then finally presented, either wholly or in part, to the class, who take notes and are examined upon these co-operative studies in the same way as on material presented by the instructor.

An interesting and valuable practice has gradually grown

up among students of historical and political science at the Johns Hopkins University, namely, that of students lecturing to their own class upon subjects connected with the course. The practice originated several years ago among undergraduate students of history and international law; it was the natural outgrowth of the topical method of study. It is a practice considerably different from that of reading formal essays, which often prove very burdensome to a class of intelligent pupils. The idea of oral reports with the aid of a brief or of a few notes, or, best of all, of an analysis written upon the blackboard, led the way to the preparation of a regular course of co-operative lectures by members of a class working conjointly with the instructor. Greater dignity was given to the efforts of students by asking them in turn to come to the front, to the map or blackboard, or else to the instructor's chair. For the time being the student became the teacher. Pretensions were seldom made to original investigations in preparing for such a class-lecture. The understanding was that students should collect the most authoritative information upon a given subject, and present it to his fellows in an instructive way. This naturally implied the selection of the best points of view, and the omission of all irrelevant matter. The success of the lecturer turned, not upon his occupying the time by reading an encyclopædic article, but upon his kindling the interest of his classmates, and keeping their attention to the end.

4. *The Seminary Method.* — The *Seminarium*, like the college and the university, is of ecclesiastical origin. Historically speaking, the seminary was a nursery of theology and a training-school for seminary priests. The modern theological seminary has evolved from the mediæval institution, and modern seminary-students, whether at school or at the university, are only modifications of the earlier types.

The Church herself early began the process of differentiating the ecclesiastical seminary for the purposes of secular education. Preachers become teachers, and the propaganda of religion prepared the way for the propaganda of science. The seminary method of modern universities is merely the development of the old scholastic method of advancing philosophical inquiry by the defence of original theses. The seminary is still a training-school for doctors of philosophy; but it has evolved from a nursery of dogma into a laboratory of scientific truth.

The transformation of the *Seminarium* into a laboratory of science was first accomplished more than fifty years ago by Germany's greatest historian, Leopold von Ranke. He was born in the year 1795, and has been Professor of History at the University of Berlin since 1825. There, about 1830, he instituted those practical exercises in historical investigation (*exercitationes historicae*) which developed a new school of historians. Such men as Waitz, Giesebrecht, Wattenbach, Von Sybel, Adolph Schmidt, and Duncker, owe their methods to this father of historical science. Through the influence of these scholars, the historical seminary has been extended throughout all the universities in Germany, and even to institutions beyond German borders.

It is easy to outline a few external characteristics of the seminary at the Johns Hopkins University, but difficult to picture its inner life. Its workings are so complex and varied, that it cannot be confined within walls, or restricted to a single library. Its members are to be found, now in its own rooms, now at the Peabody Institute, or again in the library of the Maryland Historical Society. Sometimes its delegates may be seen in the libraries of Philadelphia, or in the Library of Congress, or in some parish registry of South Carolina, or in some town clerk's office in New England. One summer the president of the university found a Johns Hopkins student in Quebec studying French parishes and Canadian feudalism. The next summer, this same student, now a teacher in Washington, D.C., was visiting Iona, and tramping through the parishes of England. He called by the wayside upon the English historian, Mr. Freeman, at his home in Somerset. Once the seminary sent a deputy in winter to a distant village community upon the extreme eastern point of Long Island, East Hampton, where he studied the history of the common lands at Montauk, with the queen of the Montauk Indians for his sovereign protectress and chief cook. Half a dozen members of the seminary have gone off together on an archaeological excursion, for example, to an old Maryland parish, like St. John's, where lies the ruined town of Joppa, the original seat of Baltimore county; or again, to North Point, the scene of an old battle-ground and the first site of St. Paul's, the original parish church of Baltimore; and still again, to Annapolis, where, with a steam launch belonging to the Naval Academy, and under the guidance of a local antiquary, they visited Greenberry's Point, upon the river Severn, the site of that ancient Puritan commonwealth which migrated from Virginia, and was originally called Providence, from which sprang the Puritan capital of Maryland. Reports of these archaeological excursions, written by members of the seminary connected with the Baltimore press, found their way into the public prints, and were read by many people in town and country, who thus became more deeply interested in the history of Maryland.

The scientific sessions of the seminary, two hours each week, are probably the least of its work, for every member is engaged upon some branch of special research, which occupies a vast amount of time. Researches are prosecuted upon the economic principles of division of labor and co-operation. This co-operation appears not merely in the inter-dependence of student-monographs, but in every-day student-life. A word is passed here, a hint is given there; a new fact or reference, casually discovered by one man, is communicated to another to whom it is of more special interest; a valuable book, found in some Baltimore library or antiquarian bookstore, is recommended, or purchased for a friend. These things, however, are only indications of that kindly spirit of co-operation which flows steadily on beneath the surface of student-life.

One of the most interesting, if not the most valuable features of the seminary library, is the so-called newspaper bureau. This consists primarily of an office wherein the newspapers of the day are reduced to their lowest terms for purposes of historical and political science. Certain files are preserved for future reference; but the great majority of papers are cut to pieces for scientific purposes. A competent force of graduate students work an hour or two each day, under direction, and mark superior articles upon economic, political, social, educational, legal, and historical subjects. These marked papers are excerpted during the succeeding week by an office-boy, pasted upon thick sheets of brown paper, octave-size, indexed at the top, and arranged alphabetically in the so-called Woodruff File-holders, which are also used for the pamphlet collections of the seminary. The choicest extracts from a few leading papers, which are clipped almost as soon as they come, are placed upon special bulletin-boards devoted each to some one department. The sub-headings under which the various clippings are grouped are changed from week to week, when the old material is cleared off and a new lot tacked up. The idea is to exhibit the current topics for a week's time, in so far as they relate to the interests of the seminary. The young men who attend to these bulletin-boards for their fellow-students are learning not only critical and orderly methods, but also the potential process of making up a journal of historical and political science. They are learning to be journalists and editors. Without professing to be a school of journalism, the seminary has furnished writers for each of the prominent papers in the city of Baltimore, and for some journals at a distance, while several of its members have secured editorial positions.

In addition to its newspaper bureau, which is a valuable auxiliary in the study of contemporary politics, economics, socialism, etc., the seminary has devoted especial attention to the collection of statistical materials, documents illustrating local, municipal, state, and national institutions; also to the collection of maps, works of historical and political geography. The beginnings of an historical museum have also been made, so that students of history find themselves surrounded by evidences of human progress from the stone age to the newspaper.

SEMINARY OF HISTORICAL AND POLITICAL SCIENCE. 147

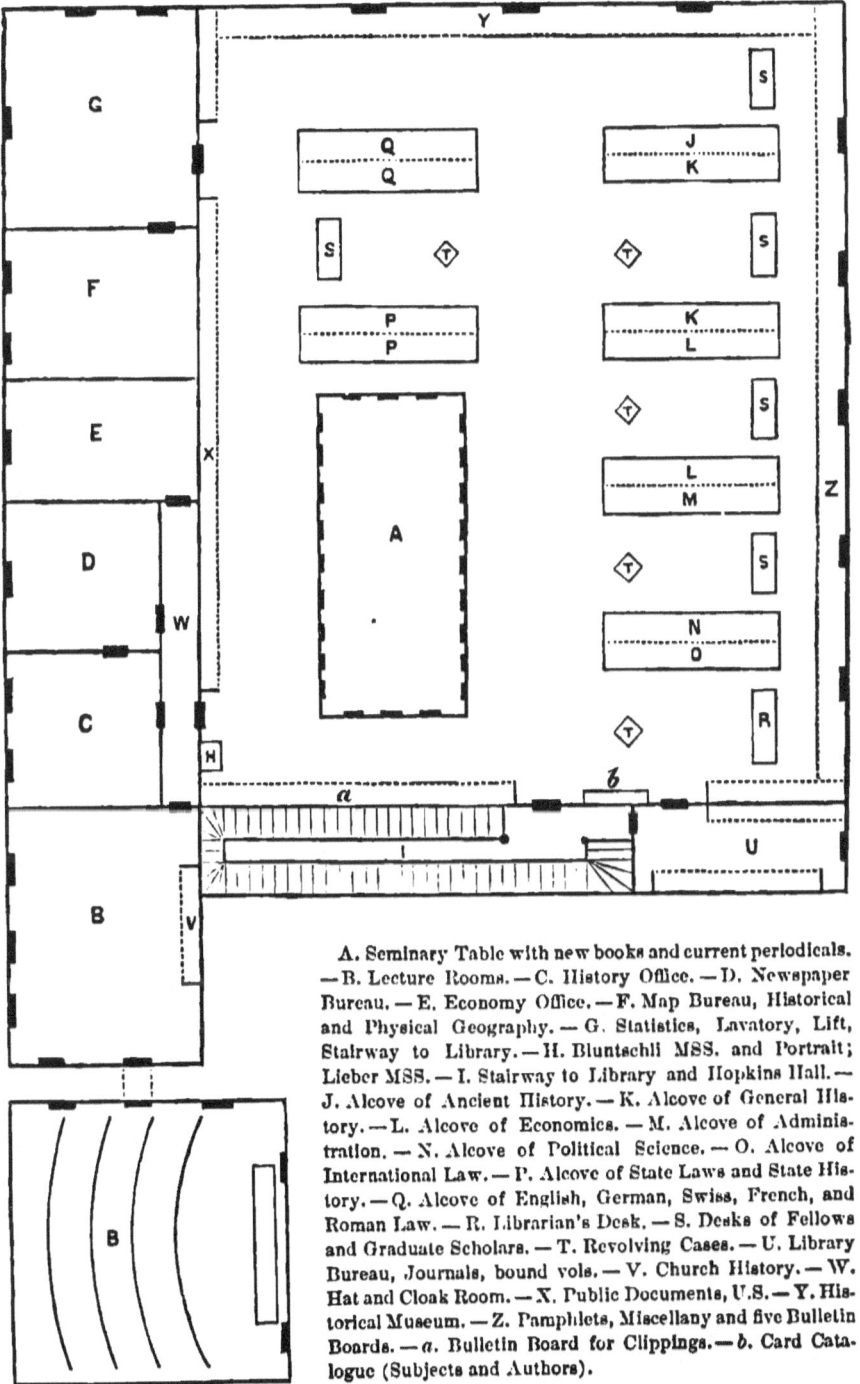

A. Seminary Table with new books and current periodicals. — B. Lecture Rooms. — C. History Office. — D. Newspaper Bureau. — E. Economy Office. — F. Map Bureau, Historical and Physical Geography. — G. Statistics, Lavatory, Lift, Stairway to Library. — H. Bluntschli MSS. and Portrait; Lieber MSS. — I. Stairway to Library and Hopkins Hall. — J. Alcove of Ancient History. — K. Alcove of General History. — L. Alcove of Economics. — M. Alcove of Administration. — N. Alcove of Political Science. — O. Alcove of International Law. — P. Alcove of State Laws and State History. — Q. Alcove of English, German, Swiss, French, and Roman Law. — R. Librarian's Desk. — S. Desks of Fellows and Graduate Scholars. — T. Revolving Cases. — U. Library Bureau, Journals, bound vols. — V. Church History. — W. Hat and Cloak Room. — X. Public Documents, U.S. — Y. Historical Museum. — Z. Pamphlets, Miscellany and five Bulletin Boards. — a. Bulletin Board for Clippings. — b. Card Catalogue (Subjects and Authors).

THE PHILOSOPHY OF THE STATE AND OF HISTORY.

GEORGE S. MORRIS.

THE ancient philosopher Heraclitus, in the fragmentary expressions of whose opinions, which alone are preserved for us, the modern speculative philosopher and the physical evolutionist alike find so many germs of the commonly received wisdom and of the scientific opinion of to-day, has left behind him one aphorism, the perception of the truth of which is the beginning of all wisdom for the student of history: πολυμαθίη νόον οὐ διδάσκει. "Multifarious learning does not instruct the mind." Nay, more, "much learning," taken merely by itself, is not only without educational or truly didactic value; it not only fails to endow the learner with real understanding; but, as was rightly implied in the address of the Roman governor to St. Paul, its tendency is to make one truly "mad."

The first impression that the world of history produces in the mind of the learner is that of an indefinite multitude of different events. One event is not another. Each is a separate fact. Each has its separate place in space or time, or both. Each is what the others are not. To be cognizant of some or all of these facts, each in its own peculiar place in space and time, and with its own peculiar individuality, is unquestionably the first mechanical condition of the acquisition of historical knowledge or science. Moreover, the circumstance that the facts in question are indeed different, that each new fact to be learned is indeed a novel fact, or, in some respect, *sui generis*, contains in part the secret of

that necessary charm by which the mind of the student is
led on from fact to fact, like the bee from flower to flower,
and so is armed with endurance to continue till the end of
the tale of "facts" is reached. But, to stop short with
this cognizance of the multitude of facts in their separation
and difference, not to see them in the unity of their relations,
is not to learn the lesson of history. The mind thus simply
filled, or crammed, is not instructed. Its sight is superficial: it is not insight. And the world of history, thus
viewed, is not comprehended as an orderly world. It is
not a "rounded world" and "fair to see." It puts intelligence to confusion. It is, indeed, my masters, "a mad
world"!

History is not simply (multifarious) events. It is the
logic of events. Historic intelligence is not merely information respecting events. It is the comprehension of their
logic.

Philosophy may be fitly described as the science of wholes.
In the last resort it is the science of *the* whole, as such, or
of the one universal drama of existence in the midst of which
man is placed, and in which he actively participates. Now,
history, according to the familiar aphorism, is "philosophy
teaching by example." Not the "example," taken by itself
as an isolated fact, is history. Thus taken, it is only a
brute fact divested of relations, and offering neither attrac-
tion nor support to intelligence. History is the example,
plus that which it exemplifies. It is the example, *plus* its
teaching. It is the "fact" seen in the relations which alone
render it comprehensible. It is the fact seen as part or member of an organic whole, and, consequently, as exemplifying
in its place and measure the law, idea, or life of the whole.
It is, in short, the fact seen as the illustration and phenomenal incarnation of a universal and livingly operative reason,

Logos, or logic, which, interior to the fact, is the ground of its reality, and, transcending the particular fact, connects it with all other facts, and so is the ground of its intelligibility. History, taken in its broadest sense, is the object-lesson of philosophy. It is the subject-matter of philosophy's demonstrations. It is the test of the correctness of her conclusions. And true "history," in the narrower or more common sense of this word, is nothing if not philosophical.

Every successful teacher of history, even with the youngest pupils, teaches in something of the philosophical spirit, and with a method more or less philosophical. He does not, indeed, neglect to insist on the acquisition, by patient mnemonic exercise, of exact information regarding particular facts; but he manages, at the same time, to engage the learner's imagination for the perception of groups of facts viewed as wholes, and having, as such wholes, to some degree, a specific character, coloring, or significance. He makes the pupil exercise, with himself, the artistic faculty of inward picturing. With immature students this is all that is possible, and it is enough. (I place under the safeguard of a parenthesis the ominous and perhaps irritating question, How many really " successful teachers of history, even with the youngest pupils," have we?) Ordinary college students, or undergraduates, who, in our commonly recognized distinction of educational grades, are treated as not yet wholly mature and independent, but as on the highway and in the doorway to such maturity, may justly claim something more. In addition to the faculty of abstract understanding, exercised in the exact and reflective discrimination and memorizing of facts, and the faculty of picturing imagination, which groups facts before the eye of the mind, as it were in larger visible wholes, that higher potency of imagination, which may be most exactly described as the synthetic reason, and for which the pictures of history possess not merely the external unity of visible wholes, but also the inward, dynamic unity of self-realizing law, idea, purpose, should be appealed to, and so, at least in some measure, trained in the appreciation of what we will here call historic truths (note the plural). Just how, and in what measure, this should be done, I will not and need not now attempt to determine. But I do not in the slightest hesitate to declare my conviction, that the university student — the graduate student, or he who, if not technically a graduate, is held to be sufficiently advanced to be permitted to pursue his studies under the specifically university *régime* — should, on the one hand, be privileged and assisted, and, on the other, required to exercise his faculty of "synthetic reason" in the fullest possible degree. In other words, in whatever department the special subject of his studies may lie, whether history, language, literature, mathematics, or the physical and natural sciences, he should be expected to accompany his study of and search for particular truths and orders of truths (the truths belonging to his "special subject") with the study of and search for the truth, the universal truth, to which all special orders of truths or "sciences," and orders of "science," are organically related; in which, as in an universal organism, they are all concretely one, "members one of another," and in the light of which alone the science of each becomes complete. Otherwise expressed, the university student should pursue, and should be taught and aided to pursue, his subject, however "special" and, at first sight, remote from philosophy it may seem to be, philosophically. And by this I mean that he should pay, and be directed and aided to pay, express and prolonged attention to the specific and universal problems of philosophy, considered both in themselves and in their relation and application to the subject of his special studies. He should, in the broadest and strictest sense, comprehend the philosophy of his subject. He who does less than this is a "university student" only in name and outward appearance, no matter where or how long he may have been enrolled as such a student, or amid what plaudits he may have been crowned with the (in this case deceptive) degree of "Doctor of Philosophy" . . . I do not, of course, stop to point out in detail how the requirement just insisted on is involved in the very conception of a university, as indicated among other things by the name "University" itself.

The justice of the requirement above mentioned is a thing which it should be easy enough to demonstrate in its relation to any of the departments of university work. It is particularly obvious in its relation to the department of history.

What is the universal truth; the truth of all truths; the truth in which all truths are united, and which reveals and realizes itself in them all; the truth of which all other truths are, in their place and kind, the concrete manifestation and evidence, and of which philosophy is the universal science? The answer that philosophy, in its most substantial and complete forms, whether ancient or modern, gives to this question, is perfectly expressed in the words of one of those writers whom the Christian world has termed sacred, "The Spirit is truth." All truth is truth of spirit. All reality is spiritually conditioned. All being has its roots in a spiritual life by which its form and nature and substance are determined. Spirit is universal, self-conscious reason. "Whatever," therefore, "is real is rational." Spirit is dynamic, living, concrete, and is the source and soul of law. Whatever is real, therefore, bears the same marks and illustrates the "reign of law" or of reason.

The spirit, or living self-conscious reason, which is the

universal truth, is not the human spirit, but it is, if this expression may here be allowed, the truth of the human spirit. The latter "lives, moves, and has its being" in the former. The spirit of man realizes its own essential nature only so far as it realizes in itself the "image" of the absolute spirit. The reason of man accomplishes its normal function in the knowledge of the truth only so far as, to use Kepler's grand expression, it "thinks the thoughts of God," and that by a process whereby it illustrates and actualizes its organic dependence upon, and so far its organic unity with, the universal spirit. The sufficiency of the individual to think, to think truly, to think and know the truth, is of God, of that absolute and concretely universal or omnipresent "spirit," which of all things is "the truth." This relation is, of course, not one in which the activity of the individual reason is suspended or rendered useless. It is the rather conditioned on the fullest and freest activity of the individual.

It will now be seen how philosophy, which is defined as the science of the universal truth, can also be called the science of self-conscious reason. It may well be considered as a common-place of philosophic science, that the fundamental, or "ground-laying" part of philosophy, is the science of intelligence or knowledge. Philosophy demonstrates that the essential and all-determining nature of intelligence is to be self-conscious reason. And it also demonstrates that true self-consciousness is something that transcends the individual, being realized only through the "objective" consciousness and progressive knowledge of the whole universe of dependent existence, and in organic dependence on an universal and absolute self-consciousness.

The universal self-consciousness, or reason, of man, which is the characteristically spiritual side of man's being, is also the essential side. It is by this and in this that man is truly man. Viewed on this side of his being, man is not a wholly completed actuality. He is not fully himself. He has not realized in full all the potentialities of his nature. He is to himself an ideal, a problem. In the progressive, active approximation to the ideal in question, or solution of the problem, man first comes to himself, and, in a measure, truly is himself. The activity by which he accomplishes this end is two-fold, theoretical and practical; theoretical, consisting, through the development of universal science, in the augmentation of his knowledge of himself and of his own possibilities; and practical, consisting in activities conditioned by this knowledge, and directed toward the use of the powers of nature and the ordering of human relations, *in magno* and *in parvo*, so that the possibilities mentioned may be more fully actualized.

These activities now are the immediate substance or the present active factors of history. The growingly self-conscious intelligence, which conditions and directs them, is the soul of history. Their end is the erection on earth of a realm of the spirit, which is a true "kingdom of heaven" or of God, and in which man gradually comes into the independent possession of his true and substantial freedom through the theoretic apprehension and practical realization of "the truth." History is the realm of man, and the realm of man is the realm of the spirit. How, then, shall not history be philosophical? How shall it not be "philosophy teaching by example"? And how shall he be pronounced a "Doctor" of history who has not comprehended history as philosophy thus teaching?

In the college, let the student, by all means, study and learn "histories"; and in the university, let not these be forgotten or neglected. But, above all things, and as the one thing indispensably needful, let the student here study and learn *history*. Let him see and know man in history, and through this knowledge let him see the absolute spirit in history.

But, it may be said, there are many well-known and not uninfluential philosophizers who contend that a true science of knowledge reveals man as possessing no other and higher categories with which to proceed to the comprehension of the whole world of reality, whether natural or moral, than the purely mechanical and sensibly conditioned ones of abstract mathematical and physical science, and that he is incapable of possessing any others. The interpretation of history then becomes for them simply equivalent to the solution of a problem in "moral" mechanics. History is, indeed, held to be one whole and a moving whole; but it is a whole, all of whose strictly knowable and scientifically determinable attributes really belong to the physical order of things alone; and it is a whole which, both as a whole and in all its parts, moves on automatically and without freedom according to simple mechanical laws, following everywhere the line of least resistance and greatest traction, and exemplifying some such general law as (say) that of universal evolution and dissolution . . . In reply, I say that I am unable to perceive that the champions of the foregoing theory are acquainted with the whole science of knowledge, or that they have once profoundly and faithfully studied the chief works which now belong to the history of philosophic science, and comprehended the lesson they contain. In so far, if my perception is correct, their opinions are deficient in value. But, supposing them to be wholly in the right, it must be allowed that they are but fulfilling an intrinsic and indefeasible requirement of historic science in seeking to found, on the basis of their mechanical conceptions, a philosophic interpretation of universal history. And, on the same supposition, it would be the duty of the university student of history to follow in their steps. The undergraduate student of history, for example, might conceivably be one of those accumulators who bring statistical grist to Mr. Spencer's mill. But it would be the duty and privilege of the university student to raise himself to the intellectual plane of the great miller himself; he should, in spirit, be a Spencer or a Buckle. Philosophy of some kind there must be; for philosophy is, in conception, nothing but the science of the whole, and, without such science, all other science — the science or knowledge of parts — remains incomplete, lacking connection, and confused. And if the philosophy that one have, or that one find current, be unfortunately one-sided, abstract, and inhospitable toward certain sides of that whole world of actuality, which it is the sole business of philosophy to comprehend, yet one must accept it, and apply it as far as it will go, and so make the best of it. Of course, it is the business of a university to see to it that philosophy is, within its precincts, comprehended, prosecuted, and taught without such defects as those just named. I hasten to add that, when this is done, the relative truth, and, within its peculiar bounds, the important truth of the mechanical philosophy in its application to the moral world, which includes the world of history, will be fully recognized. No one can shut his eyes to the mechanical aspect which belongs to all events, whatsoever, that occur within the bounds and under the forms of space and time, including, therefore, the events of history. But the eye of really concrete, catholic, and all-embracing philosophic science, sees that the mechanical aspect of events is only an aspect; that the whole event, in any case under consideration, includes more than this aspect; and that the science, or " philosophy," which regards only this aspect, is abstract; that it abstracts from something else in the event which is essential; and that it is, therefore, from the point of view of complete philosophy, fragmentary, partial, "one-sided." True philosophy perceives that, throughout the universe of living existence — and this, subject to exact definitions, must be conceived as equivalent to the whole actual universe — the mechanical is conditioned by and logically posterior to the organic; the dead is the product of the living, the phenomenal of the noumenal.

I trust I have made it sufficiently evident that the expression "philosophy of history" points to a real problem of essential importance for the student of history, and that I have sufficiently indicated what the true scope of the problem in general is. I have said nothing of the great advance made by historians during the last century in the philosophic treatment of their subjects, nor of the pains which great historians have thought it not unimportant to take to equip themselves for their work by careful training in specifically philosophic studies. There are many signs that the times are ripe, or ripening, for a more extensive introduction of the philosophic element into the treatment of history in this country. The most obvious of these is perhaps to be found in the rapid development and adoption of university methods at a number of our educational centres during the last ten or a dozen years. The true "university conception," if I may so express it, has but recently made its appearance among us; and it has evidently come to stay. And this phenomenon, by what cannot be considered as an accidental coincidence, is accompanied by (or shall I rather say accompanies?) a new and growing sense of the nature of the problems which are strictly peculiar to philosophy, and of their essential connection with that true and complete ideal of a scientifically cultured intelligence, which must serve as lodestone and guiding-star to all "higher education." Further, we have now passed the boundary of the first century of our existence as an independent nation. We are, as a people, now engaged in a confused struggle with the problem of our own national self-consciousness. We want to know what is the spirit that is in us as a nation. We must know this, in order to be properly master of ourselves and of our destiny. We must know this, in order to know our place in universal history, in order to appreciate the special task that falls to us in the solution of that universal problem of the full realization of man, of humanity "standing complete and wanting nothing," at which, whether blindly or consciously, all nations and peoples are at work, and their work upon which constitutes the living and essential substance of history. Our politicians need this, that they may become statesmen. And both statesmen and people need this, the former, in order that their labor may be truly constructive and enduring; and the latter, in order that they may willingly coöperate in the pursuit and realization of true political ideals. Here, then, is a a place where theory, in the broadest sense of this term, or the best work of intelligence, comes in contact with actuality. Here is a "living question" imperatively demanding practical solution, and where none but the best and broadest and deepest intelligence can safely serve. And it does seem as if the time had come when the university, conceived in the most liberal sense as the home and the seat of the activity of the highest intelligence, should become the radiating source and centre of ideal, and so of most truly practical, influences, by which the constructive work of the nation shall be positively furthered, and the ideal substance of the national life enriched. That our university workers in political science and history, applying themselves to their task with philosophic spirit and method, will contribute to the realization of a state of things, so much to be desired, no one should have any doubt.

And now for a few practical suggestions. For how, an interested party will naturally ask, shall I go about to study and teach the philosophy of history? I confess freely that the bank-account of my own experience in this matter is not plethoric, and that of my observation of others' work is still less so. Such as I have, with some diffidence, I will attempt to give.

It will be noticed that I have placed at the head of this article, as its title, "The Philosophy of the State and of History." Every one will readily perceive the reason for this. For though, as Droysen says, and as I have otherwise substantially expressed it in the foregoing essay, "the subject of history is the universal Ego of humanity," or "history is the γνῶθι σαυτὸν of humanity, its moral self-consciousness"; yet the concrete form in which this subject lies before the historian and student of history is that of social organizations or of states.

Of course, nothing can take the place, in the outfit of the student of the philosophy of the state and of history, of a previous course of careful training in the several "disciplines," or "subjects" (logic, both "formal" and "real," psychology, ethics, etc.), which belong to philosophy proper, and in the history of philosophy; and, in agreement with the views above expressed, such training, in an university completely organized and educationally equipped, would have to be insisted on. But now we will not, for we cannot, presuppose that this requirement has been fulfilled. As a substitute, I would propose to a student that he read carefully (say) the little book by Edwin Wallace, entitled "Outlines of the Philosophy of Aristotle" (Cambridge and London, third ed., 1883; pp. xi., 130). This work gives an epitome, with proof-texts in Greek, of logic, metaphysic, philosophy of nature, psychology, moral philosophy, political philosophy, and philosophy of art, in as many different chapters, and according to the best and ripest conceptions of ancient thought. Of all of these conceptions, that is true which is commonly said of Aristotle's logic in particular, viz., that, though antique, they can never become antiquated. The student gets, from the perusal of this epitome, a correct notion, as far as it goes, of the relation of political philosophy to philosophy in general, or of its place in the organism of philosophic science. I say "as far as it goes," for, as will be observed, no place is given in Aristotle's scheme to the philosophy of history, a subject to which the philosophy of the state is most intimately allied, but which, for obvious reasons, could scarcely be developed as a distinct discipline before modern times.

In the same spirit, I would heartily recommend the "Essays in Philosophical Criticism," edited by Seth & Haldane (London, 1883). This book, in my judgment, must be a great help to those who would get their bearings with reference to most of the leading subjects of philosophy, in the light of the best modern discussion. The student of the philosophy of the State and of history will be specially helped by the essays on "The Historical Method," by W. R. Sorley; "The Rationality of History," by D. G. Ritchie; and "The Social Organism," by Henry Jones.

Commendation no less hearty is to be given to the "Grundriss der Historik," von Joh. Gust. Droysen (Leipzig, third ed., 1882; pp. vi., 44). To this are added, as an appendix, two essays on the "Elevation of History to the Rank of a Science," reviewing Buckle's "History of Civilization in England," and on "Art and Method," by which the number of pages is increased to 90. A good translation of the "Grundriss" into English would, I should think, be one of the best services that could be rendered for the promotion of the philosophical study of history.

In teaching, now, the subjects we are considering, I would begin with the philosophy of the state. And in treating this topic, my method is to begin with the consideration of that order of theories which is apparently simplest, and which also, in the order of development of theories in modern times, stands conspicuously first in time.

All theories of the state may be philosophically classed in two groups. The one of these contains those theories which contemplate the state, either exclusively or prevailingly, from a physical or "natural" point of view, in accordance with a purely mechanical conception of the universe, or of *omne scibile*. The other will include theories which regard the state primarily and fundamentally from a spiritualistic and ethical point of view. Or, briefly, in the theories of the one group a mechanical and physical conception of the state is represented; and in those of the other, an organic and idealistic. The former conception has, at first sight, the apparent advantage in respect of simplicity and intelligibility.

From the first group, then, and for the purpose of first studying and illustrating the mechanical conception, or "philosophy," of the state, I select the "Civil Philosophy" of Thomas Hobbes ("De Cive" and "Leviathan") and the politico-philosophical writings of Mr. Herbert Spencer (chiefly his "Social Statics" and "Principles of Sociology"). In what respects the work of Hobbes is cruder and ruder than that of Spencer, how abhorrent to the latter are some of the positions of the former, and what concession Mr. Spencer himself makes in his own works, at least in appearance, to the demands of the organic conception of the state, is well known, or may be easily learned, and has, of course, in the progress of our study or teaching, to be duly recognized. It still remains that the lines of fundamental, or of quasi-philosophical agreement, are such as are implied in the classification of these two theorizers in the same group. From the works named I select such principles, or statements of principles, as are fundamental, and then seek to exhibit them, and to engage my students to study and comprehend them, both in themselves and in their collective relation to the subject-matter — the state — which they are invoked to explain. If it then appears, as I think it must, that these principles are essentially inadequate, we are prepared to go forward and try whether the theories of the other group are any more complete, and so nearer to the whole truth.

For those who are inclined to go further in the direction previously considered, and study the mechanical conception of the state in the light of modern socialistic theories founded upon it, the literature at command is abundant. The press, in certain quarters, teems with it. And one will be sure to find appropriate material among the books and pamphlets included in the "Bibliothèque Socialiste," published at Paris by Henry Oriol.

From works belonging to the second group, I am accustomed to select for consideration and study Aristotle's "Politics" and Hegel's "Philosophie des Rechts." These two works may, I think, justly be regarded as representing the high-water mark — the one in ancient times, and the other in modern — in the treatment of the philosophical conception of the state. Aristotle, certainly, cannot be wholly antiquated, for so true a child of the modern enlightenment as Mr. Frederick Pollock, has recently, in relation to this very matter of political philosophy, raised the very sane cry, "back to Aristotle." And of Hegel's work, that remains true, in spite of all its unquestionable infirmities, which is said of it by Adolf Lasson in his own recently-published "System der Rechtsphilosophie" (Berlin, 1882, p. 101), that its place is in "the foremost rank of the classical productions of the science of all times." Of the several translations of Aristotle's "Politics," the latest one, by J. E. C. Welldon (London: Macmillan & Co., 1883), is most attractive. Mr. A. C. Bradley has an essay on "Aristotle's Conception of the State," in "Hellenica," edited by E. Abbott (London, 1880). Hegel's "Philosophie des Rechts" has not been translated into English. An essay entitled "Hegel's Philosophy of Right" was published in the volume of "Oxford Essays" (1855). In vol. VI. of the "Journal of Speculative Philosophy," edited by W. T. Harris, will be found a translation of the brief summary of the Philosophy of Right, as contained in Hegel's "Philosophie des Geistes." A critical exposition of Hegel's "Philosophy of the State and of History" will be published in the series of "German Philosophical Classics for English Readers and Students," published by S. C. Griggs & Co., Chicago. The dynamic conceptions of Aristotle and Hegel, being much less abstract and, in this respect, simple than those of Hobbes and Spencer, require, for their adequate appreciation, longer study and a greater amount of time devoted to the detail of didactic exposition. In cases where German cannot be used, the work entitled "The Nation," by Elisha Mulford, LL.D. (New York, 1877), may be employed as a substitute for Hegel's "Philosophie des Rechts." In any case, the study of Dr. Mulford's book is to be most strongly urged.

On the history of political philosophy I name the following works:

Paul Janet. "Histoire de la Philosophie morale et politique dans l'antiquité et les temps modernes" (Paris, 1860;

second edition, revised and enlarged, under the title "Histoire de la science politique dans ses rapports avec la morale," 1872). This book is clearly written, with an abundance of French *bon sens*, and from the point of view of the best French type of philosophical *spiritualisme*. The author considers no writer after the time of Kant.

Frederick Pollock, "The History of the Science of Politics" (New York, 1883; No. 42 of the "Humboldt Library"; reprinted from the "Fortnightly Review," Aug., 1882, to Jan., 1883). This little work will be of value in enabling the student to familiarize himself with a considerable number of names prominently connected with the development of political philosophy in ancient and modern times. It is most valuable for its very sympathetic exposition of the doctrine of Aristotle and its account of the gist of English discussions. Spencer is excluded from the survey, and so are all Continental writers of the last hundred years.

J. C. Bluntschli, "Geschichte der neueren Staatswissenschaft. Allgemeines Staatsrecht und Politik seit dem 16. Jahrhundert bis zur Gegenwart" (Leipzig & München, third ed., 1881). This book, as the title indicates, deals only with the political philosophy of modern times. In treating of Hegel's "Philosophie des Rechts," the author is so stern to point out its confessed limitations, that the reader is in danger of being blinded to the fact of the far-reaching identity, in point of substantial content, which subsists between the fundamental conceptions of the critic himself and of him who is the object of his criticism.

Passing now to the philosophy of history, I am unable to give any counsel founded on personal experience or observation. If one were disposed to repeat or imitate the method suggested above, one might, I should suppose, well begin with Buckle's "History of Civilization in England." Though the field chosen for consideration in this work is restricted to England, yet this need not be a drawback. It may the rather be even an advantage, since it enables the student to judge the value and adequacy of the purely " mechanical conception" for the philosophic comprehension of history, applied in a field with which he is likely to be more familiar than with any other outside his own country.

I name as a work, in which the whole course of human history is treated from the materialistic point of view, F. von Hellwald's "Culturgeschichte in ihrer natürlichen Entwickelung bis zur Gegenwart."

Advancing now to the other, and, as I call it, larger point of view, to that of the *organic conception* of human history, I should take up the "Philosophie der Geschichte" of Hegel. Of this work a fairly good translation has been furnished by J. Sibree, A.M. ("Lectures on the Philosophy of History," in Bohn's "Philosophical Library," London, 1861). The most considerable systematic elaboration that the subject, so far as I have noticed, has received since the time of Hegel, is contained in Conrad Hermann's "Philosophie der Geschichte" (Leipzig, 1870). A work of still broader scope and treatment is M. Carrière's "Die Kunst im Zusammenhang der Culturentwickelung" (Leipzig. 1863–1871).

Robert Flint, in "The Philosophy of History in France and Germany" (London, 1874), gives a critical review of French and German works relating to our subject. He is, in my judgment, most successful in his appreciation of the efforts of the French and of some of the earlier Germans. The best German philosophy is beyond him.

THE COURSES OF STUDY IN HISTORY, ROMAN LAW, AND POLITICAL ECONOMY, AT HARVARD UNIVERSITY.[1]

By Henry E. Scott, Harvard University.

A DESCRIPTION of the ground covered and of the methods used in the various courses in History and Political Science at Harvard must necessarily be preceded by a brief statement of the circumstances under which these studies are pursued there.

In the first place, all the courses offered in these branches — and in almost all other branches as well — are purely elective. The University requires each year a certain amount of work from every undergraduate who is a candidate for the degree of Bachelor of Arts; but, with the exception of about two-fifths of the work of the Freshman year, and certain prescribed written exercises in English in the Sophomore, Junior and Senior years, the undergraduate has full liberty to select any course in any subject which his previous training qualifies him to pursue. The courses in History and in Political Science may therefore be elected by any undergraduate, by the Freshman as well as by the Senior; and they are also, it may be added, open to the students of the various professional schools embraced in the University, to resident graduates, and to special students whether graduates or not.

---

[1] In the preparation of the following article, the writer has been greatly assisted by the instructors in the several courses described, and their statements have been incorporated in the text with but little change.

In order to provide suitable recognition for those students who have confined their college work to one or two special fields, Honors of two grades — *Honors* and *Highest Honors* — are awarded at graduation in almost all branches in which instruction is offered. The candidate for Honors in History or in Political Science must have taken in the department selected six full courses or their equivalent, *i.e.*, he must have devoted to it about one-half of his last three years as an undergraduate, four full courses or their equivalent being the amount of elective work required each year of Sophomores, Juniors, and Seniors; and he must have passed with great credit the regular examinations in those courses, and also, shortly before Commencement, a special examination covering all the six courses in question. Students who do not care to specialize to the extent necessary to obtain Honors can yet, by doing creditably about one-half as much work (*i.e.*, by taking three full courses) in any one subject, receive at graduation Honorable Mention in that subject.

To pursue with advantage studies in History or in Political Science, the student must have easy access to books; and, in order to place within his reach the principal sources, authorities, and other helps necessary for the study of a given course, the system of "reserved books" was established some years ago in the Harvard College Library. The instructors in the various departments request the Library authorities to place upon the shelves of certain alcoves, assigned for this purpose in the reading-room of the Library, the books used by their classes for collateral reading and reference. The books thus reserved can be taken from the shelves by the students themselves without the formality of oral or written orders, and can be consulted in the Library during the day. At the close of library hours, they may, if properly charged, be taken out for the ensuing night only, the borrowers promising to return them at 9 A.M. the next day. The right to use the reserved books is not limited to those students who take the particular course for which certain books have been reserved, but all persons entitled to the privileges of the Library are likewise entitled to use *all* the reserved books, the purpose of the system being not to withdraw the works from general use for the benefit of a narrow circle, but rather so to regulate their use that the greatest possible number of students may be able to consult them. Persons engaged in special investigations can, if necessary, obtain cards of admission to the shelves where the material they wish to use is stored; but, for the ordinary student, the reserved books, together with those ordered from the Library in the usual way, are sufficient.

The courses of instruction which are now to be described are classified — as are all courses offered in the College — as courses or half-courses, according to the amount of work required of the student and the number of exercises a week, a course having either three or two exercises a week, a half-course either two or one.[1] Some of the courses are given every year, others every two years, others twice in three years. The more advanced courses can be taken only by special permission of the instructors, to obtain which students must give evidence of their ability to do the work expected of them. There are announced this year (1884–85) in the official pamphlet sixteen courses and two half-courses in History, one course and two half-courses in Roman Law, and four courses and four half-courses in Political Economy. There are actually given this year eleven courses and two half-courses in History, one course in Roman Law, and four courses and three half-courses in Political Economy,

---

[1] In the following description the half-courses are especially designated as such.

the remaining courses being omitted in accordance with the arrangements mentioned above or for special reasons. The average number of hours of instruction per week devoted this year to History is thirty; to Roman Law, three; to Political Economy, fifteen.

THE COURSES IN HISTORY.

The courses in History are not laid out on the assumption that any one student will elect all or even the greater part of them. They are themselves an historical growth rather than the result of a scheme. New courses have been added from time to time as the needs of the students and the means of the College warranted, each course as a rule covering a field which some unity of interest or some series of related movements seemed to mark out as suitable ground for connected study. Courses so built up must inevitably cross each other at various points, with an appearance of more or less confusion; nevertheless it is believed they are better adapted to the needs of the students than a more systematically arranged list would be.

HISTORY 1 (Mediæval and Modern European History, two hours a week, Assistant-Professor MACVANE) is an elementary course serving as an introduction to Courses 7, 8, 9, 10, and 11, and covering the history of Europe from the fall of the Roman Empire. In so wide a field, the work is necessarily of a very general character, the principal aim being to trace as clearly as possible the changes and stages through which Europe has passed in reaching its modern condition. The only countries for which a connected outline of political history is attempted are England, France, and Germany.

The course is designed for two classes of students: first, for those who intend to give a considerable amount of attention to history while in college; for these it serves as an introduction, as a general view of the whole field of mediæval and modern history; they are enabled to enter later on the study of selected portions or periods with some feeling of acquaintance with the surroundings. They also get some practice in using historical books and in dealing with historical terms and ideas. Secondly, the course is designed for students whose serious college work lies in other departments, who yet wish to acquire some general knowledge of history. There is, for the most part, no text-book, nor is there any attempt at recitations. Several books are usually designated for each country or period; and each student is allowed to choose from these the one best suited to his aims or to the amount of time at his disposal for the work. A certain portion of ground is laid out in advance for each exercise; and the instructor goes over this in a general way with the class, answering questions, pointing out relations and connections, explaining terms, and bringing into prominence the more important points of the narrative. A good deal of attention is given to historical geography.

HISTORY 2 (Constitutional Government in England and the United States, three hours a week for the first half-year, counting as a half-course, Assistant-Professor MACVANE) is designed as an introduction to Courses 12, 13, and 14, *i.e.*, to the study of modern constitutional government. Attention is chiefly directed to the present condition and practical working of English and American institutions; but the more prominent features of the French and German constitutions are also noted. The comparative method is followed wherever possible. The work done in the class-room is a combination of lecture and conference. Each member of the class is expected to procure either Amos's "Primer of the English Constitution" or Fonblanque's "How we are Governed"; and a pamphlet is printed for the use of the class, containing a syllabus of the course, together with the Articles of Confederation, the Constitution, and a number of selections from books, magazine articles, etc. The main objects in view are to prepare students for the profitable study of American and of modern European history, and to awaken an intelligent interest in the problems of constitutional government, both here and in other countries.

HISTORY 3. Roman History to the Fall of the Republic, with especial reference to the Development of Political Institutions in Greece and Rome, two hours a week.

HISTORY 4. Later Roman and Early Mediaeval History (from Augustus to Charlemagne), with especial reference to institutions, two or three hours a week (at the pleasure of the instructor).

HISTORY 8. Constitutional and Legal History of France to the Sixteenth Century, two or three hours a week (at the pleasure of the instructor).

These courses (all of them given by Professor GURNEY), while covering each a period having a distinct and independent interest of its own, are designed to furnish in their sequence a study of the development of society, of political, legal, and economic institutions, and in outline, too, of moral and intellectual conditions as manifested in religious beliefs, philosophy, and literature, from the cradle of patriarchal existence among the ancestors of the Greeks and Italians to the old age of a Byzantine civilization; and, again, to the repetition of this development under the greatly changed conditions produced by the legacies of Mediterranean civilization, from the primitive German society described by Cæsar and Tacitus to the reflection of imperial Rome which may be traced in the administration, law, literature, and art of France in the time of the early Renaissance.

In Course 3 this development is followed for the Roman

state from the first glimpses which we obtain, by the aid of philology, of its Indo-European ancestors to the point at which, after the conquest of the ancient world, the overtaxed energies of municipal government succumb, and the republican type of rule begins to merge in the imperial. Though the history proper of Greece forms no part of this course, the political and legal institutions of the Greeks, especially the Spartan and Athenian constitutions, and, at a later day, the first serious efforts of men at federation in the Achaean League, are all treated in detail for the light they throw upon the parallel Roman development. A secondary object of Course 3 is to qualify a student of the classics to read a book of Livy, or a public oration of Demosthenes, with somewhat the same background of information with which he would take up Bancroft or Burke.

Course 4, which deals with the whole period from Augustus to Charlemagne, falls naturally into two parts; in one of which, ending perhaps as well at the death of Theodosius the Great as at any other point, the interest continues predominately Roman, and the development of society is in every sense the sequel of Course 3; in the other the interest is predominately German; the subject of study is German institutions, and the processes and results of the combinations of these with existent Roman institutions and tendencies within the territories of the Empire, and especially in Gaul. Either half of this course may easily be pursued separately.

In Course 8, an investigation is made of the centrifugal forces which led to the disruption of the Carolingian Empire, and to the dispersion of authority which we know as the Feudal System. Upon a study of the institutions and working of that system in France, follows naturally the main subject of the course, the gradual reassertion of the royal authority over ever wider territory, and to ever more complete exclusion of all other authority, until the irresistible control of Louis XI. and his successors is reached, and, in large measure on the lines of Roman models, the framework is erected for the still more perfect structure of absolutism of the seventeenth century.

As these courses cover long periods of time — some seven hundred years each — the student is not expected to acquire a detailed knowledge of events. An account is given him of the best books accessible, great and small, upon the whole period and parts of it; but the scale on which he conducts his reading is left to his taste and discretion. The instructor, from time to time, tries to aid the student in acquiring a just historical perspective by remarks upon the relative importance of events, and upon such connections between them as might easily be missed; but, otherwise, he does not concern himself with the narrative history, except when consulted. The chief original authorities are mentioned and characterized, but no investigations in them are demanded. The history of institutions, on the other hand, is given by the instructor in informal lectures, with constant opportunity and encouragement for interruption on the part of the student for questions and discussion. The best works on the subject are described and reserved in the Library for the student's use; but for this part of the course he may, if he chooses, rely on the lectures alone. As these courses are conducted for the general student of history, no work upon the sources, Greek, Latin, or old French, could wisely be exacted. It is hoped, however, that subsidiary half-courses may be connected with them, so that properly qualified students may have opportunity and encouragement to become themselves investigators.

In HISTORY 7 (The General History of Europe from the

beginning of the Ninth to the end of the Thirteenth Century, two hours a week, Mr. SCOTT) the title does not state correctly the chronological limits of the course, or the ground covered by it. It really deals with the political and constitutional history of Continental Europe from the rise of the Carolingian line of Frankish kings to the fall of the emperors of the House of Staufen, England being omitted entirely, and France, too, receiving but little attention in comparison with Germany and Italy, since both England and France are provided for in special courses. As a necessary introduction, a rapid survey is taken of the institutions of the primitive Germans; and this is followed by a more detailed account of the constitutional and legal system that arose from the mixture of German and Roman elements in the kingdom of the Merovingians. With the Carolingian period the real work of the course begins, the Frankish Monarchy and the Mediæval Empire forming naturally the centres of interest around which the remaining historical phenomena are grouped.

In the class-room, the instructor endeavors to call attention to the points of view from which the events under consideration may be most advantageously studied, and to the relation in which these events stand to those that have gone before and to those that are to follow; but the details of political history are usually left to be worked out by the students themselves, while, on the other hand, the development of institutions is treated at length by means of lectures. An account of the principal sources for the history of each period is given, the most valuable modern works are mentioned, and specific references are made, from time to time, to these works and to important historical articles in periodicals. The students are questioned frequently and encouraged to ask questions, in order that the instructor may satisfy himself of the nature of their work, and that any special difficulties which they meet may be, if possible, removed.

HISTORY 9 (three hours a week, Assistant-Professor YOUNG) takes up the Constitutional and Legal History of England to the Sixteenth Century. The work in the class-room consists of lectures by the instructor, and of translations and explanations of extracts from Stubbs' "Select Charters," which, together with Stubbs' "Constitutional History," may be said to serve as a text-book. Students are also encouraged, but not required, to write theses on special topics.

The lecturer treats the whole subject by periods (Primitive Germany ; the Anglo-Saxon, Frankish, Norman, and Anglo-Norman periods ; Henry II. to John ; Magna Carta ; Henry III. and Edward I. ; Edward I. to Henry VII.) and by topics within each period, the study of each period being preceded by a general bibliography of that period, and of each topic by a special bibliography of that topic. The references for collateral reading are of two sorts, those which every student is expected to read as a preparation for examination, and those designed for students who take a special interest in any topic, and wish to make it the subject of special study.

The object of the lectures is (1) to give a more detailed account of some subjects than is to be found in the ordinary text-books (for example, of the institutions of the primitive Germans ; the classes of society and influence of the land-system on the social development in the Anglo-Saxon period ; the Frankish and Norman development; the legal reforms of Henry II. ; the reception of the Roman law in England, etc.) ; (2) to give a different view of some subjects from that taken by the English writers (for example, of the effect of the Norman Conquest on English constitutional development) ; (3) to arrange the subject-matter in a more convenient form.

Of the documents contained in Stubbs' "Charters," substantially all to the close of the reign of Henry II. are read (some of the special customs, some of the historical extracts and the *Dialogus de Scaccario* are omitted), together with selections from the documents of the reigns of Richard I., John, Henry III., and Edward I.

HISTORY 6 (The Legal Institutions of the Franks and the Anglo-Saxons, two hours a week, Assistant-Professor YOUNG), an advanced course in mediæval institutions, is designed (1) to teach the student the methods, and to acquaint him with the results so far attained of the new science of "Early Comparative Jurisprudence"; and for this purpose the following topics are studied: Origin of the family, of the state, of law, of courts, of judicial procedure, of criminal law, of property, and of contract; (2) to show the results so far attained by students of early German and Frankish law, and the methods used to attain them. In this connection, a study is made of legal sources, courts, procedure, criminal law, family law and law of inheritance, law of property, and law of contract: the Frankish legal sources, and especially the *Lex Salica* and the *Capitula legi Salicae addita* being critically examined in the class; (3) to apply the knowledge thus obtained of methods and results to the study of the Anglo-Saxon law. As this is a course for advanced and special study, every student is required to write a thesis on some topic of Anglo-Saxon law, a thesis based upon an independent examination of Anglo-Saxon legal sources.

It is hoped that the course may some time be extended to include the Norman and the Anglo-Norman institutions. It is given from a conviction that English legal history is yet to be written, that this cannot be done until many special investigations have been made, and that these can profitably be made only by those familiar with the methods and results of the Germanists.

HISTORY 5 [CHURCH HISTORY 1]. The Conflict of Christianity with Paganism to the Eighth Century, two hours a week.

HISTORY 10 [CHURCH HISTORY 2]. History of the Protestant Reformation and the Roman Catholic Reaction, two hours a week.

CHURCH HISTORY 3. History of Christian Doctrines, two hours a week.

HISTORY 17 [CHURCH HISTORY 4]. Practice in the Study and Use of Historical Sources, once a week (two hours).

These four courses, given by Professor EMERTON, are, in so far as they deal with ecclesiastical history, arranged with a view (1) to separate as far as possible the History of Doctrines from that of the outward life of the Church, and (2) to bring out into prominence the critical moments in this outward life rather than to attempt any comprehensive review of the whole subject. Course 5 deals with the formative period of Christianity. The purpose here is to show how the church organization grew up with the empire until the two became co-extensive, then to connect the Germanic influence in the empire with the form taken by the Church in the life of the Middle Ages. The reign of Charlemagne, in which these various tendencies reach the form they were to maintain during the whole following mediaeval period, properly closes this course.

Course 10 treats of the second great critical period, when the forms of mediaeval are changing to those of modern society. Beginning with the awakening energy of the individual mind in the fourteenth century, the various phases of this revival in literature, art, law, commerce, politics, and religion are treated as preparing the way for the protest of Luther. The religious revolt is traced from its earliest signs in the Italian Humanists, through Wiclif, Hus, Savonarola, and the Mystics, to Luther and Calvin. Finally, the reaction of Rome against the Reform, as shown in the Order of Jesuits, the Inquisition, and the Council of Trent, is followed to the point where the conditions of modern Church History appear firmly established.

Church History 3 is confined strictly to the history of doctrines, presupposing a general knowledge of the progress of the Church as an organization. But as in the earlier courses frequent reference to the doctrinal development was necessary, so here the student is constantly reminded of the reaction of politics upon the doctrine. It is believed that in this way a more thorough understanding of the essential connection between these two phases of church life can be gained than by attempting to treat them both at once, with the risk of continual confusion. The system of doctrines is considered as a development through the efforts of men to reach a solution of the problems suggested or revived by the teaching of Jesus.

All of these courses are conducted by means of lectures with occasional oral reviews, and, in Courses 10 and Church History 3, with the writing of theses upon topics connected with the course, selected by the student and approved by the instructor.

History 17 is a practice-course on the principle of the German Seminarium. Its purpose is to introduce the student into the methods of historical investigation and composition. The work consists mainly of inquiry into points of historical detail from original sources, together with the interpretation of some original document before the class.

In HISTORY 11 (European History during the Seventeenth Century and the first half of the Eighteenth, three hours a week, Assistant Professor MACVANE) attention is mainly confined to England, France, and Germany. English affairs occupy about half of the time. No uniform method of instruction is followed in all parts of the course, the instructor holding that, in teaching history, method must depend partly on the nature of the period and topic under treatment, partly on the quality of the books and other helps available for the students, partly on the size and character of the class.

In the main, the class-room exercises in this course are designed to open up the field, to bring into relief the more important features of it, and to aid the members of the class with suggestions as to their reading. An effort is made to show the significance of the great social, political, and religious movements of each period, to bring historical events as far as possible into living connection with their causes, and to point out from time to time the manner in which the movements of one country have reacted on the affairs of other countries. Special study is given to the growth and working of institutions, especially in England, Hallam's "Constitutional History" (beginning with Chapter VI.) forming an integral part of the course. References are given from time to time to the most notable passages in the works reserved in the Library for the use of the class, the aim here being as much to beget an acquaintance with historical literature and a taste for the study of it, as to aid in the present acquisition of historical knowledge.

HISTORY 12 (European History from the Middle of the Eighteenth Century, three hours a week, Assistant Professor MACVANE) is, in all essential respects, a continuation of Course 11, and is conducted on the same general plan. The proportions are different, however, considerably more time being devoted to Continental history than is the case in 11. The institutions of the Old Regime in France; the causes and course of the French Revolution, and of the later changes in France; the effects of the French Revolution upon the other countries of Europe; the German Federation, and the recent reorganization of Germany under Prussia's leadership; the consolidation of Italy into one kingdom, and the changed position of the Papacy; the growth of Russia, and the varying phases of the "Eastern Question"; — these, and many other topics, claim attention in the attempt to treat the recent history of the Continent. Time, however, is found to deal with the chief incidents of English history since the accession of George III. The attempt by George III. to revive personal government, the character and history of the various ministries, the full development of cabinet government, the reform of Parliament, the reform of the criminal laws and of the judicial system, Catholic Emancipation, the Irish land question, and other similar topics, are studied with more or less thoroughness.

In HISTORY 14 (Forms of Government and Political Constitutions, particularly in Continental Europe, since 1789, two hours a week, Assistant-Professor MACVANE [1]) the various constitutions are studied in connection with the circumstances under which they were adopted. Attention is given to the composition of the representative bodies; the relations between the legislative bodies and the executive; the methods and extent of popular control over the government; the position of the ministers; the progress of cabinet government; parliamentary procedure; the relations between local and central authorities; the federal systems of Europe; the composition and jurisdiction of the chief courts, etc. The method of comparative study is followed; the institutions of each country being brought into comparison, or contrast, with the corresponding institutions of other countries.

[For the courses in American History, numbered 18 and 13, see the separate article by the instructor on pp. 1–31.]

HISTORY 15 (Elements of Public International Law, two hours a week, Professor TORREY; Periods and Leading Events in Diplomatic History, one hour a week, Dr. CHANNING) consists of two distinct parts, — neither of which can be taken without the other, — and is designed for those students only who have shown creditable progress in their previous

---

[1] For the year 1884–85 only. The course is regularly given by Professor TORREY.

studies. As the classes are small, a close personal relation is established between teachers and students.

In the former part of the course, the lectures take largely the shape of a free commentary on Woolsey's "International Law"; but the bibliography of the subject is treated at length; and, in dealing with the principles, the important points are illustrated by references to leading writers,— such as Wheaton, Twiss, Hall, and Bluntschli, — and by extracts from their works. Particular attention is paid to weighty decisions (especially of English and American courts); questions in which the United States have been involved are discussed, the manner of dealing with concrete cases under the Constitution and laws is explained, and the bearing of the rules of International Law on questions of present interest is pointed out.

The second part of the course deals with the leading events in the diplomatic history of the last two hundred and fifty years. An analysis of each period, with a limited number of specific references, is written on the board as a foundation for the student's reading. The lecturer narrates the events leading to each important treaty, gives a bibliography of the treaty itself, together with some biographical account of the negotiators, and takes up in detail its chief provisions; considerable use being made of Woolsey's valuable synopsis of political treaties. From the beginning of the course geography receives especial attention, and a thorough knowledge of the physical conformation of Europe is insisted upon. The last four lectures are devoted to the territorial development of the United States, and are given in the College Library, where contemporary maps and other material can be used for purposes of illustration.

HISTORY 16 (Studies in the Comparative History of Religions, — particularly the Vedic, the later Brahmanic, the Buddhist, the Mazdean, and the Chinese; two hours a week, counting as a half-course, Professor EVERETT), although properly classified as an historical course, might as properly be called philosophical; for it is really a study of the philosophy of religion. It begins with a brief study of the religion of savages; then certain religions are treated that have in a marked degree a philosophical basis, and these are grouped according to psychological relations. The attempt is made to bring out the philosophical significance of each religion, special attention being given to Hindu philosophy. On the other hand, the outward form, and, to some extent, the history of the different religions, must be presented; and this involves historical detail.

The instruction is given by means of lectures, supported at every point by reference to translations and other authorities; the most important of the works referred to being placed in the reference-room of the Divinity-School Library.

THE COURSES IN ROMAN LAW.

ROMAN LAW 1 (History and Institutes of Roman Law; Institutes of Gaius and Justinian, omitting the Law of Inheritance; three hours a week, Assistant-Professor YOUNG) is an elementary course, covering the whole body of Roman private law, with the exception of the Law of Inheritance (see ROMAN LAW 3), and mainly designed to give to the historical student some familiarity with fundamental legal notions (a familiarity, the need and value of which will be recognized by every teacher of history). After a brief account of the history of the legal sources, and of the general course of Roman legal development, the instructor, following the arrangement of topics adopted by Gaius and Justinian, describes the historical development of each legal institution, and states the principal rules of law relating to it. The passages in the Institutes of Gaius and Justinian which bear on the subject are then translated and discussed in the class (Gneist's "Institutionum et regularum juris Romani syntagma" being used as a text-book), and references, which every student is expected to read, are occasionally made to the Digest. Every student is expected to follow the course in some elementary treatise on the subject, and for this purpose the following books are recommended: — in English, Moyle's "Institutes" (much the best), Poste's "Gaius," or Hunter's "Roman Law"; in French, the treatises of Maynz (the best), Van Wetter, or Demangeat; in German, Puchta or Marezoll.

ROMAN LAW 2 (The Law of Property; selections from the Digest; one hour a week counting as a half-course, Assistant-Professor YOUNG) is intended for advanced study in some special department of the law. The subject of the course may be varied from year to year, so that a student may elect it in successive years, studying, for example, in one year the Law of Obligations, and in another the Law of Property.

In ROMAN LAW 3 (The Law of Inheritance; Institutes of Gaius and Justinian; selections from the Digest; three hours every two weeks, counting as a half-course, Professor GURNEY) the principal features of the Law of Inheritance are studied, especial attention being given to the Roman Law of Wills. The portions of the Institutes of Gaius and Justinian bearing on the subject are first gone over in the class-room, and after the outlines of the subject are thus fixed, select passages from the Digest are assigned to be read by the class for the purpose of filling up the outline to the extent that time permits, the more difficult passages being interpreted by the instructor, and the hours of meeting being devoted to informal lectures on the part of the teacher, and to questions and discussions on the part of the students.

THE COURSES IN POLITICAL ECONOMY.

POLITICAL ECONOMY 1 (Mill's "Principles of Political Economy"; Lectures on Banking and the Financial Legislation of the United States; three hours a week, Professor DUNBAR and Assistant-Professor LAUGHLIN) is designed (1) to provide for those students who intend to continue their economic studies for more than one year a suitable introduction to the elementary principles of the science, and their application to questions of practical interest; and (2) to furnish students whose time is chiefly devoted to other departments of study with that general knowledge of and training in Political Economy which all men of liberal education should desire. It has, therefore, its theoretical and its practical side. In the present year (1884–85) the new edition of Mill, prepared by Professor Laughlin, serves as a text-book for the main part of the course, and the remaining time is occupied by lectures on the elements of banking and the public finance of the United States (especially in the last quarter of a century). The instructor holds that for a course in the elements of Political Economy, where it is eminently desirable that the student should assimilate principles rather than memorize explanations of each subject, neither the recitation system nor the lecture system is best fitted, but that a judicious mixture of both is necessary; for the object of the instruction is in general not merely to give men facts, but to lead them to think. The text-book is supposed to furnish to the student a clear statement of the principles that are to be taken up at a given exercise. Then in the class-room the instructor, by questions, and by drawing the men into discussion and the free expression of difficulties, endeavors as much as possible to fix the knowledge of principles in the mind of the students, and to direct their attention to the workings of these principles in concrete cases. Graphic representations of facts (such, for example, as are given by the charts in the text-book referred to) are often used to make the relation between theory and practice still clearer; and statements from the newspapers in regard to economic matters are sometimes read in the class-room, in order to test the student's ability in applying abstract principles to the affairs of every-day life. To give the students practice in making accurate statements, questions are now and then written on the blackboard and answered in writing within fifteen minutes, and at the next hour these answers are criticised and discussed.

In the lectures on the elements of banking and finance in the latter part of the year, the three functions of banking — deposit, issue, and discount — are illustrated by references to the system of National Banks, of the old United States Banks, and of the Bank of England; and the sub-treasury system, the national debt, the methods of raising revenue during the war, the issue of legal tender paper, the resumption of specie payments, etc., are some of the topics discussed, Professor Dunbar's pamphlet entitled "Extracts from the Laws of the United States relating to Currency and Finance" serving as a basis for the lectures on finance.

POLITICAL ECONOMY 2 (History of Economic Theory — Examination of Selections from Leading Writers, three hours a week, Professor DUNBAR) was in former years conducted by taking up, in the earlier part of the year, Cairnes's "Leading Principles," and, in the later part, some book of which the discussion and criticism would bring out more clearly the meaning of the generally accepted doctrines. Carey's "Social Science," George's "Progress and Poverty," Shadwell's "Principles" — books which put the "orthodox" student in a defensive attitude — were used for this purpose. In addition, lectures were given on the history of political economy, and on examples of the working in practice of its principles, such as the working of the principles of international trade in the payment of the Franco-German indemnity in 1871–73, the commercial crisis of 1857, etc.

For the present year (1884–85) the course is remodelled. Nothing in the nature of a text-book is used. The subject is treated by topics. Such questions as the wages-fund controversy, the theory of international trade, the method of political economy, the theory of value, are to be taken up in succession. On each topic references to leading writers will be submitted to the students for examination and discussion. On the wages-fund question, for example, Mill's retractation in the "Fortnightly Review" of his original views, Cairnes's restatement of the theory, F. A. Walker's position as found in his "Wages Question" and his "Political Economy," George's criticism of current views in "Progress and Poverty" will be read and discussed. The history of political economy is to be taken up in a similar way, by reference to characteristic extracts from the writings of the Physiocrats, Adam Smith, Malthus, Ricardo, Senior, Say, Bastiât, and their successors and critics in England and on the Continent. These extracts, read beforehand by the students and discussed in the class-room, will be supplemented by the comments and explanations of the instructor. By this method it is hoped that some familiarity with the literature of the subject will be obtained, as well as a more exact comprehension of its doctrines than can come from an elementary study like that of Course 1.

In POLITICAL ECONOMY 3 (Discussion of Practical Economic Questions — Lectures and Theses, three hours a week, Assistant-Professor LAUGHLIN) it is expected that the student, who is supposed now to have grasped firmly the general principles of political economy by at least one year's previous study, will apply these principles to the work of examining some of the prominent questions of the day, such as the navigation laws and American shipping, bimetallism, reciprocity with Canada, government and national bank issues, etc. At the beginning of each topic a general outline of the subject and its principal divisions is given by the instructor, together with more or less particular references to the most important authorities; but a *complete* list of books is not always furnished, the student being rather encouraged to hunt for material himself. The exercise in the class-room takes the form rather of a discussion than a formal lecture, references to authorities being given previous to each meeting, as the following examples will show: —

Standards of Value, see Jevons, "Money and the Mechanism of Exchange," chaps. iii, xxv; S. Dana Horton, "Gold and Silver," chap. iv, p. 36; F. A. Walker, "Political Economy," pp. 363-368, "Money, Trade, and Industry," pp. 56-77; Wolowski, "L'Or et l'Argent," pp. 7, 22, 207; Mill, "Principles of Political Economy," book iii, chap. xv; Walras, "Journal des Économistes," October, 1882, pp. 5-13.

The third hour of the week (and also the mid-year examination) can be omitted by men who promise to prepare one considerable thesis (due in April) on a subject connected with some practical question of the day which has not been discussed in the class-room. Examples of such subjects are: the warehousing system; a commercial treaty with Mexico; the public land system; the remedy for our surplus of revenue; municipal taxation; characteristics of socialism in the United States; co-operation in the United States (productive and distributive co-operation, industrial partnerships, and co-operative banks); advantages and disadvantages of small holdings.

POLITICAL ECONOMY 4 (Economic History of Europe and America since the Seven Years' War, three hours a week, Professor DUNBAR) serves to connect Political Economy with

History. It requires no previous study of Political Economy, although some historical knowledge of the period is presupposed. Among the more prominent subjects taken up are : the rise of the modern manufacturing system, more particularly in cottons, woolens, iron ; the steam engine : the economic effects of American Independence and of the French Revolution ; the factory system ; the migration of labor ; improved transportation by railroads and steamships ; the application of liberal ideas to international trade ; the new gold of California and Australia ; the economic effects of the Civil War in the United States ; American grain in Europe ; the Suez Canal ; the crisis of 1873, and commercial crises in general ; the development of banking ; and the resumption of specie payments in the United States.

The course is chiefly narrative, and is carried on by lectures, supplemented by references for collateral reading. A printed list of topics is distributed to the students, containing a summary of the lectures and references to books reserved in the Library. An extract from this list will most clearly indicate its character and purpose. It gives the topics and references for the first lecture on the new gold supply : —

LECTURE XLVII. — The discovery of gold in California : " Robinson's California" (see Larkin's and Mason's Reports, pp. 17, 33); also Exec. Doc. of U. S., 1848, i, 1. — The discovery in Australia : Westgarth, " Colony of Victoria," 122, 315. — Establishment of miners' customs : Wood, " Sixteen Months in the Gold Diggings," 125 ; Lalor's " Cyclopædia," ii, 851. — Increased supply of precious metals in sixteenth and seventeenth centuries small in proportion to that in nineteenth century : Soetbeer, " Edelmetall-Production " (in Petermann's " Mittheilungen "), Plate 3 ; " Walker on Money," Part I, chaps. vii, viii. — The discoveries of 1848 and 1851 needed to give effect to influences already stimulating trade and commerce.

Similar topics and references are given for each of the eighty or ninety lectures.

IN POLITICAL ECONOMY 5 (Economic Effects of Land Tenures in England, Ireland, France, and Germany — Lectures and Theses, one hour a week, counting as a half-course, Assistant-Professor LAUGHLIN) a branch of the science that has been but slightly considered in Course 1 is taken up, and, as in the other practical courses, an attempt is made to apply principles to facts. The following extract from the official pamphlet, describing the courses of study in Political Economy, will indicate the ground covered : —

"This course covers the questions now of political importance in England, Ireland, France, and Germany in their economic aspects, and embraces the following subjects : — In England : the land laws ; relative position of landlord, tenant, and laborer in the last one hundred years ; tenant-right ; leases ; prices and importation of grain ; repeal of the corn-laws ; American competition ; peasant proprietorship. In Ireland : the ancient tribal customs ; English conquests ; relations of landlord and tenant ; security of tenure ; Ulster tenant-right ; absenteeism ; parliamentary legislation ; acts of 1869, 1870, 1881, 1882 ; population ; prices of food and labor. In France : feudal burdens on land ; relation of classes, and condition of peasantry and agriculture before the Revolution ; small holdings and the law of equal division ; present condition of peasantry and agriculture ; growth of population ; statistics of production, wages, prices ; peasant proprietorship. In Germany : reforms of Stein and Hardenberg ; condition of agriculture ; peasant proprietors ; statistics of wages and prices."

A subject taken up (for example, English land tenures) is divided into topics, some of which are treated by the instructor by means of lectures, others are assigned to the individual members of the class, who are expected to present the results of their study in writing. These short theses are criticised and discussed by the instructor and the class, authorities that have been overlooked are pointed out, and suggestions are made as to the way in which the question can be better handled. Perhaps five or six of these papers are required from each student during the year, the intention being that at least one shall be handed in each week. As the natural tendency of such work is to "compile," much more consideration is given to the quality than to the quantity of the thesis.

In POLITICAL ECONOMY 6 (History of Tariff Legislation in the United States, one hour a week, counting as a half-course, Dr. TAUSSIG) the history of tariff legislation from 1789 to the present day is studied. The method of instruction is by lectures and collateral reading, specific references being given beforehand on the subjects to be taken up; for example, the references on the tariff act of 1789 are as follows: Hamilton's "Life of Hamilton," iv, 2-7; Adams, "Taxation in United States," 1-30, especially 27-30; Sumner, "History of Protection," 21-25; Young's "Report on Tariff Legislation," pp. iv-xvi. Similar references are given when the economic effects of the tariff, more particularly in recent years, are discussed. The class-room work is based on the assumption that the passages referred to have been read by the students, and, though mainly carried on by lectures, includes questioning and discussion on the references. The economic principles bearing on tariff legislation are taken up in connection with the more important public utterances on the subject, such as Hamilton's "Report on Manufactures," Gallatin's "Memorial of 1832," Walker's "Treasury Report of 1845," and the speeches of Webster, Clay, and others. These are read by the students, and discussed in the class; and at the same time with them are considered the views of writers on the theory of economic science. In the course of the year the various arguments *pro* and *con* in the protection controversy are, in one shape or another, encountered and discussed. Towards the close of the year lectures are given on the tariff history of England, France, and Germany.

POLITICAL ECONOMY 7 (Comparison of the Financial Systems of France, England, Germany, and the United States, one hour a week, counting as a half-course, Professor DUNBAR) deals with the principles of finance, and with the financial systems of the more important civilized countries. The budgets of France, Germany, and England are examined and compared, the financial methods of the United States are noted, and the principles of finance and the advantages and disadvantages of different taxes are discussed. The instruction is mainly by lectures. The course is not given in the present year (1884-85), and may be omitted in future years, though it will be retained on the elective list.

In POLITICAL ECONOMY 8 (History of Financial Legislation in the United States, one hour a week, counting as a half-course, Professor DUNBAR) the funding of the Revolutionary debt, the establishment and working of the first Bank of the United States, the financial policy of Hamilton and Gallatin, the effect of the War of 1812 on the finances and the currency, the establishment of the second Bank of the United States, the fall of the bank in Jackson's time, and the years 1836-40, the independent treasury, the State banking system, the growth of the public debt during the Civil War, and its reduction and conversion since, the establishment and working of the National Bank system, — are the topics successively considered. The method of instruction is by lectures and by reference to the public documents and other writings bearing on the subject. It is advised by the instructors that Courses 6 and 8 in Political Economy be taken together; and this advice has been followed, most students who take one of these courses being also members of the other.

THE TEACHING OF HISTORY.

BY PROFESSOR J. R. SEELEY.

I MUST ask you to be content with a few large affirmations, which may be sufficient to provoke discussion, but which, in the paper itself, can be but very inadequately supported. Perhaps you will agree with me that history, as an educational subject, is not yet past the stage at which large affirmations are necessary, that conscientious and exact research ought to prevail in history, as in other serious departments of study, that we can no longer be content with the showy, semi-fictitious narratives that satisfied a former generation, is a proposition upon which a great reform in the teaching of history has been based. We all know what has been done in this direction among ourselves; in Germany the reform was made long ago; in Paris it has, in recent years, proceeded rapidly, thanks to the exertions of the Minister Duruy and such professors as Monod, Sorel, and Lavisse. On the principle itself I shall have nothing to say, because I do not suppose that among serious men there is any difference of opinion about it. If we set out in pursuit of truth, evidently we cannot be content with anything short of truth; and we all of us by this time have enough familiarity with the rigor of scientific methods to be convinced that the discovery of truth is no child's play, no mere amusement. But, though the principle seems indisputable, I find that the application of it in education arouses much opposition, more opposition than I for a long time understood. It is allowed that such vigor of research is indispensable in the best kind of historical study, that those who intend to devote their lives to history should study it in this spirit. But the principle is of wider application. It affects also the historical studies of those who give less exclusive attention to history; in short, of the mass of students; and, further still, it affects popular views of history and our notions of the manner in which history should be written. These more indirect results of the principle of thoroughness arouse, I find, much opposition, and, when such opposition seems likely to be vain, a very sincere feeling of dismay. For this principle makes havoc of more cherished opinions than we might at first have expected, and, as it proceeds, seems to take all the poetry and all the charm out of history in such a way that we find ourselves at last asking for what purpose history so studied can serve. The admiration of great men, the elevating contemplation of noble examples, is the reward most of us expect to receive for the trouble we bestow upon history; but the principle of thoroughness soon sets us doubting whether any great men will come safe out of the critical crucible; whether the historical record is complete enough to have preserved any trustworthy memory of great men; nay, whether public affairs are not for the most part under the empire of routine, and seldom much affected by the especial qualities of an individual. Scepticism invades this department of knowledge too, and we begin after a time to perceive that another class of opinions, viz., our opinions on politics, were far more involved than we at first imagined with those opinions on historical events and historical characters about the soundness of which we have begun to feel a misgiving. Hitherto, those who have sought to elevate the minds of students and give them a noble enthusiasm by means of books, have looked mainly to historical books. It is a result of the reform in historical method, which has made it so much more rigorous, that historical books henceforth will be less available for this purpose. But, if so, it will begin to be asked what is the use of them to the majority of students. I do not myself think that such extreme scepticism with respect to history, as that which Mr. Herbert Spencer professes, is likely to prevail. I am not afraid but that history will continue to be thought important, and I believe that in the form of serious research it will flourish more and more for a long time to come. But in this form will it not be a study only adapted for the few? Ought we not, therefore, to lay it down as a fundamental rule of the teaching of history that the subject is to be struck off the general educational list of subjects?

I have remarked with anxiety of late years that some distinguished teachers appear inclined to hold this opinion. History was the favorite subject of Arnold and Temple, but some at least of those who now hold the same sort of distinguished position in the educational world, profess that they do not know how to teach history, and that there is no subject which baffles them so much. The solution of this difficulty I seem to myself to see very distinctly, and, if I seem to any to state it here indistinctly, I must ask them to impute it to the hurry in which I write, and at the same time refer them to several essays printed at different times in "Macmillan's Magazine," in which I have stated it more fully.

That historical investigations ought to be thorough is of course true, but by itself the proposition can hardly be called a truth; it is at best a half-truth. If we borrow from science its rigorous method, let us borrow at the same time what science has else to offer. History which is scientific in its exactness, but in nothing else, is a middle thing between science and literature, and will attain the ends of neither; it will be only dull literature and abortive science.

Science, when it has with such exemplary care collected and verified its facts, proceeds to generalize upon them, and thus to establish principles. It is only for the sake of such principles that science considers facts worthy of collection and exact verification. But history, when it has made its investigations, contents itself with arranging and recording the results in stately narrative composed with literary art. The historian usually asserts that the results thus recorded are of great value; he seems to assume that general principles might be deduced from them, but he professes at the same time that his business is only with the facts, and that his work is done when a narrative has been composed exactly true, and at the same time well written. The reform of which I have spoken has scarcely touched this curious division of labor. It leaves the historian in the condition of a mere investigator and narrator of facts, asserting only that of these two functions the former is far more important and more difficult than the latter.

To whom, then, does it fall to deduce conclusions from the materials furnished by the historian? To a wholly different class of persons, who at present have scarcely a name or recognized position among us, — those philosophers who are attempting to build up a system of sociology. But their speculations, being kept wholly separate from history, do not enter into the teaching of history. In education, therefore, this subject is left as a mass of building materials, out of which no edifice is ever constructed. So long as the mere literary view of the subject prevailed, this did not seem absurd; political truth was supposed to have been discovered independently by some *à priori* method, and historical examples were adduced chiefly by way of illustration; but the absurdity springs to light as soon as history begins to be classed under science rather than under literature, so soon as political truth is understood to be discovered through history, and not merely to be illustrated by it.

I should like to argue at length that it is in itself an unsound method to assign the investigation of facts to one set of workers, and the reasoning upon the facts so discovered to another class. I should like to show that if the historian is not himself a sociologist, he will not know what facts are worth investigating, and still less in what degree facts are worth investigating. I should like to call attention to the vast waste of labor on the one side, and the vast deficiency of labor on the other side, which actually arise from the fact that historians under the present system are scarcely sociologists, and therefore do not altogether know for what purpose they investigate. But I must be content to point out the bad effects which the system has in education.

Under this system facts are grouped, not according to resemblance in kind, but simply in a chronological series. What may be called a biography of some famous state is written. Such a state biography may be made very impressive by a writer of imagination, especially if he does not hamper himself with too minute research. But what can the student do with it? He can scarcely treat it as a poem, and learn it by heart. Under the reformed system he analyzes it, criticises it, traces it back to its source; a process under which most of its poetical impressiveness is likely to disappear. In return, he gets exact knowledge of important occurrences, but he does not get this in the form in which he can use it for the purpose of establishing general conclusions, for the facts of which he thus gets exact knowledge are heterogeneous. They do not belong together by their nature, but only happen to be connected chronologically.

A single example will put before you the very obvious, yet, as I think, all-important fact to which I draw your attention. Let us think of the agrarian legislation of Tiberius Gracchus, which occupies the first striking chapter in the history of the fall of Rome. What subject can be more instructive to a student, both from its own importance and from the admirable manner in which it has been treated by modern scholarship? True, but educationally it is out of its place when it comes before the student as a mere occurrence of the second century before Christ. For thus presented it stands among facts with which it has no resemblance, and which throw no light upon it, — military facts concerning the conquest of Carthage, Spain, and Greece by the Romans, facts of culture history concerning the influence of Greek literature and Greek philosophy upon the conquerors of Greece. To study it properly, we must take it out of its chronological connection and put it among facts of its own kind. It is a land question; it has nothing to do with war or with literature. It must be studied first in connection with the land system of Rome in earlier and later times; secondly, by comparison with the land systems and land revolutions of other states, both ancient and modern.

In short, science brings together phenomena of the same kind, but history brings together phenomena of different kinds, which have chanced to appear at the same time. We have given to history the conscientiousness of science, but we have not yet given it the arrangement of science. We still arrange historic phenomena under periods, centuries, reigns, dynasties, but what is wanted is a real rather than a temporal classification. The phenomena should be classed under such headings as Constitutional, International, Economical, Industrial, etc. Nor should each state be studied by itself, but all states together, the comparative method being constantly employed, and much attention being given to the classification of states.

It will be seen that this principle would be almost revolutionary, if it were at once and without reserve applied to the teaching of history. I am sensible that it needs to be explained at great length, and I am quite aware how many objections might be urged against it. But I have not time either for fuller exposition or for dealing with objections, and therefore in the remainder of this paper I shall deal with an intermediate system which might, without too great difficulty, be adopted at once.

The essential point is this, that we should recognize that to study history is to study not merely a narrative, but at the same time certain theoretical subjects. Thus, industrial facts cannot be understood without political economy, nor military facts without military science, nor legal facts without legal science, nor constitutional and legislative developments without political science. I have gone further, and laid it down that these theoretical subjects are the real object for which historical facts are collected and authenticated. But for the present it is enough that they should be recognized as inseparably connected with historical study. It has always been tacitly assumed that the historian is also an economist, an authority on constitutional law, on legislation, on finance, on strategy. Let us, then, go a single step further, and recognize that, as the historian is all this, the student of history must prepare himself to be all this — in other words, must master all these subjects. These are the great subjects of public life : these are the studies which make the citizen and train the statesman. All the poetic charm which history is losing would be amply compensated if it should acquire in exchange the practical interest that is associated with these studies.

First, then, let the most important of these subjects be taught theoretically along with history, and for the benefit of historical students. Some of them, of course, are much more important than others. I place in the foreground what we may call political philosophy (*Allgemeine Staatslehre*). After this may come that comparative study of legal institutions of which we have such excellent specimens in the works of Sir H. Maine. Next will come political economy, which in the hands of an able teacher will probably assume a somewhat new shape when it is treated from the historical point of view. International law should be added, in order to accustom the student to contemplate the mutual relations of states.

It may be said that enough would be done if the teacher or lecturer, in treating a historical period, entered fully into the economical, or juridical, or political principles suggested by the narrative. This is precisely what I wish to deny. It seems to me that in history, as hitherto written and taught, a quantity of theory has been, as it were, held in solution; I wish to see it precipitated. Whereas the investigation of historical facts has lately been made honest and careful, the reasoning about historical facts is still, it seems to me, oracular and unsatisfactory; I wish to make this, too, honest, methodical, explicit. For this end it seems to me necessary that what really is theory should be called theory and studied as such.

If it be asked by what practical measures such a change could be introduced; if it be urged, for instance, by a schoolmaster, that there is no room in the school-day for lessons on three or four new subjects, and that masters to teach them are not to be found in sufficient number, I should reply, that I have been discussing the teaching of history in general, not the teaching of history in schools. What I myself know practically is the teaching of history in universities, and I suppose it may be laid down as a general principle that reforms in education must begin at the university. The school is fettered to the university, since *to* the university the boys go, and *from* the university the masters come. Now, in the universities it is not very difficult to arrange the teaching of history on this principle. Since in a university the theoretical subjects I have mentioned are already taught, all that is required is to bring them into more direct, more formal connection with history, and to abolish that vicious division of labor under which the historian imagines that he has nothing to do with sociology, and the sociologist that he can dispense with history.

When this has once been done, each university will create a school of historians who will be as strong on the theoretical side as on the side of mere research. They will be sociologists, economists, jurists, as well as chroniclers and antiquarians, and, as at both our universities the historical school is already large, a good many of such historians will be formed. These will carry the method from the universities to the schools. They will be the masters of the future historical classes at Harrow and Rugby. From them will proceed the text-books which will, as it were, fix the method and bring it within the reach of less able teachers. They, too, will decide whether history taught in this way is to be considered as an advanced subject, fit only for the highest classes in schools, or whether it may be possible to introduce even younger boys to it.

Lastly, they will help to clear up the confusion as to the nature and objects of history which now exists in the public mind. They will separate it from biography and from mere curious information about past times. They will separate it from romance, and they will explain in what sense and in what degree it may properly be made interesting, and in what sense also it cannot be interesting without ceasing to be true. They will assert the seriousness of history, and make it the lesson-book of politics; no longer a record which partisans may garble at their pleasure, but a record of truth, not to be altered and not to be evaded, written to correct our prejudices and rebuke our party rancor. — *London Journal of Education.*

ON METHODS OF TEACHING HISTORY.

BY PROFESSOR C. K. ADAMS, MICHIGAN UNIVERSITY.

THE teaching of history, in common with instruction in all other systems of organized knowledge, should be carried on with three more or less distinct objects in view: the nature of the facts involved, the relations of those facts, and the proper methods of investigation. Though it is not possible in practice to separate these three objects completely one from another, yet each should receive its due proportion of attention, and should receive that attention in its appropriate place. First of all, therefore, the teacher of history is called upon to decide which of these three objects he ought with any given class to keep most prominently in view. The answer of this question involves nothing less than a determination of the proper succession of historical studies.

This order of succession would seem to be fixed by nature. It is certain that we must know something of the existence, if not, indeed, of the nature, of any given order of events before we can apprehend very clearly the relations of those events to one another. Indeed, it may be said that the beginning of all organized knowledge is the acquisition of a certain number of facts and truths. These facts, moreover, must not be limited in range to a single portion of the subject we are to study. They must be comprehensive in their scope. We must know something of the heavens as a whole before we can well understand the double stars or even the moon. We cannot appreciate the significance of a missing link until we have learned something of the chain of which that link is supposed to form a part. We shall be unable to explain the jubilant prosperity of a great and growing city unless we have acquired considerable knowledge of the region of which that city is the political and commercial centre. Thus we see that there is a certain necessary order of succession, an order which seems to be founded in the law, so well formulated by Herbert Spencer, "there can be no correct idea of a part without a correct idea of the correlative whole."

It is of course true that we learn something of individual facts before we can advance to a comprehension of a series. In a certain sense, therefore, we must proceed from the individual to the general. But it is also true that before our knowledge of the individual can be complete, we must have acquired some knowledge of the series of which the individual forms a part. The proper order of study, therefore, would seem to be definitely fixed at our hand. We should begin with such individual facts as form the strategic points of historical progress, and should dwell upon them only so far as to fix their general character and importance in the attention of the pupil. We should then proceed to a study of the relations of those facts in the development of society. This done, we are ready to advance to the third stage of our study, — a more careful investigation of the individual elements of social and political life, with a view to revealing the sources of their influence and power.

Having determined so much in regard to the proper order of studies, we are ready to address ourselves to the question of methods. But at the very outset we are confronted with a somewhat formidable difficulty. In the present condition of schools in the United States, there is actually, and perhaps necessarily, a broad distinction between what is desirable and what is practicable. It is probably not too much to say that the introduction of methods of ideal excellence in the teaching of history would involve a revolution in our schools which the public at present is scarcely ready even to consider. But however much we may be obliged to fall short of what we could desire, we shall always find it profitable to keep our eyes fixed upon the highest ideals. First of all, then, let us provide a standard of measurement by inquiring what is desirable.

In a school where all branches of instruction are properly distributed and organized, the pupil may profitably receive his first lessons in history when he is nine or ten years of age. But a careful distinction must be made between receiving the first instruction in history and beginning the study of it. At this age the pupil acquires information, not through his own unaided effort, but almost exclusively through the effort of the teacher. A mother has no difficulty in teaching her child the story of Joseph or Samuel, and a teacher properly qualified for his vocation ought to have no more difficulty in teaching the story of Pyrrhus or Martin Luther. Indeed, it may be said that there are only two requisites of success. The teacher must know the story, and he must understand the art of telling it in such a way as to make an impression by it. That such methods, under favorable circumstances, are entirely practicable has been clearly demonstrated in the German gymnasia. In these schools, where history has been taught with greater success than anywhere else in the world, a teacher who has been especially trained for his work takes the lowest grade of pupils over the whole range of general history in this way. The course is almost exclusively biographical. Indeed, it is little more than a succession of stories told with the especial aim of making a deep impression upon the mind of the child concerning some of the most important of the great characters of history. Such a course, continuing for two years at the rate of two lessons a week, will be found to have given the pupil considerable knowledge of a vast number of valuable facts. And, best of all, the method by which this information has been acquired, so far from taxing the strength or wearying the attention of the scholar, has been to him a positive source of recreation and pleasure.

At the age of about twelve the pupil is ready for a more substantial diet. The teacher now takes him once more over the same ground, but with a somewhat different object in view. The scholar can now put facts together, and can understand something of the relations of cause and effect. In the former course he listened to the story of Hannibal: now he is ready for the story of the Second Punic War. A little pamphlet, usually prepared by the teacher and made up almost exclusively of names and dates, is put into the hand of the pupil merely to assist him in recalling what the teacher has said. Here, as in the former course, the knowledge acquired comes chiefly from the teacher. The system keeps clearly in view the fact that the pupil is not yet ready for that development which results from hard study. It never ceases to remember that at least three-fourths of all the time spent by a boy of twelve in trying to learn a hard lesson out of a book is time thrown away. Perhaps one-fourth of the time is devoted to more or less desperate and conscientious effort; but the large remaining portion is dawdled away in thinking of the last game of ball and longing for the next game of tag. A true system must make a constant endeavor to turn these demoralizing moments to profitable account. In this effort the German system is the most successful for the reason that instead of leaving the pupil to the meagre resources of his own thoughts, it occupies his attention with direct instruction in the form of attractive and profitable narration. The result is that, through a judicious exercise of this kind of economy, the German pupil at the age of fifteen or sixteen has been able to complete two distinct surveys of universal history. In the two or three years following, he is able to supplement the knowledge already obtained in a variety of ways. He may be directed in a careful study of the history of his own country, an outline of which he has already obtained; or may make an elaborate examination of some important period like that of the Reformation or the French Revolution.

Such, stated in general terms, is the preparation in history which the German student receives before going to the university. It is founded in a philosophical appreciation of the needs and the capabilities of the pupil, and is undoubtedly the best that has ever been devised. It is equally adapted to the wants of those two classes of pupils into which every secondary school is divided. It is the best preparation for those whose scholastic studies are to terminate with the preparatory school; and the best for those who are to carry forward their studies in a university course.

The student who has received this preparation goes to the university at about the age of nineteen. He is now ready for the more careful and philosophical study of individual nations and of individual periods. In his future studies he will devote himself chiefly to the relations and significance of facts rather than to the mere existence of facts themselves. Two ways are open to him: he can attend courses of lectures, and he can become a member of an historical seminary. But, wherever he goes, he will usually find that the object is to make a very careful study of some limited period, or of some limited phase of historical development. In the lecture-room he will find that the work done by the professor has for its highest object the opening of avenues of research and the guiding of the student in certain methods of thought and investigation. In the seminary, the student will be directed here and there by the professor, with a view to avoiding gross errors, but the investigator will be left to work out his results mainly in his own way. Before he has advanced very far in carrying on his investigations, he will almost inevitably arrive at the conclusion that the historical seminary is to the study of history, what the laboratory is to the study of the natural sciences.

But as soon as we attempt to compare this ideal with the methods that now generally prevail in the United States, we find more points of difference than points of similarity. In the preparatory schools of Germany, every teacher of history is required to have received especial training by thorough courses of historical study, such as those given in the gymnasium and in the university. In the best of the preparatory schools in America, on the other hand, history is often taught by persons that have received no especial training for the work whatever. Not only have the teachers, as a rule, received inadequate outfit, but they are generally so burdened with other work, and so wearied by it, that they are quite incapable of repairing any defects that under more favorable circumstances might be removed. In Germany, moreover, history is made a constituent part of the regular intellectual nourishment of the pupil during the whole of the time of his preparatory work. In America, on the contrary, it is generally crowded into one or two terms, or, at most, into a single year. There is a strong analogy between the proper methods of feeding the body and the proper methods of feeding the mind. The arrangement of the studies in many of our schools suggests the propriety of eating roast beef and plum pudding five days in a week for six months, and then abstaining from it altogether for five or six years. The effect of such a system upon the appetite and the digestion would doubtless be very much like the effects of a similar policy in matters of education. Moreover, the teacher in America is often expected to teach not less than twenty-five or thirty hours a week, while, of the teachers in Germany, scarcely more than half of that number is required. But, if we demand twice as many hours of the teacher, we strike the balance by requiring only half as many hours of the pupil. In America, the number of lessons per week for each pupil is about fifteen; while in Germany the number regularly required is from thirty to thirty-five. Thus, in the fashion of Charles Lamb, we preserve the equation by multiplying the lessons of the teacher and dividing the lessons of the scholar by two.

These comparisons are enough to show that nothing less than a revolution will make our teaching of history equal to that which we find in Germany. Such a revolution we may not look for at present. But we can at least inquire what improvements are practicable without interference with the general organization of our schools.

In the first place, some amelioration is possible in the use of the ordinary text-book. In many schools the so-called teaching of history is literally a mere hearing of recitations. I have heard of a person, by courtesy called a teacher, who habitually kept his finger upon the line in the text-book before him, and limited his instruction to the work of correcting the trifling variations of the pupil from the phraseology of the text. Here, the function of the teacher was merely that of a watchman; though this method prevailed in a school that called itself a university. I have no hesitation in expressing the opinion that the total result of such an exercise on the mind of the pupil is more injurious than beneficial. The mere memorizing of dry facts and assertions affords no intellectual nourishment, while it is almost sure to create a distaste for historical study, and, perhaps, will even alienate the taste of the scholar forever. The first of all endeavors, therefore, should be to put life and action into what, as it stands, is a mere bundle of dry bones.

This can be done in two ways. The information of the teacher may be used to illustrate what is set before the class as a lesson. Questions hinted at in the lesson may also be assigned the class for personal investigation. The first method will always be used to some extent by every efficient teacher; but it will not ordinarily be found sufficient. A far more helpful reliance is the method of personal research. The nature of the questions assigned must, of course, depend on the intelligence and advancement of the class. But even with a class of beginners, more is likely to be accomplished by assigning certain topics than by assigning certain lessons. Questions selected with due reference to the resources of the school library are likely to prove a far more profitable means of real advancement than any slavish dependence on even the best of text-books. The most successful instruction I have ever known in any preparatory school was carried on without any text-book whatever.

But if these methods are the most efficient in the preparatory schools, they are even more emphatically to be recommended in our colleges and universities. Perhaps in neither grade of instruction would it ordinarily be quite safe to abandon the text-book altogether. But the text-book should be looked upon as an assistance, rather than as a means of support. The student ought not to be encouraged to rely on any one book as an unquestionable authority. The habit of consulting different authors on every question of importance should be early acquired and should be constantly stimulated. For the accomplishment of these ends it will ordinarily be found, I think, that the most successful instruction is made up of a judicious combination of the text-book, the lecture, and the method of personal research.

When the college student is ready to begin his studies in history, he is not yet prepared for the most advanced work. He is deficient in two very important qualifications. In the first place, he is not in possession of a sufficient number of important historical facts; and, in the second, he is not yet sufficiently familiar with what may be called the methods and laws of historical development. To supply these deficiences should be the object of the earlier historical studies during the undergraduate course.

At the outset the student may be presumed to have some knowledge of general history, and of the history of his own country. This may be a somewhat violent presumption: but it is probably not wise to occupy the time of the undergraduate with such elementary studies as are taught in all the best of our high schools and academies. Better results are likely to follow from devoting our energies to an examination of such selected periods and nationalities as hold out the most credible assurances of profit.

But what periods shall be selected, and how shall the instruction be given?

Studies in the history of our own country and in the history of England should doubtless occupy the foremost place; but they should not crowd out studies of a more general nature. I cannot better point out what I think these studies should be than by indicating what is done at the present time in the University of Michigan. Some years ago a course was provided for, by means of which two lessons a week for one year are devoted to a study of the Political and Social History of England before the close of the Napoleonic Wars. Another course of two lessons a week, for half a year, is devoted to a study of the Reforms in the English Government during the present century. This is supplemented by a course of two lectures a week, for half a year, on The Theories and Methods of the English Government. In American History, a course on The Political and Social Development of the Colonies is followed by two courses on The Constitutional History of the United States since the close of the Revolutionary War. These courses in American History occupy the student once a week during half a year, and twice a week during a whole year. Of a more general nature, and for the purpose of giving broader views of the laws of historic development, one course is given on The History of Political and Social Institutions, one on The General History of Europe from the Reformation to the French Revolution, one on The History of Civilization in the Middle Ages, and one on The Rise and Development of Prussia. Not all of these courses are absolutely prerequisite for admission to the more advanced work of the historical and political seminaries, but they may all be regarded as preliminary to it. Crowning the work of the whole are three seminaries, one being devoted to a study of the Political Institutions of England, one to those of America, and one to Comparative Methods of Local Administration.

What has already been said will afford sufficient answer, perhaps, to the question of method. But a single illustration will probably give a more definite idea. The lecture of to-day, in the course on the History of Institutions, happens to be devoted to a study of Roman Provincial Administration. The following topics were assigned to the several groups of the class for the lessons of next week: "What light is thrown on Roman Provincial methods by Plutarch's Life of Lucullus?" "What by Cicero's oration against Verres?" "What by Guizot's essay on the *Regime Municipal?*" "What by Arnold's chapter on 'The System of

Taxation?'" In this manner a class may easily be led through their own researches to see how completely the systematic practice of injustice finally dissolved all the bonds that bound the Roman provinces to the general government. This accomplished, the downfall of the Empire is no longer a question that will give any difficulty to the student.

The work of the historical seminary is of a higher order. Each class consists of not more than about ten members, and each meeting is not less than about two hours in length. Each of the questions given out for investigation is such as to occupy the attention of the student during at least half a year; and all of the questions are designed to be of such cognate significance as to be of interest to all the members of the class. At the weekly meetings each member gives an account of his own investigations, and listens to such inquiries and suggestions as may be made by the teacher and the other members of the class. The titles of two or three papers prepared during the present semester will be enough to indicate the nature of the work done. Among others, essays founded on original research have being written on "A History of the Appointing Power of the President"; "A History of the Land Grants for Education in the North-west"; and "Criminal Legislation in New England during the Colonial Period."

It need not be added that this is true university work of a high order. Of course such studies are impracticable, except in an institution where large liberties in the way of elective courses are given, and where preliminary historical studies are begun early in the student's collegiate career. But my own experience leads to the belief that if the student enters upon the proper antecedent studies in the second year of his course, he may be brought in the fourth year to a grade of work which need not shrink from comparison with that carried on in the universities of the old world.

THE METHODS OF HISTORICAL STUDY AND RESEARCH IN COLUMBIA COLLEGE.

BY PROFESSOR JOHN W. BURGESS, COLUMBIA UNIVERSITY.

IN order to a clear presentation of this subject, one which shall escape the possibilities of a misunderstanding, it will be necessary to describe briefly the general peculiarities of the educational system of that complex of institutions to which the name Columbia College is now attached. The most general principle of that system distinguishes the College into two parts ; viz. : the Gymnasium, the College according to the old signification of that name in the United States, — as we term it here, the School of Arts, and the graduate and professional courses, the University. This distinction, however, is, without further explanation, liable to a misconception ; for the last year of the School of Arts, what is generally known as the College senior year, is counted to the University in the non-professional courses of the University, — those courses which, in a German University, would be placed under the Faculty of Philosophy. It is at this point, viz., the beginning of the senior year in the School of Arts, that the courses of study become purely and wholly elective, and the methods of instruction purely and distinctively those of the University. This year, with two graduate years, forms the University period for the students who pass from the School of Arts into the University, or who come from other Colleges at the end of their junior year. If, however, they be *graduates* of other Colleges, in which the courses of the senior year correspond to, or are an equivalent for, the courses in the School of Arts, they are admitted to the second year of the University.

If, now, the reader will keep this distinction and these explanations clearly in mind, a full comprehension of the methods of historic study and research at present followed in Columbia College will be easily and rapidly attained.

In the Gymnasium, — the first three years of the School of Arts, — the method is, of course, the gymnastic method, and the purpose sought the gymnastic purpose: that is, the daily drill upon text-books and hand-books of history by recitation, question and answer, as required studies, for the purpose of fixing and classifying in the mind of the student the elements of historical geography, the chronology and outward frame of historic events, the biographies of historic characters, and the definitions of historical terms and expressions. This is, of course, the indispensably necessary preparation for every student who would come with a properly disciplined historical memory, stored with a sufficient amount of elementary historical data, to the work of the University in this branch. If this be not properly accomplished, the foundation for everything further is wanting, and the instruction received in the University will be to a large degree unappreciated, to say the least. I would venture to assert that to all persons who have taken any part in the attempt to develop a University in the United States the want of a true gymnastic training in the elements of knowledge has appeared a most crying one. And if, while so many of our Colleges, both great and small, are affecting to despise their gymnastic calling, and seeking to become Universities through the fallacious process of simply making their gymnastic studies elective and optional, some Apostle of the Gymnasium would arise and found Academies which would stand true to the gymnastic method and purpose, such an one would do for the development of the true University a far greater work than the College which ceases to be the one thing without becoming the other.

On the other hand, the methods pursued and the purposes aimed at in the *University* courses of history are more complex, as well as different, and therefore require a more minute presentation. In the first place, attendance upon these courses is purely optional with the student. There would be a great loss both in the quantity and quality of the instruction were the professor obliged to accommodate himself to the level of hearers whose tastes and talents were not in the line pursued; and, on the other hand, it would be an unnatural limitation upon, if not a total destruction of, individual genius, were the student of the University not permitted to construct the combination of his studies for himself. The discipline and general elementary instruction of the Gymnasium ought to have developed in his own consciousness a better knowledge of his own intellectual peculiarities than any other person or body of persons can have. If it has not, then it will not matter much, as a general rule, where he may fall. Consideration for him who has no genius at all must never lead us to abandon the method in the University for the cultivation of a true intellectual peculiarity; for without such a development there can be no advance in the discovery of new truth or in a fuller comprehension of old truth. It is this consideration which has led the authorities in Columbia College to permit the University students of history not only to select what courses they may choose in history, but also to combine therewith such courses in philology, literature, philosophy, natural science and law as they may desire. Our experience in the working of the method has hardly yet been long enough to pronounce with confidence upon results. So far as my own observation reaches, however, I feel entirely satisfied that the comprehension of history has been greatly broadened and deepened by the variety of combinations into which it has thus been brought, and I cannot but believe that the other elements of the combinations have experienced a like advantage.

In the second place. The method of instruction in the University branches of history is chiefly by original lecture. And this for two reasons: the one relating to the professor, the other to the student. The University professor must be a worker among original material. He must present to his student *his own view* derived from the most original sources attainable. He must *construct* history out of the chaos of original historic atoms. If he does not do this, but contents himself with simply repeating the views of others, it is probably because he is not capable of it; in which case he is no University professor at all, but at best only a drill master for the Gymnasium. While the University student must learn among his first lessons that truth, as man knows it, is no ready-made article of certain and objective character, that it is a human interpretation, and subject therefore to the fallibility of human insight and reasoning, — one-sided, colored, incomplete. Unless this thought be continually impressed upon him by the method of the instruction which he receives, he will, to a greater or less degree, make dogma of his learning, and this is the negation of progress in the wider and more perfect comprehension of truth. Now instruction by means of the text-book in the University has always the tendency to the production of this result, — unless, perchance, the professor uses the text more for the purpose of confuting than teaching, in which case he is really lecturing and not hearing recitations. What is contained in a book which has been studied by classes gone before has, in the mind of a student not yet accustomed to sharp criticism, too large a presumption in its favor. He is too ready to acquiesce in its propositions, and let memory act where the more difficult processes of criticism and judgment should be called into play. On the other hand, when he has the person of his author always before his eyes, observes his weaknesses as well as his strength, then the true scholastic skepticism and belligerency will be aroused, and criticism, judgment, reasoning, insight, be developed.

Third. But this is only what might be termed the outward form of method generally. As to the internal principles or purposes of our method of historical instruction in particular, we seek to teach the student, first, how to get hold of a historic fact, how to distinguish fact from fiction, how to divest it as far as possible of coloring or exaggeration. We send him, therefore, to the most original sources attainable for his primary information. If there be more than one original source upon the same fact, we teach him to set these in comparison or contrast, to observe their agreements and discrepancies, and to attain a point of view from which all, or if this is not possible, the most of the evidence may appear reconcilable. And we warn him not to accept a statement not well authenticated for a fact, upon the principle that it is far better for the historical investigator to think that he does not know what he may know than to think he knows what he may not know. We undertake, in the second place, to teach the student to set the facts which he has thus attained in their chronological order, to the further end of setting them in their order as cause and effect. And we seek to make him clearly comprehend and continually feel that the latter process is the one most delicate and critical which the historical student is called upon to undertake, in that he is continually tempted to account that which is mere antecedent and consequent as being cause and effect. It is just in this process, of course, that the true historical *genius* most clearly reveals itself. It is just in this process that genius is most necessary to accomplish anything valuable. It is therefore most difficult to formulate rules upon the point for the direction of the historical student who may have no genius for his work. What we most insist upon, however, is a critical comparison of the sequence of facts in the history of different states or peoples at a like period in the development of their civilizations. If this be done with patience, care, and judgment, the student who possesses a moderate degree of true logic will soon learn to distinguish, to some extent at least, antecedent and consequent merely from cause and effect.

Fourth. After the facts have been determined and the causal *nexus* established we endeavor to teach the student to look for the *institutions and ideas* which have been developed through the sequence of events in the civilization of an age or people. This I might term the ultimate object of our entire method of historical instruction. With us history is the chief preparation for the study of the legal and political sciences. Through it we seek to find the origin, follow the growth and learn the meaning of our legal, political, and economic principles and institutions. We class it therefore no longer with fiction or rhetoric or belles-lettres, but with logic, philosophy, ethics. We value it, therefore, not by its brilliancy, but by its productiveness.

Lastly. We would not consider the circle of our method as complete, did it make no provision for the public practice of the students. To this end we have established an Academy of the historic, jural, and political sciences, composed of the graduates of the University in these branches. Before this body, in its regular weekly meetings, each member has the opportunity and assumes the duty of presenting one original work each year. The work is then the property of the Academy to publish or preserve in its archives as it will. The best production of the year in the Academy, as adjudged by the University Faculty in these departments, is rewarded by a prize lectureship in the University. In this manner we seek to make our students not simply pupils but co-workers, not simply recipients but givers with interest upon what they have received and to open the way for genius, talent, and industry in these branches to positions from which they may be employed in the further development and expansion of these departments.

As I indicated above, we have hardly yet had sufficient experience with our method and system to pronounce definitely and finally upon results. They have not yet made their cycle. But we are satisfied with the progress, and encouraged by the prospects.

COLUMBIA COLLEGE,
April 27, 1883.

PHYSICAL GEOGRAPHY AND HISTORY.

A KNOWLEDGE of the structure of the earth on which we dwell should underlie and precede all our studies of history and political science. We have been accustomed to study mind psychologically, without studying the body in which the mind dwells. So we have considered the historical movements of man without considering the theatre on which he moves. Edition after edition of the historical atlases of the learned German, Von Spruner, was published, with most elaborate and exact maps of Greece, of the Roman Empire, of mediæval Europe, Germany, Italy, etc., but not a single map showing geological formations. A clearer understanding of the importance of the physical structure of the earth would have made his maps much better than they are.

It is needless to say that in any exposition of these relations, constant use must be made of maps; in fact, the work cannot be carried on without them. The difficulties in the way of preparing such representations are great, for we need to exhibit each portion of the earth's surface as something cut out by the hands of a sculptor, which has a distinct physiognomy, to be recognized and known as definitely as our own physiognomies are known. The most direct method is by the relief map or atlas. But the difficulty of representing a solid upon a plane surface has been to some extent overcome, different elevations being represented by different colors.

Observe some of the things which a good physical map of the United States tells us. You see a long extent of seaboard, with mountains receding from the coast. When the first settlers landed, they found a wall, from 3500 to 7000 feet high, hemming them in. We see here the door through which the Baltimore and Ohio Railroad goes west; also the path of the Erie Canal. We see where the Pennsylvania people found a path over the mountains, and others after them. Without a physical map of North America, the unity of the French dominions, Canada and Louisiana, would hardly be discerned; with such a map, this unity is made strikingly evident, and the process of acquisition becomes clear. A glance at the broad basin of the Mississippi, as represented upon such a map, will show that it was predestined to become one of the greatest granaries of the world. The history of the peculiar attitude of California during the civil war can be studied only in the light of its physical relations to the rest of the Union. Thus, the history of this country was largely written before man came here. It is written on the map, and every citizen ought to have it written on his mind. Every student of political history or political economy should understand these great physical features of his country, not only in broad outline, but in detail.

As examples of exposition of our physical geography, one may mention Professor Shaler's chapter in Winsor's forthcoming *Narrative and Critical History of America*, the prefatory chapter in Palfrey's *New England*, and Professor Whitney's chapter in the *Guide-Book to the Yosemite*, and in Walker's *Statistical Atlas of the United States*, whose maps also are highly useful.

If we turn to Europe, the connection between physical geography and history is presented in the same striking way, and in even greater variety. Observe on any relief map how manifestly the plain of Lombardy and Venetia, carved out at the base of the enormous wall of the Alps, seems formed to be the garden of Europe and the theatre of wars. As for Greece, it is no exaggeration to say that he who does not understand its physical conformation can have no proper conception of its political history. The connection between the two is admirably displayed in the opening pages of Curtius' *History of Greece*, and in a delightful chapter in Taine's *Lectures on Art*, in which book a similar service is also done for Flanders. Also of note is Professor Conrad Bursian's essay, *Ueber den Einfluss der Natur des Griechischen Landes auf den Charakter seiner Bewohner*, in the *Jahresberichte* of the *Geographische Gesellschaft in München*, 1877. Further west, notice the remarkable cut from the Mediterranean to the North Sea (the valleys of the Rhone and Rhine), which made a Lotharingia possible. A relief map of France makes clear the reasons for the directions taken by the several invading tribes in 406 A.D. The position of Belfort, commanding the upper Rhine valley, explains the vigor with which it was defended in 1870; we see, too, why Germany fixed her boundary where she did. Again, in England, who does not know, to mention one illustration only, how decisive was the influence of such geographical features as the great forests upon the course of the English conquest of Britain? (See Guest's *Origines Celticae*, 1882, Green's *Making of England*, and Professor Pearson's valuable Historical Maps.) For similar illustrations, one may consult with profit Professor Archibald Geikie's paper on *The Geological Influences which have affected English History*, in Macmillan, March, 1882. If we turn to Asia, the connection between its great plains and the careers of its great conquerors could scarcely be more evident than it is.

All these are isolated and random illustrations. Indefinitely multiplied, as they might easily be, they would irresistibly force the conviction that the influence of physical geography upon history is a matter which no one can afford to neglect, and that a teacher of history who does not make frequent use of physical maps commits a grave error.

It may not be amiss to mention that prominent among the standard works of general scope which may be used in such studies are, beside the books of Ritter and Peschel, Professor Guyot's *Earth and Man*, G. P. Marsh's *The Earth as Modified by Human Action*, and Frederick von Hellwald's *Die Erde und ihre Völker*. Into the minor literature it is impossible here to enter (an important specimen is Wilhelm Roscher's *Betrachtungen über die geographische Lage der grossen Städte*, in his *Ansichten*, I., pp. 317–363), but it can be found, clearly arranged, in the bibliographical lists in successive volumes of Petermann's *Mittheilungen*, the best of geographical journals. An index to the maps in Petermann is now appearing in the Harvard University *Bulletin*. As to wall-maps, the most useful are perhaps the new Kiepert series and Professor Guyot's.

WHY DO CHILDREN DISLIKE HISTORY?

BY THOMAS WENTWORTH HIGGINSON.

IT has always seemed to me creditable to the brains of children that they dislike what we call the study of history. It is surely unfair to blame them, when they certainly like it quite as well as do their parents. The father brings home to his little son, from the public library, the first volume of Hildreth's United States, and says to him, "There, my son, is a book for you, and there are five more volumes just like it." Then he goes back to his *Sunday Herald*, and his wife reverts to *But Yet a Woman*, or *Mr. Isaacs;* both feeling that they have done their duty to the child's mind. Would they ever read through the six volumes of Hildreth consecutively for themselves?

Yet it needs but little reflection to see that no study is in itself—apart from the treatment—so interesting as history. For what is it that most interests every child? Human beings. What is history? The record of human beings, that is all.

We are accustomed to say, and truly, that every child is a born naturalist. But where is the child who would not at any time leave the society of animals for that of human beings? Even the bear and the raccoon are not personally more interesting to the country boy than to hear the endless tales of the men who have trapped the one and shot the other. The boy by the seaside would rather listen to the sailors' yarns than go fishing. Even stories about animals must have the human element thrown in, to make them fully fascinating; children must hear, not only about the wolf and his den, but about General Putnam, who went into it; and they would rather hear about Indian wars than either, because there all the participants are men. The gentlest girl likes to read the *Swiss Family Robinson*, or to dress up for a "centennial tea-party." But early Puritan history is all *Swiss Family Robinson* with many added excitements thrown in; and the colonial and revolutionary periods are all a centennial tea-party. If we could only make the characters live and move, with their own costume and their own looks, in our instruction, they would absorb the attention of every child.

It is idle to say, "But children prefer fiction to fact." Not at all; they prefer fact to fiction, if it is only made equally interesting. The test is this. Tell a boy a story, which he supposes to be true, and then disclose that it is all an invention. If the boy preferred fiction to fact, he would be pleased. Not at all; he is disappointed. On the other hand, if, after telling some absorbing and marvellous tale, you can honestly add, "My dear child, all this really happened to your father when he was little, or to your respected great-grandmother," the child is delighted.

In truth, the whole situation, in respect to history, is described in that well-known conversation between the English clergyman and the play-actor. "Why is it," asked the clergyman, "that you, who represent what everybody knows to be false, obtain more attention than we who deal in the most momentous realities!" "It is," said the actor, "because you represent the truth so that it seems like fiction, while we depict fiction in such a manner that it has the effect of truth."

The moral of it all is, that the fault is not in the child, but in us who write the books and teach the lessons. History is but a series of tales of human beings. Human beings form the theme which is of all things most congenial to the child's mind. If the subject loses all its charms by our handling, the fault is ours, and we should not blame the child.

Gradation and the Topical Method of Historical Study.

By Professor W. F. Allen, Wisconsin University.

FOR instruction in history, as in other branches, there are three distinct periods to be considered: childhood, school-life, and college-life. For the first of these I have nothing to offer beyond the excellent remarks made by our author on page 139. What the child needs is to have the imagination quickened, and the memory stored with incidents and associations. It is not so necessary that there should be any definite plan or order in the acquisition of these interesting stories, great names, and important events. The mind merely needs to have associations and memories of these; their arrangement will come later.

Formal instruction in history, he goes on to say, may begin at about the age of ten; but the length of time that it is to be kept up differs very greatly with different pupils, and it is obvious that we cannot advantageously lay out the same course for those who are to go to college, those who are to pass through the high school merely, and those who have to be satisfied with a grammar-school education. The beginning, however, must be nearly the same with all, and it will be found that the longest course will, in the main, coincide with the shorter ones, so far as they go.

All alike must begin with the history of their own country, and with this a considerable proportion of the pupils must be content. So far there is no difference of opinion. When, however, we pass to the next stage, and ask what branch of history should follow that of the United States, the answers would be various. The usual practice is to take up General History at this point; but I think the practice is not a wise one. Very few pupils at this age have a sufficiently developed historical sense to follow intelligently the fortunes of several nations side by side, now studying the separate history of each country independently, then passing to the complicated international relations, which make up the current of modern history. In antiquity there was but one empire at a time. General history is, therefore, the separate histories of Egypt, Assyria, Persia, etc., taken up *successively*. In modern times these separate histories have to be taken up *contemporaneously*. There is no one thread to be followed, but a multitude of threads to be woven into a connected whole; and my experience is, that an attempt to do this, with only the preparation that the study of United States history gives, results, for most scholars, in a bewildering confusion.

Our author lays down the correct principle on page 146: "The way to that which is general is through that which is special." General history cannot be profitably studied until, first, the historical imagination has been trained and the historical sense developed by abundance of stories, and by instruction in national history; and, secondly, at least one of the separate threads has been traced by itself, and a certain degree of familiarity thus gained with the leading events which are to come under consideration. The separate annals of at least one country should be studied before general history is begun. Which country should be selected for this purpose for American schools can, of course, be no question. American citizens need to know the history of England next to that of their own country. I should even desire that a second thread should be taken up by itself — in the history of France or Germany — before general history is studied; but this is not essential.

Further details must depend upon the extent of the course and its object. If there can be but one term's work, besides United States history, I would have the history of England. If there is plenty of time, I would have ancient history, English history, and French history all precede general history, or, if need be, take its place.

But I can conceive of something better even than this. To go back to our first question: What does the American boy really need, who is to have only one term of history before he goes out into the world, and becomes an American citizen? Would not everybody admit that, while the Plantagenets are of more importance for him than the Hohenstaufen, and Oliver Cromwell than Gustavus Adolphus, the events and personages of the last hundred years are of more importance than either?

Let us pass now to the college course. Only a very small proportion of our people go through a college course, and of these only a small proportion — under our present system of elective studies — take any extended course in history. Here, too, I have tried a good many experiments, and have arrived at a scheme which appears to answer my requirements very well.

The field of history is so vast and varied that it is impossible, in any college course, to treat all the subjects that deserve to be taken up. All that we can do is to lay out a course, or a number of courses, which appear to meet, as a whole, the needs of the largest number, and which will allow selection, in accordance with tastes, to those who do not care to take it as a whole.

We require for admission, in the classical courses of this University, ancient history, the history of the United States, and the history of England. We are able, therefore, to take for granted something of an acquaintance with the leading events and characters of ancient and modern times. The only history which is required in our curriculum is a term of United States history for the juniors of the classical department. Besides this, there are three elective courses, each carried through the year: one as a full course, the others as half courses.

In laying out this work, we are not limited, as in the common schools, by the necessity of considering what is most essential for those who are soon to leave school. We are not to lay out a single course which all must follow, but a series of courses, which may be taken either in whole or in part, according to individual tastes. Even here, however, there is a natural order which should be insisted on, so far as possible, for those who take the whole course. We must begin with what is most indispensable. It is all very well to say that dates and dynasties are of only secondary importance, and that it is the history of ideas and of social progress that we want. There can be no history without dates and dynasties. They are to the nobler parts of history what the skeleton is to the body. All the beauty of the body and all its seeming energy are in the external parts; but what would they be without the framework of bones? So, in history, we can have no sure and adequate comprehension of the movement of the great forces of society, without the skeleton of the history of events. Now, all events take place in two relations, — time and place. The indispensable foundation of history is, therefore, a knowledge of chronology, — of historical distances, — and of historical geography, in connection with the changes of empire. Territorial and dynastic history — the study of the successive empires and dynastic powers of the world — forms the first course, which should precede the others.

Next to the knowledge of empires, the most necessary,

if the least important branch of history, comes the study of the organized action of mankind. The study of institutions, of their organic relation to one another in constitutions of government, and of the political conflicts that have grown out of these, forms naturally the second course. After this, and not till then, the history of thought, of society, of ideas, can be profitably taken up. We have thus three independent courses, affording an approximately complete survey of the field of history, or at least preparation for further independent study. But although this is the natural order of study, it is not necessary to adhere to it overscrupulously. The student has already, in a general way, studied the dynastic history of Greece, Rome, and England; has thus acquired a consecutive, if partial, view of ancient and modern times. He is, therefore, prepared to take up the special study of the institutions of Greece and Rome, with which, moreover, he is already somewhat familiar from his classical studies, without waiting for the extended course in dynastic history. He may even, without great disadvantage, pass at once to the study of mediæval and modern institutions.

As to method, I have also experimented a great deal. For college classes—elective classes especially—nothing seems to me a greater waste of force than to spend the hour with a text-book in my hand, hearing the students repeat what is in the book. Lecturing, however satisfactory in the German universities, I do not find suited to the wants of my students as a regular mode of *instruction*. For suggestion and for review it may be employed with great advantage; and for regular instruction in fields in which there is no suitable text-book, I am often obliged to have recourse to it. But it requires, to be efficacious, constant questioning, thorough examinations, and occasional inspection of note-books.

In the method which I have at last settled upon, my aim has been to get some of the benefits which students in the natural sciences acquire from work in laboratories. Students of the age and maturity of juniors and seniors can get the greatest advantage from historical study by doing some independent work akin to laboratory work. I would not be understood as claiming that this is original investigation, in any true sense of the term. Laboratory work in chemistry or physics is not original investigation, neither is the study of topics in history. The object, it must be remembered, is *education*, not historical investigation; and the object of the educational process is not merely to ascertain facts, but even more: to learn how to ascertain facts. For the student, as a piece of training, historians like Prescott and Bancroft may stand in the place of original authorities. To gather facts from them, really at second hand, has for the student much of the educational value of first-hand work. Of course, there is a difference in students, and the work done by some is of a much higher grade than that of others. For the best students it easily and frequently passes into the actual study of authorities at first hand.

In studying by topics I always desire that the class should have a text-book — a brief compendium — upon which they are liable to be questioned and examined, and which will serve at any rate as a basis and guide of work. My method is then to assign for every day — as long beforehand as possible — special topics to two or three students, which they are to study with as great thoroughness as possible in all the works to which they have access, and present *orally* in the class, writing out a syllabus beforehand upon the blackboard. If they write out the topic, and depend upon a written paper, they are much less likely to be certain of their ground and independent in their treatment.

The topical method here described is successful in proportion to the abundance and accessibility of books of reference. In American history it works best, and here I employ no other. In the dynastic history of ancient and modern times, it is satisfactory in most cases. I combine with it constant map-drawing, and the preparation of a synchronistic chart. In the more advanced courses, owing to the deficiency of good books of reference, it is necessary to abandon the method, or combine it with lectures, recitations, and written essays. It is, of course, impossible to assign topics which cover the whole ground. It is possible, however, to select for this purpose all the names and events of first importance, and it is one of the advantages of the topical method that it thus affords an opportunity to emphasize those facts of history which most need emphasis. It is the special function of the teacher to supplement the topics, to point out their relative importance and their connection with one another, and to help the students in acquiring a complete and accurate general view.

PART I.

HISTORICAL LITERATURE AND AUTHORITIES.

1. PRIMITIVE SOCIETY.

C. F. Keary. The Dawn of History: An Introduction to Prehistoric Study. L.* Mozley & Smith. $1.50.

‡*E. G. Tylor.* Early History of Mankind. N.Y. Holt. $3.50.

‡*Id.* Primitive Culture. 2 v. N.Y. Holt. $7.00.

‡*Id.* Anthropology. N.Y. App. $2.00.

    Mr. Tylor's books present the best picture of primitive society, and summary of the present condition of the inquiry.

‡*Sir John Lubbock.* Pre-historic Times. N.Y. App. $5.00.

    Chiefly devoted to archæology.

Id. Origin of Civilization. N.Y. App. $2.00.

‡*H. Spencer.* Ceremonial Institutions. App. $1.25.

‡*Id.* Political Institutions. App. $1.50.

    These works describe the evolution of governmental institutions.

---

* In this list only books in the English language are given, with the exception of a few of prime importance. Works written in a foreign language, whether in the original or translated, are indicated by a dagger (†). Books of especial importance are indicated by the double dagger (‡). Abbreviated titles are given, except where the full title contains a description of the book. In the abbreviations, App. stands for Appleton; B., for Boston; Ber., for Berlin; C., for Cassell; C. & H., for Chapman & Hall; Ch., for Chicago; E. & L., for Estes & Lauriat; Ed., for Edinburgh; H., for Harper; L., for London; Lip., for Lippincott; Longm., for Longmans; Lp., for Leipsic; L. & B., for Little, Brown, & Co.; L. & S., for Lee & Shepard; M., for Murray; Macm., for Macmillan; O., for Osgood; P., for Paris; Ph., for Philadelphia; Put., for Putnams; R., for Roberts; Scr., for Scribner; S. & E., for Smith, Elder, & Co.; W. & N., for Williams & Norgate. E.S. stands for Epochs Series (Scribner); and Soc., for Society for the Diffusion of Christian Knowledge (Young).

‡*L. H. Morgan.* Ancient Society. N.Y. Holt. $4.00.
>The best analysis of the structure of primitive society, based upon an intimate knowledge of the institutions of the North American Indians. The later portions less reliable.

J. F. McLennan. Studies in Ancient History. L. Quaritch.
>Controverts Mr. Morgan's theories, and finds the origin of the family in marriage by capture.

W. E. Hearn. The Aryan Household. L. Longm. $6.40.
>The most complete treatise upon the structure and development of primitive society.

‡*Fustel de Coulanges.* The Ancient City.† B. L. & S. $2.00.
>A remarkable book, affording the best key to the origin and much of the history of the Greek and Roman institutions.

‡*Sir H. S. Maine.* Ancient Law: its Connection with the Early History of Society, and its Relation to Modern Ideas. N.Y. Holt. $3.50.
>Invaluable as an introduction to the history of institutions.

Id. Village Communities. N.Y. Holt. $3.50.
>This work introduced the theory of village communities to the English public.

‡*Id.* Early History of Institutions. N.Y. Holt. $3.50.
>Devoted especially to the early institutions of Ireland.

Id. Dissertations upon Early Custom and Law. N.Y. Holt.
>A collection of essays and lectures.

‡*E. de Laveleye.* Primitive Property.† L. Macm. $3.50.
>The most complete elaboration of the theory of primitive community of property.

Sir A. C. Lyall. Asiatic Studies. M.
>Papers full of valuable observation and study.

E. Nasse. Agricultural Community of the Middle Ages.† W. & N.
>The theory of village communities applied to England.

D. W. Ross. Early History of Land-holding among the Germans. B. Soule & Bugbee.
>Controverts the theory of village communities.

John Fenton. Early Hebrew Life. L. Trübner.

A. F. Bandelier. On the Art of War and Mode of Warfare among the Ancient Mexicans. — On the Distribution and Tenure of Land, etc. — On the Social Organization and Mode of Government, etc.

> Three papers of great value, reprinted from the reports of the Peabody Museum of Ethnology for 1877-8-9.

J. J. Bachofen. Das Mutterrecht.† Stuttgart. 1861.

> A pioneer work; treats of inheritance in the female line, as an institution of primitive society.

See also the following articles: by *E. Nasse,* in Cont. Rev., May, 1872, upon Village Communities; by *J. F. McLennan,* in Fortn. Rev., 1866, upon Kinship in Ancient Greece, and in 1869-70, upon Worship of Animals and Plants [theory of totems]; by *F. H. Cushing,* in the Atl. Monthly, Sept. and Oct., 1882, upon the Nation of the Willows [the Zuñis of New Mexico]; by *W. F. Allen,* in Penn Monthly, June, 1880, upon the points at issue between Mr. Morgan and Mr. McLennan.

Authorities.

Books of travel, etc., containing graphic and accurate accounts of savage and barbarous society.

Herbert Spencer. Descriptive Sociology. — Div. 1: Uncivilized Societies; Div. 2: Ancient Mexicans, etc. 8 parts, each $4.00.

> A classified collection of facts.

L. H. Morgan. Systems of Consanguinity and Affinity of the Human Family. Vol. XVII. (1870) of the Smithsonian Contributions.

> A very extensive and remarkable collection of facts.

Id. League of the Iroquois. Rochester. 1851.

‡*F. Parkman.* The Oregon Trail. B. L. & B. $2.50.

> Perhaps the most vivid picture of Indian life.

‡*David Livingstone.* Missionary Travels and Researches in South Africa. H. $4.50.

H. M. Stanley. Through the Dark Continent. 2 v. H. $10.00.

G. Schweinfurth. The Heart of Africa. 2 v. H. $8.00.

‡ *W. G. Palgrave.* A Year's Travel in Arabia. Macm. $2.00.

J. A. McGahan. Campaigning on the Oxus. H. $3.50.
> Contains an excellent account of nomadic life.

‡ *Lord Pembroke.* Old New Zealand. L. Bentley.
> Contains a forcible picture of the evils worked by contact with civilization.

H. Rink. Tales and Traditions of the Eskimo. Ed. Blackwood.

‡ *G. W. Dasent.* Story of Burnt Njal. Ed. Edmonston. $7.50.
> Presents a vivid picture of early German society.

‡ *Homer's* Iliad, translated in prose by Lang, etc.; and Odyssey, by Butcher and Lang. Each, $1.50.
> A portrayal of early Greek society and institutions.

D. M. Wallace. Russia. Holt. $2.00.
> Contains the best account of the *Mir*, or Russian village community.

A. J. Evans. Through Bosnia and Herzegovina. Longm.
> Contains a description of the Slavonian family communities.

J. W. Probyn. Systems of Land Tenure in Various Countries. C. $1.75.
> The essays upon India, Germany, and Russia, describe systems of land community.

Sir J. B. Phear. The Aryan Village in India and Ceylon. Macm $2.25.

See also the publications of the American Bureau of Ethnology, the Peabody Museum, the American Archæological Institute, and kindred institutions; and the list of books upon the Indians of America.

2. MYTHOLOGY.

‡*Max Müller.* Chips from a German Workshop. 5 v. N.Y. Scr. $10.00.
>These essays laid the foundation for the study of comparative mythology and folk-lore.

‡*C. F. Keary.* Outlines of Primitive Belief. N.Y. Scr. $2.50.
>Especially of the Greeks, Hindoos, and Scandinavians.

J. A. Hartung. Die Religion und Mythologie der Griechen.† 4 v. Lp. Engelmann.
>The first volume contains perhaps the best introduction to the study of mythology.

Sir G. W. Cox. Introduction to Science of Comparative Mythology and Folk-lore. Holt. $2.50.

‡*Id.* Mythology of the Aryan Nations. Longm. $4.50.
>A comparative view of the Indian, Greek, and German systems of mythology.

John Fiske. Myths and Myth-Makers. Houghton. $2.00.
>A popular account of the way in which myths are formed.

A. S. Murray. Manual of Mythology. N.Y. Scr. $2.25.
>Chiefly devoted to that of Greece ; with illustrations.

‡*L. Preller.* Griechische Mythologie.† Ber. Weidmann.

‡*Id.* Römische Mythologie.† Ber. Weidmann.
>Preller's are the best and most compendious treatises.

‡*J. Grimm.* Teutonic Mythology.† 2 v. L. Bell.
>An exhaustive and invaluable treatise.

R. B. Anderson. Norse Mythology. Ch. Griggs. $2.50.

D. G. Brinton. Myths of the New World. Ph. Watts. $2.00.

Ethnic Religions.

C. P. Tiele. History of Religion. Houghton. $3.00.
>The best work of a general character.

J. F. Clarke. Ten Great Religions. Houghton. $3.00.
>A popular comparative view of the principal ethnic religions.

‡Hibbert Lectures: —
 1878. *Max Müller.* The Origin and Growth of Religion, as illustrated by the Religions of India. Scr.
 1879. *P. Le Page Renouf.* Id., Ancient Egypt. Scr.
 1881. *T. W. Rhys-Davids.* Id., Buddhism. Put.
 1882. *A. Kuenen.* National Religions and Universal Religions.

‡Non-Christian Religious Systems. Soc.
 Monier Williams. Hinduism.
 T. W. Rhys-Davids. Buddhism.
 R. K. Douglas. Confucianism and Taouism.
 J. H. W. Stobart. Islam and its Founders.
 Sir William Muir. The Coran.

‡*S. Johnson.* Oriental Religions: I. India; II. China; III. Persia. Houghton. $5.00.

A. Barth. Religions of India. Houghton.

O. Keitner. Buddha and his Doctrines. L. Trübner.

J. Edkins. Chinese Buddhism. Houghton.

J. Legge. Life and Teaching of Confucius.

M. Haug. The Religion of the Parsis. Houghton. $4.50.

‡*C. P. Tiele.* Comparative History of the Egyptian and Mesopotamian Religions. Part I.: Egypt. L.

See also articles by *Monier Williams*, on Indian Religious Thought, Cont. Rev., 1878, and on Religion of Zoroaster, 19th Cent., Jan., 1881; by *W. F. Allen*, on the Religion of the Ancient Greeks, N. Am. Rev., July, 1869; and the Ancient Romans, July, 1871; by *Jas. Darmesteter*, in Cont. Rev., Oct., 1879, on Supreme God in Indo-European Mythology; by *J. N. Hoare*, in 19th Cent., Dec., 1878, on Religion of Ancient Egyptians; in Edin. Rev., Oct., 1881, on the Koran; by *K. Blind*, in N. Am. Rev., Oct., 1872, on the German World of Gods; by *F. Lenormant*, in Cont. Rev., 1880, on the Eleusinian Mysteries; by *C. T. Newton*, in

19th Cent., June, 1878, on the Religion of the Greeks as Illustrated by Inscriptions. For the truest conception of Greek mythology: *Ruskin's* Modern Painters, Part IV., Chap. 13.

Authorities.

Sacred Books of the East. 11 vols. Macm.
The Elder Edda. L. Trübner.
The Younger Edda. Ch. Griggs.

---

3. History of Society.

‡*H. Spencer.* The Study of Sociology. App. $1.50.
W. Bagehot. Physics and Politics. $1.50.
   Analyzes the causes of progress.
‡*A. Comte.* The Positive Philosophy.† 2 v. App.
   The second volume contains an application of the positive philosophy to historical phenomena.
F. Schlegel. The Philosophy of History.†
Id. Lectures on the History of Literature, Ancient and Modern.†
   These old works are still unsurpassed in their field.
R. Flint. The Philosophy of History in France and Germany.
Baron de Montesquieu. The Spirit of Laws.† Cincinnati.
   A work of great insight, first published in 1748.
‡*J. W. Draper.* The Intellectual Development of Europe. 2 v. H. $3.00.
‡*H. T. Buckle.* Introduction to History of Civilization in England. 2 v. App. $4.00.
   Draper and Buckle write from the point of view of the controlling influence of physical causes.
G. P. Marsh. Man and Nature. Scr. $2.00.
   Treats of the influence of man and the earth upon each other.
A. Blanqui. History of Political Economy in Europe.† $3.00.
Sir T. E. May. Democracy in Europe. 2 v. Longm.
E. Viollet-le-duc. The Habitations of Man in all Ages.† L. Low.

4. GENERAL HISTORY.

W. Oncken. Allgemeine Geschichte in Einzeldarstellungen.† Ber. G. Grote. 300 marks.

A series of works by writers of high authority. The following are already published. *G. F. Hertzberg,* Hellas und Rom; Das Römische Kaiserreich. *F. Dahn,* Urgeschichte der Germanischen und Romanischen Völker. *M. Philippson,* Zeitalter Ludwigs XIV. *A. Stern,* Revolution in England. *A. Brückner,* Peter der Grosse. *W. Oncken,* Zeitalter Friedrichs des Grossen.

E. A. Freeman. General Sketch [in Freeman's Hist. Series]. Holt. $1.00.
    The best brief outline of general history.

‡*Id.* Historical Geography of Europe. 2 v. [vol. ii., maps]. $12.00.
    An elaborate and accurate work; the best there is.

‡*Leopold von Ranke.* Weltgeschichte.† 3 vols. already published.
    A summary of the best results of scholarship by the greatest living master. Translation of Vol. I. II.

K. von Spruner. Handatlas der Geschichte.† In three parts.
  1. Atlas Antiquus.
  2. Europa. Revised by Th. Menke. [English edition by W. & N., £4 14s. 6d.]
  3. Asia, Africa, America, and Australia.
    Altogether the best and completest historical atlas.

‡*N. Bouillet.* Dictionnaire Universel d'Histoire et de Géographie. P. Hachette.

‡*Id.* Atlas Universel d'Histoire et de Géographie.
    These works of Bouillet are the best books of reference.

J. Haydn. Dictionary of Dates. App. $6.00.
    The best brief compendium of chronology, revised to 1883.

H. B. George. Genealogical Tables. Macm. $3.00.
    The best in English.

‡*S. Willard.* Synopsis of History. App.
    Chronological and genealogical tables of the highest merit.

HISTORICAL LITERATURE AND AUTHORITIES. 247

C. K. Adams. Manual of Historical Literature. H. $2.50.
>The best guide to historical reading.

W. F. Allen. Reader's Guide to English History. B. Ginn, Heath, & Co.
>With a supplement giving brief references to the history of other countries and periods.

See also articles by *E. A. Freeman,* in Fortn. Rev., May, 1881, on the Study of History; by *J. Gairdner,* in Cont. Rev., Oct., 1880, on Sources of History.

Periodicals.

‡Historische Zeitschrift. By *H. von Sybel.* München (bi-monthly).
>The oldest and leading historical periodical.

‡Revue Historique. By *G. Monod* and *G. Fagniez.*† P. (bi-monthly).
>Especially valuable for its survey of current historical literature.

Mittheilungen aus der Historischen Literatur.† By *F. Hirsch.* Ber. (quarterly).
>Consists exclusively of book reviews.

Jahresberichte der Geschichtswissenschaft. Ber.
>An annual review of historical literature.

Das Historische Taschenbuch. Lp.
>An annual collection of historical essays.

The Antiquary. Published by *Elliot Stock.* L. (monthly).
>Devoted to antiquities rather than history.

‡The Magazine of American History. (Monthly.) N.Y. Barnes.
>A periodical of high excellence.

The American Antiquarian. By *S. D. Peet.* Ch. (quarterly).
>Devoted to the entire field of antiquities.

Besides these, several of the State Historical Societies publish periodicals or regular volumes of Transactions.

5. ANCIENT HISTORY.

‡*Philip Smith.* A History of the World. Ancient History. 3 v. App. $6.00.

    The best English history of antiquity.

A. H. L. Heeren. Historical Researches into the Politics, Intercourse, and Trade of the Principal Nations of Antiquity.† 6 v. Ox.

    An old but valuable book.

‡*G. Rawlinson.* A Manual of Ancient History. H. $1.25.

    A careful and accurate compendium, with abundant references to authorities and special treatises.

P. V. N. Myers. Outlines of Ancient History. H. 1882. $1.75.

    A good compendium for non-classical readers.

E. A. Freeman. Historical Essays. Second Series. Macm. $3.50.

    This series is devoted to ancient history.

J. J. Winckelmann. History of Ancient Art. 2 v.† O. $9.00.

    The starting-point of study in the history of ancient art.

‡*F. von Reber.* History of Ancient Art.† H. $2.50.

    An excellent compendium, well illustrated.

G. G. Zerffi. Manual of the Historical Development of Art. L. Hardwicke.

‡*S. R. Koehler.* Illustrations of the History of Art. Series 1: Ancient Architecture, Sculpture, etc. B. Prang. 1879. Series 5 contains the History of Painting.

K. O. Müller. Ancient Art and its Remains. L. Quaritch.

    The German edition is accompanied by two vols. of illustrations.

W. C. Perry. Popular Introduction to the History of Greek and Roman Sculpture. Longm. $12.00.

A. S. Murray. History of Ancient Sculpture. M.

James Fergusson. History of Architecture. 2 v. M. $24.00.

Ancient Classics for Modern Readers. Lipp. $1.00.
> Twenty-eight small volumes, containing excellent short accounts of the principal authors.

Classical Writers. Edited by J. R. Green. App. 60 cts.
> A similar series, containing fewer treatises, but of the highest excellence.

W. C. Wilkinson. Preparatory Greek Course in English. N.Y. Phillips & Hunt.
> Especially adapted to non-classical readers.

W. Smith. Dictionary of Antiquities. M. $6.00.

Id. Dictionary of Classical Biography and Mythology. 3 v. M. $18.00.

Id. Dictionary of Classical Geography. 2 v. M. $12.00.

Id. Classical Atlas. M. $40.00.
> The most complete works of reference. Smaller works are :—

A. Rich. Dictionary of Antiquities.

W. Smith. Classical Dictionary. H.

E. Guhl and W. Koner. The Life of the Greeks and Romans. L. Chatto & Windus. $4.00.

---

6. ORIENTAL HISTORY.

‡M. Duncker. History of Antiquity. 6 v.† L. Bentley. $50.00.
> Covers only the oriental period, but is the best compendium for this period.

F. Lenormant and E. Chevallier. Manual of the Ancient History of the East.† 2 v. L. Asher. 1869. $5.50.

F. Lenormant. The Beginnings of History.† Scr. $2.50.

G. Rawlinson. The Origin of Nations. Scr. $1.50.

‡*Id.* The Five Great Monarchies of the Ancient Eastern World [Chaldæa, Assyria, Babylon, Media, and Persia]. Dodd, Mead, & Co. $6.00.

Id. The Sixth Great Monarchy [Parthia]. Dodd, Mead, & Co. $2.00.

Id. The Seventh Great Oriental Monarchy [Sassanidæ]. $4.00.

Id. History of Ancient Egypt. 2 v. B. Cassino. $4.00.

> All Canon Rawlinson's works are marked by learning and ability. They are written from the point of view of the absolute authority of the Hebrew scriptures.

‡*H. Brugsch Bey.* Egypt under the Pharaohs. 2 v. M. $12.00.

> The best history of Egypt, by one of the most distinguished Egyptologists.

‡*Sir J. G. Wilkinson.* The Manners and Customs of the Ancient Egyptians. 3 v. M. $33.00.

> The standard work upon the subject.

‡*H. Ebers.* Egypt. C.

> An illustrated work of the highest excellence.

‡*H. Ewald.* History of Israel. 5 v. Longm. $26.00.

> By the greatest authority upon Hebrew history.

H. H. Milman. History of the Jews. 3 v. N.Y. Widdleton. $5.25.

> A popular work.

J. H. Allen. Hebrew Men and Times. R. $1.50.

E. H. Palmer. History of the Jewish Nation; from the earliest times to the present day. Soc. $1.50.

C. R. Conder. Life of Judas Maccabeus [New Plutarch]. Put. $1.00.

‡*A. P. Stanley.* History of the Jewish Church. 3 v. Scr. $7.50.

J. Kenrick. Phœnicia. L. Fellowes.

See also series of articles by *R. Stuart-Poole* in Cont. Rev., 1878–79, on Ancient Egypt.

Authorities.

Records of the Past. 6 v. L. Bagster. $18.00.
Ancient History from the Monuments. 6 v. Soc. Each, 75 cts.
I. P. Cory. Ancient Fragments. L. Reeves.

---

7. HISTORY OF GREECE.

‡*Geo. Grote.* History of Greece. 12 v. H. $18.00.
> The most complete history; from a liberal point of view.

Connop Thirlwall. History of Greece. 2 v. H.
> An excellent and scholarly work.

‡*Ernst Curtius.* History of Greece. 5 v.† Scr. $10.00.
> The best German history; a book of eloquence as well as scholarship.

Sir G. W. Cox. General History of Greece. H. $1.25.
> The best short history.

Wm. Smith. History of Greece. B. Ware. $2.00.
> The American edition, edited by Pres. Felton, contains important additions, bringing it down to the present century.

Id. Smaller History of Greece. H. 60 cts.

T. T. Timayenis. A History of Greece from the Earliest Times to the Present. 2 v. App. $3.50.
> Interesting as the work of a native Greek, and covering the period of modern history.

C. C. Felton. Greece, Ancient and Modern. 2 v. Houghton. $5.00.
> The best popular work on the history, literature, etc., of Greece.

E. A. Freeman. History of Federal Government. Vol. I. Macm. $7.00.
> This, the only volume published, is chiefly devoted to the Achæan League.

W. W. Lloyd. The Age of Pericles. 2 v. M. $6.00.
Id. History of Sicily to the Athenian War. M.

The following belong to the series of Epochs of ancient history: —

S. G. W. Benjamin. Troy. $1.00.
Sir G. W. Cox. The Greeks and the Persians. $1.00.
Id. The Athenian Empire. $1.00.
C. Sankey. The Spartan and Theban Supremacies. $1.00.
A. M. Curteis. Rise of the Macedonian Empire. $1.00.

C. Peter. Chronological Tables of Greek History. Macm. $3.00.
J. P. Mahaffy. Social Life in Greece. Macm.
W. A. Becker. Charicles. L. $3.00.
    A tale illustrating manners and customs.
W. Mure. Critical History of the Language and Literature of Ancient Greece. 5 v. Longm. $35.00.
    This is the principal work; a good short one is —
J. P. Mahaffy. History of Classical Greek Literature. II. $1.00.

---

8. ROMAN HISTORY.

‡*Th. Mommsen.* History of Rome. 4 v.† Scr. $8.00.
    The best history of Rome; reaches B.C. 46.
W. Ihne. History of Rome. 5 v.† Longm. $30.00.
    Gives less attention than Mommsen to legal and economical causes; is also more favorable to the Carthaginians. Reaches B.C. 78.
Thos. Arnold. History of Rome. App. $3.00.
    Of high literary merit, but based upon Niebuhr in its view of Roman institutions, and therefore largely superseded by later researches. Reaches B.C. 202.
Chas. Merivale. General History of Rome. App. $1.25.
    The best short history of Rome, reaching to the fall of the western empire, A.D. 476.

HISTORICAL LITERATURE AND AUTHORITIES. 253

H. G. Liddell. History of Rome. H. $1.25.
: Of a good deal of literary merit, founded chiefly upon Niebuhr. Reaches B.C. 30.

W. Smith and *E. Lawrence.* Smaller History of Rome. H. 60 cts.
: An excellent sketch, reaching A.D. 476.

A. Schwegler. Römische Geschichte. 2 v.† Tübingen. 1853–58. $4.70.
: An exhaustive cyclopædia of Roman history, indispensable for the student; reaches B.C. 390. A fourth volume, by O. Clason (Ber., Calvary), reaches B.C. 328.

T. H. Dyer. The History of the Kings of Rome. Lip. $5.00.
: Maintains the traditionary view, against Niebuhr. The same view is presented with great learning and brilliancy by

Fr. Dor. Gerlach and *J. J. Bachofen.* Geschichte der Römer.† Basel. 1851. Vol. I., $2.60.
: The first volume, containing the history of the kings, is the only one ever published.

V. Duruy. History of Rome. 6 v.† L. Kelly [now publishing].
: Magnificently illustrated; a work of high merit.

‡*Geo. Long.* The Decline of the Roman Republic. 5 v. L. Bell. $28.00.
: An exhaustive collection of facts from B.C. 154 to 44, accompanied with acute criticism.

‡*Chas. Merivale.* History of the Romans under the Empire. 7 v. App. $14.00. New edition, 4 v., $7.00.
: From B.C. 60 to A.D. 180. The best account of the period between Mommsen and Gibbon.

R. Congreve. The Roman Empire of the West. L. Parker. $1.75.
: By an eminent positivist.

‡*J. R. Seeley.* Roman Imperialism. R. $1.50.
: Three lectures on the establishment and decline of the empire.

‡*Edw. Gibbon.* History of the Decline and Fall of the Roman Empire. 6 v. Lip. $12.00.
The Students' Gibbon. H. $1.25.
: Gibbon is an indispensable guide for the twelve centuries from the accession of Commodus to the fall of Constantinople.

A. J. Mason. The Persecutions of Diocletian. L. Bell. $3.50.
  An attempt to vindicate Diocletian.
‡Thos. Hodgkin. Italy and her Invaders. 2 v. Macm. $8.00.
  A history of the Visigoths, Vandals, and Huns.
C. Kingsley. The Roman and the Teuton. Macm. $1.75.
W. E. H. Lecky. History of European Morals, from Augustus to Charlemagne. 2 v. App. $3.00.

‡The following belong to the series of Epochs of Ancient History:—
William Ihne. Early Rome. $1.00.
R. Bosworth Smith. Rome and Carthage. $1.00.
A. H. Beesly. The Gracchi, Marius, and Sulla. $1.00.
Chas. Merivale. The Roman Triumvirates. $1.00.
W. W. Capes. The Early Empire. $1.00.
Id. The Age of the Antonines. $1.00.

‡W. S. Teuffel. History of Roman Literature.† $7.50.
  The best German work. The best English works are:—
‡G. A. Simcox. History of Latin Literature. 2 v. H. $4.00.
‡C. T. Cruttwell. History of Roman Literature. Scr. $2.50.
  An excellent short manual is
L. Schmitz. History of Roman Literature. $1.25.

‡Th. Mommsen and J. Marquardt. Handbuch der Römischen Alterthümer. 7 v.† Lp. Hirzel. Vol. I., $4.40; Vol. II., Abth. 1, $4.80, Abth. 2, $3.30; Vol. III., not out yet; Vol. IV., $3.30; Vol. V., $4.05; Vol. VI., $4.05; Vol. VII., $6.60.
  Mommsen's part is Staatsrecht; Marquardt's, Staatsverwaltung. Neither is yet complete. This is the greatest work on Roman antiquities, superseding the earlier work by Becker and Marquardt (5 v. Lp.).
W. A. Becker. Gallus. $3.00.
  A treatise on antiquities in the form of a tale.

L. Lange. Römische Alterthümer. 3 v.† Ber. Weidmann. $8.45.
: This work, which is rather historical than systematic, reaches B.C. 30.

W. Ramsay. Manual of Roman Antiquities. L. Griffin. $3.00.
: Excellent when written, but now antiquated in many parts.

J. R. Seeley. First Book of Livy. Macm. $1.50.
: The introduction to this work contains the best discussion in English of the institutions of the period of the kings.

F. W. Newman. Regal Rome. N.Y. Redfield. 1852. 63 cents.
: Contains much interesting matter.

R. F. Leighton. History of Rome. N.Y. Clark & Maynard. $1.44.
: A school history, but contains the most complete statement in English of the latest results of scholarship.

W. T. Arnold. The Roman System of Provincial Administration. Macm. $1.75.

V. Rydberg. Roman Days. $2.00.
: Art and life under the empire.

Wm. Forsyth. Life of Cicero. Scr. $2.50.
: A good work; even better is that by

‡*Anthony Trollope.* 2 v. II. $3.50.
: It is distinguished for vivid and correct portraiture. Its view is favorable to Cicero.

J. A. Froude. Cæsar. Scr. $2.50.
: Brilliant, but not always accurate. It presents the most eulogistic view of Cæsar's character and career. The same view is presented in the Life of Julius Cæsar ascribed to the Emperor Napoleon III. [2 v. Scr.]

E. S. Beesly. Catiline, Clodius, and Tiberius. L. C. & H. $2.00.
: Able and interesting, by a distinguished positivist, in defence of these three characters. Tiberius also finds a defender in

F. Huidekoper. Judaism in Rome. [Note G.] N.Y. Francis. $2.25.

Thos. De Quincey. The Cæsars. Houghton. $1.50.
: An entertaining sketch.

Earl Stanhope. Life of Belisarius. L. $3.50.

Montesquieu's Grandeur and Decadence of the Romans, translated by John Baker. App. $2.00.
> An old work of much value.

See article by *Goldwin Smith* in Cont. Rev., May, 1878, on the Greatness of the Romans.

Authorities.

Translations of the classic authors may be found in Bohn's Classical Library, republished by Harper; besides these, we will mention

Herodotus, — Oriental history, and the Persian wars, — translated by Geo. Rawlinson. 4 v. $10.00.

Thucydides, — Peloponnesian War, — translated by B. Jowett. Macm. $8.00.

Xenophon, — continuation of Thucydides, and expedition of Cyrus the Younger. $2.00.

Livy. — Roman history, — [to 390] translated by Geo. Baker. N.Y. Worthington. $7.50.
> Finely illustrated.

Polybius, — the chief authority for the Second Punic War, — translated by Hampton.

Sallust. — Jugurthine War and Conspiracy of Catiline, — translated by A. W. Pollard. Macm. $1.60.

Cæsar, — civil and foreign wars, from B.C. 58 to 45. $2.00.

Tacitus. — the Roman empire, A.D. 14 to 70, with some interruptions, — translated by Church and Brodribb. Macm. $2.00.

Suetonius, — lives of the Cæsars, — translated by Thomson. $1.75.

Plutarch, — biographies, — translated by A. H. Clough. L. & B. $3.00.

Josephus, — Jewish wars. $2.00.

HISTORICAL LITERATURE AND AUTHORITIES. 257

9. MEDIÆVAL AND MODERN HISTORY.

‡*H. Hallam.* Middle Ages. 3 v. N.Y. $5.25.
A sound and scholarly work, incomplete in certain parts (*e.g.*, the north of Europe), and superseded in others by recent investigations, but still indispensable.

‡*F. Guizot.* Lectures on the History of Civilization in France and in Europe. 4 v. App. $5.60.
Likewise indispensable, and still containing the best view in English of feudal society.

J. Balmes. European Civilization.† Baltimore. Murphy. $3.00.
A comparison of Protestantism and Catholicism in their relation to civilization, by a Catholic writer.

F. Ozanam. History of Civilization in the Fifth Century.† Lip. $3.50.
A work of eloquence and spiritual power.

C. J. Stillé. Studies in Mediæval History. Lip. $2.00.
An excellent course of lectures; especially good in the history of civilization, less satisfactory in that of institutions.

‡*A. M. Curteis.* History of the Roman Empire. Lip. $1.50.
From A.D. 395 to 800; with good maps. The best brief sketch of this period.

‡*R. W. Church* The Beginnings of the Middle Ages. [E.S.] $1.00.
Covers a somewhat later period; from A.D. 500 to 1000.

P. Lacroix. Manners, Customs, and Dress in the Middle Ages.† App. $12.00.

Id. The Arts in the Middle Ages.† App. $12.00.

Id. Science and Literature in the Middle Ages.† L. Bickers. $12.00.
Finely illustrated works, of the highest value.

E. L. Cutts. Scenes and Characters in the Middle Ages. L. Virtue. $5.00.
With good illustrations of manners, customs, etc.

J. J. Sheppard. The Fall of Rome and the Rise of the New Nationalities. N.Y. $2.50.
A good manual for students.

‡*E. A. Freeman.* Historical Essays. Series 1 and 3. Macm. $3.00.
Series 1 treats of mediæval history; Series 3, of Eastern Europe.

V. *Rydberg.* Magic of the Middle Ages.† Holt. $1.75.

‡*H. von Sybel.* History and Literature of the Crusades.† C. & H. 10s. 6d.

J. F. Michaud. History of the Crusades. 4 v.† N.Y. Redfield. $3.75.

Sir G. W. Cox. The Crusades. [E.S.] $1.00.

G. Z. Gray. The Children's Crusade. Houghton. $1.50.
>Michaud's is the standard history of the crusades; Cox's, the best short sketch; Sybel's work presents the best results of scholarship.

C. Mills. History of Chivalry. 2 v. Ph. Carey & Lea. $1.25.
>The standard work upon the subject.

E. Viollet-le-duc. Annals of a Fortress.† B. $5.00.
>By a distinguished architect and historian.

E. L. Cutts. Constantine. Soc. $1.05.

Id. Charlemagne. Soc. $1.05.

F. C. Woodhouse. Military Religious Orders of the Middle Ages. Soc. $1.05.
>Excellent books of a popular character.

A. L. Koeppen. The World in the Middle Ages. 2 v. App. $3.00.
>A thorough and accurate geography of the middle ages, with an atlas.

F. de Coulanges. Institutions Politiques de l'Ancienne France.† 2 v. P. Hachette. $5.25.
>A brilliant but not always trustworthy description of political society in the beginning of the middle ages.

W. Smyth. Lectures upon Modern History. B. Mussey.

‡*T. Arnold.* Lectures on Modern History. App. $1.50.
>These courses of lectures are old, but valuable.

T. H. Dyer. History of Modern Europe. 5 v. Bell. $22.50.
>The best work, extending from 1453 to 1871.

C. D. Yonge. Three Centuries of Modern History. App. $2.00.
>A popular and interesting sketch.

James White. Eighteen Christian Centuries. App. $2.00.
An entertaining popular outline of history from the Christian era.

‡*A. H. L. Heeren.* Manual of the History of the Political System of Europe and its Colonies.† $1.50.

Id. Historical Treatises.† $5.00.
Heeren's writings are of the highest excellence.

E. J. Payne. History of European Colonies. [Freeman's Hist. Series.] Holt. $1.10.

F. C. Schlosser. History of the Eighteenth Century.† 8 v. C. & H.

---

10. ECCLESIASTICAL HISTORY.

‡*H. H. Milman.* The History of Christianity from the Birth of Christ to the Abolition of Paganism in the Roman Empire. 3 v. N.Y. Armstrong. $5.25.

‡*Id.* History of Latin Christianity. 8 v. N.Y. Armstrong. $14.00.
The best general history of the church in the middle ages; reaching the end of the pontificate of Nicholas V., 1455.

J. C. L. Gieseler. A Text-book of Church History.† 5 v. H. $5.25.
The standard complete history of the church.

J. Alzog. Manual of Universal Church History.† 3 v. Cincinnati. Clarke. $15.00.
From a Catholic point of view; fair and learned.

J. J. Döllinger. The First Age of Christianity. 2 v. $6.00.
Also by a Catholic of great learning and reputation.

E. Rénan. [Hibbert Lect., 1880.] The Influence of the Institutions, etc., of Rome upon Christianity. W. & N. $3.50.

F. D. Maurice. Lectures on the Ecclesiastical History of the First and Second Centuries. Macm. $3.50.

J. H. Newman. Historical Sketches. 3 v. L. Pickering. $6.00.
Chiefly connected with church history.

R. C. Trench. Lectures on Mediæval Church History. Scr. $3.00.
A good popular sketch.

C. Hardwick. A History of the Christian Church. Middle Ages. Macm. $2.25.
Id. The Reformation. Macm. $2.25.
> Excellent compendiums of handy reference.

A. R. Pennington. Epochs of the Papacy. L. Bell. 10s. 6d.
> A book of much merit; from the point of view of the Church of England.

J. F. Clarke. Events and Epochs of Religious History. Osgood. $3.00.

J. H. Allen. Christian History in its Three Great Periods. 3 v. R. $3.75.
> Academic lectures. Early Christianity; the Middle Ages; Modern Phases.

H. C. Lea. A History of Sacerdotal Celibacy. Houghton. $3.75.
Id. Studies in Church History [Temporal Power; Benefit of Clergy; Excommunication]. Ph. Lea. $2.75.
Id. Superstition and Force [Wager of Law and Battle; Ordeal; Torture]. Ph. Lea. $2.50.
> Books of sound and independent scholarship.

T. Greenwood. Cathedra Petri. 6 v. L. Dickinson & Higham. $3.00.
> A political history of the Papacy, ending 1420.

M. Creighton. The Papacy during the Reformation. 2 v. Houghton. $10.00.
> The two volumes published extend from 1378 to 1464.

Sir J. Stephen. Essays in Ecclesiastical Biography. Longm. 7s. 6d.
A. F. Villemain. Life of Gregory VII.† 3 v. Bentley. 26s.
J. C. Morison. Life and Times of St. Bernard. Macm. $2.00.
Baron Hübner. Life and Times of Sixtus V.† Longm. 24s.

The Fathers for English Readers. Soc. 10 v. Each, 75 cents.
The Conversion of the West. Soc. 5 v. Each, 60 cents.
> Two series of small works of merit.

The Reformation Period.

G. P. Fisher. History of the Reformation. Scr. $3.00.
: An excellent work.

‡*L. Häusser.* Period of the Reformation.† N.Y. $2.50.
: A course of lectures of high scholarship and historic insight.

M. J. Spalding. History of the Protestant Reformation. Baltimore. Murphy. $3.50.
: By the Catholic archbishop of Baltimore. See also his Miscellanies. 2 v.

‡*F. Seebohm.* History of the Protestant Revolution. [E.S.] $1.00.
: A compendium of great accuracy and value.

J. H. Merle D'Aubigné. History of the Reformation.† 5 v. N.Y. Carter. $4.50.
: Ultra-Protestant in tone.

‡*L. von Ranke.* History of the Popes.† 3 v. L. Bell. $3.75.
: The best history of the period of the Reformation, from a political point of view.

C. Beard. [Hibbert Lect., 1883.] The Reformation of the 16th Century in its Relation to Modern Thought. W. & N. 10s. 6d.

J. H. Treadwell. Martin Luther and his Work. [New Plutarch.] Put. $1.00.

R. B. Drummond. Erasmus, his Life and Character. 2 v. S. & E.

D. Strauss. Ulrich von Hutten.† L. Daldy. 10s. 6d.

H. Morley. Clement Marot. 2 v. C. & H. 18s.

K. Benrath. Bernardino Ochino of Siena.† L. Nisbet. 9s.

R. C. Christie. Etienne Dolet. Macm. $5.00.
: These are persons whose lives illustrate some special phase of the Reformation.

P. Sarpi. History of the Council of Trent.
: Ranked by Macaulay with Thucydides.

J. A. Wylie. History of Protestantism. 3 v. C. $15.00.

See essays on Luther by *Stephen, Carlyle, Froude,* and *Mozley;* also his Table Talk, and *Erasmus'* Colloquies. A life of Luther, by *Peter Bayne,* is in preparation; also a translation of *Köstlin's* popular work, to be published by Scribner.

For Reference.

W. Smith. Dictionary of Christian Antiquities. 2 v. M. $7.00.
Id. Dictionary of Christian Biography. 2 v. M. $11.00.
P. Schaff. Religious Encyclopædia [based on that of Herzog]. 3 v. N.Y. Funk & Wagnalls. $6.00.

---

11. HISTORY OF ENGLAND, IRELAND, AND SCOTLAND.

David Hume. History of England. 6 v. Lip. $6.00.
    In elegant style, with strong Tory bias; is excellent in social history, but lacks accurate scholarship.
J. Lingard. History of England. 13 v. $20.00.
    A Catholic work, able and scholarly. This, like Hume, comes down only to 1688.
C. Knight. The Popular History of England. 8 v. Ph. $10.00.
    Liberal in tone, with abundant illustrations.
‡*J. R. Green.* History of the English People. 4 v. H. $10.00.
    The best history of England; its fault is in disregarding too much the chronological order.
Id. A Short History of the English People. H. $1.75.
    An earlier work of similar character.
‡*J. F. Bright.* English History for the Use of Public Schools. 3 v. N.Y. Dutton. 17s.
    An excellent work; especially good for reference. Both Bright and Green have numerous maps and genealogical tables.
J. S. Brewer. The Student's Hume. H. $1.25.
    More than an abridgment. The editor has added accuracy and liberality of tone.
The Pictorial History of England. 8 v. £5.
    A work of solid merit, with numerous illustrations.
Sir James Mackintosh. History of England.
    In Lardner's Cyclopædia.
Miss E. Thompson. History of England. Holt. [Freeman's Historical Series.] 80 cents.

HISTORICAL LITERATURE AND AUTHORITIES. 263

‡*J. H. Burton.* History of Scotland. 8 v. and index. Ed. Blackwood. Each, 7s. 6d.
    The best history of Scotland.

Miss M. Macarthur. History of Scotland. Holt. [Freeman's Historical Series.] 80 cents.

E. M. Robertson. Scotland under her Early Kings. 2 v. Ed. Edmonston. 36s.
    Reaches the end of the thirteenth century. Able and scholarly, but confused in arrangement.

W. F. Skene. Celtic Scotland. 3 v. Ed. Edmonston. Each, 15s.
    The most complete work upon Scottish antiquities.

‡*C. G. Walpole.* The Kingdom of Ireland. II. $1.75
    An excellent history of Ireland, with very good maps; reaches 1800.

W. Dolby. History of Ireland. N.Y. Virtue. $10.00.

J. H. McCarthy. Outline of Irish History. Baltimore. Murphy. 75 cents.

---

‡*Mrs. E. S. Armitage.* The Childhood of the English Nation. Put. $1.25.
    An admirable sketch; reaches 1199.

‡*E. A. Freeman.* Old English History. Macm. $1.50.
    The Anglo-Saxon period; originally written for the young.

Id. Short History of the Norman Conquest. Macm. 60 cents.

‡*Id.* History of the Norman Conquest. 5 v. and index. Macm. $20.00.
    Mr. Freeman's greatest work, and the best history of the period.

Id. History of William Rufus. Macm. $8.00.
    A continuation of the above.

A. Thierry. History of the Norman Conquest.† 2 v. L. Bell. Each, 3s. 6d.
    Brilliant, but resting upon unsound theories.

C. Elton. Origins of English History. L. Quaritch. $8.00.
    A work of great learning and research; embracing the Celtic period and the Anglo-Saxon conquest.

‡ *J. Rhys.* Celtic Britain. Soc. 75 cents.
By an eminent Celtic scholar. It gives a history of the Celtic nationalities of Britain through the eleventh century.

‡ *Grant Allen.* Anglo-Saxon Britain. Soc. 75 cents.
The author opposes Freeman's view of an exclusively Teutonic character of the English nationality.

‡ *J. R. Green.* The Making of England. II. $2.50.
Describes graphically and in detail the events of the Anglo-Saxon conquest and the Heptarchy.

J. M. Kemble. The Saxons in England. 2 v. L. Quaritch. 24s.
Old, but full of valuable material.

Thos. Nicholas. Pedigree of the English People. Longm. 16s.
Argues for a large Celtic element in the English people.

E. Guest. Origines Celticae. 2 v. Macm. $9.00.
An unfinished work containing papers of remarkable merit, especially in relation to the Anglo-Saxon conquest.

J. M. Lappenberg. History of England under the Anglo-Saxon Kings. 2 v. L. Bell. Each, 3s. 6d.

Id. History of England under the Norman Kings. 15s.
Scholarly works, but partly superseded by later writers.

W. Longman. Lectures on the Early History of England. Longm. 15s.

C. H. Pearson. England during the Early and Middle Ages. 2 v. L. Bell. 14s.
Reaches death of Edward I.; of great value in political and constitutional history.

Id. Historical Maps of England. L. Bell. £1 11s. 6d.
Illustrates especially the social and political condition of the middle ages. Contains material not to be found elsewhere.

W. H. Blaauw. The Barons' War. L. Bell. 10s. 6d.
An excellent monograph on the times of Montfort.

Greatest of all the Plantagenets. L. Bentley. 12s.
A history of Edward I.; very eulogistic, but on the whole sound.

‡ *W. Longman.* History of the Life and Times of Edward III. 2 v. Longm. 28s.
The most important work for the history of England in the fourteenth century.

‡*C. H. Pearson.* English History in the Fourteenth Century. L. Rivingtons. 3s. 6d.
>An excellent short history.

G. M. Towle. History of Henry V. App. $2.50.

Miss C. A. Halsted. Richard III. Ph. Carey.
>An attempt to vindicate his character.

Jas. Gairdner. Life and Reign of Richard the Third. Longm. 10s. 6d.
>Sustains the traditionary view.

‡*J. A. Froude.* History of England from the Fall of Wolsey to the Death of Elizabeth. 12 v. Scr. $18.00.
>Reaches only 1588. A fascinating narration, friendly to Henry VIII.; deficient in judicial qualities.

Miss Lucy Aikin. Memoirs of the Court of Queen Elizabeth. Longm. 3s. 6d.
>An old but valuable book.

‡*L. von Ranke.* History of England.† 6 v. Macm. $16.00.
>A work of the highest value and importance; embraces the sixteenth, seventeenth, and eighteenth centuries.

‡*S. R. Gardiner.* History of England: 1. From the accession of James I. to the disgrace of Coke, 2 vols.; 2. The Spanish marriage; 3. Under the Duke of Buckingham and Charles I., 2 vols.; 4. Personal government of Charles I., 2 vols.; 5. Fall of the Monarchy of Charles I., 2 vols. Longm. Each, 12s.
>Mr. Gardiner is the highest authority upon this period. A new and cheaper edition of the combined work is now publishing.

Earl of Clarendon. History of the Rebellion. 6 v. Ox. £1 2s.
>The author, as Sir Edward Hyde, was a leading actor in the events.

‡*B. M. Cordery and J. S. Phillpotts.* King and Commonwealth. Ph. Porter & Coates. $1.75.
>An excellent sketch; from 1603 to 1660.

F. Guizot. 1. History of the English Revolution of 1640; 2. England under Oliver Cromwell, 2 v.; 3. Under Richard Cromwell, 2 v.; 4. History of Monk.† L. Per vol., 3s. 6d.

A. Bisset. History of the Struggle for Parliamentary Government in England. 2 v. 21s.

Id. History of the Commonwealth of England from the Death of Charles I. to the Expulsion of the Long Parliament by Cromwell. 2 v. 30s.
> An able exposition of the parliamentary side.

J. Forster. The Arrest of the Five Members by Charles I. M. 12s.

Id. The Grand Remonstrance. M. 12s.

‡*F. von Raumer.* The Political History of England during the 16th, 17th, and 18th Centuries. 2 v.† £1 10s.
> By a distinguished German historian.

‡*T. B. Macaulay.* History of England. 5 v. H. $2.50.
> Strongly Whig; a brilliant work; unfinished; covers the reigns of James II. and William III., with a general sketch of that of Charles II.

‡*Sir James Mackintosh.* History of the Revolution of 1688.
> An able work; also Whig. Unfinished.

C. J. Fox. History of James II. Scr. $1.25.

J. H. Burton. History of the Reign of Queen Anne. 3 v. Scr. $13.50.
> Whig; by the author of the history of Scotland.

Earl Stanhope. History of the Reign of Queen Anne. 2 v. M. 10s.

Id. History of England from the Peace of Utrecht to the Peace of Versailles [1713 to 1783]. 7 v. M.
> These two works give the history of the eighteenth century from a Tory point of view.

‡*W. E. H. Lecky.* History of England in the 18th Century. 4 v. App. $9.00.
> Not yet finished; from a Whig point of view.

J. Ashton. Social Life in the Reign of Queen Anne. Scr. $9.00.
> Graphic and accurate.

J. A. Froude. The English in Ireland in the 18th Century. 3 v. Scr. $3.00.
> Written with a strong English bias.

J. Adolphus. A History of England from the Accession of George III. to 1803. 7 v. Each, 14s.

HISTORICAL LITERATURE AND AUTHORITIES. 267

W. Massey. A History of England during the Reign of George the Third. 4 v. Each, 6s.
  Massey is Whig ; Adolphus, Tory.

Miss H. Martineau. History of the Peace [to 1854].* 4 v. B. Walker. $10.00.

S. Walpole. History of England from the Conclusion of the Great War in 1815 to 1841. 3 v. Longm. £2 14s.

W. N. Molesworth. History of England from 1830 to 1874. 3 v. C. & H. $6.00.

‡*J. McCarthy.* History of Our Own Times. 2 v. H. $2.50.

H. M. Hozier. Invasions of England. 2 v. Macm. $8.00.

‡*S. R. Gardiner.* Introduction to English History. [In English History for Students.] N.Y. Holt. 80 cents.

R. Pauli. Pictures of Old England.† Macm. 6s.
  Belonging to mediæval history.

Miss C. M. Yonge. Cameos from English History. Macm. $5.00.
  Four series, covering mediæval history.

J. Gairdner and J. Spedding. Studies in English History. Ed. Douglas. 12s.
  Belonging to the fifteenth, sixteenth, and seventeenth centuries.

A. C. Ewald. Stories from the State Papers. Houghton. $3.00.
  Belonging to the same period.

T. B. Macaulay. Essays. 4 v. Houghton. $5.00.
  Devoted chiefly to modern English history.

J. S. Brewer. English Studies. M. 14s.

‡*J. E. T. Rogers.* History of Agriculture and Prices. 4 v. Macm. $23.00.
  Covers the fourteenth, fifteenth, and sixteenth centuries.

F. Seebohm. The English Village Community. Longm.

W. Cunningham. Growth of English Industry and Commerce. C. $3.00.

C. Hole. Genealogical Stemma of the Kings of England and France. Macm. 1s.

‡*Epochs of Modern History.* Scr.

W. Stubbs. The Early Plantagenets. $1.00.
W. Warburton. Edward III. $1.00.
J. Gairdner. The Houses of Lancaster and York. $1.00.
M. Creighton. The Age of Elizabeth. $1.00.
S. R. Gardiner. The Puritan Revolution. $1.00.
E. Hale. The Fall of the Stuarts. $1.00.
E. E. Morris. The Age of Anne. $1.00.
J. McCarthy. Epoch of Reform. 1830–1850. $1.00.

Epochs of English History. E. & L. 50 cents each.

F. York-Powell. Early England [to 1066].
L. Creighton. England a Continental Power [to 1066].
J. Rowley. The Rise of the People and the Growth of Parliament [to 1485].
M. Creighton. The Tudors and the Reformation [to 1603].
B. M. Gardiner. The Struggle against Absolute Monarchy [to 1688].
J. Rowley. The Settlement of the Constitution [to 1778].
O. W. Tancock. England during the American and European Wars [to 1820].
T. Arnold. Modern England [to 1875].

Biographies.

‡Alfred the Great. By *R. Pauli.*† Scr. $2.00.
Id. By *Thomas Hughes.* [Sunday Library.] Macm. $1.75.
St. Anselm. By *R. W. Church.* [Sunday Library.] Macm. $1.75.
Id. By *M. Rule.* [Catholic.] 2 v. L. Paul. 32s.
Becket. Articles by *J. A. Froude,* Nineteenth Century, 1877.
Id. By *E. A. Freeman* [in reply; more favorable], Cont. Rev., 1878.
Richard Cœur de Lion. By *G. P. R. James.* 2 v. Scr. $2.80.

HISTORICAL LITERATURE AND AUTHORITIES. 269

‡Simon de Montfort. By *R. Pauli.*† L. Trübner. 6s.
Id. By *G. W. Prothero*. [More a history than biography.] Longm. 9s.
‡Wyclif. By *G. Lechler.*† 2 v. L. Paul. 21s.
Lives of English Popular Leaders. By *C. E. Maurice*. 1. Stephen Langton; 2. Tyler, Ball, Oldcastle. L. King. Each, 7s. 6d.
Historical Gleanings. By *J. E. T. Rogers*. 1. Walpole, Adam Smith; 2. Wyclif, Laud, Wilkes, Horne Tooke. Macm. 1st, $1.50; 2d, $1.75.
Whittington. By *W. Besant and J. Rice*. [New Plutarch.] Put. $1.00.
Sir Walter Raleigh. By *E. Edwards*. 2 v. Macm. $9.00
‡Bacon. By *J. Spedding*. 2 v. Houghton. $5.00.

For the Period of the English Revolution.

Strafford. By *Miss E. Cooper*. 2 v. L. Tinsley. 30s.
Eliot. By *J. Forster*. 2 v. C. & H. 14s.
‡Cromwell. By *Thos. Carlyle*. [Letters and Speeches.] 5 v. Scr. $18.00.
‡Id. By *J. A. Picton*. C. $2.50.
Id. By *Paxton Hood*. N.Y. Funk & Wagnalls. $1.00.
J. B. *Mozley*. Essays. [Strafford, Laud, Cromwell.] 2 v. L. 24s.
Three English Statesmen. By *G. Smith*. [Pym, Cromwell.] H. $1.50.
Statesmen of the Commonwealth. By *J. Forster*. $2.25.
Chief Actors in the Puritan Revolution By *P. Bayne*. L. Clarke. 12s.
‡Milton. By *D. Masson*. 6 v. Macm. $34.00.
Contains a minute history of the times.

W. Carstares. By *R. H. Story*. Macm. $3.00.
A prominent actor in the Scotch union.
Marlborough. By *W. Coxe*. 3 v. L. Bell. Each, 3s. 6d.

Sir R. Walpole. By A. C. Ewald. C. & H. 18s.
C. E. Stuart. By A. C. Ewald. 2 v. C. & H. £1 18s.
Lord Shelburne. By Lord E. Fitzmaurice. 3 v. Macm. 16s.
‡C. J. Fox. By G. O. Trevelyan. II. $2.50.
‡William Pitt. By Earl Stanhope. II. $2.50.
Id. By Goldwin Smith. [Three English Statesmen.] II. $1.50.

Lord Campbell. Lives of the Chief Justices. 4 v. L. & B. $7.00.
Id. Lives of the Chancellors. 10 v. L. & B. $17.50.
Mrs. A. Strickland. Lives of the Queens of England. 6 v. Lip. $12.00.
A. C. Ewald. Representative Statesmen. [Strafford to Palmerston.] 2 v. C. & H. £1 4s.
C. A. Sainte-Beuve. English Portraits.† Holt. $2.00.
D. O. Maddyn. Chiefs of Parties. [Fox, Pitt, etc.] 21s.

History of Religion.

‡R. W. Dixon. History of the Church of England. 2 v. Routledge. Each, 16s.
> The most thorough and important work; not yet completed.

‡J. H. Blunt. The Reformation of the Church of England. 2 v. N.Y. Young. $8.50.
> The best complete history; extends from 1514 to 1662. From the point of view of the Church of England.

J. J. Blunt. Sketch of the Reformation in England. Young. $1.50.
> An excellent short sketch.

Cunningham Geikie. The English Reformation: How it came about, and why we should uphold it. App. $2.00.
> A popular and rather one-sided work.

W. Cobbett. History of the Protestant Reformation in England and Ireland. N.Y. Sadlier. 75 cents.
> A violent attack upon the English Reformation, by a nominal Protestant. For the Catholic view, see Lingard and Spalding.

F. Seebohm. The Oxford Reformers. Longm. 14s.
Diocesan Histories [Canterbury, Durham, etc.]. Soc.

Constitutional History.

‡ *W. Stubbs.* Constitutional History of England. 3 v. Macm. $7.80.

‡ *H. Hallam.* Constitutional History of England. 3 v. N.Y. Armstrong. $5.25.

‡ *T. E. May.* Constitutional History of England. 2 v. N.Y. Armstrong. $2.50.

These three works form a connected series, Hallam beginning 1485, where Stubbs ends, and ending 1760, where May begins.

Sheldon Amos. Fifty Years of the English Constitution. L. & B.

T. P. Taswell-Langmead. Constitutional History of England. $7.50.

The best compendium of the subject.

P. V. Smith. History of English Institutions. Lip. $1.50.

A good short work, with a peculiar arrangement.

E. A. Freeman. Growth of the English Constitution. Macm. $2.00.

H. Adams [and others]. Essays in Anglo-Saxon Law. L. & B. $4.00.

M. M. Bigelow. History of Anglo-Norman Procedure. L. & B. $5.00.

Sir Jas. Stephen. History of the Criminal Law of England. 3 v. Macm.

See also the following articles: by *J. E. T. Rogers*, on The Black Death, Fortn. Rev., 1866; the Peasants' War, Id.; History of Rent in England, Cont. Rev., April, 1880; by *F. Seebohm*, on The Black Death, Fortn. Rev., 1865–66; by *Grant Allen*, Are we English? in Fortn. Rev., Oct., 1880 [presenting Celtic argument]; by *F. Harrison*, on Law of Treason, in Fortn. Rev., Sept., 1882; by *Goldwin Smith*, on the Greatness of England, in Cont. Rev., Dec., 1878; by *F. Seebohm*, Historical Claims of Tenant Rights, in 19th Cent., Jan., 1881; also on Land Tenures in England and in Ireland, in Fort. Rev., 1870; by *R. D. Osborn*, Another Side of a Popular Story [India], in Fort. Rev., Aug., 1882.

Authorities.

‡*J. Bass Mullinger.* Authorities [in English History for Students]. N.Y. Holt. $1.80.
: A compendious view of the principal authorities.

‡*C. K. Adams.* Questions and Notes on English Constitutional History. Ann Arbor. Sheehan.
: A complete and accurate guide to the authorities. A less full guide will be found in Prof. Short's Reference Lists, referred to elsewhere.

Jas. Gairdner. Early Chroniclers of Europe. England. Soc. $1.20.
: An interesting account of the English chronicles. Translations of most of the chronicles will be found in Bohn's Library. Bell.

Froissart's Chronicles [fourteenth century]. N.Y. Leavitt & Allen. $12.00.

J. E. T. Rogers. Loci e libro veritatis. Macm. $2.75.
: Belongs to the fifteenth century.

Id. The Paston Letters. 4 v. L. Arber.
: A collection of family letters, of the time of the War of the Roses.

D'Ewes' Autobiography and Correspondence. 2 v. L. Bentley. £1 8s.

The Fairfax Correspondence. 4 v. L. Bentley. £3.

S. Pepys. Diary and Correspondence. Scr. $2.00.

J. Evelyn. Diary and Correspondence. Scr. $1.75.
: These two works present a vivid picture of society in the last half of the seventeenth century.

H. Walpole. Letters. 9 v. Scr. $33.75.
: Full of information for the middle of the eighteenth century.

Cobbett's Parliamentary History, continued in *Hansard's* Parliamentary Debates.

Rymer's Fœdera [collection of treaties].

The publications of the Master of the Rolls.

The publications of the Camden Society, and similar societies.

12. HISTORY OF FRANCE.

‡*F. Guizot.* History of France.† 8 v. $40.00.
: Handsomely illustrated. The best large history of France in English.

‡*G. W. Kitchin.* History of France. 3 v. Macm. $7.80.
: The best English work.

H. W. Jervis. Student's History of France. II. $1.25.
: An excellent small work, with instructive illustrations.

J. Michelet. History of France. 2 v.† App. $4.00.
: Very learned, and very brilliant, but too abounding in theory.

F. Guizot and G. Masson. Concise History of France.† E. & L. $3.00.

‡*P. Lacombe.* The Growth of a People.† Holt. $1.00.
: An admirable work, descriptive of the development of the nation.

Parke Godwin. History of France. Vol. I. II. $3.00.
: An excellent history of the period before Charlemagne. No other volumes were published.

H. Martin. History of France (during the reigns of Louis XIV. and Louis XV.). 3 v.† B. E. & L. $10.50.
: Martin's is considered the best history of France.

Sir Jas. Stephen. Lectures on the History of France. II. $3.00.
: An admirable commentary upon French history.

Miss C. M. Yonge. History of France. [Freeman's Hist. Series.] Holt. 80 cents.

F. Guizot. St. Louis and Calvin. [Sunday Library.] Macm.

D. F. Jamison. Life and Times of Bertrand du Guesclin. 2 v. Lip. $14.00.

Janet Tuckey. Joan of Arc. Put. [New Plutarch.] $1.00.

Harriet Parr. Life and Death of Jeanne d'Arc. 2 v. S. & E. 6s.

T. Willert. The Reign of Louis the Eleventh. Put. $1.50.

‡*H. M. Baird.* History of the Rise of the Huguenots. 2 v. Scr. $5.00.
: The best history of the subject.

W. Besant. Coligny and the Failure of the French Reformation. [New Plutarch.] Put.

Duc d'Aumale. History of the Princes of the House of Condé.† 2 v. L. Bentley. 30s.
L. Ranke. Civil Wars and Monarchy in France.† H. $1.50.
Lady Jackson. The Old Régime. Holt. $2.25.
    A vivid picture of society under Louis XV.
Duc de Broglie. The King's Secret (Louis XV.).† 2 v. C. $5.00.
    Has special reference to Polish affairs.
G. Masson. Early Chroniclers of Europe. France. Soc. $1.20.
Memoirs of Commines (Louis XI.), Sully (Henry IV.), and others.

Revolutionary Period, etc.

A. Young. Travels in France during the Years 1787–89. 2 v.
    The best contemporary picture of the condition of France before the Revolution.
A. de Tocqueville. The Ancient Régime.† H. $1.50.
    An analysis of the political condition of France at the same time.
C. D. Yonge. Life of Marie Antoinette. H. $2.50.
    A popular work.
H. Vizetelly. Story of the Diamond Necklace. Scr. $2.25.
    A vivid picture of society under the Old Regime. See also Carlyle's essay upon the same subject.
C. K. Adams. Democracy and Monarchy in France. Holt. $2.50.
    An excellent sketch of recent French history.
H. A. Taine. The Ancient Régime.† Holt. $2.50.
Id. The French Revolution. 2 v.† Holt. $5.00.
    Not so much history as commentary; very unfavorable to the revolutionists.
‡*H. V. Sybel.* History of the French Revolution. 4 v.† M. 48s.
    The best and most important history.
T. Carlyle. History of the French Revolution. 3 v. Scr. $2.40.
    Remarkable for graphic power.
Edmund Burke. Reflections on the French Revolution.
    A bitter attack upon the revolution while still in progress; replied to by —
Sir Jas. Mackintosh. Vindiciae Gallicae.

A. Thiers. The French Revolution.† 4 v. App. $8.00.
Id. The Consulate and Empire.† 5 v. Claxton. $12.50.
>Thiers' works are written from an intensely French point of view. His excessive laudation may be balanced by —

Sir A. Alison. History of Europe from 1789 to 1815. 8 v. H. $16.00.
>Strongly Tory.

‡*P. Lanfrey.* History of Napoleon I. 4 v.† Macm. $12.50.
>An incomplete work. Impartial in tone, but severe in judgment. See also Channing's article on Napoleon Bonaparte.

W. Hazlitt. Life of Napoleon Bonaparte. 3 v. Lip. $4.50.
>Perhaps the best English work favorable to Napoleon.

H. Van Laun. The French Revolutionary Epoch. 2 v. App. $3.50.
>Comes down to 1870, but is much fullest in the earlier parts.

C. A. Fyffe. History of Europe (beginning 1879). 2 v. Holt. Vol. I., $2.50.

‡*Mrs. B. M. Gardiner.* French Revolution. [E.S.] E. & L. $1.00.
>Presents the results of the latest scholarship.

W. O. Morris. The French Revolution and First Empire. [E.S.] Scr. $1.00.
>Valuable for an admirable bibliography by Hon. A. D. White.

J. Wilson. Studies of Modern Mind and Character. Longm. 20s.
>Contains some excellent essays on French revolutionary history.

W. F. P. Napier. History of the War in the Peninsula. 5 v. N.Y. Armstrong. $7.50.

Earl Stanhope. The French Retreat from Moscow. M. 7s. 6d.
>This volume contains other valuable historical essays.

C. Adams. Great Campaigns [1796–1820]. Ed. Blackwood. 6s.
C. C. Chesney. Waterloo Lectures. Longm. 10s. 6d.
Dorsey Gardner. Quatre-Bras, Ligny, and Waterloo. Houghton. $5.00.
>The best popular history of this campaign.

Louis Blanc. History of Ten Years. 1830–40. L. £1 6s.
>By a radical republican.

A. de Lamartine. History of the Revolution of 1848. Scr. $1.40.
>Lamartine was at the head of the provisional government.

Memoirs of Mad. de Rémusat.† (1802-8.) App. $2.00.
A graphic picture of the court of Napoleon, by one of Josephine's maids of honor.

Correspondence of Prince Talleyrand and Louis XVIII. (1814-15.) Scr. $1.00.
Especially in relation to the Congress of Vienna.

13. Special Histories.

‡ The following series of works (Lip.) form a connecting link between mediæval and modern history: —

J. F. Kirk. History of Charles the Bold. 3 v. Lip. $9.00.
W. H. Prescott. History of Ferdinand and Isabella. 3 v. Lip. $4.50.
W. Robertson. History of Charles V. 3 v. [Edited by Prescott.] $4.50.
W. H. Prescott. History of Philip II. 3 v. [Unfinished.] $4.50.

‡ The following works (H.) form a good continuation: —

J. L. Motley. Rise of the Dutch Republic. 3 v. H. $6.00.
Id. History of the United Netherlands. 4 v. H. $8.00.
Id. John of Olden-Barneveldt. 2 v. H. $4.00.

J. Van Praet. Essays on the Political History of the 15th, 16th, and 17th Centuries. L. Bentley.
W. Menzel. History of Germany.† 3 v. L. Bell. $4.20.
The best large work in English.
J. Sime. History of Germany. [Freeman's Hist. Series.] 80 cents.
Bayard Taylor. History of Germany. H. $1.75.
C. T. Lewis. History of Germany. H. $1.50.
Both these short histories are based upon that of Müller.
‡ W. Coxe. History of House of Austria. 3 v. Bohn.
A book of great accuracy and value.
T. L. Kington-Oliphant. History of Frederic II. 2 v. Macm.
A valuable contribution to the history of the thirteenth century.

T. Carlyle. History of Frederick the Great. 6 v. H. $7.50.
A work of great industry, but in Carlyle's worst style, and unduly laudatory.

Duc de Broglie. Frederic the Great and Maria Theresa.† L. Low. 30s.
In the time of the First Silesian War, 1740–42.

W. Spalding. Hist. of Italy and the Italian Islands. 3 v. H. $2.25.
A good compendium; more recent is —

W. Hunt. History of Italy. [Freeman's Hist. Series.] Holt. 80 cts.

J. C. L. de Sismondi. History of the Italian Republics. H. 75 cts.
An abridgment of the author's large work.

‡*J. A. Symonds.* Age of the Despots. Holt. $3.50.
The best history of Italy in the last century of the middle ages. With "The Revival of Learning" and "The Fine Arts" it forms a series entitled "The Renaissance in Italy."

T. A. Trollope. History of the Commonwealth of Florence. 4 v. Macm. $10.00.

Mrs. Oliphant. The Makers of Florence. Macm. $3.00.
Sketches of Florentine history in the close of the middle ages.

Id. Francis of Assisi. [Sunday Library.] Macm. $1.75.

R. W. Church. Dante. Macm. $1.75.
Contains a translation of the treatise "De Monarchia."

A. v. Reumont. Lorenzo de' Medici.† 2 v. S. & E. 30s.
A scholarly work, superseding that of Roscoe.

P. Villari. Niccolo Machiavelli and his Times. 2 v.† L. Paul. 24s.
An important contribution to the history of the 15th century.

W. R. Clark. Savonarola. Soc. 3s. 6d.

J. Burckhardt. The Civilization of the Period of the Renaissance in Italy.† 2 v. Dodd. $7.50.

P. Colletta. History of Naples. 2 v. Ed. Edmonston. 24s.

W. C. Hazlitt. History of the Venetian Republic. 2 v. L. 28s.

J. T. Bent. Genoa. L. Paul. 18s.
An interesting work, but badly arranged.

J. A. Wylie. History of the Waldenses. C. $1.25.
: A good popular work.
J. Bigelow. Molinos the Quietist. Scr. $1.25.
: Episode of religious history in the seventeenth century.
Count Balzani. Early Chroniclers of Europe. Italy. Soc. $1.20.

S. A. Dunham. History of Spain and Portugal. 5 v. H. $3.75.
: An old but good work.
J. A. Harrison. Spain. B. Lothrop. $1.50.
: Excellent in parts, but of unequal merit.
‡*H. Coppée.* History of the Conquest of Spain by the Arab-Moors. 2 v. L. & B. $5.00.
: An excellent history of Spain during the middle ages.
Miss C. M. Yonge. Christians and Moors in Spain. Macm. $1.25.
: A sketch of a popular character.
J. A. Condé. History of the Arabs in Spain. 3 v. Bohn. $4.20.
: An old standard work, but of little value.
Life of Saint Teresa. Macm. $2.00.

E. C. Otté. Scandinavian History. Macm. $1.50.
: The best work; another is —
P. C. Sinding. History of Scandinavia. Pittsburgh. Haven. $3.50.
‡*E. G. Geijer.* History of Sweden. L. Whittaker. Vol. I., 8s. 6d.
T. Carlyle. Early Kings of Norway. H. $1.25.
Voltaire. History of Charles XII.† Houghton. $2.25.
: With many inaccuracies in detail, a book of positive historical merit.

---

‡*A. Rambaud.* History of Russia.† 2 v. E. & L. $11.00.
: A work of the highest merit.
W. R. S. Ralston. Early Russian History. L. 5s.
: Four lectures of great value.
Frances A. Shaw. Brief History of Russia. O. 50 cents.
S. A. Dunham. History of Poland. L. 3s. 6d.

HISTORICAL LITERATURE AND AUTHORITIES. 279

Jas. Fletcher. History of Poland. H. 75 cents.

Hungary and its Revolutions [with life of Kossuth]. Bohn. $1.40.

H. Zschokke. History of Switzerland.† Armstrong. $1.50.

Harriet D. S. Mackenzie. History of Switzerland. B. Lothrop. $1.50.

T. C. Grattan. History of the Netherlands. II. $1.00.

C. M. Davies. History of Holland. 3 v. L. Willis. 36s.

J. Geddes. Administration of John De Witt. Vol. I. H. $2.50.
    The period of the invasion of Holland by Louis XIV.

---

‡*G. Finlay.* History of Greece, from its Conquest by the Romans (B.C. 146) to the Present Time (1864). 7 v. Macm. $17.50.
    A work of the highest merit and authority.

L. Sergeant. New Greece. C. $3.50.

Sir E. Creasy. History of the Ottoman Turks. Holt. $2.50.

E. A. Freeman. The Ottoman Power in Europe. Macm. $2.00.
    Freeman's view is less friendly than that of Creasy.

J. Blochwitz. Brief History of Turkey. O. 50 cents.

There is a history of the Turks in Vol. II. of *J. H. Newman's* Historical Sketches.

---

‡*Sir W. Muir.* Life of Mahomet. S. & E. 14s.

Id. Annals of the Early Caliphate. S. & E. 16s.

W. Irving. Mahomet and his Successors. 2 v. Put. $2.00.

‡*R. Bosworth Smith.* Mohammed and Mohammedism.

E. A. Freeman. History of the Saracens. Macm. $1.50.
    A book of merit, but old.

S. Ockley. History of the Saracens. Bohn. $1.40.
    A fascinating narrative.

R. D. Osborn. Islam under the Arabs. Longm. 12s.

Id. Islam under the Caliphs of Bagdad. Seeley. 10s. 6d.

E. H. Palmer. Haroun al Raschid. [New Plutarch.] Put. $1.00.
A. Crighton. History of Arabia. 2 v. H. $1.50.

James Mill. History of British India. 9 v. £2 16s.
    The standard work. Excellent short ones are—
‡ *W. W. Hunter.* Short History of India. $6.40.
‡*J. T. Wheeler.* Short History of India. Macm. $3.50.
L. J. Trotter. History of India. Soc. 10s. 6d.
R. G. Watson. History of Persia. S. & E. 15s.
H. H. Howorth. History of the Mongols from the Ninth to the Nineteenth Century. 3 v. $28.00.
D. C. Boulger. History of China. 2 v. L. Allen. $14.40.

---

14. NINETEENTH CENTURY.

R. Mackenzie. The Nineteenth Century. L. Nelson. $1.00.
    An excellent general sketch.
Memoirs of Prince Metternich. (1773-1815.)† 2 v. Scr. $5.00.
    Valuable in the diplomatic history of the time.
Sir A. Alison. History of Europe from 1815. 4 v. H. $8.00.
    A work of great literary merit, written with a strong Tory bias.
Memoirs of Baron Stockmar. 2 v. L. & S. $5.00.
    Baron Stockmar was a leading adviser of Prince Albert.
Cardinal Wiseman. The Last Four Popes. [Pius VII., Leo XII., Pius VIII., Gregory XVI.] L. Hurst & Blackett. 5s.
G. S. Godkin. Life of Victor Emmanuel II., First King of Italy. $2.00.
N. W. Senior. Journals Kept in France and Italy. 2 v. L. Paul. 24s.
    Mr. Senior's journals and letters are full of intelligent and instructive observations upon current history.

HISTORICAL LITERATURE AND AUTHORITIES. 281

L. v. Kossuth. Memoirs of My Exile. App. $2.00.

Francis Deák: an Hungarian Statesman. Macm. $3.00.

Chas. de Mazade. Cavour. Put. $3.00.

‡*J. R. Seeley.* Life of Stein. 2 v. R. $7.50.

Id. Life of E. M. Arndt. R. $2.25.

Id. Lectures and Essays. Macm. 10s. 6d.

Jos. Mazzini: His Life and Writings. Houghton. $1.75.

J. G. L. Hezekiel. Prince Bismarck. Fords. $3.50.

J. Klaczko. Two Chancellors. [Bismarck and Gortschakoff.] Houghton. $2.00.

W. Bagehot. Biographical Studies. Longm. 12s.

Lord Stratford de Redcliffe. The Eastern Question. M. 9s.

A. W. Kinglake. The Invasion of the Crimea [1854]. 4 v. H. $8.00.

H. M. Hozier. The Seven Weeks' War. [1866.] Macm. $2.00.

A. Borbstaedt and F. Dwyer. The Franco-German War [1870]. L. Asher. 21s.

A military history; popular illustrated works are—

Edmund Ollier. The Franco-German War. 2 v. C. $7.50.

Id. The Russo-Turkish War. 2 v. C. $8.00.

F. V. Greene. The Russian Army and its Campaigns in Turkey in 1877-78. App. $6.00.

With atlas of maps.

T. W. Higginson. Brief Biographies. Put. $1.50 a vol.

1. English Statesmen. By *T. W. Higginson.*
2. English Radical Leaders. By *R. J. Hinton.*
3. French Political Leaders. By *Edw. King.*
4. German Political Leaders. By *Herbert Tuttle.*

See also lists 11 and 12, England and France.

282 HISTORICAL LITERATURE AND AUTHORITIES.

15. HISTORY OF THE UNITED STATES.

‡*Geo. Bancroft.* History of the United States. 10 v. (to 1783), $25.00; two additional vols. to 1789, $5.00.
> The standard work; democratic in tone. Centenary edition (to 1783) in 6 v., $13.50; complete edition now publishing in 6 v., $15.00.

‡*R. Hildreth.* History of the United States. 6 v. (to 1820). H. $12.00.
> Sound and generally accurate; Federalist in proclivities.

Geo. Tucker. History of the United States. 4 v. (to 1841). Lip. $10.00.
> A Southern view; begins with the Revolution

Wm. C. Bryant and S. H. Gay. Popular History of the United States. 4 v. Scr. $24.00.
> Handsomely illustrated. The early parts are the best.

B. J. Lossing. Cyclopædia of United States History. 2 v. H. $12.00.
> A valuable book of reference, but badly arranged.

S. G. Drake. Dictionary of American Biography. Houghton.

J. J. Lalor. Cyclopædia of Political Science. 2 v. Ch. Cary. Each, $6.00.

J. Winsor. Memorial History of Boston. 4 v. O. $25.00.
> A collection of monographs by various writers.

Mrs. Martha J. Lamb. History of New York. 2 v. Barnes. $20.00.
> A work of very great merit.

J. C. Ridpath. Popular History of the United States. Cincinnati. Jones. $3.00.
> The best history of an intermediate size.

S. Eliot. History of the United States (to 1850). B. Ware. $1.35.
> Very judicious and accurate, but dry.

J. A. Doyle. History of the United States. [Freeman's Historical Series.] Holt. $1.00.
> An excellent English work.

HISTORICAL LITERATURE AND AUTHORITIES. 283

R. Mackenzie. America. L. Nelson. $1.00.
Another good English work, embracing all America.

J. T. Short. Historical Reference Lists. Columbus. Smythe. 40 cts.
Chiefly having reference to American history.

J. T. Short. North Americans of Antiquity. II. $3.00.
The best book upon the ethnology, etc., of the Indians.

√ *J. W. Foster.* Prehistoric Races of the United States. Ch. Griggs. $3.00.
The best work upon American archæology.

G. E. Ellis. The Red Man and the White Man. L. & B. $3.50.

F. A. Walker. The Indian Question. $1.50.

G. W. Manypenny. Our Indian Wards. Cincinnati. Clarke. $3.00.

Mrs. Jackson (H. H.). A Century of Dishonor. H. $1.50.

‡*H. H. Bancroft.* Native Races of the Pacific States. 5 v. San Francisco. Each, $4.50.
A cyclopædia of information.

H. R. Schoolcraft. Indian Tribes of the United States. 6 v. Lip. $75.00.
Contains much information, with much useless matter.

G. W. Williams. History of the Negro Race in America. 2 v. Put. $7.00.

Colonial Period. 1607 to 1763.

Jas. Grahame. History of the United States of North America. 4 v. L. £2 10s.
A fair and friendly English account, reaching 1776.

E. D. Neill. The English Colonization of America. L. 14s.
Of especial value for the Middle States.

‡*H. C. Lodge.* Short History of the English Colonies. H. $3.00.
An excellent compendium, arranged by colonies.

‡*J. A. Doyle.* English Colonies in America. Vol. I. Holt. $3.50.
Vol. I. contains the Southern colonies. It is a very good work.

F. F. Charlevoix. History of New France.† 6 v. N.Y. $15.00.

‡*F. Parkman.* France and England in North America. 7 v. L. & B. Each, $2.50.
1. The Pioneers of France in the New World.
2. The Jesuits in North America.
3. The Discovery of the Great West.
4. The Old Regime in Canada.
5. Count Frontenac and New France.
The Conspiracy of Pontiac. 2 v.
> A series of the highest excellence.

T. Mante. History of the Late War in North America. L. 1772.
> An authentic account of the French and Indian war.

‡*J. G. Palfrey.* History of New England. 4 v. L. & B. $14.50.
> The best history of New England.

Massachusetts and her Early History. L. & B.
> An instructive series of lectures by different persons.

Peter Oliver. The Puritan Commonwealth. L. & B. $2.50.
> Hostile to the Puritans.

J. H. Trumbull. The True Blue Laws of Connecticut and New Haven, and the False Blue Laws, invented by the Rev. Samuel Peters. Hartford. Am. Pub. Co.

‡*R. Frothingham.* Rise of the Republic. L. & B. $3.50.
> A history of the growth of the sentiment of union.

E. G. Scott. The Development of Constitutional Liberty in the English Colonies of America. Put. $2.50.

‡*J. G. Shea.* Discovery and Exploration of the Mississippi Valley. $6.00.
> Indispensable to the student of western history.

R. Blanchard. Discovery and Conquests of the Northwest. Ch. MacCoun. $3.00.

Mrs. Anne Grant. Memoirs of an American Lady. Albany. Munsell. $3.00.
> A graphic picture of life in Albany before the revolution.

See also articles by *T. W. Higginson, John Fiske,* and *Edw. Eggleston* in Harper's Monthly and the Century for 1882 and 1883.

HISTORICAL LITERATURE AND AUTHORITIES. 285

Revolutionary Period. 1763 to 1789.

‡*J. Winsor.* Handbook of the American Revolution. Houghton. $1.25.
: An exhaustive list of authorities.

J. M. Ludlow. The War of American Independence. E. & L. $1.00.
: An English work belonging to the Epochs Series.

‡*G. W. Greene.* Historical View of the American Revolution. Houghton. $1.50.
: An instructive series of lectures.

Id. The German Element in the War of Independence. Houghton. $1.50.

‡*B. J. Lossing.* Field-book of the Revolution. 2 v. H. $14.00.
: A description of the battle-fields, etc.

H. B. Carrington. Battles of the Revolution. Barnes. $6.00.
: By an army officer; with plans of battle-fields, etc.

Thos. Jones. New York during the Revolutionary War. 2 v. App. $15.00.
: By a Tory; its unfairness shown by H. P. Johnston.

L. C. Draper. King's Mountain and its Heroes. Cincinnati. Thomson. $4.00.
: A valuable monograph.

W. L. Stone. Border Wars of the American Revolution. 2 v. H. $1.50.

C. W. Butterfield. The Washington-Irvine Correspondence. Madison (Wis.). Atwood.
: An important work for the history of the North-west.

W. H. Trescot. Diplomacy of the Revolution. App. 75 cents.

A. S. Bolles. Financial History of the United States. (1774–1860.) 2 v. App. $6.00.

‡*G. T. Curtis.* History of the Constitution. 2 v. H. $6.00.

L. Sabine. History of the American Loyalists. 2 v. L. & B. $7.00.
: A work of great merit and value.

Familiar Letters of John and Abigail Adams. Houghton. $2.00.

Period of the Republic.

‡*J. B. McMaster.* History of the People of the United States. App. $2.50.
: Only one vol. published; gives special attention to social history.

Jas. Schouler. History of the American Republic. Washington. Morrison. $5.00.
: Two volumes published, reaching 1817.

W. R. Houghton. Hist. of American Politics. Indianapolis. Neely.
: With numerous illustrative diagrams.

A. W. Young. The American Statesman. N.Y. Goodspeed. $5.00.
: Contains a good summary of congressional debates, etc.

E. Williams. Statesman's Manual. N.Y.

‡*Alex. Johnston.* History of American Politics. Holt. $1.00.
: A brief compendium of high merit.

J. Marshall. Life of Washington. 2 v. Ph. Claxton. $6.00.
: Contains the best political history of Washington's administration.

W. H. Trescot. Diplomatic History of the Administrations of Washington and Adams. L. & B. $1.25.

‡*H. von Holst.* Constitutional History of the United States. Ch. Callaghan. $11.50.
: The three volumes published reach 1850.

H. Adams. Documents Relating to New England Federalism. $1.00.
: Throws much light upon the history of the party.

B. J. Lossing. Field-book of the War of 1812. H. $7.00.

G. W. Cullum. Campaigns of the War of 1812–15. N.Y. Miller. $5.00.
: By an army officer.

R. Johnson. History of the War of 1812. Dodd, Mead, & Co. $1.25.
: A shorter and popular work.

‡*Theodore Roosevelt.* The Naval War of 1812. Put. $2.50.
: An accurate and impartial account.

R. S. Ripley. The War with Mexico. 2 v.

W. G. Sumner. History of American Currency. Holt. $3.00.

The First Century of the Republic. 1876. H. $5.00.
: A valuable collection of essays surveying the period.
T. H. Benton. Thirty Years in the United States Senate. 2 v. App. $6.00.
: Covering the period from 1821 to 1851.
Nathan Sargent. Public Men and Events. 2 v. Lip.
: Reminiscences from 1817 to 1883; Whig in tone.
H. Wilson. History of the Rise and Fall of the Slave Power. 3 v. Houghton. Each, $3.00.

W. H. Prescott. History of the Conquest of Mexico. 3 v. Lip. $11.50.
Id. History of the Conquest of Peru. 2 v. Lip. $3.00.
A. Helps. The Spanish Conquest of America. 4 v. H. $6.00.
C. A. Washburn. History of Paraguay. 2 v. L. & S. $7.50.
See also *Carlyle's* article on Dr. Francia.
C. R. Markham. The War Between Peru and Chili, 1879-82. N.Y. Worthington.

The Civil War.

‡*Comte de Paris.* History of the Civil War. 3 v. published. Ph. Porter & Coates. $3.50 a vol.
: The best history of the war, so far as completed.
‡Campaigns of the Civil War. Scr. $1.00 per vol.
  1. *J. G. Nicolay.* The Outbreak of Rebellion.
  2. *M. F. Force.* From Fort Henry to Corinth.
  3. *A. S. Webb.* The Peninsula.
  4. *J. C. Ropes.* The Army under Pope.
  5. *F. W. Palfrey.* The Antietam and Fredericksburg.
  6. *A. Doubleday.* Chancellorsville and Gettysburg.
  7. *H. M. Cist.* The Army of the Cumberland.
  8. *F. V. Greene.* The Mississippi.
  9. *J. D. Cox.* The Campaign of Atlanta.
  10. *Id.* The March to the Sea.
  11. *G. E. Pond.* The Shenandoah Valley in 1864.
  12. *A. A. Humphreys.* The Campaigns of Grant in Virginia.

The Navy in the Civil War. Ser. $1.00 per vol.
1. *J. R. Soley.* The Blockade and the Cruisers.
2. *Daniel Ammen.* The Atlantic Coast.
3. *A. T. Mahan.* The Gulf and Inland Waters.
> These fourteen small vols. are all by persons specially qualified to write upon their subjects, and form an admirable condensed history of the war.

Supplementary volumes : —
  F. Phisterer. Statistical Record of the Armies of the United States.
  A. A. Humphreys. Gettysburg to the Rapidan.

J. W. Draper. History of the American Civil War. 3 v. H. $10.50.
> With an introduction upon the influence of physical causes upon American history.

H. Greeley. The American Conflict. 2 v. Hartford. Case. $10.00.

Jeff. Davis. Rise and Fall of the Confederate Government. 2 v. App. $10.00.

A. H. Stephens. Constitutional View of the Late War between the States. Nat. Pub. Co. $5.50.
> These two volumes, by the president and vice-president of the Confederacy, present the Southern view. See also —

E. A. Pollard. The Lost Cause. N.Y. Treat. $5.00.   and
J. E. Johnston. Narrative of Military Operations. App. $5.00.
A. Badeau. Military History of U. S. Grant. 3 v. App. $12.00.
W. T. Sherman. Memoirs. 2 v. App. $5.50.
W. Swinton. Campaigns of the Army of the Potomac. N.Y. Richardson. $4.00.

For original documents : —
The War of the Rebellion. Published by Congress.
Frank Moore. The Rebellion Record. 12 v. Put.

HISTORICAL LITERATURE AND AUTHORITIES. 289

*Histories of the States.**
Maine. By *W. D. Williamson.* 2 v. Hallowell. $9.00.
New Hampshire. By *Jeremy Belknap.* 3 v. B. $7.50.
Vermont. By *Zadock Thompson.* Burlington. $4.50.
Massachusetts. By *J. S. Barry.* 3 v. B. $8.50.
Rhode Island. By *S. G. Arnold.* 2 v. App. $6.00.
Connecticut. By *B. Trumbull.* 2 v. New Haven. $9.00.
Id. By *G. H. Hollister.* 2 v. New Haven. $5.00.
New York. By *J. R. Brodhead.* 2 v. H. $6.00.
New Jersey. By *J. O. Raum.* 2 v. Ph. Potter. $6.00.
Pennsylvania. By *Robert Proud.* 2 v. Ph. $12.00.
Id. By *W. H. Egle.* Harrisburg. $5.50.
Maryland. By *J. L. Bozman.* 2 v. Baltimore. $5.00.
Virginia. By *R. R. Howison.* 2 v. Richmond. $6.00.
North Carolina. By *J. W. Moore.* 2 v. Raleigh. $5.00.
South Carolina. By *D. Ramsay.* 2 v. Charleston. $4.00.
Id. By *W. G. Simms.* N.Y. Redfield. $2.25.
Georgia. By *W. B. Stevens.* 2 v. Ph. $5.00.
Florida. By *G. R. Fairbanks.* Lip. $2.50.
Alabama. By *A. J. Picket.* 2 v. Charleston. $7.50.
Mississippi. By *J. F. H. Claiborne.* Jackson. 2 v. $7.00.
Louisiana. By *C. Gayarré.* 3 v. N.Y. $12.00.
Texas. By *H. Yoakum.* 2 v. N.Y. Redfield. $8.00.
Tennessee. By *J. G. M. Ramsey.* Lip. $2.50.
Kentucky. By *Humphrey Marshall.* 2 v. Frankfort. $14.50.
Ohio. By *Jas. W. Taylor.* [Unfinished; ends 1787.] Cincinnati. $6.00.
Id. By *J. S. C. Abbott.* Detroit. $4.00.
Indiana. By *John B. Dillon.* Indianapolis. $3.00.

---

* For this selected list I am principally indebted to Mr. D. S. Durrie, Librarian of the Wisconsin Historical Society.

Illinois. By *A. Davidson and B. Sturé.* Springfield. $5.00.
Michigan. By *Jas. V. Campbell.* Detroit. $1.50.
Id. By *J. H. Lanman.* H. 75 cents.
Minnesota. By *E. D. Neill.* Minneapolis. $2.50.
Wisconsin. By *W. R. Smith.* [Unfinished.] Madison.
Kansas. By *D. W. Wilder.* Topeka. $5.00.
Missouri. By *W. F. Switzler.* St. Louis. Barns. $2.50.
California. By *Franklin Tuthill.* San Francisco. Bancroft.
Oregon. By *W. H. Gray.* Portland. $4.00.
‡American Commonwealths. Houghton.
   Virginia. By *John Esten Cooke.*
History of the Pacific States. By *H. H. Bancroft* [now publishing]. San Francisco. Bancroft.

Biographies.

George Washington. By *W. Irving.* 5 v. Put. $5.00.
Alexander Hamilton. By *J. T. Morse.* 2 v. L. & B. $4.50.
John Adams. By *J. Q. and C. F. Adams.* Lip. $2.00.
Thomas Jefferson. By *H. S. Randall.* 3 v. Lip. $9.00.
Id. By *Jas. Parton.* Houghton. $2.00.
Benjamin Franklin (autobiography). By *J. Bigelow.* 3 v. Lip. $7.50.
Id. By *Jas. Parton.* 2 v. Houghton. $4.00.
General N. Greene. By *G. W. Greene.* 3 v. Put. $12.00.
Israel Putnam. By *I. N. Tarbox.* Lockwood, Brooks, & Co. $2.50.
F. W. Steuben. By *Fred Kapp.* H.
Patrick Henry. By *W. Wirt.* Ph. Claxton. $1.50.
Timothy Pickering. By *O. Pickering and C. W. Upham.* 4 v. L. & B. $11.00.
James Madison. By *W. C. Rives.* 3 v. L. & B. $10.50.
John Jay. By *Wm. Jay.* H.
Gouverneur Morris. By *Jared Sparks.* L. & B.
William Pinkney. By *Henry Wheaton.* $1.25.

Albert Gallatin. By *H. Adams.* Lip. $5.00.
George Cabot. By *H. C. Lodge.* L. & B. $3.50.
Aaron Burr. By *Jas. Parton.* 2 v. Houghton. $4.00.
Andrew Jackson. By *Jas. Parton.* 3 v. Houghton. $6.00.
Daniel Webster. By *G. T. Curtis.* 2 v. App. $4.00.
Josiah Quincy. By *Edmund Quincy.* O. $3.00.
W. L. Garrison. By *O. Johnson.* B. Russell.
W. H. Seward. By *F. W. Seward.* App. $4.25.
Charles Sumner. By *E. L. Pierce.* 2 v. R. $6.00.
James Buchanan. By *G. T. Curtis.* 2 v. H.
Abraham Lincoln. By *H. J. Raymond.* N.Y. Derby. $1.50.
Id. By *C. G. Leland.* [New Plutarch.] Put. $1.00.
Library of American Biography. Edited by *Jared Sparks.* 10 v. H. $12.50.

Theodore Parker. Historic Americans. [Washington, Jefferson, Franklin, Adams.] B. Fuller. $1.50.

‡American Statesmen. Houghton. Per vol., $1.25. Contains:—
Alexander Hamilton. By *H. C. Lodge.*
J. Q. Adams. By *J. T. Morse.*
J. C. Calhoun. By *H. von Holst.*
Andrew Jackson. By *W. G. Sumner.*
John Randolph. By *H. Adams.*
James Monroe. By *D. C. Gilman.*
Thomas Jefferson. By *J. T. Morse.*
Daniel Webster. By *H. C. Lodge.*
See also the next list.

Authorities.

W. Bradford. History of the Plymouth Plantation. $2.25.
Alex. Young. Chronicles of Plymouth.
Id. Chronicles of Massachusetts. 2 v. $5.00.
Records of the Governor and Company of Massachusetts Bay. Edited by *J. W. Thornton.*

292 HISTORICAL LITERATURE AND AUTHORITIES.

John Winthrop. History of New England. 1630–49. 2 v. $5.00.
      By the first governor of Massachusetts.

Thos. Hutchinson. History of the Province of Massachusetts Bay. $4.00.
      The author was lieutenant-governor of the colony, and a strong Tory.

Documents Relating to the Colonial History of the State of New York. 11 v. Albany. Published by the State.

American Archives. Edited by *Peter Force.*

American State Papers.

Congressional Documents, etc.

Elliot's Debates [of the Constitution]. 5 v. Lip. $12.50.

Annals of Congress.

Archæologia Americana.

T. H. Benton. Abridgment of Debates of Congress. 1789–1856. 16 v. App.

The Federal and State Constitutions, etc. Compiled by *B. P. Poore.* Washington. 1878.

Treaties and Conventions, etc. Washington. 1871.

Life and Writings of George Washington. 12 v. II. $18.00.

Life and Works of John Adams. 10 v. L. & B. $30.00.

Works of Alexander Hamilton. 7 v. N.Y. Trow. $21.00.

Letters and Other Writings of James Madison. 4 v. Lip. $16.00.

Writings of Thomas Jefferson. 9 v. Lip. $23.50.

Life and Writings of Benjamin Franklin. 10 v. Ch. $20.00.

Papers of James Madison. 4 v. Ph. $16.00.

Works of Daniel Webster. 6 v. L. & B. $18.00.

Life and Works of John C. Calhoun. 6 v. App. $15.00.

Works of Henry Clay. 6 v. $18.00.

16. Selected List of Historical Novels, Poems, and Plays, arranged Chronologically.

A. Lang. Helen of Troy. (Poem.)
W. Morris. Jason. (Poem.)
Id. The Earthly Paradise.
    A collection of poems narrating Greek and German legends.
C. Kingsley. Andromeda. (Poem.)
A. C. Swinburne. Atalanta in Calydon. (Poem.)

B.C.
15th century. — *Ebers.* Uarda [Rameses II.].
6th century. — *Id.* Daughter of an Egyptian King.
5th century. — *Landor.* Pericles and Aspasia.
2d century. — *Ebers.* The Sisters.
1st century. — *Shakespeare.* Julius Cæsar (Drama).

A.D.
1st century. — *J. F. Clarke.* Thomas Didymus.
    Philochristus. Onesimus.
    Bulwer. The Last Days of Pompeii.
2d century. — *Ebers.* The Emperor [Hadrian].
3d century. — *Cardinal Newman.* Callista.
    Cardinal Wiseman. Fabiola [The Catacombs].
    Mrs. Hunt. The Wards of Plotinus.
    W. Ware. Zenobia. Aurelian.
4th century. — *Ebers.* Homo Sum [330, Sinai].
    V. Rydberg. The Last Athenian [361].
5th century. — *C. Kingsley.* Hypatia [Alexandria].
    Wilkie Collins. Antonina, or the Fall of Rome.
8th century. — *G. Freytag.* Our Forefathers: Ingraban.
10th century. — *Scheffel.* Ekkehart [The Monks of St. Gallen].
    Taylor. Edwin the Fair (Drama).
11th century. — *Bulwer.* Harold, the Last of the Saxon Kings.
    Kingsley. Hereward, the Last of the English.
12th century. — *Scott.* The Betrothed. The Talisman. Ivanhoe.
    Lessing. Nathan the Wise (Drama).

12th century. — The Luck of Ladysmede.
E. E. Hale. In his Name [Waldenses].
13th century. — Shakespeare. King John (Drama).
C. Kingsley. The Saints' Tragedy.
G. P. R. James. Forest Days [Simon de Montfort].
Mrs. Hemans. The Vespers of Palermo (Drama).
14th century. — Schiller. Wilhelm Tell (Drama).
Bulwer. Rienzi, the Last of the Tribunes.
Taylor. Philip van Artevelde (Drama).
Shakespeare. Richard II. (Drama).
15th century. — Id. Henry IV., V., VI. Richard III. (Dramas).
Schiller. Die Jungfrau von Orleans (Drama).
Scott. Fair Maid of Perth. Quentin Durward. Anne of Geierstein.
Bulwer. The Last of the Barons [Warwick].
C. Reade. The Cloister and the Hearth.
Geo. Eliot. Romola [Savonarola].
16th century. — Shakespeare. Henry VIII. (Drama).
Scott. Marmion. Lady of the Lake. Lay of the Last Minstrel (Poems). — The Monastery. The Abbot. Kenilworth.
Kingsley. Amyas Leigh, or Westward Ho!
Schiller. Maria Stuart (Drama).
Gœthe. Egmont (Drama).
17th century. — Scott. Fortunes of Nigel. Legend of Montrose. Woodstock. Peveril of the Peak. Old Mortality. — Rokeby (Poem).
Manzoni. The Betrothed [Milan, 1628].
Schiller. Wallenstein (Drama).
Shorthouse. John Inglesant.
Browning. Strafford (Drama). The Ring and the Book (Poem).
Ainsworth. Old Saint Paul's.
Auerbach. Spinoza.
Blackmore. Lorna Doone.
18th century. — Thackeray. Henry Esmond. The Virginians.
Scott. Rob Roy. The Heart of Midlothian. Waverly. Redgauntlet.

HISTORICAL LITERATURE AND AUTHORITIES. 295

18th century.—*Browning.* King Victor and King Charles (Drama).
Dickens. Barnaby Rudge (1780).
Miss Burney (Mad. D'Arblay). Evelina.
Revolutionary epoch:—
Victor Hugo. Ninety-three. Les Misérables.
Mrs. Gaskell. Sylvia's Lovers.
Geo. Eliot. Adam Bede.
Blackmore. The Maid of Sker. Alice Lorraine.
Dickens. Tale of Two Cities.
Erckmann-Chatrian. The States General. The Country in Danger. Madame Thérèse. Year One. Citizen Bonaparte.
Miss Roberts. On the Edge of the Storm. Noblesse Oblige.
Fritz Reuter. In the Year Thirteen.
Erckmann-Chatrian. The Conscript. The Invasion of France. The Siege of Phalsburg. Waterloo.

American History.

17th century.—*Longfellow.* The Courtship of Miles Standish.
Hawthorne. The Scarlet Letter.
Paulding. The Dutchman's Fireside.
Miss Sedgwick. Hope Leslie.
Whittier. Mogg Megone.
18th century.—*Simms.* The Yemassee (S.C., 1715).
Longfellow. Evangeline (Poem).
Mrs. Stowe. The Minister's Wooing.
J. E. Cooke. The Virginia Comedians.
Cooper. Leather-Stocking Tales.
Revolution.—*Cooper.* The Spy. The Pilot.
Kennedy. Horseshoe Robinson.
Winthrop. Edwin Brothertoft.
Simms. The Partisan, etc.

PART II.

BOOKS FOR COLLATERAL READING IN CONNECTION WITH CLASS WORK.*

1. GENERAL HISTORY.

E. *Clodd.* The Childhood of the World. App. 75 cents.
Id. The Childhood of Religions. App. $1.25.
    Designed to give children correct notions of primeval times.
J. *Bonner.* Child's History of Greece. 2 v. H. $2.50.
Id. Child's History of Rome. 2 v. H. $2.50.
Mrs. *C. H. B. Laing.* The Seven Kings of the Seven Hills. Ph. Porter & Coates. $1.00.
Id. The Heroes of the Seven Hills. Ph. Porter & Coates. $1.25.
    These two books contain the legends of early Roman history.
Chas. *Dickens.* Child's History of England. $1.00.
J. *Bonner.* Child's History of England. H.
S. R. *Gardiner.* English History for Young Folks. Holt. $1.00.
    A work of the greatest soundness and accuracy.
L. *Creighton.* Stories from English History. N.Y. Whittaker.
J. R. *Green.* Readings in English History. Macm. $1.50.
Sir W. *Scott.* Tales of a Grandfather.
    Stories from Scotch and French history.
Sarah *Brook.* French History for English Children. Macm. $2.00.
    An admirable book with good maps.
Miss *C. S. Kirkland.* Short History of France. Ch. Jansen. $1.50.
S. *Lanier.* The Boys' Froissart. Scr. $3.00.
    A selection of the best stories from the prince of chroniclers.
Belt and Spur. Scr. $2.00.
    Stories from the mediæval chronicles; excellently illustrated.

---

* In this list I have derived much assistance from "Books for the Young," by Miss C. M. Hewins of the Hartford Library.

BOOKS FOR COLLATERAL READING. 297

G. M. Towle. Heroes of History. [Marco Polo, Vasco da Gama, Magellan, Pizarro, Drake, Raleigh.] L. & S.
>An excellent series of biographies. Each, $1.25.

Historical Biographies. Rivington. Each, $1.00: —
Simon de Montfort. By *M. Creighton.*
The Black Prince. By *L. Creighton.*
Sir Walter Raleigh. By *L. Creighton.*
Marlborough. By *L. Creighton.*

M. J. Guest. Lectures on English History. Macm. $1.50.
>Good for young people above the age of children.

Mrs. M. E. Green. The Princesses of England. 6 v. Each, 10s. 6d.

The Young Folks' History. E. & L. Each, $1.50. Includes: —
America. By *H. Butterworth.*
Russia. By *N. H. Dole.*
Queens of England. By *Rosalie Kaufman.*
Mexico. By *F. A. Ober.*
England, Germany, France, Greece, Rome, and Bible History. By *Miss Yonge.*

A. J. Church. The Last Days of Jerusalem. L. Seeley. $2.00.

J. Abbott. Biographies of Famous Persons (about thirty in all). H. Each, $1.00.

Brooke Herford. The Story of Religion in England. Ch. Jansen. $1.50.

Thos. Archer. Decisive Events in History. C. $1.75.
>Handsomely illustrated.

Mrs. H. R. Haweis. Chaucer for Children. L. Chatto & Windus. $2.25.

Id. Spenser for Children. $3.75.
>Beautifully illustrated; instructive for manners, costumes, etc.

2. AMERICAN HISTORY.

N. Hawthorne. True Stories. [Grandfather's Chair, etc.] Houghton. $1.00.
    The early history of New England.

C. C. Coffin. Old Times in the Colonies. Il. $3.00.

Id. The Boys of '76. Il. $3.00.

Id. The Building of the Nation. Il. $3.00.

Id. The Boys of '61. Il. $3.00.
    A handsomely illustrated series of works.

E. Eggleston. Famous American Indians. [Montezuma, Pocahontas, etc.] N.Y. Dodd, Mead, & Co. Each, $1.25.

M. Schele de Vere. Romance of American History. Put. $1.25.

J. D. Champlin. Young Folks' History of the War for the Union. Holt. $2.75.
    An excellent book, well illustrated.

J. Bonner. Child's History of the United States. 3 v. Il. $3.75.

Mrs. A. S. Richardson. History of Our Country. Houghton. $4.50.

T. W. Higginson. Young Folks' History of America. L. & S. $1.50.
    Bonner's is designed for younger children than the others; Mrs. Richardson is superior in narration; Higginson in completeness of view.

Id. Young Folks' History of Explorers. L. & S. $1.50.

C. H. Woodman. Boys and Girls of the Revolution. Lip. $1.25.

J. K. Hosmer. The Color Guard. B. Fuller. $1.50.

Id. The Thinking Bayonet. B. Fuller. $1.75.
    Belong to the war of the rebellion.

C. K. True. Life of Captain John Smith. N.Y. Phillips & Hunt. $1.00.

Centenary History of the United States. N.Y. Barnes. $5.00.
    An excellent family history.

3. Myths and Legends.

N. Hawthorne. Wonder-book. Houghton. $1.00.
Id. Tanglewood Tales. Houghton. $1.00.
    Tell the story of several Greek myths in a charming manner.
Chas. Kingsley. The Heroes. Macm. $1.50.
    The Greek heroic legends.
Thos. Bulfinch. The Age of Fable. L. & S. $2.50.
    A new edition, well illustrated, edited by Rev. E. E. Hale.
C. Witt. Classical Mythology. Holt. $1.25.
    Not a complete mythology, but a collection of legends, with their explanation.
A. J. Church. Stories from Homer. L. Seeley. $2.00.
Id. Stories from Virgil. $2.00.
Id. Stories from the Greek Tragedies. $2.00.
Id. Stories [of the East] from Herodotus. $2.00.
Id. Stories from Livy. $2.00.
Id. Stories of the Persian War. $2.00.
Id. Travellers' True Tales from Lucian. $2.00.
Id. Heroes and Kings. $2.00.
M. Frere. Eastern Fairy Legends. (Old Deccan Days.) Lip. $1.25.
A. B. Mitford. Tales of Old Japan. Macm. $2.00.
W. E. Griffis. Japanese Fairy World. $1.50.
P. W. Joyce. Old Celtic Romances. $3.00.
J. F. Campbell. Popular Tales of the West Highlands. 4 v. Ed. Edmonston. 32s.
W. R. S. Ralston. Russian Folk-tales. N.Y. Worthington. $1.50.
W. H. J. Bleek. Hottentot Fables. L. Trübner. 3s. 6d.
J. C. Harris. Uncle Remus. [Negro stories.] App. $1.50.
H. W. Longfellow. Hiawatha. (Poem.) $1.00.

Thos. Bulfinch. Legends of Charlemagne. L. & S. $3.00.
Id. The Age of Chivalry. [King Arthur.] $2.50.
C. H. Hanson. Stories of the Days of King Arthur. L. Nelson. $1.50.
S. Lanier. The Boys' King Arthur. Scr. $3.00.
Id. The Boys' Mabinogion. Scr. $3.00.
    Admirable collections of old legends.
J. & W. Grimm. German Popular Tales. Macm. $2.00.
G. W. Dasent. Popular Tales from the Norse. Ed. Edmonston. $2.50.
A. & E. Keary. Heroes of Asgard. Macm. $1.00.
W. Wägner. Asgard and the Gods. Lip. $2.50.
Id. Epics and Romances of the Middle Ages. Lip. $2.50.
    Interesting and handsomely illustrated works.
H. W. Mabie. Norse Stories retold from the Edda. R. $1.00.
R. B. Anderson. Viking Tales of the North. Ch. Griggs. $2.00.
Miss A. A. Woodward [Auber Forestier]. Echoes from Mist-land. Ch. Griggs. $1.50.
    A pleasing presentation of the story of the Nibelungs.
Jas. Baldwin. The Story of Siegfried. Scr. $2.00.
Id. The Story of Roland. Scr. $2.00.
F. Mallet. Northern Antiquities. Bell. $2.00.
    An old but valuable work.
Sir G. W. Cox and E. H. Jones. Popular Romances of the Middle Ages. Holt. $2.25.
    A valuable collection of legends.
S. Baring Gould. Curious Myths of the Middle Ages. Lip. $2.50.

4. Tales Illustrating History.

Miss Yonge. Historical Dramas [at several epochs]. 1s.

Mrs. Charles. Early Dawn. [A series, covering several centuries.] $1.00.

10th century.— *Miss Yonge.* The Little Duke [Richard the Fearless]. $1.25.

Crake. Edwy the Fair. Soc. $1.00.

11th century.— *Id.* Alfgar the Dane. Soc. $1.00.

Id. The Rival Heirs. Soc. $1.00.

Id. The Andreds-weald. [Norman conquest.] $1.00.

Edgar. Danes, Saxons, and Normans. $3.00.

12th century.— *Ballantyne.* Erling the Bold. [Iceland.] $1.25.

13th century.— *Edgar.* How I Won my Spurs. $3.00.

Miss Yonge. Prince and Page. [Edward I.] $1.25.

14th century.— *Miss Aguilar.* Days of Bruce. $1.00.

Miss Yonge. Lances of Linwood. [Edward III.] 75 cents.

15th century.— *Miss Yonge.* Caged Lion. [James I. of Scotland.] $1.25.

Howitt. Jack of the Mill. [Henry V.] $1.75.

Edgar. War of the Roses. $1.20.

Miss Yonge. Dove in the Eagle's Nest. [Maximilian.] $1.00.

Miss Aguilar. Vale of Cedars. $1.00.

16th century.— *Mrs. Charles.* Schönberg-Cotta Family. [Luther.] $1.00.

Miss Manning. Household of Sir Thomas Moore. $1.00.

Id. The Faire Gospeller. $1.00.

Id. Colloquies of Edward Osborne. [Edward VI.] 75 cents.

16th century.—*Miss Manning.* Good Old Times. [Auvergne, 1549.] 7s. 6d.

Mrs. Charles. The Martyrs of Spain. [1561.] } $1.25.
Id. The Liberators of Holland.

Miss Yonge. Chaplet of Pearls. [Charles IX.] $1.50.

Id. Unknown to History. [Mary Queen of Scots.] $1.50.

17th century.—*Marryat.* Children of the New Forest. $1.25.

Mrs. Davis. Diary of Lady Willoughby. $3.00.

Miss Manning. Married and Maiden Life of Mary Powell [wife of John Milton]. $1.00.

Macdonald. St. George and St. Michael. $1.50.

Mrs. Charles. The Draytons and Davenants. $1.00.

Id. On Both Sides of the Sea [continuation]. $1.00.

Miss Manning. Cherry and Violet. $1.00.

Id. Deborah's Diary. 1s.

Id. Jacques Bonneval. [The Dragonnades.] 75 cts.

Henty. The Cornet of Horse. $1.50.

18th century.—*Mrs. Charles.* Diary of Mrs. Kitty Trevylyan. $1.00.

Miss Manning. Old Chelsea Bun-house. 1s.

Miss Martineau. Peasant and Prince. [Louis XVII.] 50 cents.

Miss Tytler. Citoyenne Jacqueline. $2.00.

Mrs. Charles. Against the Stream. [Wilberforce.] $1.00.

19th century.—*Miss Yonge.* Kenneth. $1.00.

Henty. The Young Buglers. [Peninsular war.] $2.25.

Miss Manning. The Year Nine. [Andreas Hofer.] 7s. 6d.

PART III.

SCHOOL TEXT-BOOKS.

1. GENERAL HISTORY.

A Brief History of Ancient ($1.17), Mediæval, and Modern Peoples ($1.17). N.Y. Barnes.
Especially good in the history of civilization.

J. J. Anderson. New General History: 1. Ancient, $1.20; 2. Mediæval and Modern, $1.38. N.Y. Clark & Maynard. In 1 v., $1.92.
Distinguished for clearness and accuracy.

Miss M. E. Thalheimer. An Outline of General History. Cincinnati. Van Antwerp. $1.40.
Illustrated with excellent maps.

W. Swinton. Outlines of History. N.Y. Ivison. $1.66.
A book of much practical merit.

Marcius Willson. Outlines of History. N.Y. Ivison. $1.66 and $2.49.
A work of solid merit, but rather heavy.

Miss Emma Willard. Universal History. N.Y. Barnes. $1.87.
Entertaining in style, but diffuse.

S. G. Goodrich [*Peter Parley*]. Pictorial History of the World. Ph. Butler. $1.46.
Particularly suited to young children.

M. J. Kerney. Compendium of Ancient and Modern History. Baltimore. Murphy. $1.25.
A Catholic work of merit; in too fine type.

George Weber. Outlines of Universal History. B. Ware. $2.00.
A full and valuable compendium, but dry and badly translated.

R. H. Labberton. Outlines of History, $2.00. — Questions on History, $1.75. — Historical Atlas. N.Y. MacCoun. $1.50.
An original and admirable method of instruction, but too extensive for most schools.

Id. Historical Chart; or, History Taught by the Eye.
A wall-chart; very useful for instruction in dynastic history.
A. S. Lyman. Historical Chart. Van Antwerp & Co. $3.50.
A useful chart for reference; not accurate in all details.
W. F. Collier. Great Events of History. N.Y. Barnes. $1.40.
An excellent outline, but in too fine type.
A. Gilman. First Steps in General History. Barnes. $1.25.
A short and agreeable outline.
E. A. Freeman. History Primer of Europe. App. 45 cents.
Carl Ploetz. Epitome of Ancient, Mediæval, and Modern History. Houghton. $3.00.
A very full and accurate book of reference, excellently translated, and with valuable additions.

———◆———

2. ANCIENT HISTORY.

Miss M. E. Thalheimer. Ancient History. Cincinnati. Van Antwerp & Co. $1.87.
An excellent work, but too large for most schools.
R. F. Pennell. Ancient Greece. B. Allyn. 60 cents.
Id. Rome. B. Allyn. 60 cents.
Good and accurate compendiums.
History Primers. Edited by *J. R. Green.* App. Each, 45 cents.
Greece. By *C. A. Fyffe.*
Rome. By *M. Creighton.*
Classical Geography. By *H. F. Tozer.*
Old Greek Life. By *J. P. Mahaffy.*
Roman Antiquities. By *A. S. Wilkins.*
E. Abbott. Skeleton Outline of Greek History. Rivingtons.
P. E. Matheson. Skeleton Outline of Roman History. Rivingtons.
Contain very useful chronological and other tables.
O. Seeman. Mythology of Greece and Rome. H. 60 cents.
E. M. Berens. Myths and Legends of Ancient Greece. N.Y. Clark & Maynard. $1.08.
Seeman's is best in connection with the history of art; Berens', for interest of narrative.

Classical Atlas. B. Ginn, Heath, & Co. $2.30.
Student's Atlas of Classical Geography. Put. $1.50.
Johnston's Wall-maps of Classical and Scriptural Geography. B. Ginn, Heath, & Co. 10 maps, $4.00 each.
Guyot's Classical Wall-maps. Scr. 3 maps, $35.00.

---

3. Modern History.

Miss M. E. Thalheimer. Mediæval and Modern History. $1.87.
Id. History of England. $1.17.
    The best history of England for common schools.
J. J. Anderson. A Short Course in English History. N.Y. Clark & Maynard. $1.08.
    A good and accurate compendium.
David Morris. Class-book History of England. App. $1.25.
    A larger work, also excellent; well illustrated.
Miss Annie Wall. History of England. St. Louis. Jones. $1.00.
    A good short work.
E. M. Lancaster. Manual of English History. N.Y. Barnes. $1.17.
    Well written, and provided with good apparatus.
W. M. Lupton. Concise English History. R. $1.50.
    Crowded with names and dates; very useful for reference.
Mrs. Markham. History of England. App. $1.30.
    A well-known English school-book.
Brief History of France. N.Y. Barnes. $1.17.
    A book of great merit.
J. Michelet. Modern History. Macm. $1.10.
    Excellent, but too crowded with names and dates.
Students' Atlas of Historical Geography. Put. $1.50.
C. S. Halsey. Chronological and Genealogical Chart of the Rulers of England, Scotland, France, and Germany. B. Ginn, Heath, & Co. 25 cents.

There are no wall-maps of Modern History, except the German ones of *Bretschneider*.

4. AMERICAN HISTORY.

Marcius Willson. History of the United States. N.Y. Ivison. $1.25.

Emma Willard. History of the United States. N.Y. Barnes. 88 cents.
> These two books have the same qualities as the general histories of the same authors.

D. B. Scott. School History of the United States. H. 80 cents.
> Excellent, especially for arrangement.

J. C. Ridpath. History of the United States. Cincinnati. Jones. $1.00, $1.50, $3.00.
> Illustrated with serviceable diagrams.

J. J. Anderson. Popular School History of the United States. N.Y. Clark & Maynard. $1.11.
> Containing a large number of illustrative extracts from different authors.

C. A. Goodrich. History of the United States of America. B. Ware. $1.30.
> Well adapted to *memoriter* recitations.

B. J. Lossing. Outline History of the United States. N.Y. Sheldon. $1.11.
> Entertaining and well illustrated; too crowded with detail.

G. P. Quackenbos. Illustrated School History of the United States. App. $1.25.
> Very well written, but poorly arranged.

Miss M. E. Thalheimer. Eclectic History of the United States. Cincinnati. Van Antwerp. $1.17.
> With very good maps and illustrations.

Excelsior Studies in the History of the United States. N.Y. Sadlier. $1.25.
> A Catholic work; also has excellent maps.

A. H. Stephens. Compendium of the History of the United States. N.Y. Hale. $1.50.
> From a Southern point of view.

J. W. Leeds. History of the United States of America. Lip. $1.54.

H. E. Scudder. History of the United States of America. Ph. Butler.
>These two books are especially valuable in the history of civilization. Leeds is from a Quaker point of view; Scudder is beautifully illustrated.

L. J. Campbell. Concise School History of the United States. B. Ware. 87 cents.
>Based upon the work of C. A. Goodrich.

W. Swinton. Condensed School History of the United States. N.Y. Ivison. $1.04.
>A brief skeleton of events.

J. C. Martindale. History of the United States. Ph. Eldredge. $1.17.
>Of the same general character.

Primer of United States History. N.Y. Armstrong. 50 cents.
>With very good historical maps.

E. Abbott. Paragraph History of the United States. R. 50 cents.
Id. Paragraph History of the American Revolution. R. 50 cents.

See also Doyle (p. 282), Higginson, and others (p. 298).

The following are for younger scholars:—

Brief History of the United States. N.Y. Barnes. $1.17.
>Well arranged and written.

W. H. Venable. History of the United States. Cincinnati. Van Antwerp & Co. $1.00.
>A good book, with excellent maps.

A. B. Berard. School History of the United States. Ph. Cowperthwait. $1.10.
>A book of great merit, written in an interesting style.

S. G. Goodrich. Pictorial History of the United States. Ph. Butler. $1.46.
>Entertaining, but badly arranged.

One Thousand Questions in American History. Syracuse. Bardeen.
>A useful aid to teachers.

R. Blanchard. Historical map of the United States. Ch.

W. R. Houghton. Wall-chart of United States History.

Id. Conspectus of the History of Political Parties.
>An ingenious diagram, containing much information.

J. J. Anderson. United States Reader. N.Y. Clark & Maynard. $1.30.
>Well selected extracts from historians, poets, and orators, illustrating the history of the United States.

L. H. Porter. Outlines of the Constitutional History of the United States. Holt. $1.50.
>Contains many valuable and interesting documents.

SUPPLEMENT.

CONTAINING ADDITIONAL BOOKS, CHIEFLY FRENCH AND GERMAN, OR WORKS PUB-
LISHED SINCE THE EARLIER LIST, ARRANGED UNDER THE SAME HEADS.

PART I.

HISTORICAL LITERATURE AND AUTHORITIES.

1. PRIMITIVE SOCIETY.

D. G. Brinton. Library of Aboriginal American Literature. Ph. [Published by the editor.]
> Invaluable for the study of native institutions and religion; three volumes already published: 1. Chronicles of the Mayas; 2. Iroquois Book of Rites; 3. The Comedy-ballet of Guegence.

Capt. J. C. Bourke. The Snake Dance of the Moquis of Arizona. Scr. $5.00.
> An important contribution to the study of native Indian institutions.

J. G. Wood. The Uncivilized Races of Men in all Countries of the World. Hartford. Burr. $3.50.
> A very valuable collection of facts.

See also article upon the Zuñis, by *F. H. Cushing*, in the Century for 1883.

2. MYTHOLOGY.

W. H. Roscher. Ausführliches Lexicon der griechischen und römischen Mythologie. Lp. Teubner.
> Appearing in parts.

C. G. Leland. The Algonquin Legends of New England. Houghton.

Ethnic Religions.

Albert Réville. The Native Religions of Mexico and Peru. [Hibbert Lecture. 1884.] Scr. $1.00.

James Freeman Clarke. Ten Great Religions. Part II.: A comparison of all religions. Houghton.

3. HISTORY OF SOCIETY.

W. E. H. Lecky. History of European Morals from Augustus to Charlemagne. 2 v. App.

K. T. v. Inama-Sternegg. Deutsche Wirthschaftsgeschichte. Vol. I.: Zum Schluss der Karolingerperiode. Lp. Duncker & Humblot.
    The first complete study of economic phenomena for this period.

E. Bonnemère. Histoire des Paysans. 2 v. P. Sandon et Fischbacher.
    Extends from the earliest times to the Revolution.

C. Dareste de la Chavanne. Histoire des classes agricoles en France. P. Guillaumin.

Henri Doniol. Histoire des classes rurales en France. P. Guillaumin.
    La Chavanne is most complete for the middle ages, Doniol for the modern period.

Samuel Sugenheim. Geschichte der Aufhebung der Leibeigenschaft und Hörigkeit in Europa. Lp. Voss.
    The best work upon serfdom and its abolition.

J. E. T. Rogers. Six Centuries of Work and Wages. Put.
    A history of the English laboring classes, based upon an exhaustive study of economic facts.

Toulmin Smith. English Gilds: with Introduction upon the History, etc., of Gilds, by *Lujo Brentano* [which can be had separate]. Early English Text Society. L.

G. Fagniez. Etudes sur l'industrie et la classe industrielle à Paris au xiiie et au xive siécle. P. Viewig.

W. Stieda. Zur Entstehung des deutschen Zunftwesens. Jena. Dufft.

HISTORICAL LITERATURE AND AUTHORITIES. 311

G. Schanz. Zur Geschichte der deutschen Gesellenverbände im Mittelalter. Lp. Duncker & Humblot.
    These ten works, selected from a large literature, give a tolerably complete view of the industrial classes in the middle ages.

4. GENERAL HISTORY.

W. Assmann. Handbuch der allgemeinen Geschichte. 5 v. Braunschweig. Vieweg.
    Valuable for its references to authorities; especially full for the middle ages.

Georg Weber. Allgemeine Geschichte für die gebildeten Stände. 14 v.
    The best complete universal history. The "Lehrbuch," by the same author, is regarded as the best German text-book.

W. Oncken. Allgemeine Geschichte in Einzeldarstellungen. The following works have been added: *F. Justi,* Geschichte des alten Persiens. *B. Kugler,* Geschichte der Kreuzzüge. *S. Ruge,* Zeitalter der Entdeckungen. *L. Geiger,* Renaissance und Humanismus. *A. Brückner,* Katharina die Zweite.

F. Laurent. Etudes sur l'Histoire de l'Humanité. 18 v. Bruxelles.
    A series of monographs. Probably the most suggestive general history.

C. G. Wheeler. The Course of Empire. O.
    A brief summary of history by centuries, with abundant selections; an outline map for each century.

L. Weisser. Bilderatlas zur Weltgeschichte. Stuttgart. Neff. 50 numbers at 50 pf. = $6.50.
    A very large and useful collection of historical illustrations; of unequal value.

5. ANCIENT HISTORY.

A. Baumeister. Denkmäler des Klassischen Alterthums zur Erläuterung des Lebens der Griechen und Römer in Religion, Kunst und Sitte: lexikalisch bearbeitet. R. Oldenbourg. München. 40 numbers at 1 mark = $10.00.

H. A. Wallon. Histoire de l'Esclavage dans l'Antiquité. 3 v. P.
    The only complete treatise upon the subject.

W. C. Wilkinson. Preparatory Latin Course in English; College Greek Course; College Latin Course. Phillips & Hunt.

Quellenbuch zur alten Geschichte. Lp. Teubner. 2 v. 1. Griechische Geschichte. 2. Römische Geschichte.
    Contains all the important authorities on classical history, in selections, chronologically arranged.

6. Oriental History.

A. H. Sayce. The Ancient Empires of the East. Scr.
    A compendious statement of the present condition of knowledge.

G. Rawlinson. Ancient Empires of the East. Student's edition. 5 v. Dodd, Mead, & Co. $6.25.

7. History of Greece.

G. Gilbert. Handbuch der griechischen Staatsalterthümer. Lp. Teubner.
    The best compendium of the subject.

K. Fr. Hermann. Lehrbuch der griechischen Antiquitäten. 4 vol. Staats-, Gottesdienstliche- und Privatalterthümer. Freiburg. Mohr.
    The standard work; a revised edition has been published.

E. Kuhn. Ueber die Entstehung der Städte der Alten. Komenverfassung und Synoikismos. Lp. Teubner.
    The best treatise upon the formation of political communities among the Greeks.

8. Roman History.

G. Boissier. Cicéron et ses Amis. P.

Id. La Religion romaine d'Auguste aux Antonins. 2 v. P.

P. B. Watson. Marcus Aurelius Antoninus. H.
    An able and scholarly production.

L. Friedländer. Darstellungen aus der Sittengeschichte Roms. 3 v. Lp. Hirzel.

H. Schiller. Geschichte des römischen Kaisserreichs unter der Regierung des Nero. Ber. Weidmann.

J. N. Madvig. Verfassung und Verwaltung des römischen Staates. 2 v. Lp. Teubner.

P. Willems. Le Droit public romain. Louvain.
: These are the two best compendiums of Roman antiquities.

E. Kuhn. Die städtische und bürgerliche Verfassung des römischen Reichs bis auf die Zeiten Justinians. 2 v. Lp. Teubner.

R. J. A. Houdoy. Le Droit Municipal. P. 1876.
: These two works treat of the municipal constitution: Kuhn from an historical, Houdoy from a legal point of view.

J. Beloch. Der italische Bund. Lp. Teubner.
: Treats of the relation of Rome to the other Italian communities.

B. Heisterbergk. Die Entstehung des Colonats. Lp. Teubner.
: Discusses the subject from an economical point of view.

E. C. Clark. Early Roman Law. The Regal Period. Macm.

James Hadley. Lectures on Roman Law.

R. von Jhering. Der Geist des römischen Rechts. 3 v. Lp. Breitkopf and Härtel.

F. C. Savigny. Geschichte des römischen Rechts im Mittelalter. 7 v. Heidelberg.

Orelli and *Henzen.* Inscriptionum Latinarum selectarum amplisima collectio. 3 v. Turici [Zurich].

9. MEDIÆVAL HISTORY.

M. A. Geffroy. Rome et les barbares. P. Didier.
: A study upon the Germania of Tacitus.

Charles Kingsley. The Roman and the Teuton. Macm.
: An interesting and suggestive course of lectures.

G. Waitz. Deutsche Verfassungs Geschichte. 8 v. Kiel. Homann.
: The great standard work upon German constitutional history, reaching the twelfth century.

P. Roth. Geschichte des Beneficialwesens. Erlangen. Palm.
: The most important work for the beginnings of Feudalism.

R. Sohm. Altdeutsche Reichs und Gerichtsverfassung. Weimar. Böhlau.
: Treats of the constitution of the Frank Empire.

P. E. Fahlbeck. La royauté et le droit royal francs. Lund.
> The best sketch of the constitutional history of the early Merovingian period; agrees essentially with Sohm.

E. Secretan. Essai sur la Féodalité. Lausanne.
> The most complete description of the Feudal System.

H. G. Gengler. Germanische Rechtsdenkmäler. Erlangen. Deichert.
> A collection of illustrative extracts from documents, with a good introduction.

Id. Deutsche Stadtrechts Alterthümer. Erlangen. Deichert.

A. Heusler. Der Ursprung der deutschen Stadtverfassung. Weimar. Böhlau.
> The best single treatise of a general nature. The best special work is perhaps:

C. Hegel. Verfassungsgeschichte von Cöln im Mittelalter. Lp. Hirzel.

A. Wauters. Les libertés communales. Bruxelles. Lebègue.
> Treats of municipal institutions in northern France and Belgium.

A. Kremer. Culturgeschichte des Orients unter den Chalifen. 2 v. Vienna.
> The best history of Mohammedan civilization.

10. Ecclesiastical History.

Count de Montalembert. The Monks of the West: from St. Benedict to St. Bernard. 7 v. Ed. Blackwood.
> The best history of monasticism.

A. H. Wratislaw. John Hus. Soc.

Julius Köstlin. Life of Martin Luther. Scr.
> The best popular life of Luther; with contemporary illustrations.

E. D. Mead. Martin Luther: A Study of Reformation. B. Ellis.

W. Smith. Dictionary of Christian Biography. 3 v. Murray.

Id. Dictionary of Christian Antiquities. 2 v. Murray [also Hartford. Burr. $7.00].

S. E. Herrick. Some Heretics of Yesterday. Houghton.
> Popular lectures; extend from Tauler to Wesley.

11. HISTORY OF ENGLAND, ETC.

J. R. Green. The Conquest of England. H.
: Properly a continuation of "the Making of England," completing the history of the Anglo-Saxon period.

J. R. Seeley. The Expansion of England. R.
: Two courses of lectures of remarkable suggestiveness.

Coote. The Romans in Britain.
: Devoted to establishing the survival of Roman institutions, etc.

H. M. Scarth. Roman Britain. Soc.

William Hunt. Norman Britain. Soc.
: Two valuable short treatises.

J. S. Brewer. The Reign of Henry VIII. 2 v. $12.00.
: Papers written during the work of editing the documents belonging to this reign.

P. Friedmann. Anne Boleyn: A Chapter of English History. 1527-1536. 2 v. Macm.

S. R. Gardiner. History of England. 1603-1642. 10 v. Longm.
: A revised and cheaper edition of his great work.

J. McCarthy. A History of the Four Georges. Vol. I. II. $1.25.
: Reaches the year 1729.

Id. Short History of Our Own Times. H.
: An abridgment of his larger work.

J. H. McCarthy. Outline of Irish History. Baltimore. Murphy.
: Particularly good for the nineteenth century.

Edw. Smith. Story of the English Jacobins. C.
: A popular account of the treason trials, etc., at the close of the eighteenth century.

R. B. Smith. Life of Lord Lawrence. 2 v. Scr.

R. Schmidt. Die Gesetze der Angelsachsen. Lp. Brockhaus.
: The best edition of these laws, with a glossary.

A. S. Cook. Extracts from the Anglo-Saxon Laws. Holt.
: The most important passages, in the original.

W. Stubbs. Select Charters: Documents Illustrative of English History. Macm.
: A valuable selection of documents, with introduction; extends to Edward I.

K. E. Digby. Introduction to the History of the Law of Real Property.
    An excellent treatise, with illustrative documents.
F. Pollock. The Land Laws. Macm.
    A good short history of these laws.

12. History of France.

L. Häusser. Geschichte der französischen Revolution. Ber.
    A course of lectures reported stenographically.
A. Schmidt. Tableaux de la Révolution Française.
    A valuable collection of documents, presenting a vivid picture of society during the revolution.
J. F. Crane and S. J. Brun. Tableaux de la Révolution Française. Put.
    An historical French reader. With an introduction by Pres. A. D. White.
Sarah Tytler. Life of Marie Antoinette. [New Plutarch.] Put.
K. Hillebrand. Geschichte Frankreichs von der Thronbesteigung Louis Philippes bis zum Falle Napoleons III. Gotha.
    The second volume reaches the year 1840.

13. Special Histories.

Geschichte der europäischen Staaten, edited by *Heeren, Ukert,* and *Giesebrecht:* Geschichte der Teutschen, by *Pfister,* 5 v.; der italienischen Staaten, by *Leo,* 5 v.; des preussischen Staates, by *Stenzel,* 5 v.; von Sachsen, by *Böttiger,* 2 v.; von Spanien, by *Lembke and Schäfer,* 3 v.; der Niederlande, by *van Kampen,* 2 v.; Russland, by *Strahl and Herrmann,* 7 v.; Schwedens, by *Geijer and Carlson,* 4 v.; Englands, by *Lappenberg and Pauli,* 5 v.; des österreichischen Kaiserstaats, by *Mailath,* 5 v.; Portugals, by *Schäfer,* 5 v.; Frankreichs, by *Schmidt,* 4 v.; von Dänemark, by *Dahlmann,* 3 v.; Frankreichs, by *Wachsmuth,* 4 v.; des osmanischen Reichs, by *Zinkeisen,* 8 v.; Polens, by *Röpell and Caro,* 3 v.; Deutschlands (1806–30), by *Bülau.*

HISTORICAL LITERATURE AND AUTHORITIES. 317

W. Arnold. Deutche Urzeit. Gotha, Perthes.
> A later volume brings the history down to the time of Charles the Great. A work of great value.

G. Kaufmann. Deutsche Geschichte bis auf Karl den Grossen. 2 v. Lp. Duncker & Humblot.
> An excellent compendium of the present condition of knowledge.

W. von Giesebrecht. Geschichte der deutschen Kaiserzeit. 5 v. Braunschweig. Schwetschke.
> The best history of the empire; reaches the twelfth century.

F. von Raumer. Geschichte der Hohenstaufen und ihrer Zeit. 6 v.
> A standard work of great literary merit.

Konrad Maurer. Island von seiner ersten Entdeckung bis zum Untergange des Freistaates. München.
> By far the most valuable work upon the history of Iceland.

O. Lorenz. Deutschlands Geschichtsquellen im Mittelalter. 2 v. Ber. Hertz.

C. Müller. Der Kampf Ludwig des Baiern mit der römischen Curie. 2 v. Tübingen.

E. Werunsky. Geschichte Kaiser Karls IV. und seiner Zeit. Innsbruck.

T. Lindner. Geschichte des deutschen Reiches unter König Wenzel. 3 v. Braunschweig.

F. Krones. Handbuch der Geschichte Oesterreichs. 3 v. Ber. Grieben.

F. Palacky. Geschichte v. Böhmen. 4 v. (in several parts). Prag.
> By the great Bohemian historian; the German view is given by

L. Schlesinger. Geschichte Böhmens. Lp. Brockhaus.

L. von Szalay. Geschichte Ungarns. 3 v. Pest. Lauffer.
> Reaches the close of the middle ages; a brief complete history is

M. Horváth. Kurzgefasste Geschichte Ungarns. Buda-Pest.
> Both of these are Hungarian works. The German view will be found in

J. A. Fessler. Geschichte von Ungarn. 5 v.

B. von Kállay. Geschichte der Serben. 2 v. Buda-Pest. Lauffer.
> A good history of this important Slavonic people.

Jos. von Hammer. Geschichte des osmanischen Reiches. 8 v. Pesth.
: The highest authority upon this history.

Vulliemin. Histoire de la Suisse.
: The best history of Switzerland.

F. Gregorovius. Geschichte der Stadt Rom im Mittelalter. 8 v. Stuttgart. Cotta. $20.00.

F. T. Perrens. Histoire de Florence. 6 v. Paris.
: The most important recent contribution to Italian history.

G. Sartorius. Geschichte des hanseatischen Bundes. 2 v. Göttingen.
: An old work, but still the best on the subject.

E. Worms. Histoire commerciale de la ligue hanséatique. P. Guillaumin.

H. Tuttle. History of Prussia to the Accession of Frederick the Great. 1134-1740. Houghton.
: An interesting and scholarly work.

F. Eberty. Geschichte des preussischen Staates. 7 v. Breslau. [to 1871].

J. G. Droysen. Geschichte der preussischen Politik. 2 v. Lp.
: Of the highest historical merit, but strongly absolutist.

L. von Ranke. Memoirs of the House of Brandenburg. 3 v. L.
: Chiefly devoted to the history of the eighteenth century. The original work has been completely revised and re-written under the title "Zwölf Bücher preussischen Geschichte."

C. F. v. Stälin. Wirtembergische Geschichte. 4 v. Stuttgart. Cotta.
: Regarded as one of the very best histories of a single state.

A. Young. History of the Netherlands. E. & L.
: A good short history; chiefly of the 16th and 17th centuries.

L. Vanderkindere. Le siècle des Artevelde. Bruxelles. Lebègue.

P. Fredericq. Le Rôle politique et social des ducs de Bourgogne. Gand. Hoste.

A. Gindely. History of the Thirty Years' War. 3 v.
: A popular work by the highest living authority.

John L. Stevens. History of Gustavus Adolphus. Put.

Carl van Noorden. Europäische Geschichte in achtzehuten Jahrhundert: I. Der spanische Erbfolgekrieg. 3 v. Düsseldorf.
: The most important work upon the subject.

A. Schäfer. Geschichte des siebenjährigen Kriegs. 2 v. B.
Especially valuable in diplomatic history.
C. B. Brackenbury. Frederick the Great. [New Plutarch.] Put.
F. W. Longman. Frederick the Great. [E.S.] Scr.
L. Häusser. Deutsche Geschichte vom Tode Friedrichs des Grossen bis zur Gründung des deutschen Bundes. 4 v.
Learned, impartial, and graphic.
Eugene Schuyler. Peter the Great. Scr.
An excellent work; handsomely illustrated.
F. W. Horn. History of the Literature of the Scandinavian North. Ch. Griggs.
W. E. Griffin. Corea, the Hermit Nation. Scr.

14. NINETEENTH CENTURY.

Staatengeschichte der neuesten Zeit, ed. by *Baumgarten*: France (1814–52), by *Rochau*, 2 v.; England (since 1814), by *Pauli*, 3 v.; Germany (19th. century), by *Treitschke;* Italy (modern period), by *Reuchlin*, 2 v.; Spain (since French Revolution), by *Baumgarten,* 3 v.; Austria (since 1809), by *Springer*, 2 v.; Greece (since 1453), by *Mendelssohn*, 2 v.; Turkey (1826–52), by *Rosen*, 2 v.; Russia (1814–31), by *Bernhardi*, 3 v.
Baron Henry Worms. The Austro-Hungarian Empire (since 1866). L.
C. Bulle. Geschichte der neuesten Zeit. 1815–71. 2 v. Lp.
A work of great merit.
Cesare Cantù. Les trente dernierès années. (1848–78). P.
The work of a Republican and Catholic.
Th. Juste. La Révolution belge de 1830. 2 v. Bruxelles.
W. Müller. Political History of Recent Times, 1816–75 (with appendix, 1876–81). H.
Id. Politische Geschichte der Gegenwart. B.
An annual publication of great merit.
Count de Maupas. Story of the Coup d'Etat. App.
D. M. Wallace. Egypt and the Egyptian Question. Macm.

15. HISTORY OF THE UNITED STATES.

Arthur Gilman. History of the American People. Lothrop. $1.50.
C. C. Jones. History of Georgia. Houghton.
    Gives special attention to the social history of the colony.
American Commonwealths. Houghton.
    Oregon, by *W. Barrows.*
    Maryland, by *William Hand Browne.*
W. E. Foster. Stephen Hopkins, a Rhode Island Statesman; a study in the political history of the eighteenth century. Providence. Rider.
Richard Markham. King Philip's War [Lesser Wars]. Dodd, Mead, & Co.
C. W. Baird. History of the Huguenot Emigration to America. Dodd, Mead, & Co. $5.00.
Works of John Smith. Birmingham. Edward Arber.
Francis Parkman. Montcalm and Wolfe. 2 v. L. & B.
Frederick Kapp. Life of John Kalb. Holt.
E. J. Lowell. The Hessians and the other German Auxiliaries of Great Britain in the Revolutionary War. H.
American Statesmen. Houghton.
    James Madison, by *S. H. Gay.*
L. G. Tyler. Letters and Times of the Tylers. Richmond. Whittet.
    A series of pictures, from the Revolution to 1861.
H. O. Ladd. History of the Mexican War [Lesser Wars]. Dodd, Mead, & Co.
Mrs. C. E. Cheney. Young Folks' History of the Civil War. E. & L.
W. H. Seward. Diplomatic History of the Civil War in America. Houghton. $3.00.
    Vol. III. of Seward's Works.
J. G. Blaine. Twenty Years of Congress, from Lincoln to Garfield. 2 v. Norwich.
Gen. E. D. Keyes. Fifty Years' Observations of Men and Events, Civil and Military. Scr.

T. V. Cooper. American Politics. Ch. Brodix.
A valuable collection of facts and documents.

H. C. Adams. Taxation in the United States. (1789–1816.) Baltimore.

Johns Hopkins University Studies in Historical and Political Science. Edited by *H. B. Adams.* Baltimore.
Chiefly devoted to the history of American institutions.

See also Battles and Leaders of the Civil War, in the Century, 1883–84.

PART II.

BOOKS FOR COLLATERAL READING.

Sir G. W. Cox. Tales of Ancient Greece. Ch. Jansen.
Miss Beesly. Stories from the History of Rome. Macm.
A. J. Church. Stories of the Old World. Ginn, Heath, & Co.
    A selection from the several collections of classical tales.
Id. Stories of the Persian War. Dodd, Mead, & Co.
Id. Roman Life in Days of Cicero. Dodd, Mead, & Co.
J. S. White. Herodotus for Boys and Girls. Put.
Id. Plutarch for Boys and Girls. Put.
Rosalie Kaufmann. Our Young Folks' Plutarch. Lip.
W. Shepard. Our Young Folks' Josephus. Lip. $2.50.
R. Markham. Chronicle of the Cid. Dodd, Mead, & Co.
E. C. Kindersley. History of the Good Knight, the Lord de Bayard. Dodd, Mead, & Co.
    These six books are large and handsomely illustrated.
H. C. H. Calthrop. Paladin and Saracen [Tales from Ariosto].
Helen Zimmern. Tales from the Eddas. L. Swan.
Lady Calcott. Little Arthur's History of England. N.Y. Crowell.
Philips' Historical Readers. 1. Stories from English History; 2. Early England; 3. Middle England; 4. Modern England. B. School Supply Co.
W. H. Rideing. Young Folks' History of London. E. & L.
Miss C. M. Yonge. Aunt Charlotte's Stories of American History. App.
E. E. Hale. Stories of Discovery, told by Discoverers. R. $1.00.
F. S. Drake. Indian History for Young Folks. H. $3.00.
Capt. Charles King. Famous and Decisive Battles of the World. Ph. McCurdy.

HISTORY TOPICS.

ANCIENT HISTORY.

I. ORIENTAL PERIOD, TO B.C. 500.

1. **Egypt and Palestine.**—*a.* The Mediterranean system of lands. *b.* The valley of the Nile (with map). *c.* The early empire; the 4th and 12th dynasties. *d.* The Hyksos. *e.* The 18th and 19th dynasties. *f.* The 26th dynasty. *g.* The Hebrew monarchy. *Solomon*, B.C. 1000. *h.* The kingdoms of Israel and Judah.—*i.* The exodus of the Israelites. *k.* Æthiopia.—*Map:* The Mediterranean sea; the Orient; B.C. 1500.

2. **The Orient.**—*a.* The Chaldean empire. *b.* The Assyrian empire. *c.* Babylon. *d.* Media. *e.* Asia Minor; the kingdom of Lydia. *f.* Cyrus; the Persian empire. *g.* Darius Hystaspes; B.C. 500. *h.* Phœnicia; Tyre and Sidon.—*i.* Cyprus. *k.* Armenia. *l.* Cambyses in Egypt.—*Map:* B.C. 650 and 600.

II. GRECIAN PERIOD. B.C. 500–300.

3. **Greece.**—*a.* The geography and races of Greece. *b.* The Greek colonies. *c.* The Spartan hegemony. *d.* The Persian invasion. *e.* The Athenian empire; the age of Pericles. *f.* The Peloponnesian war. *g.* Epaminondas; the hegemony of Thebes. *h.* Philip of Macedon.—*i.* The return of the Heraclidæ. *k.* Themistocles. *l.* The battle of Marathon; of Salamis; of Leuctra. *m.* The peace of Antalcidas, B.C. 387.—*Map:* Greece; the Orient; B.C. 500.

4. **The Macedonian Empire.**—*a.* Alexander; the conquest of Persia. *b.* The expedition to India. *c.* Greece after Alexander. *d.* The Achæan league. *e.* The kingdom of Pergamus. *f.* The Seleucidæ; the kingdom of Syria. *g.* The Ptolemies in Egypt; Lagidæ. *h.* The Parthian empire; Arsacidæ.—*i.* The battle of Ipsus, B.C. 301. *k.* The Ætolian league. *l.* Agis and Cleomenes. —*Map:* B.C. 275.

III. ROMAN PERIOD. B.C. 300 TO CHRISTIAN ERA.

5. **Italy.** — *a.* The geography and races of Italy. *b.* The Etruscans. *c.* Magna Graecia. *d.* Rome under the kings. *e.* The hegemony of Rome in Latium. *f.* The capture of Rome by the Gauls, B.C. 390. *g.* The Latin war, B.C. 340. *h.* The Samnite wars. *i.* The war with Pyrrhus. — *k.* The Æquians and Volscians. *l.* The conquest of Veii. *m.* The Caudine Forks; B.C. 321. — *Map:* Italy; B.C. 500 and 275.

6. **The Conquest of the World.** — *a.* Carthage and the First Punic war. *b.* The Second Punic war; Hannibal. *c.* The Macedonian wars. *d.* The war with Antiochus. *e.* The conquest of Spain. *f.* The wars of Pompey in the East. *g.* The conquest of Gaul. *h.* The Social war, B.C. 90. — *i.* The battle of Cannæ; of Cynoscephalæ. *k.* The Ligurians. *l.* The Illyrians. *m.* The Numidians. *n.* The Maccabees. — *Map:* B.C. 200 and 100. List of the provinces in the order of their acquisition.

IV. ROMAN EMPIRE. THE CHRISTIAN ERA TO A.D. 500.

7. **The Early Empire.** — *a.* The civil war of Cæsar and Pompey. *b.* The Second Triumvirate. *c. Augustus;* the Empire; B.C. 27. *d.* The wars with the Germans. *e.* The conquest of Britain. *f.* The destruction of Jerusalem, A.D. 70. *g. Trajan;* A.D. 100. *h.* Marcus Aurelius, d. 180. — *i.* Relations with Parthia. *k.* Mauretania. *l.* The defeat of Varus by Arminius, A.D. 9. — *Map:* B.C. 27; A.D. 14 and 100. Genealogy of the family of Augustus.

8. **The Later Empire.** — *a. Septimius Severus;* A.D. 200. *b. Diocletian;* A.D. 300. *c.* Constantine the Great, d. 337. *d. Honorius;* A.D. 400. *e.* The new Persian empire; Sassanidæ. *f.* Palymra; Zenobia. *g.* The battle of Hadrianople, 378. *h.* The . Alemanni. — *i.* Aurelian, d. 275. *k.* Julian the Apostate, d. 363. *l.* Theodosius the Great, d. 395. *m.* Constantinople. — *Map:* A.D. 350 and 400.

9. **The Migrations of the Barbarians.** — *a.* The Visigoths (*West Goths*); Alaric, d. 412. *b.* The Vandals; Genseric, d. 477. *c.* The Burgundians. *d.* The Angles and Saxons. *e.* Attila and

the Huns. *f.* Odoacer; the fall of the Empire, 476. *g.* Theodoric the Ostrogoth (*East Goth*), d. 526. *h.* The Lombards; Alboin, 568. — *i.* Stilicho, d. 408. *k.* The battle of the Peoples (*Châlons*), 451. *l.* The Gepidæ. — *Map:* 420 and 476. List of the barbarian kingdoms in the order of their settlement.

MEDIÆVAL HISTORY. A.D. 500-1500.

I. THE FRANK PERIOD. A.D. 500-900.

10. **The Merovingian House.** — *a. Clovis;* A.D. 500. *b.* Justinian and his conquests. *c.* The Slavs and Avars. *d. Pope Gregory the Great;* A.D. 600. *e.* Heraclius, d. 641. *f.* Mohammed and his successors. *g.* The Ommeyades, 661. *h.* Austrasia and Neustria. *i.* The hegemony of Northumbria. — *k.* Belisarius, d. 565. *l.* Penda of Mercia, d. 655. *m.* The Scots and Picts. — *Map:* 510 and 565.

11. **The Carolingian House; A.D. 752.** — *a. Pipin of Heristal;* A.D. 700. *b.* Leo the Isaurian, d. 741. *c.* The battle of Tours, 732. *d.* The kingdom of the Asturias. *e.* The Abassides, 750. *f. Charles the Great;* A.D. 800. *g.* The treaty of Verdun, 843. *h.* The Normans. *i. Alfred the Great;* A.D. 900. — *k.* The hegemony of Mercia. *l.* Egbert of Wessex, d. 836. *m.* Harold Haarfager, d. 936. *n.* The kingdom of Scotland. — *Map:* A.D. 750 and 843. Genealogy of the Carolingian house.

II. PERIOD OF GERMAN ASCENDENCY. A.D. 900-1250.

12. **The Saxon House; A.D. 919.** — *a.* Otto the Great; emperor, 962. *b.* The kingdom of Burgundy. *c.* The Capetian house, 987. *d. St. Stephen of Hungary;* A.D. 1000. *e.* The Macedonian dynasty. *f.* The Russian monarchy. *g.* The Fatimites in Egypt. *h.* The Danish conquest of England, 1016. — *i.* Gorm the Old of Denmark, d. 936. *k.* St. Olaf of Norway. *l.* The kingdom of Bulgaria. *m.* The Saracens in Sicily. — *Map:* A.D. 1000. Genealogy of the Saxon house.

13. **The Franconian House; A.D. 1024.**—*a. Henry IV. of Germany;* A.D. 1100. *b.* Pope Gregory VII., d. 1086. *c.* The Norman conquest of England, 1066. *d.* The Norman conquests in Italy. *e.* Alfonso VI. of Castile, and the Cid. *f.* The Almoravides in Spain. *g.* The Seljukian Turks. *h.* The first crusade, 1096.—*i.* Sancho III., *the Great,* of Navarre, d. 1035. *k.* The States of North Africa. *l.* The Concordat of Worms, 1122.—*Map:* The countries about the Mediterranean; A.D. 1100. Genealogy of the Franconian house.

14. **The Swabian House (Hohenstaufen); A.D. 1138.**—*a.* A contest with the Welfs. *b.* The Lombard league. *c.* The kingdom of Sicily; 1130. *d.* The third crusade, 1189. *e.* The fourth crusade, 1204. *f.* Pope Innocent III.; A.D. 1200. *g.* The house of Plantagenet; 1154. *h.* The kingdom of Portugal; 1139.—*i.* The Almohades in Spain. *k.* The second crusade, 1147. *l.* The mark of Brandenburg. *m.* The duchy of Austria. *n.* Henry the Lion. —*Map:* Germany; A.D. 1138; Europe; A.D. 1200. Genealogy of the Welfs.

15. **The Great Interregnum; A.D. 1250.**—*a.* Frederic II., d. 1250. *b.* Rudolf of Hapsburg, d. 1291. *c.* Ottocar II. of Bohemia, d. 1278. *d.* St. Louis of France, d. 1270. *e.* Ferdinand III. of Castile, d. 1252. *f.* The Teutonic knights. *g.* The Albigensian crusade. *h.* Genghis Khan, d. 1227.—*i.* The seventh crusade, 1270. *k.* Iceland.—*Map:* Spain in 1050 and 1250. Genealogy of the Hohenstaufen.

III. PERIOD OF FRENCH ASCENDENCY. A.D. 1250–1500.

16. **The Fourteenth Century, to 1328.**—*a. Philip IV., the Fair;* A.D. 1300. *b.* The house of Anjou in Naples. *c.* Venice. *d.* Genoa. *e.* The Popes at Avignon. *f.* The independence of Scotland. *g.* The Swiss confederacy. *h.* Casimir the Great of Poland, d. 1370. *i.* Louis the Great of Hungary, d. 1382.—*k.* The conquest of Wales. *l.* Henry VII. in Italy. *m.* Louis IV. and John XXII.—*Map:* Germany; A.D. 1300. Genealogy of the house of Anjou.

17. **The Hundred Years' War, to 1360.**—*a.* The house of Valois. *b.* The treaty of Bretigny, 1360. *c.* The Jacquerie. *d.* The house of Luxemburg in Germany. *e.* The house of Palæ-

ologus in Constantinople. *f.* The Ottoman Turks. *g.* Tamerlane, d. 1405. *h.* The duchy of Milan. — *i.* Rienzi, the last of the tribunes, d. 1354. *k.* Stephen Dushan of Servia, d. 1356. — *Map:* France in the 14th century. Genealogy of the house of Valois.

18. **The Great Schism; A.D. 1378.** — *a.* The rival "obediences," Rome and Avignon. *b.* The council of Constance, 1414. *c.* The Hussite wars. *d.* The civil wars of Armagnac and Burgundy. *e.* Henry IV. *of England;* A.D. 1400. *f.* Joan of Arc, d. 1431. *g.* The Hanseatic league, 1360. *h.* The union of Calmar, 1397. — *i.* Philip van Artevelde, d. 1382. *k.* The battle of Agincourt, 1415. *l.* Pedro the Cruel of Castile, d. 1369. *m.* The battle of Nicopolis, 1396. — *Map:* 1400. Genealogy of descendants of John II. of France.

19. **The Fifteenth Century, to 1483.** — *a.* Louis XI., d. 1483. *b.* The duchy of Burgundy. *c.* Charles the Bold, d. 1477. *d.* The wars of the Roses. *e.* The capture of Constantinople, 1453. *f.* The revival of learning. *g.* The discovery of the East Indies. *h.* The invention of printing. — *i.* John Hunyady of Hungary, d. 1456. *k.* Scanderbeg, d. 1467. *l.* The kingmaker Earl of Warwick, d. 1471. — *Map:* The east of Europe. Genealogy of descendants of Edward III.

20. **The End of the Middle Ages, to 1517.** — *a.* Ferdinand and Isabella; A.D. 1500. *b.* The house of Aragon in Naples. *c.* The Italian expedition of Charles VIII., 1494. *d.* Florence. *e.* The house of Tudor, 1485. *f.* The league of Cambrai, 1508. *g.* Ivan the Great of Russia, d. 1505. *h.* The discovery of America, 1492. — *i.* Pope Alexander VI., d. 1503. *k.* Francesco Sforza, d. 1466. *l.* Gonsalvo di Cordova, d. 1515. *m.* The Holy League, 1512. — *Map:* Italy in the 15th century. Genealogy of Charles V. (his parents and grandparents).

MODERN HISTORY. FROM 1500.

I. PERIOD OF RELIGIOUS WARS. 1500-1650.

21. **The Reformation Period, 1517-55.** — *a.* The Ladies' peace [of Cambrai], 1529. *b.* The peace of Câteau-Cambresis, 1559. *c.* The Schmalkaldic league. *d.* The peace of Augsburg, 1555.

e. The duchy of Prussia. *f.* The house of Austria. *g.* The knights of St. John. *h.* Gustavus Wasa; king, 1523. — *i.* The battles of Marignano and Pavia. *k.* The field of the cloth of gold, 1520. *l.* The sack of Rome, 1527. *m.* Andrea Doria, d. 1560. *n.* The seizure of the three bishoprics, 1552. *o.* The battle of Mohacs, 1526. *p.* The duchy of Florence, 1531. — *Map:* 1500.

22. **The Spanish Supremacy; to 1598.** — *a.* The revolt of the Netherlands, 1572. *b.* The Invincible Armada, 1588. *c.* The Huguenot wars, 1562–72. *d.* The war of the Henries, 1585. *e.* The annexation of Portugal, 1580. *f.* Pope Sixtus V., d. 1590. *g.* Mary Queen of Scots, d. 1586. *h.* Henry IV. of France; A.D. 1600. — *i.* The battle of Lepanto, 1571. *k.* Sir Philip Sidney, d. 1586. *l.* Alexander Farnese, Prince of Parma, d. 1592. *m.* Ivan the Terrible, d. 1584. *n.* The edict of Nantes, 1598. — *Map* of the Spanish possessions. Genealogy of the house of Tudor.

23. **The Thirty Years' War; to 1648.** — *a.* The Cleve succession. *b.* The war in Bohemia. *c.* Gustavus Adolphus, d. 1632. *d.* Wallenstein, d. 1634. *e.* The peace of Westphalia, 1648. *f.* Cardinal Richelieu, d. 1612. *g.* The English revolution. *h.* The house of Romanof. — *i.* The Donauwörth affair, 1607. *k.* The independence of the Netherlands, 1609. *l.* The war with La Rochelle. *m.* The independence of Portugal, 1640. *n.* The colonization of America. *o.* Transylvania. — *Map:* 1648.

II. PERIOD OF DYNASTIC WARS.

24. **The Age of Louis XIV.; to 1697.** — *a.* Louis XIV.; A.D. 1700. *b.* The peace of the Pyrenees, 1659. *c.* The treaty of Nymwegen, 1678. *d.* The treaty of Ryswick, 1697. *e.* The English revolution of 1688. *f.* Frederick William, the Great Elector, d. 1688. *g.* The treaty of Oliva, 1660. *h.* The treaty of Carlowitz, 1699. — *i.* The invasion of the Netherlands, 1672. *k.* The devastation of the Palatinate, 1688. *l.* The triple alliance; Sir William Temple, 1668. *m.* John Sobieski, d. 1696. *n.* The war of the Fronde. — *Map:* The countries about the Baltic, 1660. Genealogy of the house of Stuart.

25. **The Eighteenth Century; to 1763.** — *a.* The treaty of Utrecht, 1713. *b.* The pragmatic sanction. *c.* The treaty of Aix-

la-Chapelle, 1748. *d.* The treaties of Paris and Hubertsburg, 1763. *e.* Charles XII. of Sweden, d. 1718. *f.* Peter the Great of Russia, d. 1725. *g.* Frederick the Great of Prussia, d. 1786. *h.* The English empire in India. — *i.* Cardinal Alberoni, d. 1752. *k.* The quadruple alliance. *l.* The family compact. *m.* The treaty of Vienna, 1738. *n.* The treaty of Nystadt, 1721. *o.* The kingdom of Prussia, 1701. *p.* The kingdom of Sardinia, 1720. — *Map:* The east of Europe, 1750. Genealogy of the Spanish succession.

III. Revolutionary Period.

26. **The French Revolution; to 1799.** — *a.* The first partition of Poland, 1772. *b.* The national assembly, 1789. *c.* The declaration of Pilnitz, 1791. *d.* The legislative assembly, 1791. *e.* The national convention, 1792. *f.* The first coalition, 1793. *g.* The second and third partitions of Poland, 1793 and 1795. *h.* The peace of Basle, 1795. — *i.* Count Mirabeau, d. 1791. *k.* The battle of Valmy, 1792. *l.* The American revolution. *m.* Catherine II. of Russia, d. 1796. — *Map:* Europe in 1789. Genealogy of the house of Romanof.

27. **The Wars of Napoleon; to 1815.** — *a.* Napoleon Bonaparte; A.D. 1800. *b.* The armed neutrality, 1800. *c.* The treaty of Luneville, 1801. *d.* The peace of Presburg, 1805. *e.* The confederation of the Rhine, 1806. *f.* The peace of Tilsit, 1807. *g.* The peace of Schönbrunn, 1809. *h.* The peace of Vienna, 1815. — *i.* The duchy of Warsaw and kingdom of Poland. *k.* Napoleon's continental system. *l.* The French annexations in their order. — *Map:* 1800; 1810.

28. **The Period of Peace, 1815-1848.** — *a.* The holy alliance, 1815. *b.* The French revolution of 1830. *c.* The kingdom of Belgium, 1831. *d.* The kingdom of Greece, 1831. *e.* The extinguishment of Poland, 1831. *f.* Mehemet Ali, d. 1849. *g.* The war of the Sonderbund, 1846. — *h.* The opium war, 1840. *i.* The Afghan war, 1839-41. *k.* The French occupation of Algiers, 1830. *l.* Prince Metternich, d. 1859. — *Map:* Europe in 1820. Genealogy of the Bourbons.

29. **The Second Empire; to 1870.** — *a.* The French revolution of 1848. *b.* The Hungarian revolution. *c.* The Crimean

war. 1854. *d.* The Sepoy revolt, 1857. *e.* The Italian war, 1859. *f.* The Schleswig-Holstein war, 1864. *g.* The seven weeks' war, 1866. *h.* Count Cavour, d. 1861. *i.* The revolution in Rome. *k.* The revolution in Venice. *l.* The Greek revolution, 1862. *m.* The Mexican empire, 1863. — *Map:* Italy in 1850 and 1870.

30. **The German Empire.** — *a.* The Franco-Prussian war, 1870. *b.* Prince Bismarck. *c.* The Turko-Russian war, 1876. *d.* The Afghan war, 1878. *e.* The Greek question. *f.* The Spanish republic, 1873. *g.* The Egyptian troubles, 1882. — *h.* The Abyssinian war, 1867. *i.* The Zulu war, 1878. *k.* The French in Tunis, 1881. *l.* The Dalmatian revolt, 1882. — *Map:* Germany in 1860, 1866, and 1871.

AMERICAN HISTORY

INTRODUCTION.

1. **The Discovery of America.** — *a.* The fifteenth century; formation of States. *b.* The renaissance. *c.* The great discoveries and inventions. *d.* Commerce with the East in the middle ages. *e.* The Portuguese navigators. *f.* The voyages of Columbus. *g.* The Cabots.

2. **Relation of American to European History.** — *a.* 16th cent.; rivalry between Spain, France, and England. *b.* 17th cent.; ascendency of France and Holland. *c.* Thirty years' war; rise of Sweden. *d.* The Puritan revolution in England. *e.* The revolution of 1688. *f.* 18th cent.; rivalry of France and England. *g.* The French encyclopædists. *h.* Reaction of America upon Europe. *i.* Federalist and republican sympathies.

3. **Spanish Explorations and Colonies within the Limits of the United States.** — *a.* De Soto's expedition, 1539. *b.* Coronado's expedition, 1540. *c.* Cabrillo's expedition, 1542. *d.* explorations and settlements in Florida.

4. **French Settlements in North America.** — *a.* Cartier's discoveries. *b.* The Huguenots in Carolina. *c.* The settlement of Acadia, 1604. *d.* Champlain's discoveries and settlements. *e.* The discovery of the Mississippi, 1673.

AMERICAN HISTORY. 331

Period of Colonization. 1607-1688.

5. **Virginia and Maryland.**— *a.* The London company and the Virginia charter. *b.* The Maryland grant. *c.* The government of Virginia. *d.* Bacon's rebellion, 1676. *e.* The controversy with Clayborne. *f.* The nature of proprietary government. *g.* The Puritan revolution in Maryland.

6. **The Dutch Colonies.**— *a.* The Dutch land grants. *b.* The Jerseys. *c.* The Pennsylvania boundary. *d.* New Sweden. *e.* The controversy with Connecticut. *f.* The nature of the royal province.

7. **New England.**— *a.* Patents and charters in New England. *b.* The settlement of Massachusetts bay. *c.* The nature of charter government. *d.* Territorial history of Maine and New Hampshire. *e.* The New England confederacy. *f.* The Indian wars. *g.* The Quakers in Massachusetts. *h.* The blue laws of Connecticut.

8. **The Southern Colonies.**— *a.* Locke's plan of government. *b.* The colonization of Georgia. *c.* The Huguenot refugees.

9. **Chronological Review of the Period.**— *a.* Order of settlement of the colonies. *b.* Map of the colonies in 1688. *c.* History of religious toleration.

Period of Colonial Life. 1688-1763.

10. **New France and Florida.**— *a.* Extent of French and Spanish occupation. *b.* Wars of Count Frontenac. *c.* The North American Indians.

11. **The Revolution of 1688.**— *a.* The new charter of Massachusetts. *b.* Leisler's rebellion. *c.* Salem witchcraft. *d.* Sir Edmund Andros.

12. **King William's and Queen Anne's Wars.**— *a.* The war of the Spanish succession. *b.* The treaty of Utrecht, 1713. *c.* Sir William Phips, d. 1695. *d.* The changes in colonial government.

13. **Wars of George II.**— *a.* The seven years' war. *b.* The treaty of Paris, 1763. *c.* Hostilities in 1754 and 1755. *d.* The campaign of 1758. *e.* The conquest of Canada. *f.* Franklin's plan of union, 1754. *g.* The conspiracy of Pontiac, 1763.

14. **Review of the Period.**—*a.* Map of the colonies in 1763. *b.* Nationalities in the colonies. *c.* Education. *d.* Industry. *e.* Slavery. *f.* Literature. *g.* Church organizations.

REVOLUTIONARY PERIOD. 1763–1789.

15. **1763 to 1770.**—*a.* The navigation acts and writs of assistance. *b.* The stamp act, 1765. *c.* The congress of 1765. *d.* Acts of Grafton's administration, in relation to America. *e.* Troubles in New York. *f.* Affairs in the South. *g.* The British administrations. *h.* James Otis, d. 1783.

16. **1770 to 1774.**—*a.* Lord North's financial acts and the Boston tea-party. *b.* The acts of parliament of 1774. *c.* The Continental congress of 1774. *d.* The Boston massacre, March 5, 1770. *e.* The burning of the Gaspé, June 10, 1772. *f.* Patrick Henry, d. 1799. *g.* Samuel Adams, d. 1803.

17. **1775.**—*a.* The acts of congress. *b.* Hostilities down to June. *c.* The battle of Bunker Hill, June 17. *d.* The expedition to Canada. *e.* George Washington, d. 1799.

18. **1776.**—*a.* Acts of independence and union. *b.* The siege of Boston. *c.* Military operations about New York. *d.* Washington in New Jersey. *e.* The military organization.

19. **1777.**—*a.* Burgoyne's expedition. *b.* The occupation of Philadelphia. *c.* The operations in the South, 1774–77. *d.* The Conway cabal. *e.* The finances of the war. *f.* The treaty with France, Feb. 6, 1778. *g.* Benjamin Franklin, d. 1790.

20. **1778 and 1779.**—*a.* The battle of Monmouth, June 28, 1778. *b.* Sullivan's expedition against the Six Nations, 1778. *c.* The expedition of George Rogers Clark, 1779. *d.* The capture of Stony Hook, July 15, 1779. *e.* The operations about Savannah. *f.* John Paul Jones, d. 1792.

21. **1780.**—*a.* The battle of Camden, August 16. *b.* The battle of King's Mountain, October 7. *c.* The capture of Charleston, May 12. *d.* Arnold's treason.

22. **1781.**—*a.* The battle of Cowpens, January 17. *b.* Greene's retreat, and the battle of Guilford, March 25. *c.* Campaign of Gen. Greene after Guilford. *d.* Campaign of Lord Cornwallis. *e.* The siege of Yorktown. *f.* Marquis Lafayette, d. 1834.

AMERICAN HISTORY.   333

23. **Close of the War.**—*a.* The armed neutrality. *b.* The treaty of peace. *c.* The Newburgh addresses. *d.* The formation of state governments. *e.* The cession of the public lands.

24. **The Confederacy, 1781-89.**—*a.* The articles of confederation. *b.* The financial troubles. *c.* Shay's rebellion. *d.* The ordinance of 1787. *e.* The formation of the constitution.

25. **The Constitution.**—*a.* The distinctive features of the constitution. *b.* The establishment of the new government. *c.* Settlement and early history of Kentucky. *d.* The Vermont controversy. *e.* Formation of state government in Tennessee.

26. **Review of the Period.**—*a.* Hamilton's theory of government. *b.* Madison's theory of government. *c.* Luther Martin's theory of government. *d.* Party divisions at the close of the period.

PERIOD OF THE REPUBLIC.   1789-1876.

I. FOREIGN RELATIONS, TO 1820.

27. **Washington's First Administration, 1789-93.**—*a.* The amendments to the constitution. *b.* The legislation of the first congress. *c.* Hamilton's financial policy. *d.* The Indian troubles. *e.* A permanent seat of government.

28. **Washington's Second Administration, 1793-97.**—*a.* Jay's treaty, 1795. *b.* The French complications. *c.* The whiskey insurrection, 1794. *d.* Washington's farewell address. *e.* Alexander Hamilton, d. 1804.

29. **John Adams' Administration, 1797-1801.**—*a.* The war with France. *b.* The alien and sedition acts. *c.* The Virginia and Kentucky resolutions. *d.* The presidential election of 1800-1. *e.* The schism in the Federalist party; the Essex junto.

30. **Jefferson's First Administration, 1801-5.**—*a.* The purchase of Louisiana, 1803. *b.* The war with Tripoli, 1801. *c.* The north-western territory. *d.* The amendment to the constitution.

31. **Jefferson's Second Administration, 1805-9.**—*a.* Burr's conspiracy, 1806. *b.* Relations with France and England. *c.* The embargo, 1807.

32. **Madison's First Administration, 1809-13.**—*a.* Causes

of the war of 1812. *b.* The Indian hostilities; Tecumseh. *c.* Naval operations in 1812. *d.* Hull's surrender, August 16.

33. **Madison's Second Administration, 1813-17.** — *a.* Campaigns on the northern frontier. *b.* Military operations in 1814. *c.* Jackson's campaigns in the South. *d.* Naval operations. *e.* The attack upon Washington and Baltimore. *f.* The Hartford convention, 1814. *g.* The treaty of Ghent, Dec. 24, 1814. *h.* The war with Algiers, 1815.

34. **Monroe's Administration, 1817-25.** — *a.* The Missouri compromise. *b.* The purchase of Florida, 1819. *c.* The Seminole war. *d.* The settlement of the northern boundary.

35. **Review of the Period.** — *a.* The era of good feeling. *b.* The bank of the United States. *c.* Tariff legislation until 1815. *d.* Foreign relations. *e.* Slavery and the slave-trade.

II. Economic Questions, to 1845.

36. **John Quincy Adams' Administration, 1825-29.** — *a.* The Panama congress and the Monroe doctrine. *b.* Georgia and the Creek Indians. *c.* The tariff of 1828.

37. **Jackson's First Administration, 1829-33.** — *a.* Nullification. *b.* The anti-Mason party. *c.* Black-hawk's war, 1832. *d.* The "kitchen cabinet." *e.* John C. Calhoun, d. 1850.

38. **Jackson's Second Administration, 1833-37.** — *a.* The removal of the deposits. *b.* the anti-slavery movement. *c.* The farewell address. *d.* The Seminole war. *e.* The French spoliation claims.

39. **Van Buren's Administration, 1837-41.** — *a.* The subtreasury. *b.* The crisis of 1837. *c.* The repudiation movement. *d.* The affair of the *Caroline.*

40. **Harrison and Tyler's Administrations, 1841-45.** — *a.* The Webster-Ashburton treaty, 1842. *b.* The tariff of 1842. *c.* The annexation of Texas, 1845. *d.* Dorr's rebellion, 1842. *e.* The Mormon troubles in Illinois, 1844. *f.* Daniel Webster, d. 1852.

III. The Slavery Controversy, to 1876.

41. **Polk's Administration, 1845-49.** — *a.* The campaigns of the Mexican war. *b.* The occupation of the Pacific coast. *c.* The

treaty of Guadalupe-Hidalgo, 1848. *d.* The north-western boundary. *e.* The tariff of 1846. *f.* The Wilmot proviso.

42. Taylor and Fillmore's Administrations, 1849-53.—
a. The omnibus bill, 1850. *b.* The free-soil party. *c.* The fugitive-slave law. *d.* The Japan expedition. *e.* The correspondence of Webster and Hülsemann. *f.* Henry Clay, d. 1852. *g.* The Cuban filibusters.

43. Pierce's Administration, 1853-57.—*a.* The Nebraska bill, 1854. *b.* The know-nothing party. *c.* The Gadsden purchase. *d.* Diplomatic relations with Great Britain. *e.* The Ostend manifesto.

44. Buchanan's Administration, 1857-61.—*a.* The Kansas question. *b.* The Dred Scott decision, 1857. *c.* The personal-liberty bills. *d.* The Mormons in Utah. *e.* The acts of secession. *f.* John Brown, d. 1859.

45. Lincoln's Administration; to July, 1862.—*a.* The peninsular campaign. *b.* Operations in the West until Shiloh. *c.* The capture of New Orleans. *d.* The *Merrimac* and *Monitor*. *e.* The arrest of Mason and Slidell. *f.* The national bank system. *g.* The policy towards slavery. *h.* The constitution of the Confederacy. *i.* Operations on the seaboard.

46. Lincoln's Administration; July 1862, to Jan. 1864.—
a. Pope's campaign. *b.* McClellan's Antietam campaign. *c.* Fredericksburg and Chancellorsville. *d.* Murfreesboro'. *e.* Gettysburg. *f.* The opening of the Mississippi. *g.* Chickamauga and Chattanooga. *h.* The emancipation proclamation.

47. Lincoln's Administration, 1864-65.—*a.* Grant's campaign in Virginia. *b.* Sherman's campaign in the South. *c.* Hood's advance into Tennessee. *d.* The Shenandoah campaign. *e.* The Confederate cruisers. *f.* The policy towards the seceded states. *g.* The sanitary commission. *h.* The Freedmen's Bureau.

48. Johnson's Administration, 1865-69.—*a.* Reconstruction. *b.* The impeachment of the president, 1868. *c.* The purchase of Alaska, 1867. *d.* The constitutional amendments.

49. Grant's Administration, 1869-77.—*a.* The Santo Domingo treaty, 1870. *b.* The resumption of specie payments. *c.* The Geneva congress, 1872. *d.* The Crédit Mobilier.

50. **Review of the Period.** — *a.* The tariff question. *b.* The slavery controversy. *c.* The public lands. *d.* The Indian policy. *e.* The civil service. *f.* The Pacific railroad. *g.* The fisheries. — *Maps:* 1688, 1763, 1783, 1803, 1820, 1850, 1876. List of the states admitted to the union, with dates. List of the vice-presidents, with state, full name, and date. List of the secretaries of state, with same.

BIBLIOGRAPHY OF CHURCH HISTORY.

CONTENTS.

	PAGE.
I. INTRODUCTORY	343
II. GENERAL CHURCH HISTORY	344

A. *Eastern.*
1. Armenian 344
2. Coptic 344
3. Georgian 344
4. Græco-Russian 344
5. Nestorian 345
6. Syrian 345

B. *Western.*
1. North African 345
2. European 345

III. EARLY CHRISTIANITY 350
1. General 350
2. Catacombs 354
3. Charity 355
4. Controversies and Heresies 355
5. Patristics 355
6. Persecutions 355

IV. MEDIÆVAL CHRISTIANITY 356
1. General 356
2. Celibacy of the Clergy 357
3. Crusades 357
4. Lollards 357
5. Myths 358
6. Waldenses 358

	PAGE.
V. Modern Christianity	358
1. General Histories of the Reformation Period	358
2. The Roman Catholic Church	360
I. General	360
II. The Inquisition	361
III. Jansenists	361
IV. Jesuits	361
V. Port Royalists	361
VI. Ultramontanism and Vaticanism	362
3. Old Catholics	362
4. Modern Ecclesiastical History, by Countries	362
I. Bohemia	362
II. England	362
A. The Church of England established by Law	362
B. Dissenters	363
III. France	364
IV. Germany	365
V. Holland	365
VI. Hungary	365
VII. Ireland	365
VIII. Italy	365
IX. Poland	365
X. Scandinavia	366
XI. Scotland	366
XII. Spain	366
XIII. Switzerland	366
XIV. United States of America	366
A. General	366
B. Denominational	367
VI. Special Topics	371
1. Art	371
2. Biography	372
A. Biblical	372
I. Lives of Christ	372
II. Lives of Apostles	373
B. General	374
I. Collections	374
II. Individual	375

VI. SPECIAL TOPICS — *Continued.* PAGE.
   3. Church and State 377
   4. Councils 377
   5. Creeds 378
   6. Doctrines 378
   7. Fiction.. 379
   8. Liturgies 381
   9. Martyrs 382
  10. Miracle Plays and Mysteries 382
  11. Missions 382
  12. Monastic Orders 383
  13. Rationalism 383
  14. Reference Books 383
  15. Sacred Seasons 385
  16. Symbolism 385

A SELECT BIBLIOGRAPHY OF ECCLESIASTICAL HISTORY.[1]

BY JOHN ALONZO FISHER,
GRADUATE STUDENT OF CHURCH HISTORY AND PHILOSOPHY AT
JOHNS HOPKINS UNIVERSITY.

I. INTRODUCTORY.

Crooks, G. R., and *Hurst, J. F.* Theological Encyclopædia and Methodology. Based on Hagenbach. 8vo. pp. 596. N.Y. Phillips & Hunt. 1884. $4.00.
 An admirable introduction to all departments of theological study. It contains valuable bibliographies, German and English.

Dowling, John G. An Introduction to the Critical Study of Ecclesiastical History, attempted in an account of the progress, and a short notice of the sources of the history of the church. L. 1838.

Hitchcock, R. D. The True Idea and Uses of Church History. N.Y. 1856.

Newton, J. Review of Ecclesiastical History, etc. Works, p. 369 (pp. 88).

Schaff, Philip. General Introduction to Church History, Bibliotheca Sacra, v. 6, 1849, p. 409 (pp. 33); and Progress of Church History as a Science, Bib. Sac., v. 7, 1850, p. 54 (pp. 37).

Id. What is Church History? A vindication of the idea of historical development. 12mo. pp. 128. Ph. Lip. 1846.

Smith, H. B. Nature and Worth of the Science of Church History. Andover. 1851. In Bib. Sac., v. 8, 1851, p. 412 (pp. 50).

---

[1] For abbreviations, see page 239, foot-note.

Smyth, Egbert C. Value of the Study of Church History in Ministerial Education. A lecture delivered to the senior class of Andover Theological Seminary. pp. 31. Andover. Draper. 1874. Paper, 25 cents.
>Of practical value to pastors.

Stanley, A. P. Three Introductory Lectures on the Study of Ecclesiastical History. 8vo. Oxford. J. H. & J. Parker. 1857. Republished as an introduction to the American edition of the author's History of the Eastern Church. 1861. N.Y.: Scr., 1867. Scribner, Armstrong, & Co., 1873, $2.50.
>Compare the introductory pages of the church histories by the Roman Catholic writers *Fleury, Möhler, Alzog, Döllinger,* and *Hergenröther,* and the Protestant writers *Mosheim, Schroeckh, Gieseler, Hase, Niedner, Kurtz,* and *Schaff.*

II. GENERAL CHURCH HISTORY.

A. EASTERN. — 1. *Armenian.*

Davis, (Mrs.) Tamar. A General History of the Sabbatarian Churches. Embracing accounts of the Armenian, East Indian, and Abyssinian Episcopacies. 8vo. pp. 255. Ph. Lindsay & Blakiston. 1851.

2. *Coptic.*

Malan, S. C. A Short History of the Copts and of their Church. 12mo. pp. 115. L. Nutt. 1873. 2s. 6d.

3. *Georgian.*

Joselan, P. A Short History of the Georgian Church. Translated from the Russian, and edited with additional notes by *S. C. Malan.* 8vo. L. Saunders. 1865. $1.50.

4. *Græco-Russian.*

Neale, J. M. A History of the Holy Eastern Church, the Patriarchate of Antioch, etc. Edited, with an introduction, by *George Williams.* 8vo. L. 1873. $5.00.

Stanley, A. P. Lectures on the History of the Eastern Church. L. & N.Y., 1862. N.Y.: Scribner, Armstrong & Co., 1873. $2.50.
  Contains three introductory lectures on Church history. These lectures were delivered at Oxford. Not a continuous and exhaustive history, but, like all of Dean Stanley's writings, fascinating and scholarly. The sections on the Arian controversy are, according to Dr. Schaff, who also criticizes Stanley's omission to discuss the Nestorian and the other Christological controversies of the Eastern Church, "more brilliant than solid."

5. *Nestorian.*

Badger, Geo. Percy. The Nestorians and their Rituals. Illustrated (with colored plates). 2 v. L. 1852.

6. *Syrian.*

Wortabet, John. Researches into the Religions of Syria; or, Sketches, Historical and Doctrinal, of its Religious Sects. 8vo. L. Nisbet. 1860.
  Cf. paper by *H. H. Jessup* in Proceedings of the Sixth Session of the Evangelical Alliance. N.Y. H. 1874.

B. WESTERN.—1. *North African.*

Lloyd, Julius. The North African Church. 8vo. With map. L.. Soc. 1880. 3s. 6d.

2. *European.*

Allen, Joseph Henry. Christian History in its Three Great Periods. 16mo. 3 v. B. R. $1.25 each.
  Convenient; liberal; readable.

Alzog, John. A Manual of Universal Church History. Translated from the ninth enlarged and improved German edition, and edited and brought down to the present time, by *F. J. Pabisch* and *Thomas S. Byrne.* 3 v. I. Early Church History; II. The Middle Ages; III. To the Present Time. 8vo. Cincinnati.. Clarke & Co. $15.00.
  At once the latest and the highest Roman Catholic authority: " Alzog aims to be the Roman Catholic Hase as to brevity and

condensation. . . . The American translators censure the French translators for the liberties they have taken with Alzog, but they have taken similar liberties, and, by sundry additions, made the author more Romish than he was." — P. SCHAFF.

Arnold, Matthew. St. Paul and Protestantism; with an Introduction on Puritanism and the Church of England. 12mo. N.Y. 1875. $1.75. L. Smith, Elder, & Co. 4s. 6d.

Blackburn, W. M. History of the Christian Church, from its Origin to the Present Time. 8vo. pp. 719. Cincinnati. Hitchcock & Walden. 1879. $2.50.

Comprehensive and convenient. By a Presbyterian.

Döllinger, John Joseph Ignatius. Manual of Church History. Translated from Dr. Döllinger's unfinished Handbook of Christian Church History, 1833, and Manual of Church History, 1836, by *Edw. Cox.* 4 v. 8vo. pp. 287, 375, 351, 245. L. Dolman. 1840–42.

This work extends to the Reformation. Dr. Döllinger, since 1870 the leader of the Old Catholic movement, is the most learned Roman Catholic historian of the nineteenth century.

Gieseler, John C. L. Text-Book of Church History. 5 v. Bonn. 1824–56. Fourth edition, 1844 sqq. "Translated into English first by *Cunningham*, Ph., 1846; then by *Davidson* and *Hall* in England; and last and best, on the basis of the former, by *Henry B. Smith*. 5 v. N.Y. H. 1857–80. The fifth and last volume of this edition was completed after Dr. Smith's death (1877) by Prof. *Stearns* and Miss *Mary A. Robinson*, with an introductory notice by *Philip Schaff*." Vols. 1, 2, 3, and 4, $2.25 each; vol. 5, $3.00.

"Profoundly learned, acute, calm, impartial, conscientious, but cold and dry." — P. SCHAFF. "The standard complete history of the church." — W. F. ALLEN. The great merit of this work is its wealth of choice extracts from the original authorities. It is generally considered the best of all the text-books on church history.

Guericke, H. E. F. Handbook, etc. Translated, in part, by *W. G. T. Shedd.* 8vo. 2 v. pp. xvi, 433; pp. viii, 160. Andover. Draper. 1857 and 1870. Vol. I. (to A.D. 590), $2.75; Vol. II. (to A.D. 1073), $1.25.

The tone of the book is that of a Lutheran polemic.

Hardwick, Charles. A History of the Christian Church. 2 v. 12mo. Vol. I.: Middle Ages, with maps constructed for the work by *A. Keith Johnson.* Vol. II.: The Reformation. 12mo. Cambridge and London. 1861–65. $3.00 per vol.

> Written for students by a representative of the Church of England.

Hase, Charles. A History of the Christian Church. Translated from the seventh and much improved German edition, by *C. E. Blumenthal* and *C. P. Wing.* 8vo. N.Y. 1855; 1870. $3.50.

> Since the publication of the translation, the German work has been revised. Condensed, skilfully arranged, and well written.

Hurst, J. F. Outlines of Church History. N.Y. Philips & Hunt. 1884. 50 cents.

Kurtz, John Henry. Text-Book of Church History. Translated from the German by *Schaeffer*, 2 v., Ph., 1860; revised edition, 1875; eighth edition, 1880. (Translated by *Edersheim*, and completed by *Bomberger*, Ed. and Ph., 1861.) $3.00.

> Evangelical Lutheran. Concise.

Lawrence, Eugene. Historical Studies. 8vo. pp. 508. N.Y. H. 1876. Contents: The Bishops of Rome; Leo and Luther; Loyola and the Jesuits; Ecumenical Councils; The Vaudois; The Huguenots; The Church of Jerusalem; Dominic and the Inquisition; The Conquest of Ireland; The Greek Church.

> Protestant. Clear, strong, and accurate.

Lea, Henry C. Studies in Church History: The Rise of the Temporal Power; Benefit of Clergy; Excommunication. 8vo. pp. xiii, 518. Ph. H. C. Lea. 1869. $2.50.

Milman, H. H. History of Latin Christianity; including that of the Popes to the Pontificate of Nicholas V. 8 v. 12mo. pp. 554, 551, 525, 555, 530, 539, 570, 561. N.Y. Armstrong & Son. 1881. $14.00.

> Of great value alike to students and to general readers. See under Mediæval Christianity.

Milner, Joseph. History of the Church of Christ. L. 1794–1812. New corrected edition, 4 v., 1847, 1860, etc. L. 1875. 18s.

> Pietistic; neither scholarly nor polemic.

Mosheim, John Lawrence. Institutes of Ecclesiastical History, Ancient and Modern. A new and literal translation from the original Latin, with copious additional notes, original and selected, by *James Murdock.* 3 v., fifth edition, N.Y., 1854; 3 v. in one, 8vo, pp. 470, 485, 506. N.Y. Carter & Bros. 1881. $5.00. (There is a translation by *A. Maclaine.* N.Y. II. $1.00.)

> The distinguished author, a moderate Lutheran, is "the father of church historiography as an *art*, unless we prefer to concede this merit to Bossuet." Skilful, clear, impartial. Mosheim wrote in unrivalled Latin. He died in 1755.

Neander, J. Augustus W. General History of the Christian Religion and Church. Translated from the second improved German edition by *Joseph Torry.* 5 v., 8vo, Boston, 1854; also, 8 v., 12mo, L. & N.Y., 1861. Twelfth edition: B. Houghton. 1881. $18.00.

> This well-known history is "distinguished for thorough and conscientious use of the sources, critical research, ingenious combination, tender love of truth and justice, evangelical catholicity, hearty piety, and by masterly analysis of the doctrinal systems and the subjective Christian life of men of God in past ages. . . . The political and artistic sections, and the outward machinery of history, were not congenial to the humble, guileless simplicity of Neander. His style is monotonous, involved, and diffuse, but unpretending, natural, and warmed by a genial glow of sympathy and enthusiasm." — P. SCHAFF, his pupil.

Newman, John Henry. Essays Critical and Historical. 2 v., with notes. Poetry; Rationalism; De la Mennais; Palmer on Faith and Unity; St. Ignatius; Prospectus of the Anglican Church; The Anglo-American Church; Countess of Huntingdon; Catholicity of the Anglican Church; The Antichrist of Protestants; Milman's Christianity; Reformation of the Eleventh Century; Private Judgment; Davison; Kemble. L. Pickering. 1872-77. 12s.

> By the able Roman Catholic prelate, formerly of the Church of England.

Id. Historical Sketches. 3 v. Primitive Christianity; Church of the Fathers; St. Chrysostom; Theodoret; St. Benedict, etc. L. Pickering. 1873 *sqq.* 18s.

ECCLESIASTICAL HISTORY. 349

Robinson, James E. History of the Christian Church (A.D. 64–1517). 4 v., 1854 *sqq.*; 8 v., 12mo, L., 1874.
> The best general history yet written from the Anglican point of view.

Schaff, Philip. History of the Apostolic Church. 8vo. N.Y. 1853, etc. $3.75.
> Excellent, but superseded by his *magnum opus*, History of the Christian Church.

Id. History of the Christian Church. 3 v. 8vo. 1859–67. Revised and enlarged, with maps: Vol. I., Apostolic Christianity (A.D. 1–100), pp. 863; Vol. II., Ante-Nicene Christianity (A.D. 100–325), pp. 866; Vol. III., Nicene and Post-Nicene Christianity (A.D. 311–600), pp. 1039. N.Y. Scr. 1882–84. (Other volumes are promised.) $4.00 per volume.
> The greatest monument of American scholarship in the field of church history. Orthodox, liberal, readable. Though designed especially for students, it meets the wants of studious men in all the walks of life. It is peculiarly rich in bibliographies.

Smith, Philip. The Student's Manual of Ecclesiastical History. A history of the Christian church from the time of the Apostles to the full establishment of the Holy Roman Empire and the Papal power. Illustrated. 12mo. N.Y. H. 1879. $1.50.
> An excellent manual. It contains chronological tables, and has an index.

Stanley, A. P. Essays on Ecclesiastical Subjects: Baptism and the Eucharist, Absolution, Ecclesiastical Vestments, the Basilica, the Clergy, the Pope, the Litany, the Roman Catacombs, the Creed of the Early Christians, the Lord's prayer, the Council and Creed of Constantinople, and the Ten Commandments. 12mo. N.Y. H. 50 cents.
> By a scholarly genius.

Waddington, George. History of the Church, from the Earliest Ages to the Reformation. 8vo. N.Y. H. $2.00.

Washburn, E. A. Lectures on the Apostolic Age, the Nicene Age, the Latin Age, the Reformation, the English Church, the Church of America, the Church of the Future, Richard Hooker, etc. 12mo. pp. 400. N.Y. Dutton & Co. $1.75.

Whately, Richard. A General View of the Rise, Progress, and Corruption of Christianity. 12mo. pp. 288. N.Y. W. Gowans, 1860. N. Tibbals & Sons, 1876. $1.50.

White, James. The Eighteen Christian Centuries. 12mo. L. & N.Y. Second edition. 1862. App. $2.00.

"Its merit is in the fact that the spirit of each age is generally well apprehended and correctly represented; while its weakness shows itself in what must be considered an altogether artificial division of history into exact periods of a hundred years each. The author's style is at all times bright and vigorous." — C. K. ADAMS.

III. EARLY CHRISTIANITY.

(*See Lives of Christ, under Biography.*)

1. GENERAL.

Baumgarten, M. Apostolic History. The Acts of the Apostles; or, the History of the Church in the Apostolic Age. Translated by A. J. W. Morrison. 3 v. 8vo. Ed. 1854. $9.00.

Baur, Ferd. Christ. The Christians and the Christian Church of the First Three Centuries. Tübingen, 1853. 2d rev. ed., 1860 (pp. 536). The 3d ed. is a reprint of the second, forming Vol. I. of Baur's General Church History, edited by his son, in 5 v., 1863. Tr. by A. Menzies. 8vo. 2 v. L. W. & N. 1878, 1879. 10s. 6d.

"The last and ablest exposition of the Tübingen reconstruction of the Apostolic History from the pen of the master of that school.... Baur's critical researches have compelled a thorough revision of the traditional views on the apostolic age, and have so far been useful, notwithstanding their fundamental errors." — P. SCHAFF.

Blunt, J. H. A Christian View of Christian History, from Apostolic to Mediæval Times. 12mo. L. Rivingtons. 1866. New edition, 1872. 1s. 6d.

Delitzsch, Franz. Jewish Artizan Life in the Time of Jesus. Translated by *Bernhard Pick.* 12mo. N.Y. Funk & Wagnalls. 1884. Paper, 15 cts.; cloth, 75 cts.

Scholarly; but entertaining as a romance. The author refers, in foot-notes, to his authorities. Well translated.

Döllinger, Johann Joseph Ignaz. The First Age of Christianity. Translated by *H. N. Oxenhams.* 2 v. 8vo. L. 1866. $8.00.
"Dr. Döllinger has long been held as one of the ablest historians in the Roman Catholic Church; and this work may be regarded as the most successful representation of the early history of the Church from the Catholic point of view." — C. K. ADAMS.

Eusebius. Ecclesiastical History (Greek). Translated by *C. F. Crusé;* with an Historical View of the Council of Nice, by *Isaac Boyle.* 8vo. L., 1842. Ph., 1860. Lip. $2.50. Another translation in Greek Ecclesiastical Historians of the First Six Centuries, *q.v.*
Eusebius, "the Christian Herodotus," was intimately associated with Constantine the Great. Died 340.

Farrar, F. W. Early Days of Christianity. N.Y. Funk & Wagnalls. Paper, 40 cts.; cloth, 75 cts.
A standard work.

Fisher, George P. The Beginnings of Christianity, with a View of the State of the Roman World at the Birth of Christ. 8vo. pp. 580. N.Y. Scr. 1877. $3.00.
Scholarly, but popular. In this volume the orthodox but liberal author incidentally discusses the theories of the Tübingen school.

Id. Supernatural Origin of Christianity, with special reference to the theories of Renan, Strauss, and the Tübingen school. 8vo. pp. 620. N.Y. Scr. New and enlarged edition, 1870. $3.00.
Suited to the needs of all classes of readers. Clear, strong, readable.

Gibbon, Edward. Decline and Fall of the Roman Empire. See chapters on the Growth of Christianity. Numerous editions.
Contains many depreciatory references to the Christian church. "To counteract the influence of these arguments and insinuations of Gibbon, both Milman and Guizot have edited special editions of this history, with abundant notes. The Student's Gibbon, prepared by *W. Smith* in a similar spirit, is an edition greatly abridged." — N. PORTER. The best edition is Milman's.

Hatch, E. The Organization of the Early Christian Churches. Bampton Lectures for 1880. 8vo. pp. 216. Oxford and Cambridge. Rivingtons. 1881. 10s. 6d.
Learned, eloquent. Shows the development of church polity from a democracy into a monarchy.

Historians (Greek) of the First Six Centuries. Translations in Bohn's Ecclesiastical Library. 4 v. 8vo. L. 1851. Eusebius, Socrates, Sozomen, Theodoret, and Evagrius. 6 v. L. 1843–47. $2.00 each.

> Cf. *Geo. A. Jackson*: The Apostolic Fathers of the Second Century, with extracts. pp. 203. N.Y. 1878.

Jackson, Samuel M. Lipsius on the Roman Peter-Legend. In the Presb. Quar. and Princeton Rev. (N.Y.) for 1876. p. 265 *sqq.*

> A summary of the views of R. A. Lipsius, who has examined "carefully the heretical sources of the Roman Peter-legend, and regards it as a fiction from beginning to end."

John, St. The Fourth Gospel.

> See *Baur, Strauss, Renan,* and their followers. The genuineness of this Gospel has been defended by *Priestley, Andrews & Norton, Van Oosterzee* (trans. by *Hurst*), *Lange* (Com. trans. by *Schaff*), *Sanday* (Authorship and Historical Character of the Fourth Gospel, London, 1872), *Lightfoot* (in Cont. Rev., 1875–77), *George P. Fisher* (Beginnings of Christianity, chap. x., and art. "The Fourth Gospel" in the Princeton Rev. for July, 1881, pp. 51–84), *Westcott* (Introduction to the Gospels, 1862, 1875, and Commentary, 1879), *McClellan* (The Four Gospels, 1875), *Milligan* (in the Cont. Rev. for 1867, 1868, 1871, and in his Moulton's Commentary, 1880), and *Ezra Abbot* (The Authorship of the Fourth Gospel, External Evidences, Boston, 1880; paper, 50 cents. A work of great merit).

Lightfoot, J. B. In Contemporary Review, 1875–77. A series of articles against "Supernatural Religion," *q.v.* Cf. the reply of the anonymous author in the preface to the sixth edition of S. R.

Maurice, F. D. Lectures on the Ecclesiastical History of the First and Second Centuries. 8vo. Camb., 1854. L. Macm. $3.50.

Milman, Henry Hart. The History of Christianity, from the Birth of Christ to the Abolition of Paganism in the Roman Empire. 3 v. 8vo, L.; and 12mo, N.Y. New and revised edition: N.Y. Armstrong. 1871. $5.25.

> For the person that can read but one church history, this, perhaps, is the best. It is pervaded by the spirit of enlightened faith. It treats especially of the relations of Christianity to the Roman Empire.

Mosheim, J. L. History of the Ante-Nicene Period. Translated from the Latin by *Vidal.* 3 v. 1813 *sqq.* 2 v. New Haven, 1852. New edition. 2 v. N.Y., 1853.

Neander, J. A. W. History of the Planting and Training of the Christian Church. Translated by *J. E. Ryland.* Ed., 1842; and in Bohn's Standard Library, L., 1851; reprinted in Ph., 1844; revised by *E. G. Robinson,* N.Y., 1865. $4.00.

"This book marks an epoch, and is still valuable." — P. SCHAFF.

Priestley, J. General History of the Christian Church to the Fall of the Western Empire. In Works, Vols. 8–10.

Pressensé, Edmund de. The Early Years of Christianity. Translated by *Annie Harwood-Holmden.* 4 v. 12mo. L., Hodder & Stoughton, and N.Y. 1870 and 1879. $1.50.

By a scholarly Protestant pastor. Written in a popular style.

Renan, Ernest. The Apostles. 12mo. N.Y. Carleton. 1870. $1.75.

Id. The Influence of the Institutions, etc., of Rome upon Christianity. The Hibbert Lectures for 1880. L. W. & N. 1880. $3.50.

In Renan's best spirit. He shows, clearly and conclusively, that in its external organization, the early church was by degrees conformed to the existing institutions of the Roman Empire, and that these institutions thus have been perpetuated to the present day.

Simcox, Wm. H. Lectures on the Beginnings of the Christian Church. 12mo. L. 1881. $3.00.

Supernatural Religion, an Inquiry into the Reality of Divine Revelation. Anonymous. L., 1873; 2 v., 8vo, B., R., 1875, $8.00; 7th ed., "carefully revised," 1879, 3 v., 8vo, L., Longm., 36s.

"An English reproduction and repository of the critical speculations of the Tübingen School of Baur, Strauss, Zeller, Schwegler, Hilgenfeld, Volkmar, etc. . . . Dr. Schürer, in the 'Theol. Literatur Zeitung' for 1879, No. 26 (p. 622), denies to this work scientific value for Germany, but gives it credit for extraordinary familiarity with recent German literature, and great industry in collecting historical details. Drs. Lightfoot, Sanday, Ezra Abbot, and others, have exposed the defects of its scholarship and the false premises from which the writer reasons." — P. SCHAFF.

Taylor, Isaac. Ancient Christianity and the Doctrine of the Oxford "Tracts for the Times." Fourth edition, with a supplement. 2 v. 8vo. L. Bohn. 1844.
    By an Independent. Polemic; against "Puseyism" and the Roman Catholic Church.

Wadsworth, Charles. A Church History. [To the Council of Chalcedon, A.D. 451.] 4 v. 12mo. L. and N.Y. 1881(?). Vol. I., $2.50; II., III., and IV., $2.00 each.
    Churchly; not critical.

2. CATACOMBS.

    The best original authorities are in Italian. The highest is Rossi. The works of Padre-Marchi and Perret are superbly illustrated. D'Agincourt wrote from a personal knowledge of fifty years.

Lundy, John P. Monumental Christianity; or, the Art and Symbolism of the Primitive Church as Witnesses and Teachers of the one Catholic Faith and Practice. N.Y. Bouton. 1876. New edition; enlarged, 1882, pp. 453. Illustrated. $7.50.
    The writer is an Episcopalian.

Mommsen, Theodor. Roman Catacombs, in The Contemporary Review, Vol. XVII. (1871), pp. 160–175.

Northcote, J. S., and *Brownlow, W. R.* Roma Sotterranea. L. Longmans, Green & Co., 1869. Second edition, "rewritten and greatly enlarged." 1879. 2 v. $22.50.
    Northcote, Canon of Birmingham, and Brownlow, Canon of Plymouth, here present to English readers the results of Commendatore De Rossi's celebrated researches. The book is liberally illustrated with chromo-lithographic plates and with wood engravings.

Northcote, J. Spencer. Epitaphs of the Catacombs; or, Christian Inscriptions in Rome during the First four Centuries. L. Burns & Oates. 10s. (Vol. III. of B. & O.'s edition of *Roma Sotterranea.* Vols. I. and II. £1 4s. each.)

Parker, John Henry. The Archæology of Rome. Illustrated. Oxford and L. 1877. (Parts IX. and X., $6.00; and XII., $6.00.)
    Standard. Consult, also, *Kip, Maitland, McCaul, Stanley* (in his Christian Institutions), *Smyth* (pamphlet, 1882), *Stokes* (in Contemporary Review, 1880, 1881), *Venables* (in Smith and Cheetham, I. 294–317), *Marriott*, and *Withrow*.

3. CHARITY.

Uhlhorn, Gerhard. Christian Charity in the Ancient Church. 8vo. N.Y. Scr. $2.50.
The best work on the subject. Cf. *Chastel:* Charity of the Primitive Churches. Trans. by *G. A. Matiles.* Ph. Lip. 1857. $1.25.

4. CONTROVERSIES AND HERESIES.

Döllinger, J. J. I. Hippolytus and Callistus. In German, 1853. Translated by *Alfred Plummer.* 8vo. Ed. 1876. pp. 360. $3.60.
"An apology for Callistus and the Roman See against Hippolytus, the supposed first anti-Pope." See Wordsworth for a defence of Hippolytus.

Mansel, Henry L. The Gnostic Heresies. Edited by *J. B. Lightfoot.* L. Murray. 1875. $4.75.
Mansel was dean of St. Paul's. Cf. Dr. *Lightfoot's* Excursus in his Commentary on Colossians and Philemon for a satisfactory account of Gnosticism. *C. W. King's* Gnostics and their Remains (L., 1864) contains illustrations of Gnostic symbols and works of art. See, also, *Norton:* History of the Gnostics. B. 1845.

Newman, J. H. The Arians of the Fourth Century. L. 1838. Second edition, unchanged, 1854; third edition, 12mo. L. 1871. $3.50.

De Soyres, J. Montanism and the Primitive Church: a Study in the Ecclesiastical History of the Second Century. (Hulsean Prize Essay, 1877.) 8vo. pp. 163. L. Bell & Son. 1878. 6s.

5. PATRISTICS.

Donaldson, James. A Critical History of Christian Literature and Doctrine from the Death of the Apostles to the Nicene Council. L., 1864-66. 8vo, 3 v., L., Macm., 1874. $8.00.
Valuable. Cf. *Blunt* and *Jackson.*

6. PERSECUTIONS.

Mason, A. J. The Persecutions of Diocletian. (Hulsean Prize Essay, 1874.) 8vo. pp. 370. L. Bell & Sons. 1876. 10s. 6d.
In defence of Diocletian.

Uhlhorn, Gerhard. The Conflict of Christianity with Heathenism. Translated by *Egbert C. Smyth* and *J. C. H. Ropes.* 8vo. pp. 508. N.Y. Scr. $2.50.

IV. MEDIÆVAL CHRISTIANITY.

1. GENERAL.

Bryce, James. The Holy Roman Empire. Seventh edition, 12mo. pp. xxvii, 479. N.Y. Macm. 1877. $3.00.
    Standard. An excellent introduction to mediæval history, both ecclesiastical and secular.

Church, R. W. The Beginnings of the Middle Ages. With three Maps. 16mo. L. and N.Y. Longm. 1877. $1.00.
    Small, but readable and instructive. Discusses the relation of the Franks to the Church, and the ecclesiastico-political relations of Gregory the Great, Charlemagne, and Otto the Great.

Creighton, M. A History of the Papacy during the Period of the Reformation. 8vo. 2 v. L., Longm.; B., Houghton, Mifflin & Co. 1882. $10.00.
    The volumes treat of the events that led to the Reformation. Vol. II. ends with the death of Pius II., in 1464.

Greene, G. W. Lectures on the Middle Ages. 12mo. N.Y. App. $1.50.
    " A useful and trustworthy manual." — N. PORTER.

Hallam, Henry. State of Europe during the Middle Ages. 8vo. N.Y. H. $2.00. Student's edition, 12mo, $1.25.
    " Though exceedingly dry and condensed in its matter and manner, it is indispensable, even to a general reader." — N. PORTER.

Hardwick, C. A History of the Christian Church. Middle Ages. L. Macm. $2.25.

Lacroix, Paul. Works on the Middle Ages. 5 v. Imperial 8vo. L. 1880. N.Y. App. $12.00 per volume.
    The title of the third volume is " Military and Religious Life in the Middle Ages and at the Period of the Renaissance." Well translated, and richly illustrated. In collecting materials for his work, the author made good use of his opportunities as curator of the Imperial Library at the Arsenal of Paris.

Milman, Henry Hart. History of Latin Christianity. Including that of the Popes to the pontificate of Nicholas V. (For price, etc., see under General Church History, European.)
> "To the student of the middle ages this work is second in importance only to that of Gibbon. . . . Of the numerous works on the history of the church in the Middle Ages, this will generally be found at once the most readable, the most impartial, and the most satisfactory."— C. K. ADAMS.

Trench, Richard C. Lectures on Mediæval Church History. Being the substance of lectures delivered at Queen's College, London. 8vo. N.Y. Scr. 1878. $3.00.
> "A good popular sketch." — W. F. ALLEN.

Ullmann, C. Reformers before the Reformation. Principally in Germany and the Netherlands: I. John of Goch; II. John of Wesel; III. The Brethren of the Common Lot and the German Mystics; IV. John Wessel. Translated by *Robert Menzies.* 2 v. 8vo. pp. xxv, 416; xiv, 636. Ed. T. & T. Clark. 1855. $3.00 per volume.

Woodhouse, F. C. Military Religious Orders of the Middle Ages. Soc. 1879. 3s. 6d.

2. CELIBACY OF THE CLERGY.

Lea, Henry C. Historical Sketches of Sacerdotal Celibacy in the Christian Church. 8vo. pp. 601. B. Houghton, Mifflin & Co. 1884. Ph. Lip. $3.75.
> Highly valued, as embodying the results of independent and thorough research.

3. CRUSADES.

(*See Professor W. F. Allen's Bibliography.*)

4. LOLLARDS.

Wyckliffe, John de. Apology for Lollard Doctrine, attributed to Wyckliffe. With introduction and notes by *J. H. Todd.* 4to. L. Camden Soc. 1842.
See Biography, Wyckliffe.

5. MYTHS.

Baring-Gould, S. Curious Myths of the Middle Ages. 12mo, L., 1866; 16mo, B., R., 1880. $1.50.
> "The book is instructive, but it entertains and amuses even more than it instructs." — C. K. ADAMS.

Cox, George W., and *Jones, E. H.* Popular Romances of the Middle Ages. First American, from the second London, edition. 8vo. N.Y. Holt & Co. 1880. $2.25.
> "Probably the most valuable of the several manuals on the subject of the folk-lore of Europe." — C. K. ADAMS.

Döllinger, J. J. I. Fables Respecting the Popes of the Middle Ages, together with Dr. Döllinger's essay on the Prophetic Spirit and the Prophecies of the Christian Era. Translated by *Alfred Plummer*, with an introduction and notes by *H. B. Smith.* 12mo. N.Y. Dodd, Mead, & Co. 1872. $2.25.

6. WALDENSES.

Wylie, J. A. History of the Waldenses. L. Cassell. 2d edition. 1880. $1.25.

Worsfold, J. N. The Vaudois of Piedmont, A Visit to their Valleys, with a Sketch of their History to the Present Date. 8vo. L. J. F. Shaw & Co. 1873. 3s.

V. MODERN CHRISTIANITY.

1. GENERAL HISTORIES OF THE REFORMATION PERIOD.

Balmes, James. European Civilization: Protestantism and Catholicism Compared in their Effects on the Civilization of Europe. 8vo. 16th edition. Baltimore. Murphy. 1850. $2.50.
> By a learned Spanish priest, whose purpose in writing was to refute Guizot's reflections upon the Roman Catholic Church. Controversial. Contains interesting chapters on "Tolerance in Matters of Religion," "The Right of Coercion," and "The Inquisition in Spain."

Bossuet, J. B. The History of the Variations of the Protestant Churches. Translated from the last French edition. 2 v. 8vo. pp. 432, 424. Dublin. R. Coyne. 1829.
> Translated from the classic French of a celebrated Roman Catholic prelate.

D'Aubigné, J. H. Merle. History of the Great Reformation of the Sixteenth Century in Germany, Switzerland, etc. Translated from the French. 5 v. 12mo. N.Y. Carter Bros. 1846, etc. $4.50.
> The most widely read, but by no means the best, history of the Reformation. C. K. Adams justly pronounces it "simply one side of a great question, presented with great power by a skilful and brilliant advocate." D'Aubigné was an ardent Protestant.

Fisher, George P. The Reformation. 8vo. N.Y. Scr. 1873. $3.00.
> Perhaps the best short history of the Reformation.

Froude, J. A. Short Studies. 12mo. 3 v. N.Y. Scr. $1.50 each.
> Contain essays on "Erasmus and Luther," "Influence of the Reformation on Scottish Character," "Philosophy of Catholicism," and on "Calvinism."

Hagenbach, Karl Rudolph. History of the Church in the Eighteenth and Nineteenth Centuries. Translated by *John F. Hurst.* 2 v. 8vo. N.Y. Scr. 1869. $6.00.
> Impartial; popular. There is a translation by Miss Evelina Moore, 2 v., Ed., 1879; though good, it is not equal to the one by Bishop Hurst.

Hardwick, C. The Reformation. 8vo. L. Macm. 1873. $2.25.

Häusser, Ludwig. Period of the Reformation (1517–1648). 12mo. L. and N.Y. 1874. $2.50.
> "A course of lectures of high scholarship and historic insight." — W. F. ALLEN. Eleven of the fifty lectures discuss the Thirty Years' War. Not controversial. The book is translated by Mrs. G. Sturge, and edited by Prof. Wm. Oncken.

Hurst, John F. Short History of the Reformation. pp. 120. N.Y. H. 1884. 40 cts.
> The shortest history of the Reformation, and, for a beginner, the best. It contains portraits and maps.

Ranke, Leopold von. The History of the Popes, their Church and State, and especially of their Conflicts with Protestantism in the Sixteenth and Seventeenth Centuries. Translated by *E. Foster,* 3 v., 12mo, L., 1840. Translated by *Sarah Austin,* 3 v., 8vo, pp. 385, 414, 481. L., Murray, 1866. L., Bell. $3.75.

> "First published as early as 1837, this great work did more than any other to raise its author to that supreme rank among historians, which he has now long enjoyed. . . . As a portrayal of the interior policy of the church, and of the course that led to the reaction against the Reformation, these volumes have no equal." — C. K. ADAMS.

Seebohm, Frederic. The Era of the Protestant Revolution. Second edition, with notes on books in English relating to the Reformation, by *George P. Fisher.* 16mo. N.Y. Scr. 1875. $1.00.

> "A convenient and popular summary. . . . The book is less comprehensive in scope and less able in manner of treatment, than the work of Häusser." — C. K. ADAMS. The book is one of the Epochs of History series.

Spalding, M. J. History of the Protestant Reformation in Germany and Switzerland; and in England, Ireland, Scotland, the Netherlands, France, and Northern Europe. 8vo. Baltimore and N.Y. 1860. Many other editions. $3.50.

> By the late archbishop of Baltimore. Intended as a reply to D'Aubigné. "It is consequently too controversial to be of the greatest historical value, but it is scarcely more one-sided than the work of D'Aubigné, and it is perhaps the strongest presentation we have of the Catholic side of the Reformation." — C. K. ADAMS.

2. THE ROMAN CATHOLIC CHURCH.

I. *General.*

Wiseman, (Cardinal) N. Recollections of the last four Popes and of Rome in their Times. 12mo. N.Y. P. O'Shea. 4 v. $1.50 each.

> See under the Reformation Period, Church and State, and Councils.

II. The Inquisition.

"The Catholic Inquisition is best described by Llorente, is most heartily justified by Balmes, and most vigorously denounced by Buckle." — C. K. ADAMS.

Llorente, D. Jean Antoine. The History of the Inquisition of Spain, from the time of the Establishment to the Reign of Ferdinand VII. Composed from the original documents in the archives of the Supreme Council, and from those of subordinate tribunals of the Holy Office. 8vo. L. 1826.
> An abridged translation from the Spanish. There is no more authentic history of the Spanish Inquisition.

Rule, William H. History of the Inquisition, from its Establishment in the Twelfth Century to its Extinction in the Nineteenth. 2 v. 8vo. L. Hamilton. 1874. 25s.
> By a Wesleyan minister. Controversial, but fair, and ably written.

III. Jansenists.

Neale, J. M. History of the so-called Jansenist Church of Holland. 8vo. Oxford. Parker. 1858. 5s.

Tregelles, S. P. The Jansenists: their Rise, Persecutions by the Jesuits, and Existing Remnant. 12mo. L. Bagster. 1851. $1.60.

IV. Jesuits.

Carlyle, Thomas. See his essay on Jesuitism in his "Latter-day Pamphlets." 8vo. L. C. & H. 9s.

Macaulay, T. B. See his essay on Ranke, in which he maintains that the Jesuits, in their history, represent the Catholic reaction from the Protestant Reformation.

Stephens, (Sir) James. See his essay on Loyala, in Ecclesiastical Essays.
> "The best brief account of the rise of the Jesuits." — C. K. ADAMS.

V. Port Royalists.

Beard, Charles. Port Royal. A Contribution to the History of Religion and Literature in France. New edition. 2 v. 8vo. L. W. & N. 1873. $4.80.
> Cf. Stephen's Essays.

VI. *Ultramontanism and Vaticanism.*
(See Church and State, under Special Topics.)

3. OLD CATHOLIC.

"*Theodorus.*" The New Reformation; a narrative of the Old Catholic movement from 1870 to the present time, with an historical introduction. 8vo. L. Longm.(?) 12s.
For periodical literature, consult Poole's Index.

4. MODERN ECCLESIASTICAL HISTORY, BY COUNTRIES.

I. *Bohemia.*

Gillett, E. H. The Life and Times of John Huss; or, the Bohemian Reformation of the Fifteenth Century. 2 v. 8vo. pp. 632, 651. B., Gould & Lincoln, 1863; N.Y., Randolph. $7.00.

II. *England.* — A. *The Church of England established by Law.*

Bede. Historia Ecclesiastica. Oxford. 1846. In Bohn's Antiquarian Library, with the Anglo-Saxon Chronicle, $2.00.

Blunt, J. H. The Reformation of the Church of England. 2 v. N.Y. Young. $8.50.
"The best complete history. Extends from 1514 to 1662. From the point of view of the Church of England." — W. F. ALLEN.

Id. Sketch of the Reformation in England. Young. $1.50.

Cobbett. Reformation in England and Ireland. 12mo. Baltimore, Murphy, 1851, 75 cts.; N.Y., Sadlier, $1.25.
Roman Catholic. Wholly unsympathetic.

Diocesan Histories. Maps. [Canterbury, Chichester, Durham, Sheffield, Oxford, Peterborough, Salisbury, Worcester, York.] L. Soc. N.Y. Young. 2s. 6d. each, except Canterbury and York, 3s. 6d.
Valuable. Intended to form a complete library of English Ecclesiastical History.

Dixon, R. W. History of the Church of England. 2 v. Routledge. 16s. each.
"The most thorough and important work; not yet completed." — W. F. ALLEN.

ECCLESIASTICAL HISTORY. 363

Fuller, Thomas [edited by *J. S. Brewer*]. The Church History of Britain; from the Birth of Jesus Christ until the year 1648, etc. 6 v. 8vo. Clarendon Press, Oxford. 1845. £1 19s.

Geikie, Cunningham. The English Reformation, How it came about and why we should uphold it. 12mo. pp. xviii, 512. N.Y. App. 1869 and 1879. $2.00.

Haddan and *Stubbs.* Councils and Ecclesiastical Documents relating to Great Britain and Ireland. 8vo. 3 v. pp. 704, 285, 660. Oxford. Clarendon Press. 1869-78. Vols. 1 and 2, £1 1s. each; vol. 2, part 1, 10s. 6d.; vol. 2, part 2, 3s. 6d.

Herford, Brook. The Story of Religion in England. 12mo. pp. 391. Ch. Jansen, McClurg, & Co. $1.50.

Perry, G. G. A History of the Church of England from the Accession of Henry VIII. to the Silencing of Convocation in the Eighteenth Century. With an Appendix containing a Sketch of the History of the Protestant Episcopal Church in the United States of America, by *J. A. Spencer.* 8vo. N.Y. H. 1879. $2.50.
Excellent. "The best that has yet been written." — N.Y. CHURCHMAN.

Short, (Bp.) Thomas V. Sketch of the History of the Church of England, to the Revolution, 1688. 8th edition. 8vo. L. Longm. 1870. 7s. 6d.

Stanley, A. P. Historical Memorials of Canterbury Cathedral. 8vo. L. Murray. 1855. 5th edition, 1869. 7s. 6d.

Id. Historical Memorials of Westminster Abbey. 8vo. L. Murray. 1867. 4th edition, 1874. 15s.
Important; entertaining.

Strype, J. Works: Ecclesiastical Memorials, Annals, etc. [Orig. fol. 1694-1733.]
An excellent edition is that of the Clarendon Press, 1820-28, 8vo, 27 v., including two index volumes, £7 13s. 6d. Important.

For histories of the Book of Common Prayer, see Liturgics.

B. *Dissenters.*

Neal, Daniel. The History of the Puritans; or, Protestant Non-Conformists, from the Reformation (1517) to the Revolution in

1688. Reprinted from the Text of Dr. Toulmin's edition, with his life of the author, etc. Revised, corrected, and enlarged. 3 v., 8vo, L., Tegg. 1837; and with notes by J. O. Choules, 2 v., 8vo, N.Y., H., 1863. $1.00.

See Denominational Histories of the United States, for American churches having their origin in England.

III. France.

Baird, Henry M. History of the Rise of the Huguenots of France. Maps. 2 v. 8vo. N.Y. Scr. 1879. $3.50.

"An excellent account . . . from . . . 1515 to . . . 1574. . . . Written with judicial moderation." — C. K. ADAMS.

Poole, Reginald Lane. A History of the Huguenots of the Dispersion at the Recall of the Edict of Nantes. 12mo. L. Macm. 1880. 6s.

"A very learned, and a very successful, attempt to show what became of the Huguenots after the dispersion." — C. K. ADAMS.

Pressensé, E. de. Religion and the Reign of Terror; or, the Church during the French Revolution. Translated by J. P. Lacroix. 12mo. pp. 416. N.Y. Carlton and Lanahan. 1869. $1.75.

Smiles, S. The Huguenots in France. 8vo. N.Y. H. $2.00.

Id. The Huguenots in England, Ireland, and America. 8vo. N.Y. H. $2.00.

Weiss, Charles. History of the French Protestant Refugees. Translated from the French by H. W. Herbert. With an American Appendix. 2 v. 8vo. pp. 382, 419. N.Y. Stringer & Townsend. 1854.

A fine work, well translated.

White, Henry. The Massacre of St. Bartholomew, preceded by a History of the Religious Wars in the Reign of Charles IX. With illustrations. 8vo. N.Y. H. 1871. $1.75.

"Written in a judicious spirit. . . . Adopts the view of Ranke and of Soldan in believing that the famous massacre was not the result of a long-premeditated plot. . . . Many new materials tending to confirm this view. . . . The book, however, does not show the same intellectual grasp as that manifested in the pages of Baird." — C. K. ADAMS.

IV. Germany.

Lloyd, Julius. Sketches of Church History in Germany. L. Soc. 1882. 1s. 6d.

See, also, Doctrines, Biography, and General Histories of the Reformation Period.

V. Holland.

Martyn, W. C. The Dutch Reformation: a History of the Struggle in the Netherlands for Civil and Religious Liberty in the Sixteenth Century. 12mo. pp. 823. N.Y. American Tract Society. 1868. $1.75.

VI. Hungary.

D'Aubigne, J. H. Merle. History of the Protestant Church in Hungary to 1850. Translated by the Rev. J. Craig, D.D., with an introduction by J. H. Merle D'Aubigne, D.D. 8vo. pp. xxviii, 464. L. J. Nisbet & Co. 1844.

VII. Ireland.

Mant, Richard. History of the Church of Ireland, from the Reformation to the Revolution, with a Preliminary Survey from the Papal Usurpation in the Twelfth Century to its legal abolition in the Sixteenth. Large 8vo. 2 v. pp. 809, 844. L. Parker. 1845. 17s each.

VIII. Italy.

Baird, Robt. Sketches of Protestantism in Italy. 12mo. B. 1845. $1.75.

McCrie, Thos. History of the Progress and Suppression of the Reformation in Italy in the Sixteenth Century. Including a Sketch of the History of the Reformation in the Grisons. 12mo. Ph. Presb. Bd. of Pub. $1.00.

IX. Poland.

Krasinski, Valerian. Historical Sketch of the Rise, Progress, and Decline of the Reformation in Poland. 2 v. 8vo. pp. xxi, 415; xxiii, 573. L. Murray. 1838.

X. Scandinavia.

Crichton, A., and *Wheaton, H.* Scandinavia, Ancient and Modern: being a History of Denmark, Sweden, and Norway; comprehending . . . an account of the Mythology . . . Religion, etc. 2 v. 16mo. pp. xvii, 373; x, 403. N.Y. H. 1872. $1.50.

XI. Scotland.

Lawrence, E. The Scottish Covenanters. pp. 14. Harper's Magazine, v. 46, 1873, p. 103.

Stanley, A. P. Lectures on the History of the Church in Scotland. 8vo. pp. 180. L. Murray. 1872. 7s. 6d.
"Delighted the moderate and liberal, but displeased the orthodox" people of Scotland.

XII. Spain.

McCrie, Thos. History of the Progress and Suppression of the Reformation in Spain in the Sixteenth Century. 8vo. pp. viii, 424. Ed. Blackwood & Son. 1829.
Cf. Prescott's History of the Reign of Philip II.

Yonge, (Miss) C. M. Christians and Moors of Spain. L. Macm. $1.25. N.Y. H. Paper. 10 cents.
A popular sketch.

XIII. Switzerland.

D'Aubigné, J. H. Merle. Reformation in Switzerland. 2 v. 1864.
See Biographies of Calvin, Servetus, and Zwinglius.

XIV. United States of America. — A. General.

Baird, Robert. Religion in America. 8vo. pp. 338. N.Y. H. 1844. $3.00.
By a Presbyterian minister. The best book on the subject.

Belcher, Joseph. The Religious Denominations in the United States. Illustrated. New and revised edition. Large 8vo. pp. 1024. Ph. John E. Potter. 1861. $5.00.
A voluminous and somewhat crude work, which is, nevertheless, useful for reference. It contains many extracts from official documents not elsewhere easily accessible.

ECCLESIASTICAL HISTORY. 367

Mather, Cotton. Magnalia Christi Americana. [1702.] With notes and translations by *Robbins* and *Robinson*. 2 v. 8vo. pp. 622, 682. Hartford. S. Andrews & Son. 1853.
> Confined chiefly to New England. Editions without critical notes are misleading.

Rupp, I. D. An Original History of the Religious Denominations in the United States. 8vo. pp. 734. Ph. Humphreys. 1844.
> Chapters contributed by prominent members of the several churches.

Sprague, William B. Annals of the American Pulpit. 8 v. 8vo. N.Y. 1859-65.
> Biographical; impartial. Vols. 1 and 2, Trinitarian Congregationalists; vols. 3 and 4, Presbyterians; vol. 5, Episcopalians; vol. 6, Baptists; vol. 7, Methodists; vol. 8, Unitarians. There is a later edition published by Carter in 9 v. ($36.00).

B. *Denominational.*

BAPTIST.

Backus, I. History of New England, with Particular Reference to the Denomination of Christians called Baptists. 8vo. B.; 1777: Providence, 1784; B., 1796; Newton, 1871. 2 v. pp. x, 538; vi, 584. Ph. Am. Bap. Pub. Society. 90 cents.

Moss, Lemuel [Ed.]. The Baptists and the National Centenary. A Record of Christian Work. 8vo. Ph. 1876. $1.75.

Stewart, J. D. The History of the Free Will Baptists, for Half a Century. 12mo. pp. 479. Dover, N.H. Free Will Baptist Printing Establishment. 1862.

CHRISTIAN.

Summerbell, N. History of the Christians. Dayton, O. Christian Publishing Association.

CONGREGATIONAL.

Bacon, Leonard. The Genesis of the New England Churches. 8vo. N.Y. H. $2.50.

Dexter, Henry Martyn. Congregationalism. 8vo. pp. 1082. N.Y. H. 1880. $6.00.
> A complete bibliography is appended. Cf. *Waddington* (London, 1880) and *Punchard* (Boston, 1865-80). These three are the best authorities on general Congregational history.

FRIENDS.

Hodgson, Wm. The Society of Friends in the Nineteenth Century. 8vo. 2 v. pp. 349, 441. Ph. Smith, English & Co. 1875.
Cf. *Penn* and *Wagstaff.*

LUTHERAN.

Schmucker, S. S. The American Lutheran Church, Historically, Doctrinally, and Practically Delineated in Several Occasional Discourses. 12mo. Ph. 1852. 75 cents.
Cf. *Hazeline* (Zanesville, O., 1846) and Cong. Quar., 1862, article Lutheran Church in the United States.

Seiss, Joseph A. Ecclesia Lutherana. A Brief Survey of the Lutheran Church. 32d edition. 12mo. Ph. Luth. Bd. of Pub. 1867. (Cf. *Krauth.* $5.00.)

METHODIST.

Simpson, Matthew. Cyclopedia of Methodism. Revised edition. 4to. pp. 1031. Ph. L. H. Evarts. 1880.
Valuable as a work of reference.

Stevens, Abel. History of Methodism. 3 v. 12mo. N.Y. Methodist Book Concern. 1858–61. $4.50.

Id. History of the Methodist Episcopal Church in the United States of America. 4 v. 12mo. N.Y. Methodist Book Concern. 1864. $6.00.
Dr. Stevens is the highest authority on Methodist history.

Wood, E. M. Methodism and the Centennial of American Independence. With a brief History of the Various Branches of Methodism, and full Statistical Tables. 12mo. pp. 412. N.Y. Nelson & Phillips. 1876. $1.50.
Cf. *Atkinson, John:* Centennial History of American Methodism, N.Y., 1884. $2.00.

MORMON.

Stenhouse, (Mrs.) T. B. H. Rocky Mountain Saints: History of the Mormons. 8vo. pp. xxiv, 761. N.Y. App. 1873. $5.00.

Tucker, Pomeroy. Origin, Rise, and Progress of Mormonism. 12mo. N.Y. App. 1867. $1.25.

MORAVIAN.
Schweinitz, E. de. The Moravian Manual, containing an Account of the Protestant Church of the Moravian United Brethren. 12mo. Ph. 1869. $1.00.
   Cf. *Reichel*, Memorials. Ph., Lip., 1870.

PRESBYTERIAN.
Gillett, E. H. History of the Presbyterian Church in the United States of America. 2 v. Ph. 1864. $5.00.
Hodge, Charles. The Constitutional History of the Presbyterian Church in the United States. 8vo. Ph. Presb. Bd. of Pub. $3.00.
Presbyterian Reunion: A Memorial Volume, 1837-1871. By the Rev. Drs. *Miller, Stearns, Sprague, Humphrey, Adams, Jacobus, Fowler, Hall, Irving, Hatfield,* and *Knox,* and the Rev. *G. S. Plumley.* Illustrated. Large 8vo. pp. 568. N.Y. Lent & Co. 1870.
   Valuable for the history of Old School and New School Presbyterian Churches from the separation in 1837 to the reunion in 1871.

PROTESTANT EPISCOPAL.
Perry, W. S. [editor in chief]. The History of the American Episcopal Church, 1587-1883. 2 v. 4to. Illus. B. O.
   In course of preparation. It will surpass all existing histories of the Protestant Episcopal Church.
Wilberforce, (Bp.) S. A History of the Protestant Episcopal Church in America. 2d edition. 12mo. N.Y. Stanford & Swords. 1846. 12mo. pp. 357. 1849. Pott. $3.50.
   Cf. *White's* Memoirs, 1836, and *Hawk's* Contributions, 1836.

REFORMED EPISCOPAL.
Aycrigg, Benjamin. Memoirs of the Reformed Episcopal Church, and of the Protestant Episcopal Church, with Contemporary Reports respecting these and the Church of England, extracted from the Public Press. 5th edition. 8vo. pp. lxvi, 373. N.Y. and Passaic, N.J. Aycrigg. 1880.
   A collection of materials. Indexed. This work is not of a popular character, but will be invaluable to future historians of the Protestant Episcopal and the Reformed Episcopal Churches.

Cummins, (Mrs.) G. D. Memoir of G. D. Cummins, First Bishop of the Reformed Episcopal Church. 12mo. pp. 544. N.Y. Dodd, Mead, & Co. 1879. $2.50.
> It contains an excellent account of the origin and organization of the Reformed Episcopal Church.

REFORMED CHURCH IN AMERICA (DUTCH).
Demarest, David D. History and Characteristics of the Reformed Protestant Dutch Church. 12mo. pp. xxviii, 221. N.Y. 1856, 1859. $1.00.

REFORMED CHURCH IN THE UNITED STATES (GERMAN).
Mayer, Lewis. The History of the German Reformed Church. Vol. I. 8vo. pp. 477. Ph. Lip. 1851.
> Cf. article by *E. V. Gerhart* in Bib. Sac., vol. XX., 1863.

ROMAN CATHOLIC.
Clarke, R. H. Lives of the Deceased Bishops of the Catholic Church in the United States. 2 v. 8vo. N.Y. P. O'Shea. 1872. $8.00.
Murray, J. O. A Popular History of the Catholic Church in the United States. 8vo. pp. 619. 2d edition. N.Y. Sadlier & Co. 1876. $2.50.
> An Appendix contains valuable statistical tables and biographical sketches. Cf. *Le Clercq*, translated by *Shea*, Cin. ($12.00); and *Parkman*, Jesuits in North America.

SHAKERS.
Evans, F. W. Compendium of the Origin, History, etc., of the United Society of Believers in Christ's Second Coming. 16mo. N.Y. App. 1859.

UNITED BRETHREN.
Lawrence, John. History of the Church of the United Brethren in Christ. 2 vols. in one. 8vo. Dayton, O. U. B. Pub. House. $2.50.
> Cf. *Spayth*, Circleville, Ohio; Conference Office, 1851.

UNITARIAN.
Ellis, Geo. E. A Half Century of the Unitarian Controversy. B. American Unitarian Association. 1859. $1.50.
> Cf. *Ware*, American Unitarian Biography. 2 v. B. 1850–51.

UNIVERSALIST.
Thomas, Abel C. A Century of Universalism. B. Universalist Publishing House.
Cf. *Adams*, Fifty Notable Years; and *Eddy*, Universalism in America.

VI. SPECIAL TOPICS.

1. ART.

Heaphy, Thomas. The Likeness of Christ. Being an Inquiry into the Verisimilitude of the Received Likeness of Our Blessed Lord. Edited by *Wyke Bayliss*. With 12 colored plates. Folio. pp. 78. L. David Bogue. 1880. £3 6s.
Cf. *Schaff*, History of the Christian Church. N.Y. 1882. Vol. I, pp. 167-170.

Jameson, (Mrs.) Anna. Sacred and Legendary Art. Portrait of Leonardo da Vinci. 2 v., 32mo, $3.00; 6 v., 8vo, L., Longm., £5 15s. 6d.
Popular.

Jameson, (Mrs.) Anna, and Eastlake, (Lady). The History of Our Lord as Exemplified in Works of Art. Illustrated. 2 v. L. Longm. 2d edition. 1865. 42s.

Lübke, W. Ecclesiastical Art in Germany during the Middle Ages.
High authority.

Norton, C. E. Studies of Church Buildings in the Middle Ages. 8vo. pp. 331. N.Y. II. 1880. $3.00.
The result of careful study. Written in good style.

Poole, Geo. A. History of Ecclesiastical Architecture in England. 8vo. L. 1848. $3.50.

Scott, G. G. Lectures on the Rise and Development of Mediæval Architecture. Illustrated. 2 v. 8vo. pp. xv, 365; xvi, 347. L. Murray. 1879. 42s.

Id. An Essay on the History of English Church Architecture, prior to the Separation of England from the Roman Obedience. Illustrated. 4to. pp. 195. L. Simpkin, Marshall, & Co. 1881.

Tyrwhitt, R. St. John. The Art Teaching of the Primitive Church. L. Soc. 8vo. 7s. 6d.

2. BIOGRAPHY.

A. Biblical. — I. Lives of Christ.

Ebrard, A. Wissenschaftliche Kritik der Evangelischen Geschichte. Condensed translation. 8vo. Ed. Clark. 1869. 10s. 6d.
    Against Strauss, Bruno Bauer, etc.

Ewald, H. Geschichte Christus' und seiner Zeit. (Vol. 5 of his History of Israel.) Tr. by O. Glover. Cambridge. Bell. 1865. 9s.

Farrar, Frederic W. Life of Christ. 2 v. L. 1874. About thirty editions have since appeared, many of them in America. One is illustrated. $1.00.

Geikie, C. The Life and Words of Christ. L. Strahan & Co. 1878. 2 v. Illustrated. 30s. Several editions. N.Y. Munro. Paper, 40 cts.

Hardwick, Chas. Christ and Other Masters. L. Macm. 4th edition. 1875. 10s. 6d.
    A comparison of Christ with founders of Eastern religions.

Keim, Theodore. Geschichte Jesu von Nâzara. Zurich. 1867-72. 3 v. Translated into English by *Geldart* and *Ransom.* L. W. & N. 2d edition. 1873-79. 2 v. 10s. 6d. each.
    Based chiefly upon Matthew. In the preparation of this work the Fourth Gospel was not used.

Lange, John Peter. The Life of the Lord Jesus Christ : a Complete Examination of the Origin, Contents, and Connection of the Gospels. New edition. 4 v. 8vo. Ph. 1872. $10.00.
    By a distinguished German commentator.

Neander, J. A. W. The Life of Jesus. Translated by *McClintock* and *Blumenthal.* N.Y. H. 1848. $2.50.
    " A positive refutation of Strauss." — P. SCHAFF.

Pressensé, E. de. Jesus Christ : His Times, Life, and Work. 4th edition. Revised. 8vo. L. 1871. $3.40.
    Written in reply to Renan.

Renan, Ernest. Life of Jesus. Translated by *E. Wilbour.* 12mo. pp. 376. N.Y. Carleton & Co. 1864, 1870. $1.75.
> Renan professed to write without any other passion than a very keen curiosity. "This book created even a greater sensation than the *Leben Jesu* of Strauss, but is very superficial, and turns the gospel history into a novel with a self-contradictory and impossible hero. Eloquent, fascinating, superficial, and contradictory." — P. SCHAFF. "In it the learning of the Orientalist vied with the enrapturing rhetoric of the fine writer to warp the judgment of sentimental amateurs." — J. F. HURST in "Crook's & Hurst's Theological Encyclopædia and Methodology."

Strauss, D. F. Life of Jesus. Translated by *Marian Evans (George Eliot).* L. 1846. 3 v. Republished in N.Y., 1850. Authorized translation. 2d edition. 2 v. 8vo. pp. xxii, 440; iv, 439. L. W. & N. 1879. 24s.
> Refuted by Neander, *q.v.*

Weiss, Bernard. The Life of Christ. Translated by *John W. Hope.* 3 v. 8vo. Ed. 1883–4. $3.00 each.
> Liberal evangelical. Dr. Weiss is professor of theology at Berlin.

Young, J. The Christ of History. L. & N.Y. 1855. 5th edition. 1868. L. Strahan. 6s.
> Evangelical. Popular.

These are excellent lives of Christ, original and translated, by *Lyman Abbott, S. J. Andrews, H. W. Beecher, C. E. Caspari, Howard Crosby, C. F. Deems, Z. Eddy, C. J. Ellicott, Fleetwood, Wm. Hanna, Carl Hase, Mrs. Jameson* ("as exemplified in works of art"), *E. H. Plumptre, Chr. Fr. Schmid, D. Schenkel,* and *J. R. Seeley.* Cf. *G. Uhlhorn*: Modern Representatives of the Life of Jesus. Translated by *Grinnell.* 16mo. B. L. & B. 1868.

II. *Lives of the Apostles.*

Baur, Ferd. Chr. Paul the Apostle of Jesus Christ. Translated by *Allan Menzies.* 2 v. L. W. & N. 1873 and 1875. 10s. 6d. each.
> The standard work of the Tübingen school.

Conybeare and *Howson*. Life and Epistles of St. Paul. L. 1853.
Many reprints, both English and American.
> A standard work; of especial value to Christian teachers.

Farrar, F. W. Life and Work of St. Paul. 2 v. L. & N.Y.
1879, and other editions. N.Y. Funk & Wagnalls. 1880.
Paper, 50 cts.
> Canon Farrar is a learned and rhetorical writer.

Pearson (Bp.). Annales Paulini. Works. Also separately.
Cambridge. 1824.

Renan, E. St. Paul. Translated by *Ingersoll Lockwood.* 12mo.
pp. 422. N.Y. Carleton. 1869. $1.75.
> Entertaining, but fanciful and illogical.

Tholuck, Aug. The Life, Character, and Style of the Apostle
Paul. In Selections from German Literature (pp. 1–72). Translated by *B. B. Edwards* and *E. A. Park.* 8vo. pp. iv, 472.
Andover. Gould, Newman, & Saxon, 1839.

B. General. — I. Collections.

Baring-Gould, Sabine. Lives of the Saints. 15 v. 12mo. N.Y.
Pott, Young, & Co. 1879. $2.50 each.

Butler, Alban. Lives of the Fathers, Martyrs, and other Saints.
12 v. 24mo. L. Duffy. 1866. First American edition, 2 v.
8vo. Baltimore. J. Murphy & Co. 1850. $7.00.
> Roman Catholic.

Hook, W. F. Lives of the Archbishops of Canterbury from St.
Augustine to Juxon. 12 v. 8vo. L. R. Bentley & Son.
1860–76. 15s. each; vol. 12, 21s.
> In two series. The last volume is an index to the others.

Piper, Ferdinand. Lives of the Leaders of our Church Universal
from the Days of the Succession of the Apostles to the Present
Time. Translated from the German, with valuable American
additions, by *McCracken.* 8vo. J. & T. Clark. 1880. 2 v.
pp. 430, 413. $3.00.
> For popular use, this is the best book of Christian biography. Its
> tone is Protestant, but not sectarian.

Sprague, W. B. See General Histories, under *United States.*

Stephen, (Sir) J. Essays in Ecclesiastical Biography. 1st edition. 1850; 4th, 1860. L. Longm. 7s. 6d.
Few subjects, but well treated.

Tulloch, John. Leaders of the Reformation : Luther, Calvin, Latimer, and Knox. 2d edition. 8vo. Ed. W. Blackwood & Sons. 1860. 3d edition, enlarged, $3.00.

II. Individual.

Ambrose, St. *R. Thornton.* Soc. 2s.
Anselm, St. By *R. W. Church.* Macm. $1.75.
Arnold, Thomas. *A. P. Stanley.* Scr. 1880. $2.50.
Augustine, St. *E. L. Cutts.* Soc. 1880. Cf. *Clark*, Pott, 75 cts.
Id. *Possidius* (personal friend of Augustine); *Pressensé*, in Smith and Wace; *Schaff*, 1854; *Poriarty* and *Tulloch*, in Encycl. Brit.
Basil, St. *R. T. Smith.* Soc. 1879. 2s.
Becket. *J. A. Froude* in Nineteenth Century, 1877.
Id. By *E. A. Freeman* in Contemporary Review, 1878.
A reply to Froude's article in the Nineteenth Cent.; more favorable.
Bede. *G. F. Browne.* Soc. 2s.
Calvin. *Wm. Blackburn.* 2 books. Ph. Presb. Bd. 70 and 75 cts.
Chrysostom, John. *Aug. Neander.* Translated by *Stapleton.* Bohn. 1845.
Id. *W. R. W. Stephens.* L., 1872; 2d ed., 1880. L., Murray, 12s.
Constantine. *E. L. Cutts.* L., Soc. N.Y., 1881.
Erasmus. *R. B. Drummond.* 2 v. S. & E. 21s.
Farel. *Wm. Blackburn.* Ph. Presb. Bd. of Pub. $1.50.
Fox, George. *J. Marsh.* B. 1847.
Id. *S. M. Janney.* Ph. Lip. $1.25.
Gregory the Great. *J. Barmby.* Soc. 2s.
Gregory VII. *A. F. Villemani.* 3 v. Bentley. 26s.
Huss, John. *E. H. Gillet.* 2 v. N.Y. 1864. $7.00.
A learned monograph.
Id. *A. H. Wratislaw.* L. Soc. 3s. 6d.

Hutten. Ulrich von. *D. F. Strauss.* L. Daldy & Isbister. 1874. 10s. 6d.
Jerome. *E. L. Cutts.* 12mo. Soc. 1878. 2s.
Julian. *Randall.* L. 1879.
Kempis, Thomas à, and the Brothers of the Common Life. *S. Kettlewell.* 8vo. 2 v. N.Y. Put. 1882. $8.00.
Knox, John. *Thomas McCrie.* Ph. Presb. Bd. of Pub. $2.00. Cf. *Carlyle,* Hero Worship.
Laud. *Peter Bayne* in the Chief Actors in the Puritan Revolution. Originally in the Contemporary Review. Cf. *Mozley's* Essays, 2 v., L., 21s.; and *J. E. T. Roger's* Historical Gleanings, L., Macm., $1.75.
Leo the Great. *C. H. Gore.* Soc. 2s.
Louis, St., and Calvin. *F. Guizot.* 8vo. Macm. 6s.
Luther. *Audin* (strongly denunciatory); *Peter Bayne*, *T. Carlyle*, in Hero Worship; *J. A. Froude* (Longm., 1883); *Julius Kœstlin* (Longm., 16s.); *Rein,* based on *Kœstlin* and translated by *Behringer* (N.Y., Funk & Wagnalls, 25 cts. and $1.00); and *J. H. Treadwell* (Put., $1.00). Cf. Essays by Mozley.
Patrick, St. *Wm. M. Blackburn.* Ph. Presb. Bd. of Pub. $1.00.
Savonarola. *W. R. Clark.* 3s. 6d. N.Y., 1879, Pott, $1.50.
Id. *Villari.*
Schleiermacher, F. E. Autobiography and Letters. L. S. & E. 1860.
Sixtus V. *Baron Hübner.* L. Longm. 24s.
Swedenborg. *Hobart,* B., 1832; *R. L. Tafel* (translated; the most complete); Worcester, B., R., 1883. $2.00.
Theresa, St. L. Macm. $2.00.
Wesley, John. *Robert Southey,* with notes by *S. T. Coleridge.* N.Y. 1820.
Id. *Luke Tyerman.* 3 v. N.Y. H. 1872. $7.50.
The best that has yet been written.
Id. *R. Denny Urlin.* (The Churchman's Life of Wesley.) L. Soc. 3s. 6d. Cf. *J. Hampson,* 2 v.; *H. Moore,* 2 v.; and *R. Watson* (best edition, with notes in reply to Southey, 6s.).

Whitefield, George. *Luke Tyerman.* 2 v. N.Y. Randolph & Co. 1878. $2.00.

Wyclif. *G. V. Lechler,* tr. by *Peter Lorimer.* 2 v. L. Paul. 21s.

Id. *J. E. T. Rogers.* Vol. II. of Historical Gleanings. L. Macm. $1.75.

Zwingli. *Jean Grob.* Translated. 12mo. N.Y. Funk & Wagnalls. 25 cts. and $1.00. Cf. *Blackburn.* Presb. Bd., $1.25.

Xavier. *Coleridge.* Also *Venn,* and *Bouhours* (translated by *Dryden,* 1688).

3. CHURCH AND STATE.

Bryce, James. Holy Roman Empire. L. Macm. 7s. 6d.
"Invaluable for clearing up the relations of Germany and Rome."
— C. K. ADAMS.

Geffcken, Heinrich. Church and State; their Relations Historically Considered. Translated and edited, with the assistance of the author, by *Edward Fairfax Taylor.* 2 v. 8vo. L. 1877. 42s.
"For knowledge, acumen, and fairness, the work is worthy of high praise."— C. K. ADAMS. The author, a conservative Protestant, is professor of international law in the University of Strasburg.

Thompson, R. W. The Papacy and the Civil Power. 8vo. N.Y. II. 1876. $3.00.
"Carefully prepared. . . . A powerful indictment of the temporal policy of the Catholic Church. It contains several ecclesiastical documents that enhance its value. . . . It is the best easily accessible sketch of the subject of which it treats." — C. K. ADAMS.

4. COUNCILS.

Bungener, L. F. History of the Council of Trent. Edited by *John McClintock.* 12mo. N.Y. H. 1855. $1.50.

Hefele, C. J. A History of the Councils of the Church. 4 v. have been translated by *W. R. Clark* and *H. N. Oxenham.* Ed. T. & T. Clark. 1871–1884. $4.80 each.
By a Roman Catholic bishop of great learning. Independent, original, authoritative. Vol. V. covers the Nestorian and Eutychian controversies. Cf. *E. H. Landon* (Anglican). 12mo. L. 1846.

Pusey, E. B. The Councils of the Church, from the Council of Jerusalem, A.D. 51, to the Council of Constantinople, A.D. 381; chiefly as to their Constitution, but also as to their Object and History. 8vo. L. 1857. $3.50.
 By the Tractarian leader. Died 1882.
Sarpi, P. Council of Trent. Tr. by *N. Brent.* 4to. pp. 889. L. 1676.
 "A work of genius, concerning which see Dr. Johnson's account in his 'Lives of Eminent Persons'; also a charming account in Howell's 'Venetian Life.'" — C. K. ADAMS. "Ranked by Macaulay with Thucidides." — W. F. ALLEN.

5. CREEDS.

Schaff, P. The Creeds of Christendom, with a History and Critical Notes. 8vo. 3 v. I. The History of Creeds; II. The Greek and Latin Creeds, with Translations; III. The Evangelical Protestant Creeds, with Translations. N.Y. II. 1877. $15.00.
 Of great value.

6. DOCTRINES.

Alger, William R. A Critical History of the Doctrine of a Future Life. 1st edition, Ph., 1864. 6th edition, 8vo, pp. 676, N.Y., Widdleton, 1869. New edition, with additions, 1878, $3.50.
 A valuable bibliography, by Dr. *Ezra Abbot*, is appended.
Donaldson, James. A Critical History of Christian Literature and Doctrine, from the Death of the Apostles to the Nicene Council. 3 v. 8vo. London. 1864-66. $12.00.
Dorner, J. A. History of the Development of the Doctrine of the Person of Christ. With a Review of the Controversies on the Subject in Britain since the Middle of the Seventeenth Century. Translated by *W. Lindsay Alexander*, D.D., and *D. W. Simon*, D.D. 5 v. 8vo. pp. xviii, 467; viii, 544; 456; viii, 462; xxviii, 502. Ed. T. & T. Clark. 1862-64. £2 12s. 6d.
 "By far the most learned and instructive discussion of the theme which has ever been undertaken. . . . The book is a fine example of the mingling of intellectual freedom with due reverence, and of the spirit of science with genuine devoutness." — G. P. FISHER, in the *The Independent*, July 24, 1884.

Id. History of Protestant Theology; particularly in Germany. Translated by *G. Robson* and *Sophia Taylor.* 2 v. 8vo. pp. xxiii, 444; 511. Ed. T. & T. Clark. 1871. 21s.

> By a popular and profound theologian, who died in 1884.

Hagenbach, K. R. Text-Book of the History of Doctrine. The Edinburgh translation of *C. W. Bush,* revised, with additions from the fourth German edition, by *Henry B. Smith, D.D.* 2 v. 8vo. pp. 478, 558. N.Y. Sheldon & Co. 1861-62. $6.00.

> The additions are from Neander, Gieseler, Baur, etc. An edition of Hagenbach's History of Christian Doctrine, translated from the fifth German edition, with an introduction by *E. H. Plumptre,* is published by T. & T. Clark, Edinburgh. Vol. II. 8vo. pp. 466. 1880. $3.00.

Neander, A. Lectures on the History of Christian Dogmas. Translated by *J. E. Ryland.* 2 v. 12mo. pp. 356, 264. L. H. G. Bohn. 1858. $3.00.

Mackay, R. W. The Tübingen School and its Antecedents. A Review of the History and Present Condition of Modern Theology. 8vo. L. W. & N. 1863.

Reuss, Edward. History of Christian Theology in the Apostolic Age. Translated by *Annie Harwood.* With preface and notes by *R. W. Dale.* 2 v. 8vo. L. Hodder & Stoughton. 1872-74. 24s.

Shedd, W. G. T. A History of Christian Doctrines. 3d edition. 2 v. 8vo. pp. viii, 412; vi, 508. N.Y. Scr. 1869. $5.00.

> Clear, Calvinistic, and vigorous. Dwells on theology, anthropology, and soteriology, and entirely omits the doctrines that relate to the sacraments. There are other important omissions, which greatly lessen its value.

Tulloch, John. Rational Theology and Christian Philosophy in England in the Seventeenth Century. 2 v. 8vo. Ed. Blackwoods. 1872. 28s.

Wiggers, G. F. An Historical Presentation of Augustinianism and Pelagianism from the Original Sources. Translated from the German, with notes and additions, by *Ralph Emerson.* 8vo. pp. 383. Andover. Draper. 1840. $1.25.

7. FICTION.

(*Illustrating Periods of Church History.*)

Anonymous. Arius, the Libyan. 12mo. N.Y. App. 1884. $1.50.
Entertaining, but in many historical points inaccurate. See Boston *Watchman* for Aug. 14, 1884.

Anonymous. The Days of Knox. L. 1869. $3.00.

Banvard, Joseph. Priscilla; or, Trials for the Truth. An Historic Tale of the Puritans and the Baptists. 8vo. pp. 406. B. 1855.

Bungener, L. The Priest and the Huguenot. An historical novel of the time of Louis XV. B. Lothrop. 1874. $1.50.

Id. The Preacher [Bourdaloue] and the King [Louis XIV.]. $1.50.

Carpenter, Boyd. Narcissus. A Tale of Early Christian Times. 8vo. L. Soc. 3s 6d.
By the author of "The Chronicles of the Schönberg-Cotta Family."

Charles, (Mrs.) Elizabeth. Diary of Kitty Trevilyan. A Story of the Times of Whitfield and the Wesleys. 12mo. pp. 304. L. T. Nelson & Sons. 1865. N.Y. Dodd. 1864. $1.00.

Clarke, James Freeman. The Legend of Thomas Didymus, the Jewish Sceptic. [Life of Christ as it appeard to co-temporaries.] 12mo. pp. 418. B. L. & S. 1881. $1.75.

Croly, Geo. Salathiel. Cincinnati. U. P. James. $1.50.

Davies, Samuel. From Dawn to Dark in Italy. A Tale of the Reformation in the 16th Century. Ph. Presb. Bd. of Pub. $1.25.

Ebers, G. Homo Sum. [A tale of the early Anchorites.] N.Y. Munro. 10 cents.

Eliot, George [*Marion Evans*]. Romola. [Savonorola.] N.Y. Munro. 15 cents.
"Deserving all the high encomiums it has received." — N. PORTER.

Hale, E. E. In His Name. [Waldenses.] B. 1877. 40 cents.

Kingsley, C. Hypatia. [Alexandria.] L. and N.Y. Macm. $1.75.

Lockhart, J. G. Valerius. Ed. and L. Blackwood & Son. 1849. 3s. Excellent.

Mille, J. de. Helena's Household. 8vo. N.Y. Carter. 1869. $1.50.
"Gives an interesting and faithful picture of the workings of Christianity in a Roman household, and interweaves also much of the history of a part of the first and second centuries." — N. PORTER.

Newman, (Cardinal) J. H. Callista. 8vo. L. B. & O. 1873. 5s. 6d.
Reade, C. Cloister and the Hearth. [Germany, 15th cent.] 2s. 6d.
Spindler, C. The Jew. [Council of Constance, 1414–18.] N.Y. H. 75 cents.
Wallace, Lew. Ben-Hur, a Tale of the Christ. N.Y. H. $1.50.
> Recognized as a work of unusual worth.

Ware, W. Aurelian, Julian, and Zenobia. 3 v. N.Y. Miller. $2.00 each.
> "Excellent examples of good historical tales of the earlier Christian centuries." — N. PORTER.

Webb, (Mrs.). Pomponia; or, the Gospel in Cæsar's Household. [Rome, Nero, and Britain.] Ph. Presb. Bd. of Pub. $1.25.
Id. Alypius of Tagaste. Ph. Presb. Bd. of Pub. $1.25.
Wiseman, (Cardinal) N. Fabiola. [The Catacombs.] N.Y. Sadlier. $1.50.

8. LITURGIES.

Hammond, C. E. Liturgies, Eastern and Western: being a Reprint of the Texts, either Original or Translated, of the most representative Liturgies of the Church from various sources. With Introduction, Notes, and a Liturgical Glossary. 12mo. L. Macm. 1878. 10s. 6d.

Humphrey, Wm. G. An Historical and Explanatory Treatise on the Book of Common Prayer. 12mo, cloth. L. Bell & Sons. 1856, 1875. 4s. 6d.
> Excellent.

Maskell, W. The Ancient Liturgy of the Church of England, according to the Uses of Sarum, Bangor, York, and Hereford, and the Modern Roman Liturgy, arranged in parallel columns. 3d ed. 8vo. pp. lxxxiv, 338. Oxford. Clarendon Press. 1882. 15s.

Neale, J. M. Essays on Liturgiology and Church History. 8vo. pp. 527. L. Saunders, Otley, & Co. 1863 and 1867.
> Scholarly. Dr. P. Schaff says of Neale that he was a "most learned Anglican ritualist and liturgist, who studied the Eastern liturgies daily for thirty years, and almost knew them by heart. . . . The . . . work of . . . the English Episcopal divine, Freeman, . . . treats much of the old liturgies, with a predilection for the Western, while Neale has an especial reverence for the Eastern ritual."

Neale, J. M. The Liturgies of St. Mark, St. James, St. Clement, St. Chrysostom, St. Basil, or according to the use of the Churches of Alexandria, Jerusalem, Constantinople. L. 1859 (in the Greek original, and the same liturgies in an English translation, with an introduction and appendices, also in L., 1859). 2d edition. 12mo. L. Hayes. 1868. 6s.
    Of permanent value.

9. MARTYRS.

See works by *Fox* (standard, comprehensive, Protestant; best edition by G. Townsend, 8 v., L., 1843), *Bulkley*, *Chateaubriand* (translated by O. W. *Wight*; not critical, very poetical), and *Pressensé* (translated, L., 1871).

10. MIRACLE PLAYS AND MYSTERIES.

See *Wm. Hone*, 1823; *J. P. Jackson* (Passion Play at Oberammergau, historical introduction), 1873, and *Marriott* (A Collection of English Miracle Plays or Mysteries), 1858.

11. MISSIONS.

Christlieb, Theodor. Protestant Foreign Missions. Translated from the Fourth German edition, by *David Allen Read*. 16mo, pp. 264, N.Y., Randolph, 1880; 16mo, pp. 280, B., Cong. Pub. Soc. $1.00.
    Compact, but complete. Sufficient for the needs of the general reader.

Maclear, G. F. Apostles of Mediæval Europe. 8vo. L. Macm. 4s. 6d.
    Protestant; standard.

Merivale, C. Conversion of the West. 5 v. Maps. 16mo. I. The Continental Teutons, by *C. Merivale*, pp. 180; II. The Celts, by *G. F. Maclear*, pp. 189; III. The English, by *G. F. Maclear*, pp. 186; IV. The Northmen, by *G. F. Maclear*, pp. 202; V. The Sclavs, by *G. F. Maclear*, pp. ii, 202. L. Soc. N.Y. Pott, Young, & Co. 1879. 60 cts. each.

Seelye, J. H. Christian Missions. 12mo. pp. 207. N.Y. Dodd, Mead, & Co. 1876. $1.00.

Smith, Thomas. History of Mediæval Missions. 12mo. L. Hamilton. 1880. 4s. 6d.
> Protestant; standard.

12. MONASTIC ORDERS.

> The development of Monastic institutions is impartially and skilfully traced by *Milman*, in his History of Latin Christianity.

Montalembert, Count de. The Monks of the West, from St. Benedict to St. Bernard. Translated from the French. 7 v. 8vo. Ed. and L. Blackwoods. 1860-70. Vols. 6 and 7, 25s. B. Noonan. 2 v. $6.00.
> "The ablest plea that has ever been made for the several orders of monks, being at once scholarly, sympathetic, and conscientious." — C. K. ADAMS. Cf. Sir *James Stephen's* Ecclesiastical Essays, and Mrs. *Jameson's* Legends of the Monastic Orders.

Ruffner, H. The Fathers of the Desert; or, an Account of the Origin and Practice of Monkery among the Heathen Nations, its passage into the Church; and some wonderful stories of the fathers concerning the primitive monks and hermits. 2 v. N.Y. 1850.
> The author, a Presbyterian, is by no means friendly to monastic institutions.

13. RATIONALISM.

Hurst, John F. History of Rationalism. Embracing a Survey of the Present State of Protestant Theology. With appendix of literature. 8vo. N.Y. Scr. 1865. 9th rev. ed. 1875. $3.50.

Lecky, W. E. H. History of the Rise and Influence of the Spirit of Rationalism in Europe. 2 v. 8vo. L. & N.Y. App. 1865. $4.00.
> "His sympathies are obviously rationalistic, though he usually succeeds in maintaining a moderate and judicious spirit." — C. K. ADAMS.

14. REFERENCE BOOKS.

Abbott, Lyman, and *Conant, T. J.* A Dictionary of Religious Knowledge, for Popular and Professional Use; comprising full Information on Biblical, Theological, and Ecclesiastical Subjects. With nearly One Thousand Maps and Illustrations. Royal 8vo. pp. 1000+. N.Y. H. $6.00.
> Adapted to the needs of general students.

Bingham, Joseph. Origines Ecclesiasticæ; or, the Antiquities of the Christian Church. With two sermons and two letters on the Nature and Necessity of Absolution. Edited by *R. Bingham.* 8vo. L. Macm. Also in 7 vols. in Bingham's complete works. 9 v. 1840. L. W. Straker. 1843. 10 v. Oxford. Clarendon Press. 1855. £3 6s.

Standard.

Blunt, J. H. Dictionary of Sects, Heresies, Ecclesiastical Parties, and Schools of Thought. Imperial 8vo. pp. 618. $10.00.

Anglican. Not always unprejudiced and impartial.

Edwards, B. B., and Brown, J. N. Encyclopædia of Religious Knowledge; comprising Dictionaries of the Bible, Theology, Biography, Religious Denominations, Ecclesiastical History, and Missions. Illustrated. Imperial 8vo. pp. 1276. Brattleboro. Vt. 1850.

"This valuable work comprises a complete library in itself, on the above subjects, from the most authentic sources; with copious original articles by the ablest American writers, — Episcopal, Congregationalist, Presbyterian, Methodist, and Baptist." — NICHOLAS TRÜBNER, in his "Bibliographical Guide to American Literature," published in London, 1859. Now superseded, in most points, by *Abbott* and *Conant, McClintock* and *Strong,* and *Schaff-Herzog.*

McClintock, John, and *Strong, J. A.* Cyclopædia of Biblical, Theological, and Ecclesiastical Literature. Maps. Illustrated. 10 v. 8vo. N.Y. H. 1867 sqq. $5.00 each.

Contains many articles on American biography and history, — too large a proportion being upon Methodist subjects, as might be expected from the church relations of its editors. Notwithstanding this imperfection, and the inferior literary qualifications of some of its contributors, it is the largest and most useful work of the kind that has yet appeared in the English language.

Schaff, Philip. A Religious Encyclopædia; or, Dictionary of Biblical, Historical, Doctrinal, and Practical Theology. 3 v. Royal 8vo. N.Y. Funk & Wagnalls. 1882-84. $6.00 each.

A condensed and otherwise greatly modified translation of the Real-Encyclopädie für Protestantische Theologie und Kirche, by *Herzog, Pitt,* and *Hauck.* In the work of translation, Dr. Schaff was aided by his son, *D. S. Schaff,* and *Samuel Jackson.* The work is convenient and authoritative.

Smith, Henry B. History of the Church of Christ in (16) Chronological Tables. N.Y. Scr. 1860. $5.00.

> Useful as an introduction to the study of church history: also valuable for reference and review. Nowhere else can be found a more clear and impartial outline of American church history to A.D. 1858.

Smith, William. Bible Dictionary. 3 v. L. 1860–64. American edition much enlarged and improved by *H. Hackett* and *E. Abbot.* 4 v. pp. 3667. N.Y. Hurd & Houghton. 1868–1870. $20.00.

> Valuable for topics in early church history. An excellent bibliography of ecclesiastical history concludes the article *Church.* Another standard Bible Dictionary is *Kitto's*, edited by *W. L. Alexander.* 3 v. Ed. A. & C. Black. 1862–65. £2 2s.

Smith, W., and *Cheetham, S.* A Dictionary of Christian Antiquities. The History, Institutions, and Antiquities of the Christian Church; Being a Continuation of the "Dictionary of the Bible." 2 v. Royal 8vo. L. Murray. 1875–1880. $7.00.

> All that Dr. *Smith* has edited is valuable.

Smith, William, and *Wace, Henry.* A Dictionary of Christian Biography, Literature, Sects, and Doctrines. 5 v., royal 8vo, L., Murray, 31s. 6d. each. 4 v., B., L. & B., 1877 *sqq.*, $5.50 each.

> "By far the best patristic biographical dictionary in the English or any other language. A noble monument of the learning of the Church of England, to which nearly all the contributors belong." — P. SCHAFF.

15. SACRED SEASONS.

Grant, Alex. H. The Church Seasons, Historically and Poetically Illustrated. 2d edition. Revised. 12mo. pp. 506. N.Y. Whittaker. 1881. $1.50.

16. SYMBOLISM.

Audsley, W. and *G.* Handbook of Christian Symbolism. Illustrated. Small 4to. pp. x, 145. L. Day & Son. 1865. 12s. 6d.

O'Brien, John. A History of the Mass and its Ceremonies in the Eastern and the Western Church. 12mo. N.Y. 4th edition. Revised. pp. xix, 414. Cath. Pub. Soc. Co. 1879. $1.50.

> More comprehensive than its title would indicate. It aims to point out the symbolical meaning of all the ceremonies of the eastern and the western churches.

Press of
Berwick & Smith,
Boston.

BOOKS FOR TEACHERS.

PEDAGOGICAL LIBRARY.

Edited by G. STANLEY HALL, Professor of Psychology and Pedagogy in Johns Hopkins University.

Vol. I. Methods of Teaching and Studying History.

[*Second Edition to be ready in December.*

Consists of independent contributions by the following prominent teachers of history: Dr. A. B. HART, Harvard University; Prof. E. EMERTON, Harvard University; Prof. CHAS. K. ADAMS, University of Michigan; Prof. W. F. ALLEN, University of Wisconsin; Prof. HERBERT B. ADAMS of Johns Hopkins University; Prof. RICHARD T. ELY, Johns Hopkins University; Pres. ANDREW D. WHITE of Cornell University; Prof. J. W. BURGESS of Columbia College, N.Y.; Prin. W. C. COLLAR, Roxbury Latin School; JOSEPH THACHER CLARKE; W. E. FOSTER, Providence Public Library; and others; also an article on "The Relation of Physical Geography and History"; with a very carefully selected and discriminated bibliography by Prof. ALLEN of Wisconsin University; a "Bibliography of Church History," by Rev. J. A. FISHER, Baltimore, Md.; and an introduction by the Editor. It is thought that this volume will be indispensable to every teacher and student of history in the country.

The Nation: The general excellence and helpfulness of the book before us ought to secure it many readers. We can heartily recommend it as well to teachers who are conscious of deficiencies in their preparation, as to principals and school boards who wish for assistance in laying out courses of study. It contains few details of fact, but an excellent summary and analysis of principles.

The American: The volume is certainly an excellent one, and one that ought help to fill a need where a need has been felt, and to create a desire for something better where indolence or brainlessness has brought about a perverse satisfaction. The question is whether the proportion of teachers anxious for and capable of something better will outnumber those "who merely hear recitations, keeping the finger on the place in the text-book, and only asking the questions conveniently printed for them in the margin or back of the book."

Yale Courant: It would certainly be a most decided improvement on the cut-and-dried text-book recitations that some of us have known.

Vol. II. Methods of Teaching and Studying Ancient

Languages and Literature. [*In preparation.*

Vol. III. Methods of Teaching and Studying Natural Science. [*In preparation.*]

Vol. IV. Methods of Teaching and Studying Reading, English Literature and Language. [*In preparation.*]

Each of these volumes will contain special and general bibliographies, contributions by eminent and widely-known American and foreign educators, and a conspectus and digests of the best pedagogical literature on the respective subjects. The Editor will spare no pains to make each volume indispensable to every teacher.

EDUCATIONAL CLASSICS.

Under this general title we shall publish from time to time translations and reprints of books that have contributed so much toward the solution of educational problems as to make them indispensable to every teacher's library.

Suggestions from teachers, as to what books such a series should contain, will be gratefully received.

The first volume in the series is

Extracts from Rousseau's Émile.

Containing the Principal Elements of Pedagogy. With an Introduction and Notes, by JULES STEEG, Paris, Député de la Gironde. Translated by ELEANOR WORTHINGTON, late of the Cook County Normal School, Ill.

"**There are fifty pages of the Émile that should be bound in velvet and gold.**" — *Voltaire.*

"Émile" is like an antique mirror of brass; it reflects the features of educational humanity no less faithfully than one of more modern construction. In these few pages will be found the germ of all that is useful in present systems of education, as well as most of the ever-recurring mistakes of well-meaning zealots. Price to Teachers, 80 cts.

The second volume will be

Pestalozzi's Lienhard und Gertrud.

A work that has proved the genius and assured the immortality of this great teacher of teachers. Translated and abridged by EVA CHANNING.

The following Books should find a place in every Teacher's Library:—

Minto's Manual of English Prose Literature.

Biographical and Critical. Designed mainly to show characteristics of style. Price to Teachers, $2.00.

Arnold's Manual of English Literature.

Historical and Critical: With an Appendix on English Metres, and summaries of the different literary periods.

The student of this manual will receive just impressions of the relative value of names and books, as well as political and religious influences. Price to Teachers, $1.50.

Craik's English of Shakespeare.

Illustrated in a Philological Commentary on Julius Cæsar.

Gives an exposition of the language and style of Shakespeare. Price to Teachers, 90 cts.

Hudson's Life, Art, and Characters of Shakespeare.

In 2 vols. Price to Teachers, $1.60 per vol.

These two volumes contain:—

1. *The Life of Shakespeare.*
2. *An Historical Sketch of the Origin and Growth of the Drama in England*, discussing under this head Miracle-Plays, Moral-Plays, and Comedy and Tragedy.
3. *Shakespeare's Contemporaries.*
4. *Shakespeare's Art*, discussing under this head Nature and Use of Art, Principles of Art, Dramatic Composition, Characterization, Humour, Style, Moral Spirit.
5. *Shakespeare's Characters*, containing critical discourses on twenty-five of the Plays.

Hudson's Essays on Education, English Studies,

and Shakespeare.

The first Essay gives good reasons why foot-notes are better for the young Shakespeare student than a mass of annotation at the end of the play; discusses the comparative value of verbal and æsthetic criticism ; and protests, with all possible earnestness, against the course now too commonly pursued in studying and teaching English Literature. The second discusses the questions: " Why should English Literature be taught in our Schools?" and " What is the best way of teaching it?" The third explains how Shakespeare should be adapted to school use, and at what age the study should be undertaken. The fourth was instigated by numerous letters asking for advice or suggestions as to the best way of using Shakespeare in classes. The author details his own methods, deduced from an experience of more than thirty years in teaching Shakespeare in schools, and shows how the study ought to be, and can be, "a pastime, a recreation, a delight." In passing, he shows up some of the glaring faults of our present high-pressure system of education. Price to Teachers, 25 cts.

Thom's Two Shakespeare Examinations.

It contains also an essay on the limitations of teaching and studying Shakespeare in schools, and suggestions as to method, as well as some notes on text-books. It is hoped that the book will prove of especial value to teachers who must do their work on Shakespeare within prescribed limits of time, and without advantages of access to good libraries. Price to Teachers, 45 cts.

Allen's History Topics, for High Schools & Colleges.

The first object of the topical method is to give prominence to the most important names and events of history, and concentrate the reading of the students upon certain selected ones of these. A second object is to encourage independent research.

In an appendix is given a classified list of those books which are considered most serviceable in connection with this method. Price to Teachers, 25 cts.

Allen's Reader's Guide to English History.

A classified list of works in English History, including poems, dramas, and works of fiction, arranged by periods, for convenience of reference. It has a Supplement, extending the plan over ancient, modern, European, and American history. Price to Teachers, 25 cts.

Lambert's Memory Gems in Prose and Verse.

Contains *three hundred and forty-six "gems" selected from more than one hundred and fifty authors, and embracing a wide range of thought.* Arranged in three groups, — for *primary, intermediate,* and *advanced classes.*

Designed to encourage the excellent practice, now generally introduced into schools, of committing to memory choice passages from the best English and American authors. Teachers do not always have at hand original sources from which to make selections, and young pupils should not be allowed to select for themselves. Price to Teachers, 30 cts.

Knox's Guide to Teachers of Elementary Lessons
in *English.*

In a preliminary chapter will be found a discussion of the Pestalozzian principles of education and instruction, of the art of questioning and the laws of questioning, of methods of correcting oral and written mistakes, and of oral lessons — how to prepare them, and how to give them. It includes also material and plans for Oral Lessons in Language for the first, second, third, and fourth years in school, observation lessons, dictation and test exercises, questions for oral and written reviews, materials for composition exercises, plans for conducting picture lessons, a story lesson, etc., etc., etc. There is no book published in this country which is so clear, direct, and complete a manual for the use of teachers. Price to Teachers, 60 cts.

Bigsby's Elements of English Composition.

Intended to give children habits of thought and observation, a knowledge of the uses of words, and the power to express their ideas.

Part First deals with the Elements of Grammar.
Part Second, the Formation of Sentences.
Part Third, the Construction of Paragraphs.
Part Fourth, the Figures of Speech.
Part Fifth, the Structure of Themes.

Price to Teachers, 35 cents.

Bancroft's Method of English Composition.

A brief system of instruction in the preparation of essays or compositions. The second part consists of lists of classified themes, with specimens of plans of compositions; also reference lists for reading, with hints from experienced librarians on the use of the library by young writers. Price to Teachers, 60 cts.

Gilmore's Outlines of the Art of Expression.

It is intended to help prepare students in English for admission to college; or to give them, after they have entered college, such preliminary training as will enable them to profit by higher and more systematic instruction in Rhetoric. Price to Teachers, 60 cts.

Tomlinson's Manual for the Study of Latin Grammar.

Designed for all Latin classes in the preparatory course. It does not aim to supplant, but supplement, the other work. With its use, time and labor will be saved, knowledge will be increased, and better habits of study will be formed. Price to Teachers, 20 cts.

Whiton's Auxilia Vergiliana; or, First Steps in Latin Prosody.

Intended to facilitate the mastery of metre and rhythm at the very outset of the study of Latin poetry. Price to Teachers, 15 cts.

King's Latin Pronunciation.

Contains a few explanatory and historical paragraphs on the Roman, Continental, and English methods of pronouncing Latin, and a brief presentation of the main features of each. Price to Teachers, 25 cts.

Allen's Remnants of Early Latin.

Chiefly inscriptions. The object is to bring together, in small compass and convenient shape for reading, the most remarkable monuments of archaic Latin, with enough explanation to make them generally intelligible. Price to Teachers, 75 cts.

Bender's Brief History of Roman Literature.
Contains terse, suggestive, and admirable characterizations of the Roman writers and of their times, and suggests much for the teacher to enlarge upon. Price to Teachers, $1.00.

Shumway's Latin Synonymes.
It is designed to meet the needs not only of the college student, but also of the preparatory school. The study of synonymes should begin with the earliest lessons in Latin, and never cease. By no other method can a vocabulary be so speedily and surely mastered, or so great interest aroused. Price to Teachers, 30 cts.

Madvig's Latin Grammar.
Whatever may be the preferences for one or another modern Latin Grammar, the scholars of the country agree in placing *Madvig's Latin Grammar* as the highest authority for reference. Price to Teachers, $2.25.

Parkhurst's Latin Verb.
The *immediate* aim is to introduce to the study of Comparative Grammar. Price to Teachers, 35 cts.

Halsey's Etymology of Latin and Greek.
It presents side by side for each group of related words the form of the root in Indo-European, Sanskrit, Greek, and Latin, with the meaning of the root. Following these roots are the most practical Greek words and the most practical Latin words, with their meanings. It may be used without confusion in connection with any grammar or lexicon; and it supplies thoroughly what they may lack in the important department of Etymology. Price to Teachers, $1.12.

Ginn & Heath's Classical Atlas and Geography
of the Ancient World.

Comprising in twenty-three plates, colored maps and plans of all the important countries and localities referred to by classical authors. Embodies the results of the most recent investigations. Brief suggestions to teachers are added, to assist in the work of the class-room. Price to Teachers, $2.00.

White's Junior Student's Latin-English Lexicon.
Price to Teachers, $2.00.

White's Junior Student's Latin-English and
English-Latin Lexicon. Revised edition. Price to Teachers, $3.00.

White's Junior Student's English-Latin Lexicon.
Price to Teachers, $1.75.

Goodwin's Greek Moods and Tenses.
The object of the work is to give a plain statement of the principles which govern the construction of the Greek Moods and Tenses, — the most important and the most difficult part of Greek Syntax. Price to Teachers, $1.50.

Keep's Essential Uses of the Moods in Greek
and Latin.

Describes clearly and accurately, in language not too technical, the actual use of moods in Latin and Greek. Price to Teachers, 25 cts.

White's Stein's Summary of the Dialect of Hero-
dotus.

Makes a complete statement of the euphonic and inflexional peculiarities which distinguish the language of Herodotus from Attic Greek, and is suitable for use with any edition of Herodotus. Price to Teachers, 10 cts.

White's Schmidt's Rhythmic and Metric of the
Classical Languages.

Teachers will probably differ in opinion in regard to the extent to which such a book as this should be used in school and college instruction; but certainly no teacher can afford to ignore the subject of which it treats. Price to Teachers, $2.50.

Liddell & Scott's Greek-English Lexicon.
Unabridged. Price to Teachers, $9.40.

Liddell & Scott's Greek-English Lexicon.
Abridged. Price to Teachers, $1.90.

Wentworth & Hill's Examination Manual.
I. *Arithmetic.* Price to Teachers, 35 cts.

Wentworth & Hill's Examination Manual.
II. *Algebra.* Price to Teachers, 35 cts.

Wentworth & Hill's Exercise Manual.
II. *Algebra.* Price to Teachers, 35 cts.

Wentworth & Hill's Exercise Manual of Geometry.
Price to Teachers, 70 cts.

These, and others to follow, are a series of short Manuals, intended to cover the main subjects studied in our schools and colleges. Each Manual is confined to one subject, and consists of two parts: the first containing about 100 examination papers made from the best collections of questions; the second containing recent papers actually set in English and American schools and colleges. Each Manual also contains a paper completely worked out, as a model.

Byerly's Syllabus of a Course in Plane Trigonometry.
Price to Teachers, 10 cts.

Byerly's Syllabus of a Course in Plane Analytic Geometry.
Price to Teachers, 10 cts.

Byerly's Syllabus of a Course in Plane Analytic Geometry.
(*Advanced Course.*) Price to Teachers, 10 cts.

Byerly's Syllabus of a Course in Analytical Geometry of Three Dimensions.
Price to Teachers, 10 cts.

Byerly's Syllabus of a Course in the Theory of Equations.
Price to Teachers, 10 cts.

The Fitz Globe.

Clearly illustrates all the phenomena produced by the sun's relations to the earth, and is the first globe to illustrate the sun's daily course, or indicate the interval of twilight, or represent one's horizon, without falsifying the existing relation of the earth's axis to its orbit.

  Price of Six-inch Globe . . . . $12.00.
  Price of Twelve-inch Globe . . . 25.00.

The Joslin Terrestrial, Celestial, & Slated Globes.

  Six-inch Globe, Semi-Frame . . . $4.00.
  Nine-inch Globe, Semi-Frame . . . 9.00.
  Twelve-inch Globe, Semi-Frame . . . 13.00.

Mounted on Full Wood Frames and suited to the working of problems, $4.00 more on each Globe.

The Celestial Globes are sold at the same prices as the Terrestrial.

Slated Globes of each style, 15 per cent less.

Johnston's Wall Maps.

If returned free of expense, a set will be sent for examination. Retail Price, $5.00 each; Introduction Price for three or more, $3.00 each. If mounted on spring rollers, 85 cts. extra per map; and in cases (seven maps in a case), $1.10 extra per map.

Adopted by nearly every School Board in Great Britain, and by such cities as Chicago, Cincinnati, Minneapolis, etc., and also in use in over five thousand schools in the United States.

Guides for Science Teaching.

Intended for the use of teachers who desire to practically instruct their classes in Natural History, and supplies such information as they need in teaching and are not likely to get from any other source. In addition to many simple illustrations, and instruction in modes of presentation and study, there are, in each pamphlet, hints which will be found useful in purchasing, collecting, preserving, and preparing specimens.

These *Guides* were prepared solely as aids to teachers, — not as text-books. The plan of teaching followed throughout is based upon the assumption that, —

Seeing is the first step on the road to knowledge; that, —
How much the child learns in his early years is of little importance, — *how he learns, everything;* that, —
The teacher's work is not to teach the facts, but to lead the mind of each pupil to work out for itself the simple physical problems witnessed or described, and to cultivate the habit of observation and of perseverance in investigation.

No. I. Hyatt's About Pebbles.

An illustration of the way in which a common object may be used profitably in teaching. It contains all the suggestions necessary to enable any teacher to make the lessons a complete success. Price to Teachers, 10 cts.

No. II. Goodale's Concerning a Few Common Plants.

Gives an account of the organs or "helpful parts" of plants, and shows how these can be cultivated and used in the school-room for the mental training of children. The appliances recommended are of the most trifling cost. Even simple lenses are not absolutely required for any of the studies suggested. Price to Teachers, 10 cts.

No. III. Hyatt's Commercial and Other Sponges.

Gives an account of the Sponges in common use, and of their structure, etc. The skeletons are present to the eye every day, and even the dullest scholar will undertake with interest to find out their different qualities, their common names, where they come from, and how they are formed. Price to Teachers, 20 cts.

No. IV. Agassiz's A First Lesson in Natural History.

Gives, in narrative form, for very young children, a general history of hydroids, corals, and echinoderms. Scientifically accurate and clear, it is as simple and fascinating as a wonder story. No fairies could more completely win the interest of children than do sea-anemones, corals, jelly-fishes, star-fishes, and sea-urchins, as described and depicted in this little book. Price, 25 cts.

No. V. Hyatt's Common Hydroids, Corals, and Echinoderms.

Shows throughout how the studies, or observations, are to be most satisfactorily made. The illustrations are remarkably clear and suggestive. Price to Teachers, 20 cts.

No. VI. Hyatt's Mollusca. Oyster, Clam, and Other Common Mollusks.

Apart from its usefulness as holding in compact form all that need be taught beginners about the oyster, clam, and other common mollusks, this book is invaluable as illustrating in detail the natural method of teaching. From first to last, the pupil is a discoverer; the teacher is simply the guide,—the pupil is self-taught. The author condescends to the simplest things, and tells in the plainest way just how to lead the class to make, in proper order, the necessary investigations and discoveries. The most inexperienced will be able, with this manual, to give these lessons with success. Price to Teachers, 25 cts.

No. VII. Hyatt's Worms and Crustacea.

The space given to the description of the lobster (and fresh water crayfish) will, it is hoped, incite teachers to occupy more time in dealing with some one common animal, and thus cultivating the habit of close observation. In these lessons, as in the preceding, the children are to be discoverers, not mere learners,—they are to be taught by experience the value and the pleasure of direct personal observation. Price to Teachers, 25 cts.

No. XII. Crosby's Common Minerals and Rocks.

Especial prominence is given to the easy identification of the common minerals and rocks, and to the constant association, in the mind, of the rocks and rock-structures with the agencies by which they have been formed. Price to Teachers, 25 cts.

Complete sets of specimens of minerals and rocks referred to in the Guide, have been prepared by the author. Price per set, $2.00.

No. XIII. Richard's First Lessons in Minerals.

A valuable introduction to Guide No. 12. The outline of the lessons was first worked out by Mrs. Richards with three successive classes of children, from six to eight years old, just out of the Kindergarten. The lessons were then given to classes in two public schools in the city of Boston; after which they were written out and printed for private distribution. During the two years which have since elapsed, the lessons have been given to about one thousand children of the fourth classes of several of the Boston Grammar Schools. Price to Teachers, 10 cts.

Sets of Specimens, illustrating Science Guides III.-VII, have been prepared, and can be obtained at the following prices:—

Guide III. (7 specimens) . . . . . $1.00.
" IV., V. (15 specimens) . . . . 2.00.
" VI. (12 specimens) . . . . . 1.00.
" VII. (10 specimens) . . . . . 1.00.

Orders should be addressed to SAMUEL HENSHAW, *Boston Society of Natural History, Boston, Mass.*

Shaler's First Book of Geology. *Teacher's Edition.*

There are general directions for the guidance of teachers in their work in giving lessons on natural history; then each chapter of the book is taken up in turn, and the instructor is told how to supplement the lessons by reference to facts that may be easily accessible in the nature about the school.

The Teacher's Edition will be found interesting by those who desire to get a glance at geology, and a general notion of its bearings on ordinary life. It is believed that these instructions will open a new field for the better use of the text-book in teaching geology. The instructor who will make proper use of these pages will find it possible to enliven the printed page with many an illustration that will be of value to his students. Price, $1.00.

Hill's Questions and Exercises on Stewart's
Physics. With Answers and occasional Solutions.

Will be found serviceable for purposes of review and examination. It will stimulate original thought on the part of the student, and give the teacher the means of testing thoroughly the student's knowledge of principles. Price to Teachers, 35 cts.

Mason's National Music Teacher.

The precise work of the teacher and class is shown, each step being carefully explained. In fact, the basis of the book is a series of verbatim reports of actual lessons given to little children by the author. The words of both teacher and pupils are reported, so that the exercise is brought vividly to the mind of any intelligent instructor. Price to Teachers, 40 cts.

Mason & Holt's Manual for Music Teachers.

An aid to teachers who know but little about music. It contains also appendices on "French Time-Names" and the "Management of the Voice." Price to Teachers, 40 cts.

Harvard Examination Papers.

These are all the questions (except on the subject of Geometry), in the form of papers, which have been used in the examinations for admission to Harvard College since 1860. They furnish an excellent series of Questions in Modern, Physical, and Ancient Geography; Grecian and Roman History; Arithmetic and Algebra; Plane and Solid Geometry; Logarithms and Trigonometry; Latin and Greek Grammar and Composition; Physics and Mechanics. They have been published in this form for the convenience of Teachers, classes in High Schools, and especially for pupils preparing for college. Price to Teachers, $1.00.

Yale Examination Papers.

This book is published for the convenience of teachers and pupils in preparatory schools, and may profitably be used as a text-book for review. Price to Teachers, 75 cts.

Halsey's Genealogical and Chronological Chart

of the Rulers of England, Scotland, France, Germany, and Spain.

33 × 50 inches in size.

Has just been revised and brought down to the present year. It is printed very distinctly on tough rope paper; and the price has been made only 25 cts., postpaid, placing within reach of every student of history what has been recognized as a most valuable help.

The Teachers' Improved Class-Books.

No. I. 90 pages. This is arranged for five days' record each week, the names of twenty pupils on a page, and for terms not exceeding fifteen weeks in length. Price to Teachers, 30 cts.

No. II. 120 pages. This provides for six days' record each week, for the names of twenty-four pupils on a page, and for terms not exceeding fifteen weeks in length. Price to Teachers, 40 cents.

Three advantages result from the arrangement of pages adopted in the Improved Class-Books: 1. The names of pupils in any class need to be entered *but once for an entire term.* 2. The standing for the three months, instead of needing to be compiled from different parts of the book, is present to the eye at one view. 3. In connection with each month's record is a blank for temporary memoranda, which may be cut out when no longer of use.

N.B.— These books are not only more convenient in form, but are one-third less expensive than any similar book on the market.

Monoyer's Sight-Test for Schools.

A ready means of detecting the presence of near-sight among school children. Full directions for using are given on the back of each chart. Size 11½ × 30 inches. *Unmounted*, on thick paper: Price to Teachers, 12 cts. *Mounted*, on Manilla board: Price, 32 cts.

The Question of a Division of the Philosophical

Faculty. Inaugural Address on assuming the Rectorship of the University of Berlin, delivered in the Aula of the University, Oct. 15, 1880, by Dr. AUGUST WILHELM HOFMANN, Prof. of Chemistry.

Deals chiefly with a question which excites great interest and no little controversy in the German Universities, and will, it is hoped, interest all in this country who are devoted to the educational problems of the day. The action of Germany in dealing with the question of dividing the great Philosophical Faculty cannot fail to be weighty and lasting in its effect on the education of the world. The Address, however, as Prof. Hofmann remarks, owes its general interest mainly to its discussion of a question closely connected with the principal subject,— that of admitting students to the universities without the literary training which a German *Gymnasium* affords, and especially without a knowledge of Greek. Price, 25 cts.

Wood-Working Tools: How to Use Them.

A Hand-book for Teachers. Edited (for the *Industrial School Association*) by CHANNING WHITAKER, Professor of Mechanical Engineering at the Massachusetts Institute of Technology.

A course of simple lessons in the use of the universal tools: the hammer, knife, axe, plane, rule, chalk-line, square, gauge, chisel, saw, and auger. The lessons are so amply illustrated that any bright boy will find the book alone a great help in his endeavors to learn the right way of using common tools. Price to Teachers, 50 cts.

Warren's True Key to Ancient Cosmology and
Mythical Geography.

This little book should be in the hands of every teacher of the classics. The remarkable light which the work throws upon the Odyssey renders it indispensable to every student of that poem. Price to Teachers, 20 cts.

Straight's Aim of Industrial Education in the
Public Schools, and its Proper Relation to the Regular Studies.

Price to Teachers, 10 cts.

Seelye's Hickok's Empirical Psychology; or, The
Human Mind as Given in Consciousness.

The publishers believe that the book will be found to be remarkably comprehensive, and at the same time compact and clear. It gives a complete outline of the Science, concisely presented, and in precise and plain terms. Price to Teachers, $1.12.

Seelye's Hickok's Moral Science.
Price to Teachers, $1.12.

Lotze's Outlines of Metaphysic.
Translated and Edited by Prof. GEO. T. LADD of Yale College.

The German from which the translation is made consists of the dictated portions of his latest lectures (at Göttingen, and for a few months at Berlin) as formulated by Lotz himself, recorded in the notes of his hearers, and subjected to the most competent and thorough revision of Professor Rehnisch of Göttingen. The "Outlines" give, therefore, a mature and trustworthy statement, in language selected by this teacher of Philosophy himself, of what may be considered as his final opinions upon this subject. It has met with no little favor in Germany. Price to Teachers, 80 cts.

GINN, HEATH, & CO., Publishers,

13 TREMONT PLACE, BOSTON.   4 BOND STREET, NEW YORK.

150 WABASH AVENUE, CHICAGO.

www.ingramcontent.com/pod-product-compliance
Lightning Source LLC
Chambersburg PA
CBHW030601300426
44111CB00009B/1057